Trincheras Sites in Time, Space, and Society

Amerind Studies in Archaeology

SERIES EDITOR **John Ware**

Volume 1

Trincheras Sites in Time, Space, and Society

Edited by Suzanne K. Fish, Paul R. Fish, and M. Elisa Villalpando

Trincheras Sites in Time, Space, and Society

Edited by Suzanne K. Fish, Paul R. Fish, and M. Elisa Villalpando

The University of Arizona Press
Tucson

The University of Arizona Press

Library of Congress Cataloging-in-Publication Data
Trincheras sites in time, space, and society / edited by
Suzanne K. Fish, Paul R. Fish, and M. Elisa Villalpando.
p. cm. — (Amerind studies in archaeology)
Includes bibliographical references and index.
ISBN 978-0-8165-2540-9 (hardcover : alk. paper)
1. Indians of Mexico—Religion. 2. Indians of North
America—Arizona—Religion. 3. Religion, Prehistoric—
Mexico. 4. Religion, Prehistoric—Arizona. 5. Indians
of Mexico—Rites and ceremonies. 6. Indians of North
America—Arizona—Rites and ceremonies. 7. Indians
of Mexico—Antiquities. 8. Indians of North America—
Arizona—Antiquities. 9. Excavations (Archaeology)—
Mexico. 10. Excavations (Archaeology)—Arizona. 11. Mexico—
Antiquities. 12. Arizona—Antiquities. I. Fish, Suzanne K.
II. Fish, Paul R. III. Villalpando, M. Elisa, 1954–
F1219.3.R38T85 2007
972'.01—dc22 2007009473

Manufactured in the United States of America on acid-free,
archival-quality paper containing a minimum of 50% post-
consumer waste and processed chlorine free.

CONTENTS

FOREWORD

This volume on trincheras archaeology of northwestern Mexico and the U.S. Southwest launches a new archaeological series for the Amerind Foundation, as well as a new and promising relationship between the Amerind and the University of Arizona Press. The series, *Amerind Studies in Archaeology*, will publish the synthetic results of professional seminars held each year at the Amerind Foundation in Dragoon, a program that was begun in 1987 to encourage and support archaeological scholarship in the Western Hemisphere. In recent years the focus of Amerind's seminar program has expanded to embrace the Old World as well as the New, and a collaboration between the Amerind Foundation and the Society for American Archaeology promises to bring many outstanding symposia to Dragoon in the years to come. With these changes in the direction and scope of our seminar program, we felt it was an appropriate time to launch this new series.

There is perhaps no better topic for the first contribution in *Amerind Studies in Archaeology* than that of a region that has long been a focus of Amerind's research efforts: the southwestern and northern Mexican borderlands. Hilltop trincheras are one of several archaeological manifestations that were unfortunate enough to span an international border and, in consequence, have not received the concerted attention they deserve. The symposium on Enduring Borderlands Traditions held at the Amerind Foundation in the winter of 2002 was designed to address this neglect. Chaired by Paul and Suzy Fish of the Arizona State Museum and Elisa Villalpando of INAH Sonora, the Trincheras symposium brought together scholars from the United States and Mexico who have conducted original research on hilltop trincheras sites in the four adjoining states of Chihuahua, Sonora, Arizona, and New Mexico. By the end of the five-day symposium, there remained considerable disagreement among participants about what trincheras are and are not, but there was, I think, a new appreciation for the geographic, temporal, and cultural range of these enigmatic hilltop sites, and many new and provocative ideas about their functions and historical contexts. Much more work remains to be done on trincheras sites, but the synthetic effort of this symposium and book are an important contribution to a continuing effort.

My sincere thanks to Suzy, Paul, and Elisa for conceiving and chairing the symposium and editing the book, and to the participants in the symposium and authors of the chapters whose original research and synthetic efforts are contained herein. I thank George Gumerman, former director of the Arizona State Museum in Tucson, who set aside funds to help make the symposium and book possible. Thanks also to Amerind's board of directors for their continuing support of our seminar and publishing programs, and to the tireless efforts of Amerind staff. I suspect that longtime Amerind director Charlie Di Peso would have encouraged and applauded this contribution to borderland studies, even as he, no doubt, would have disagreed with some of its results.

John Ware
Director of the Amerind Foundation

PREFACE

This Amerind Series volume brings together the latest archaeological research on trincheras sites, hilltop locations with stone architecture in the U.S. Southwest and Mexican Northwest that have excited interest and comment since earliest Colonial times. The volume had its conceptual beginnings in conjunction with a binational museum exhibit on trincheras sites. Initial chapter drafts were prepared for an Amerind Foundation Advanced Seminar in January 2002, and shortened versions were presented immediately thereafter as a session of the eighth biannual meeting of the Southwest Symposium in Tucson. The volume editors organized the interrelated exhibit, seminar, symposium session, and resulting publication to digest and disseminate a remarkable body of new data about and interpretation of this distinctive class of sites. The authors of the following chapters are researchers who have conducted the major trincheras projects in recent decades, and two prominent scholars who have investigated hill sites of Mesoamerican affiliation to the south.

The opening of the exhibit, "In Flight: Adriel Heisey's Images of Trincheras Archaeology," at the Arizona State Museum closely preceded the Amerind Advanced Seminar and the Southwest Symposium. It celebrated Heisey's remarkable, close-up aerial photography of trincheras sites from his ultralight aircraft (Heisey plates 1–11). His images, also seen in this volume, capture the visual essence of trincheras sites in Sonora, Arizona, Chihuahua, and New Mexico. The Arizona State Museum, University of Arizona, and the Instituto Nacional de Antropología e Historia, Centro Sonora, cosponsored the exhibit. George Gumerman and Fernando Tapia, the respective directors of these two institutions, strongly supported the opportunity for binational cooperation in presenting and interpreting the common cultural heritage of the borderlands.

Suzanne Fish, Paul Fish, and Elisa Villalpando served as exhibit curators, in collaboration with Russell Varineau of Arizona State Museum Public Programs. Harald Eeckels, Director of the Museo de Sonora, administered exhibit travel and installation as it moved from Tucson to its second venue in Hermosillo later in 2002. Jose Luis Punzo, Director of the Museo de las Culturas del Norte, facilitated the third exhibit venue in Casas Grandes, Chihuahua, in 2003. Laura LaPere was instrumental in producing the permanent online version of the exhibit, available at http://www.statemuseum.arizona.edu.

John Ware, Director of the Amerind Foundation, hosted the advanced seminar in its spectacular, historic conference facilities in Dragoon, Arizona. He and his staff created the optimal surroundings for scholarly interaction and exchange. Funding was provided by the Arizona State Museum and the Amerind Foundation. The seminar was scheduled to immediately precede the Southwest Symposium in Tucson. At the invitation of Barbara Mills, 2002 program chair, the volume editors organized a session by seminar participants to communicate their findings and initiate feedback from the archaeological community.

Advanced Seminar participants were asked to prepare a paper placing their current research in broad problem-oriented frameworks and to circulate it prior to the meeting. Trincheras investigators in attendance were Christian Downum, Paul Fish, Suzanne Fish, Robert Hard, Randall McGuire, John Roney, Elisa Villalpando, Henry Wallace, and David Wilcox. Stephen Kowalewski and Ben Nelson acted as discussants, providing comparative perspectives based in Mexican archaeology. John Ware aided the volume editors in moderating deliberations. The present publication reflects the intense, productive interchange of information, argumentation, and interplay of ideas that transpired during the memorable days and nights in Dragoon.

A generous gift to the Arizona State Museum from Arch and Laura Brown made possible the publication of Adriel Heisey's photographs. Allyson Carter and Nancy Arora of the University of Arizona Press skillfully guided us through the publication process. We thank Lisa Williams, who copyedited the book manuscript, and Andrew Christenson, who prepared the index. Matthew Hill prepared figures for publication. Todd Pitezel made substantive comments and compiled the comprehensive bibliography. Stephen Lekson and an anonymous reviewer offered valuable suggestions to chapter authors and contributed significantly to the quality of the volume.

Elisa Villalpando, Instituto Nacional de Antropología e Historia, Centro Sonora
Suzanne K. Fish, Arizona State Museum, University of Arizona
Paul R. Fish, Arizona State Museum, University of Arizona

Trincheras Sites in Time, Space, and Society

1

Introduction

Paul R. Fish, Suzanne K. Fish, and Elisa Villalpando

This volume addresses a common theme, but it is the lively and occasionally contentious product of authors with differing theoretical orientations and research objectives. The central purposes of this book and the events leading up to it were: (1) to bring together the extensive and often unanticipated results of recent trincheras studies in the Mexican Northwest and U.S. Southwest; (2) to document the considerable variability among these sites in age, geographic location, and cultural affiliation; (3) to examine the role of trincheras sites in their contemporary societies; and (4) to begin to synthesize these findings. The term *trincheras*, with its various meanings, and the study of the corresponding archaeological manifestations have a long scholarly history in the U.S.–Mexico borderlands, as we will presently outline. The list of known hilltop locations included under this rubric has grown substantially over the past 20 years, with dramatically expanding chronological and geographic boundaries. The "trincheras phenomenon," by most definitions, now spans almost three millennia, from 1250 BC to AD 1450, encompasses substantial portions of Chihuahua, New Mexico, Sonora, and Arizona and, during much of this interval, represents the northern reaches of an extensive continuum of hill sites to the south (see chapters by Nelson and Kowalewski, this vol.).

The chapters in this book offer new syntheses and take great strides toward common ground but, as a whole, are far from achieving final understandings or consensus. They reflect the surge of information and intellectual ferment touched off by accelerating investigations of these intriguing hill sites. Authors begin with different assumptions and arrive at different conclusions, sometimes with regard to the same set of archaeological facts. At the same time, interpretations arising from their investigations have regional ramifications that go well beyond the interpretations of trincheras sites.

Together, the chapters represent a textbook-like array of current research issues and methodologies in the archaeology of the Northwest/ Southwest. Scales of focus range from intensive intrasite sampling to the largest contiguous survey in the region. Authors incorporate spatial analyses, artifact studies, environmental and subsistence data, ethnographic analogues, ethnohistorical records, cross-cultural comparisons, experimental archaeology, and archival resources. The result is a book-length, multifaceted exercise in archaeological inference, hypothesis testing, and argumentation.

By merging insights from shifting scales of analysis and combining approaches from anthropological archaeology, the authors frame trincheras studies within a variety of broader issues. They relate trincheras developments to the consequences of early agriculture, the emergence of village life, the appearance of differentiated site types, and tendencies toward centralization in settlement systems. Trincheras sites figure in discussions of social complexity, territorial organization, settlement pattern primacy, and the spread of local and transregional ideologies. Topics addressed by multiple authors also include the role of warfare in shaping regional societies, the layout of cultural landscapes, the importance of place, and Mesoamerican interactions with the Northwest/ Southwest.

The term *trincheras* has a bewildering array of applications in the archaeological literature. Originally referring to defensive entrenchments, the Spanish word was first used for prehispanic stone walls and terraces built on hills, but it came to designate the hill sites themselves (e.g., Fontana et al. 1959:41–42; Hoover 1941:; Sauer and Brand 1931:67; Stacy 1974:20). The term is frequently folded into the composite term *cerro de* (hill of) *trincheras*, which emphasizes the combination of stone features and placement on a hill. Cerro de Trincheras is also the name of the late prehistoric hill site with the most massive and abundant terraces in the entire region, located in the modern town of Trincheras along the Rio Magdalena in northwest Sonora. Downum and others (1994:272) previously used the term *cerros de trincheras* to refer specifically to sites with dry-laid masonry terraces on hills or low mountain peaks in the desert basins of southern Arizona and northern Sonora. This usage is too limiting, however, to include what would otherwise be termed trincheras sites outside this volume's geographic purview, as well as occasional hill sites within these boundaries that have stone features but no terraces.

Further confusing the situation with terminology, the word *trincheras* also has been used to denote terraces, check dams, and related linear features that served for water control and planting. This application includes sets of large check dams in mountain drainages surrounding Casas Grandes in Chihuahua (Di Peso 1974; Herold 1965; Hoover 1941; Howard and Griffiths 1966) and even ethnographically recorded garden terraces at Hopi in northern Arizona (Hack 1942). In addition, the Trincheras culture or tradition is the prehistoric sequence distinguished by Trincheras Purple-on-red/brown pottery in an extensive area of northwest Sonora centered on the basin of the Rio Magdalena (Johnson 1960, 1963). The characteristic painted wares were no longer produced during the El Cerro phase of this sequence after AD 1300, but it too is subsumed within the Trincheras tradition (McGuire et al. 1999).

In the volume, the minimal criteria for a "trincheras site" or *cerro de trincheras* are location on a hill and the presence of dry-laid masonry (cobble) features. This general definition does not effectively circumscribe the scope of the book, however, in that stone features of one sort or another occur on hills beyond the designated region in all directions. Additional, largely implicit referents are needed to bind a large body of otherwise disparate hill sites into a cohesive realm of inquiry. The primary referent is scholarly tradition. Even though the unanticipated diversity of trincheras sites in time, space, and affiliation is one of the major revelations of recent research, there is a strong legacy in borderlands archaeology of considering them as a unitary phenomenon. A second commonality is geographic extent. Although multiple authors acknowledge potentially related hill occupations in adjacent regions, and may draw differing classificatory boundaries, the chapters in this volume examine cases from central Arizona and New Mexico on the north through the central portions of Chihuahua and Sonora to the south (fig. 1.1). It is now abundantly clear that the overall distribution and duration of these sites does not reflect historical relationships in any direct or simple manner, but, in the largest sense, they embody an enduring regional tradition.

Sites meeting the criteria for a trincheras classification in the border-

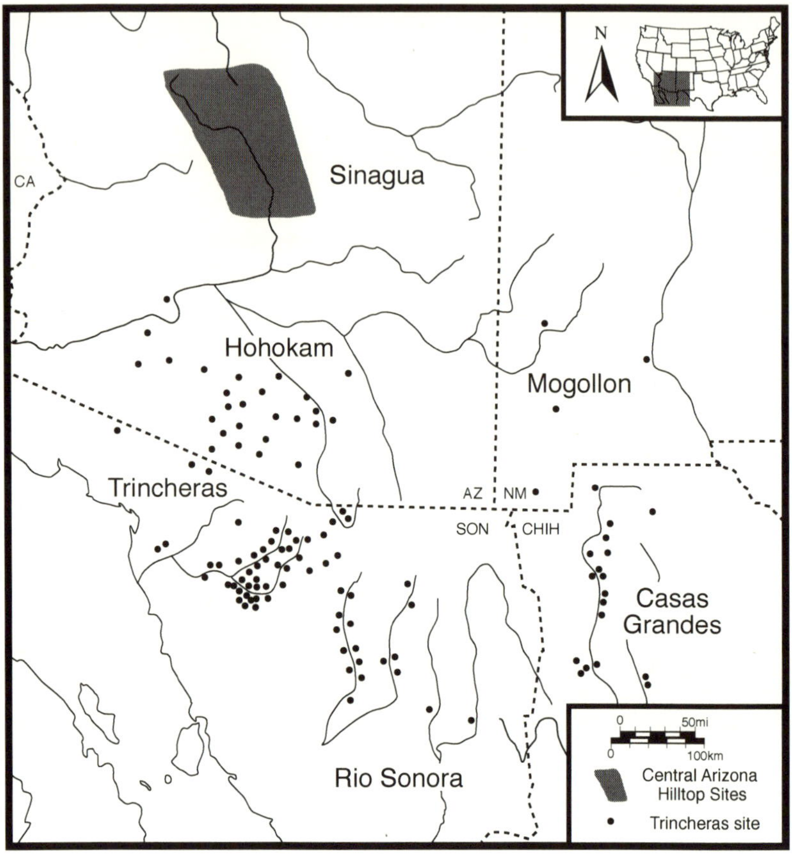

1.1 Distribution of trincheras and Central Arizona hill sites and major culture areas of the Northwest/Southwest.

lands usually occur on dark volcanic hills or low peaks. Because local populations in all periods occupied non-masonry structures on basin floors and lower slopes, elevated trincheras sites built with stone always stand out as distinctive elements of their settlement systems. Terraces typically are the predominant form among an additional variety of walls, structures, and other stone features. Individual hill sites exhibit great variability in the types, abundance, and arrangements of such features (Downum et al. 1994:272).

From Spanish Colonial times (Mange 1926:21), a recurring interpretation of trincheras sites has been as places of refuge, and of their terraces and walls as fortifications (e.g., Hoover 1941; Sauer and Brand 1931; Wallace and Doelle 2001; Wilcox 1979). Defensive interpretations are based on reported cases of retreat to prehispanic trincheras sites during postcontact conflicts, difficulty of access by virtue of location on a hill, and a view of terraces and walls as defensive structures. Alternative interpretations over the years have emphasized other dimensions of hillside settlement and architecture, including residence (e.g., Braniff C. 1990:177–179; Downum 1986; Downum et al. 1994; Tanner 1936; Hard et al. 1999:140–141; Huntington 1914; McGuire et al. 1999; Sauer and Brand 1931:118–119); terrace agriculture and dooryard gardens (e.g., Fish et al. 1984; Huntington 1914:69; Katzer 1993; Stacy 1974:194–205); monumentality, specialized site function, and visual prominence within a settlement system (e.g., Downum 1993; Downum et al. 1994; Fish and Fish 2004; Fontana et al. 1959:292–293; Haury 1976; McGuire et al. 1999:142); and line-of-site signaling (e.g., Braniff C. 1992:177; Fontana et al. 1959:43; Johnson 1960:50).

Prior to the 1980s, most investigations of trincheras sites were conducted through relatively brief reconnaissance (e.g., Fontana et al. 1959; Huntington 1913, 1914; McGee 1898; Sauer and Brand 1931) and even systematic studies were based almost exclusively on surface observations (e.g., Stacy 1974; Wallace 1983; Wilcox and Larson 1979, but see Tanner 1936 and Greenleaf 1975 for exceptions). Since that time, excavated data, absolute determinations and other refined dating, comprehensive and detailed maps, discoveries in new regional sectors, and the ability to place trincheras sites within contemporary settlement patterns have reversed many prior assumptions and demonstrated a previously unsuspected degree of variability in every aspect. Perhaps most significantly, new evidence has shown that trincheras occupations began in preceramic times (Fish et al. 1986; Hard and Roney 1999), recurred intermittently almost until the time of Spanish contact (McGuire et al. 1999), and crosscut the major cultural divisions of the region (figs. 1.1 and 1.2).

Despite significant advances in knowledge, a major axis of debate continues to be the nature of principal site function. Although no authors make a claim for unitary and exclusive trincheras function, a division is evident between those who champion defense and those who favor alternative explanations for hill location and features such as central place functions and ideological motivations. Proponents frame this

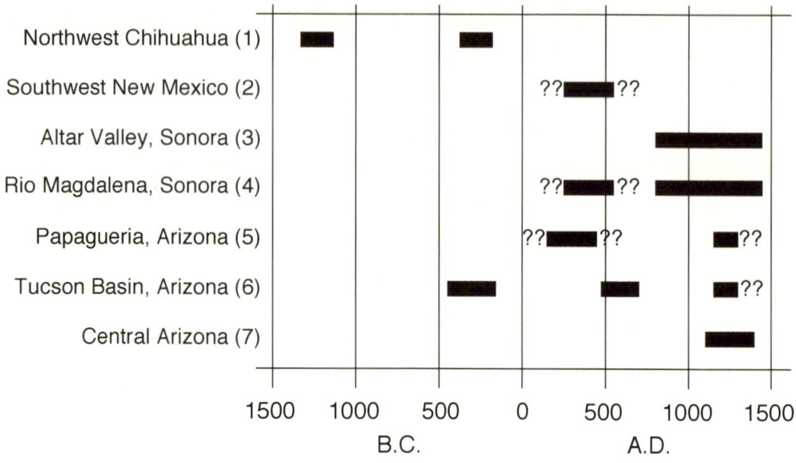

1.2 Chronology of trincheras and Central Arizona hill sites. (1) Hard and Roney 1998; (2) Roney 1999; (3) McGuire and Villalpando 1993; (4) Fish and Fish 2004; McGuire and Villalpando, this volume; (5) Stacy 1974; Wallace et al., this volume; (6) Downum et al. 1994; (7) Wilcox et al., this volume.

debate in data-rich and theoretically informed arguments about specific times and places. Hard and Roney appeal to a cross-cultural, comparative methodology in reviewing worldwide hill sites; authors such as Nelson and the Fishes find insights in regional ethnography and ethnohistory.

Even though temporal assignments are sometimes preliminary, and the discrimination of multiple components may present unresolved problems, chronologically diagnostic patterns have begun to emerge that resemble horizon styles in their cross-cultural and geographic extent. Massive and nearly continuous encircling walls and terraces around hill summits occur in late Preceramic and earliest Ceramic trincheras occupations, including a series of sites in northwest Chihuahua, Canador Peak in southwest New Mexico, and Tumamoc Hill in southern Arizona (fig. 1.3). Similar constructions have not been recorded for later Ceramic trincheras sites. Likewise, unroofed stone enclosures or *corrales* on hill summits are typical of the later Ceramic trincheras sites in Sonora, but not of the earliest ones. Fish and Fish (this vol.) suggest trends in the placement and associations of such summit features in northwest Sonora, southern Arizona, and perhaps beyond. After ca. AD 1100–1200, both isolated enclosures with sparse artifacts and residential settlements occur separately on hills in distant sectors of the Northwest/Southwest (Fish and Fish, this vol.; Wilcox et al., this vol.). Future analysis undoubtedly will reveal additional chronological and geographic patterning in trincheras attributes, much like the temporal change in terrace types described by Kowalewski (this vol.) for highland Mexico.

The chapters by Hard and Roney and Wallace et al. describe extensive occupations between approximately 3000 and 2000 BP that represent the initial appearance of residential hill sites in the Casas Grandes area and the Tucson Basin. In both archaeological sequences, the huge encircling walls and terraces represent the earliest forms of public archi-

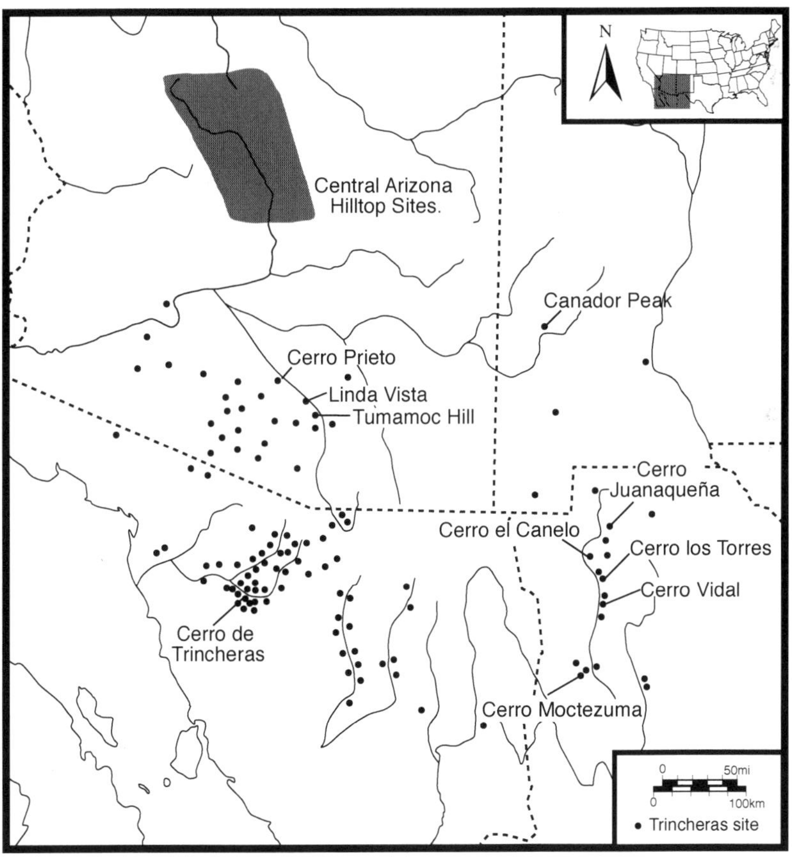

1.3 Trincheras sites discussed in this volume.

tecture, in the sense that their construction entailed widely shared labor. The first coordinated building efforts by these societies appreciably postdates their adoption of corn, documented in Tucson by 4000 BP and likely somewhat earlier farther south in Chihuahua. Inhabitants of the Tucson Basin had cooperated in canal construction for centuries, but prior structures serving limited communal purposes in their villages had been low-cost in labor and materials (Mabry 1998, 1999). The authors of the two chapters consider how the earliest trincheras sites fit into the increasingly differentiated settlement patterns, social trajectories, and centralized tendencies of developing village life.

Trincheras sites are among the most populous, spatially complex settlements known for their times, beginning with those of the Preceramic and Early Ceramic periods (Hard and Roney, this vol.; Wallace et al., this vol.). The role of individual trincheras sites as central places is addressed in detail for later Ceramic times. The chapters by Downum and by Fish and Fish examine the complex layout of Hohokam trincheras settlements as a specialized site type within the territorial entities of the Classic period. McGuire and Villalpando describe the differentiated residential and public precincts of Cerro de Trincheras in the Magdalena Basin. This remarkable site transcends the usual regional implications of central place and stands out as the unparalleled primate center for a broad cultural sphere throughout northwest Sonora.

Enhanced inventories of hill sites provide a new basis for distributional observations and analyses. Hard and Roney note line-of-sight relationships among early sites in Chihuahua. Wilcox and his colleagues combine extensive archival and field research in reporting a far-flung network of hilltop sites across central Arizona marked by strategic location and intervisibility. Fish and Fish discuss the distribution and functions of secondary trincheras sites in the settlement system surrounding Cerro de Trincheras. They propose a relationship between the distinctive *corrales* at these sites and similar enclosures on hills extending to the north and east beyond Sonora, against the backdrop of transregional ideologies in the Southwest/Northwest during late prehistoric times.

From a comparative perspective, Nelson and Kowalewski review ethnohistoric and archaeological evidence for hill site attributes, scale, and significance among the societies of Mesoamerica and its northern fringes. They illustrate configurations related to militarism, tenets of

Mesoamerican ideology, monumentality, a diversity of central place activities, and settlement specialization. Nelson analyzes markers for relative social complexity from the vantage of La Quemada in Zacatecas. Kowalewski considers volume themes, directions, and unresolved issues in light of the archaeology of Oaxaca and highland Mexico.

Despite a quantum leap in knowledge and analysis, little progress has been made in defining historical continuities among successive intervals of hill usage in the Northwest/Southwest. The title *Trincheras Sites in Time, Space, and Society* speaks to conscious connections, but the manner of transmission remains elusive. Intrinsic properties of hills undoubtedly have relevance too: view of the countryside, visibility by populations below, sense of closeness to the sky, intervisibility among hills, and the microclimatic and other environmental effects of elevation. The emerging record of multicomponent trincheras sites attests to the potential for persistent or recurrent occupations. The manipulation of social memory very likely motivated reuse in some instances. Evidence for prolonged postoccupational visits to former trincheras locations further suggests their historical roles in subsequent cultural landscapes, in which they remained prominent and meaningful elements. Mechanisms of conceptual and ideological interchange that could account for cross-cultural and transregional trincheras attributes likewise await further inquiry.

Trincheras studies of recent decades have done much to strengthen ties among U.S. and Mexican scholars with shared interests in the borderlands. Research has progressed in tandem to both the north and the south. Archaeologists from the two countries have collaborated as principal investigators, and many projects have incorporated binational students as well as local personnel. Thanks to this productive and ongoing interchange, the chapters that follow take a broader vision of the archaeology of trincheras sites than ever before.

2

Cerros de Trincheras in Northwestern Chihuahua

The Arguments for Defense

Robert J. Hard and John R. Roney

Recently we have been investigating a series of 14 *cerros de trincheras* in northwestern Chihuahua (Hard and Roney 1998, 2004, 2005, 2007; Roney and Hard 2002, 2003, 2004). The sites consist of terraces and other dry-laid stone features on the summits and slopes of isolated hills. In this presentation we emphasize the four sites that we have tested or excavated: Cerro Juanaqueña (Heisey, plate 2), Cerro el Canelo, Cerro los Torres, and Cerro Vidal (Heisey, plate 3). The largest of these, Cerro Juanaqueña, includes more than 8 km of terrace walls, and its features cover more than 11 ha. AMS radiocarbon dates from the four sites suggest that they were built and occupied during two distinct episodes. The earlier and more substantial lasted some 200 years, about 1300 to 1100 BC. There is evidence of a second occupation at about 300 BC on two sites.

Macrobotanical analyses show that these are among the earliest sites in the Southwest/Northwest with a substantial dependence on maize agriculture. Excluding wood charcoal, maize is the most abundant plant taxon (Adams 1998, 1999a, 1999b, 2000), and we have found possibly domesticated amaranth in some samples (Fritz et al. 1999). All four sites that we have tested include evidence of intensive residential occupation. We suspect that Cerro Juanaqueña was occupied by a group of about 200 people, and that a large part of the population lived there for at least nine months each year. We have documented 13 other cerros de trincheras in northwestern Chihuahua. The others are smaller than Cerro Juanaqueña and were used less intensively, but the three that we tested are all clearly part of the same pattern, dating to the Late Archaic period and yielding a similar range of artifacts, faunal remains, and macrobotanical materials.

The construction of each of these sites represents a substantial investment of energy. On the basis of a replication experiment, we estimate conservatively that at least 30 person years were required to build the terraces at Cerro Juanaqueña (Hard et al. 1999), and that Cerro el Canelo, Cerro los Torres, and Cerro Vidal each received perhaps one-quarter to one-half of that total. Aside from their initial construction, considerable effort was required to sustain occupation in these inconvenient settings. All fuel, water, food, and construction materials had to be carried, some on a daily basis, as much as 160 vertical m from floodplains at the foot of the hills. Moreover, the hilltop settings are exposed to strong winds in the spring; extreme heat in the early summer; wind, rain, and lightning during the monsoon season; and cold winds and inclement weather in the winter. Despite such costs, people chose to live in these settings, and they must have had strong reasons to do so. We believe that understanding this phenomenon is an important key to understanding the social and material processes surrounding the initial diffusion of agriculture into this region.

Agriculture

Three general explanations have been offered for cerros de trincheras: agriculture, display, and defense. In the case of the Late Archaic cerros de trincheras in northwestern Chihuahua, it is unlikely that the terraces were built for agricultural purposes. Extensive agricultural terrace systems were built in this region about AD 1200, but the late prehistoric features are very different. They were constructed along small drainages and on alluvial slopes where runoff is concentrated and where sediment can be trapped. The terraces that were built on cerros de trincheras, in contrast, show no concern with availability of runoff. They were also built in areas with as little as 230 mm of annual precipitation, which is marginal for direct rainfall farming. Finally, we have computed the total area of potential farmland created by the terraces at Cerro Juanaqueña and have estimated the agricultural production that might be expected, based on yields in the Sierra Tarahumara. This exercise suggests that if planted in corn, Cerro Juanaqueña could have fed four adults for one year (Hard et al. 1999). This is a small payoff for a project that required 30 person years of labor to construct.

Display

It is has also been proposed that cerros de trincheras were constructed as a form of display (Haury 1962). The concept of display includes a wide range of behavior. In this context the specific interpretation is that cerros de trincheras represent a form of monumental architecture, construction which in scale and elaboration exceeds the requirements of any practical function (Trigger 1990). O'Donovan (2002, 2004) proposes, for example, that domestic terraces at Cerros de Trincheras in Sonora were built in monumental proportions to convey messages regarding ethnicity and power, and that the town served as a major social and ritual focal point. The occurrence of monumental construction at 1500 BC in the Southwestern culture area would be quite unexpected. Such behavior is usually associated with higher population densities and with levels of social integration that we do not envision for this period.

Defense

Defense is the third explanation for the construction and residential use of cerros de trincheras. In the remainder of this chapter, we will consider the Late Archaic cerros de trincheras of northwestern Chihuahua from this point of view. We will develop three basic points. First, in a worldwide ethnographic sample, most residential occupation of hilltop settings is associated with raiding and warfare. Second, many of the conditions associated with increased raiding and warfare were present in northwestern Chihuahua 3,000 years ago. Third, many specific characteristics of cerros de trincheras in northwestern Chihuahua conform to criteria for recognition of defensive sites.

Cross-Cultural Study of Hilltop Settlements

Although these three hypotheses have been in the literature for decades, they have been difficult to evaluate, and investigators' biases toward particular hypotheses are sometimes evident. In order to gain further insight into these hypotheses, we conducted an ethnographic cross-cultural study of hilltop settlements. A number of specific questions motivated this project, including: (1) Why do people live on hills? and (2) Are settlements located on hills for single reasons, multiple reasons, or no particular reason? In our own culture, elevated locations are preferred for reasons of status, view, climate, elite access, recreation, and personal preference. Are these reasonable alternatives to consider for traditional societies without low cost or motorized transport? Are the conditions that motivate the original siting of a settlement the same as causes for continuing to occupy a location? Can the ethnographic literature offer any further insights toward an improved understanding of archaeological hilltop sites?

Methods

Using the microfiche and Web-based Human Relations Area Files (HRAF), we examined the settlement patterns of 186 cultures around the world for cases of residential use of hills and other elevated landforms. This sample represents more than 50 percent of all the cultures in the HRAF files and includes all cultures available on the Web-based eHRAF in 2002 and all microfiche cases at the University of Texas at San Antonio library. The eHRAF sample includes a statistically representative sample of the world's cultures.

This portion of our study focused on ethnographic residential sites, that is, locations where the normal residential unit lives for at least part of the year. Systematically pursuing ethnographic nonresidential uses of hills was beyond the scope of this study, but we did record such use by the same groups that residentially use hills. We also focused on only the residential hilltop aspect of each ethnographic group's settlement pattern, as opposed to sites in all settings.

The initial step in the study was to identify cultures that used elevated landforms for residential settlements. Using the HRAF system of cultural materials codes (Outline of Cultural Materials), we searched under codes related to settlement patterns. For the microfiche files this required reading all sections related to settlement patterns for all groups. For the Web-based eHRAF, we used the full-text search engine to locate synonyms and their variants (e.g., hill, bluff, mountain, ridge, terrace, escarpment, mesa) that co-occur with settlement pattern information.

Selecting cases for inclusion in the study required a number of definitional decisions. A case was identified if its normal settlements included residential use of the top or sides of any pronounced elevated landform, high or low. However, cases where settlements simply went up the lower slopes of a valley were not considered. Similarly, small knolls, slight slopes, low rises or other situations where it appears that slopes were gentle and/or elevations slight were not considered to be "pronounced elevated landforms." We accepted cases with settlements on hillocks, for example, while rejecting those on gentle rises. We also required that settlements be on particular elevated landforms, not simply "in the mountains." A number of pastoralist groups were excluded on this basis. Cases also had to belong to an identifiable ethnic group for a known time and place. Hill uses that appeared to be atypical for a group or were nonresidential were also excluded, as were rockshelters. Field houses and herding camps were considered to be special use sites rather than residential sites, as they were typically utilized by a subset of the usual domestic unit. Note that for ease of discussion we use the term *hill* generically to mean the top or slopes of any of these pronounced elevated landforms. Applying the procedures discussed above to 186 cases, we identified 42 ethnographic groups that use elevated landforms for residential sites.

Once cases were selected, we returned to the HRAF files for more detailed examination of each case in order to identify explanations of the hill use. As we reviewed each case, we read or electronically searched all sections identified by cultural material codes on settlement pattern, land use, architecture, public structures, political organization, religious practices, sacred objects, warfare, agriculture, and monuments, searching for references to use of hills using the hill synonyms.

A typical cross-cultural approach searches for correlations between variables such as presence of warfare and the presence of hill residential locations. For the purposes of this study, such correlations would have been seriously misleading, because even when warfare does occur, hill use may be unrelated to that circumstance. In order to understand the reasons for hill use, we had little choice but to rely on the observers' explanations. After eliminating two cases with insufficient information, we were left with 40 ethnographic groups. These 40 cases are listed in appendix 2.1, which also tabulates the ethnographic explanations given for residential use of elevated landforms.

Limited Options. We used the term *limited options* to signify cases in which there appear to be few alternatives to living on hills. In most cases the ethnographers drew this inference, but in a few cases, such as the Inca, we made the inference ourselves, based on descriptions of topography, as well as the location and context of other settlements. In extremely steep, mountainous terrain where most settlements are on steep slopes and little bottomland is available, such an inference is justified. "Limited options" was also identified under conditions of population pressure where authors clearly indicate that all potential settlement locations are occupied, as is the case with the Thai Miao. There were also cases in which hills are occupied because low-lying ground floods or remains damp, such as among the Ganda of Uganda.

Defense. Ethnographic explanations for all categories were critically evaluated, corroborated with additional sources as needed, and in most cases accepted. However, we were careful not to accept unsubstantiated statements about defense or warfare. We required specific discussions of fortifications, raiding, or other direct evidence of the defensive nature of a location before an inference of defense was accepted. There were a few instances in which an elevated settlement location was attributed to warfare without any corroborating evidence, and those explanations were not accepted. However, we did accept physical evidence of defense at a hilltop location, such as fortifications and city walls, as prima facie evidence that defense was at least one of the reasons for using a hilltop location.

Agriculture. Agriculture was accepted as an explanation if hill residences provided access to terraced or unterraced hill slope fields and there were statements to that effect. Sometimes both limited options and agriculture were accepted as explanations if there was little bottomland and hill slopes were both farmed and lived on. However, agriculture, rather than limited options was accepted as an explanation in cases where people could have lived on lowlands but instead elected to live near their hillslope fields, as among the Ifugao of the Philippines.

Environment. Environmental explanations were accepted whenever hill residences provided access to particular resources other than fields, such as food resources, protection from wind, access to springs for domestic water, a location to watch for game, avoidance of insects, etc. Examples include the Mbuti, Copper Inuit, Pawnee, and the Khasi of India.

Symbolism. We added this explanatory category after reading about spiritual linkages and ethnic identification strongly associated with particular landforms. Examples occur among the Hopi and the Dogon of Mali.

In a number of cases, explanations for hill uses varied by time or place within a given culture group. The analysis does not treat every context within a culture as a separate case with a separate explanation, but rather lists the one case as having multiple explanations. While this procedure sacrificed precision, we felt it was a more conservative approach that minimized assumptions. However, notations in appendix 2.1 distinguish among the various uses and their explanations. We accepted cases that were tied to ruins and other abandoned locations if they appeared to be well understood and it was clear that the ruins belonged to the same culture as the case being examined. For example, the pre-Columbian hilltop ruins in the Aymara region of Bolivia were not considered, as they probably do not belong to the ancestors of the Aymara and there was little information about the ruins in the HRAF documentation. On the other hand, ruins of thirteenth- to sixteenth-century hilltop castles in Okinawa were included as an element of that case, because their Okinawan use was documented. Certainly not all cases had similar levels of information, but cases were accepted when there was sufficient oral history, historical, ethnographic, and/or archaeological information in the HRAF files to achieve a basic understanding. Only in the cases of the Maori, Akan/Ashanti, and the Okinawans did we pursue literature outside the HRAF records. We expect that further research on other cases will corroborate our findings, while at the same time contributing additional explanations that we did not discover. For example, we considered fifteenth-century Slovenian hilltop castles as placed on hills for defensive reasons, but more detailed historical or archaeological research may reveal additional explanations related to agriculture, environmental resources, etc. However, it is unlikely that the defensive component of the explanation will be rejected based on further research. Appendix 2.2 presents bibliographic citations for the appendix 2.1 entries.

Appendix 2.1 also indicates whether or not monumental construction occurs on the elevated landforms. Such concerns were outside the repertoire of nineteenth- and twentieth-century observers, and the criteria for identifying monumentality are not always clear. We identify monumental architecture as large public buildings (including palaces) that required major labor investments and involved centralized control or planning (McGuire 1998; Nelson, this vol.; O'Donovan 1997). Following O'Donovan (1997), we considered the visual impact of monumental construction. However, visual impact was difficult to evaluate, as in no case was the visual impact on members of an ethnographic group recorded, only the visual impact on the investigator. Because they are not public structures, neither the massive domestic structures among the Garo of India nor Iroquois longhouses were considered monumental, nor were the enormous terraced fields of the Ifugao, despite their scale and visual impact. In keeping with the emphasis of this study, we focus on constructions that were elements of towns or other residential centers, and exclude monuments that were isolated from towns. Therefore, huge mountaintop shrines to Buddha and isolated temples are not considered. Notations in appendix 2.1 also identify the nature of these monumental works as political, religious, or ritual. Large temples, churches, and mosques are considered religious monuments. Palaces, castles, elaborate city gates, massive encircling screens or fences, and administrative centers are considered political monuments. Maori large, carved posts are monumental ritual objects.

Results

Figure 2.1 is a graph showing the various ethnographic explanations given for residential use of hills and other elevated landforms. In 38 percent (15) of the cases, defense was the only reason for selecting upland residential locations. These cases include, for example, the Shluh/Berbers of Morocco, who fortified settlements on hilltops; the Maori, who constructed elaborate hilltop fortified villages; and the Hadramaut of South Yemen, who constructed walled sultans' palaces on clifftops. Three cases (8 percent) are attributed solely to limited options. These include the Amhara, who live on the deeply incised Shoan plateau of Ethiopia; the Pomo, who live on sides and tops of ridges due to the deep, narrow canyons of the Sierra Nevada in California; and the Ganda

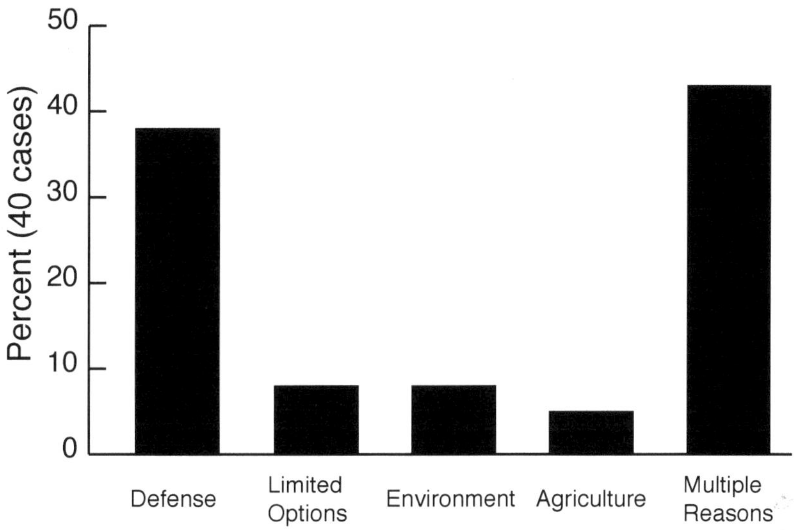

2.1 Single and multiple explanations for hill residential use.

of Uganda, who must select low, flat-topped hills because the lowlands in the vicinity of Lake Victoria are all swampland. Another three cases (8 percent) can be attributed solely to environmental conditions or access to resources excluding agriculture. These include the Mbuti, who seasonally establish camps to obtain honey on hills; the Kuna of Panama, who locate some villages on 30-foot-high bluffs to avoid river floods; and the Tzeltal of Chiapas, Mexico, who live on small hills to take advantage of improved drainage. In only two cases (5 percent) do people choose to live on hill locations only in order to gain access to elevated agricultural fields. These examples include the Ifugao of the Philippines, who live close to their elaborate, irrigated rice terraces; and Serbs, who live on high alluvial terraces near their fields. The remaining 17 cases, or 43 percent, are associated with multiple explanations.

Considering only the 17 cases with multiple explanations, the number of explanations for a single case ranges from two to five. The number of explanations for a given case is related to the complexity in the circumstances of hill living, to the changing history of hill occupation, and to the amount of information for each case. Among these 17 cases, limited options, defense, and access to agricultural land were each represented 11 times, or 65 percent of 17 cases. Environmental reasons

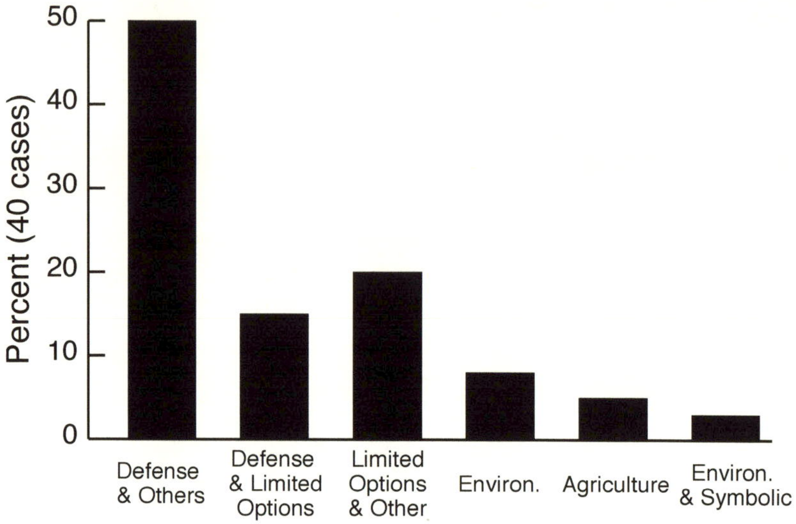

2.2 Multiple explanation cases are distributed among the major categories of explanations.

were given in 10 (59 percent) cases, and 3 of 17 (18 percent) ethnographic groups chose to live on hills or other elevated landforms in part for symbolic reasons.

Sixteen of these 17 multiple-explanation cases include defense and/or limited options as explanations. The most common co-occurrence among the 17 is agriculture and limited options, with 10 examples. Defense and limited options co-occur in six instances. Figure 2.2 includes all cases and distributes the multiple-explanation cases among the single-explanation defense and limited options as appropriate. Fifty percent involve defense, including 5 cases that are defense associated with a variety of other reasons plus the 15 defense-only cases. In addition, 6 more cases (15 percent) are associated with defense and limited options. An additional 20 percent include limited options without defense. Therefore, 65 percent of all cases (26) of hilltop living can be explained by defense, and another 20 percent can be accounted for due to limited options, although many of these are associated with additional explanations as well.

The role of warfare in siting villages and towns on elevated landforms is further emphasized as specific shifts in land use patterns are documented following cessation of warfare. In 13 of the 26 defense-related cases, residents wholly or partly relocated to lower elevations following the end of hostile threats. These cases include the Dogon (in part), Alor, Maori, Tanala, Siwans, Eastern Toraja, Garo, Khasi (relocated to slopes), Copper Inuit, Hopi (in part), Iroquois, Lau Fijans, and Maya of Icaiche. We had information on the circumstances that prevailed when hilltop locations were settled in only two cases, those of the Hopi and the Icaiche Maya, and both were defensive reactions to conflict. It is notable that substantial segments of the Dogon and Hopi populations continue to occupy elevated locations due to other resources accessible from their elevated locations, limited options for moving elsewhere (Dogon), and the symbolic value that their traditional homes offer. Unfortunately, information is lacking on shifts or persistence in settlement pattern for many of the remaining cases.

Eleven (28 percent) of the 40 ethnographic cases included monumental architecture at the hill residential locations. Nine cases include political monuments, including castles, palaces, and city gates. These cases included the two African kingdoms of the Ashanti and Ganda, which build enormous palaces surrounded by screens several kilometers in length but not fortified. Only two cases have only religious or ritual monuments, the Siwan mosques and the Maori huge carved posts.

Do hilltop settlements with monumental architecture have explanations that suggest their circumstances are significantly different from nonmonumental sites? In seven of the 11 monumental cases, defense is considered the only explanation, and defense is among the explanations in two additional cases. Therefore, in nine (82 percent) of these cases, defense is one of the reasons for use of hills. Three (27 percent) ethnographic cases with monumental architecture are related to limited options, two (18 percent) are related to agriculture, one (9 percent) is related to environmental reasons, and one (9 percent) includes symbolism as a reason for locating on hills (the Ashanti). Defense is strongly related to hilltop settlements whether or not monumental architecture is present. In fact, nine of the 11 monumental cases contain massive defensive structures such as castles or city walls. There appears to be little difference in the explanations for cases that have monuments versus those without monuments.

We found no cases suggesting that people take advantage of elevated landforms principally as a form of display or to enhance the effects of monumental constructions. However, the Ashanti case is particularly relevant to issues of monumentality and symbolism, as chiefly centers are sometimes established on hills where enormous enclosed palaces are built for the king, retainers, and wives (including the Ashanti capital of Kumasi). While it appears that in this case low hills are sometimes preferred in order to avoid constantly damp valleys, some hills are also imbued with symbolic significance related to ancestors and royal descent. In one case following British destruction of symbolic fetishes and elimination of the office of priest-king, the inhabitants abandoned the hill and settled at its foot, suggesting that the elevated location was preferred due to its symbolic ties to kingship. However, in all but this and the Ganda case, examples of monumental constructions are strongly linked to defensive functions, and it is difficult to argue a dominant role for the symbolic impact of monuments on hills.

We noted the nonresidential use of elevated landforms, and they are listed in appendix 2.1. Twenty-four (60 percent) of the 40 cases included the practice of some type of hillside agriculture, and in eight of these 24 cases agricultural terraces are constructed. It is also clear that elevated locations are favored for an array of religious activities, including: shrines (28 percent of 40 cases), funerary locations (25 percent), temples and other communal religious structures (23 percent), ritual locations without construction (10 percent), homes of spirits (10 percent), and sacred natural objects such as trees (10 percent). Secular activities were not as common as religious ones and included: herding or field stations (10 percent), communal secular buildings such as schools (13 percent), fortifications (15 percent), and lookouts (10 percent). Note that some of these special locations are occupied, but not by a typical residential social unit (for example, Buddhist temples in Korea).

Discussion

These results are highly patterned. Eight-five percent of cases can be accounted for by the presence of one or two conditions, defense and/or limited options. There is clear evidence that defense was the principal factor motivating hilltop living once the threat of warfare passed. In half of the 26 defensive cases the settlements shifted to lower elevations once hostilities ended.

How do these findings apply to residential occupation on cerros de trincheras? Of our 40 ethnographic cases in which people choose to live on hills or other elevated landforms, 14 examples are groups whose territory is located in rugged settings where there are no alternative residential locations (our limited options explanation). Clearly this circumstance is not present in the basin and range topography where the cerros de trincheras are located. Defense is a factor in 20 (77 percent) of the 26 remaining cases, and is the sole explanation for this behavior in 15 (58 percent) cases. Environmental reasons are the second most common ethnographic explanation for residential occupation of hills, being cited in nine (35 percent) examples, five of which include defense and are also included in the above count (77 percent). The four remaining environmental cases include Mbuti honey camps plus three other cases that use low, elevated landforms to avoid flooding or for improved drainage (Ashanti, Kuna, and Tzeltal). Proximity to agricultural fields is cited in only three (12 percent) of the 26 cases; they include the Serbs, the Ifugao, and the Hopi, and the latter included defense as an explanation. Finally, in two of the 26 ethnographic cases people chose to live on hills for symbolic reasons, and in each of these cases other factors were also involved.

Returning again to the entire set of 40 ethnographic groups, in no case are hills residentially occupied for solely symbolic reasons. No case was found in which occupied hills appeared to have been elaborated as monuments. Agriculture is a common factor in hill living only when associated with conditions of limited options or under unique circumstances. However, we did find that many special use functions of hilltops were related to ritual activities. These findings strongly suggest that in the absence of any other information, raiding and warfare are the most likely explanation for residential use of the cerros de trincheras, although independent archaeological data and methods for evaluating these sites must continue to be pursued.

From our work some characteristics of defensive sites emerge. The high frequency of abandonment of hilltop locations following the end of warfare is consistent with LeBlanc's (1999) suggestion that defensive locations may be characterized by short use lives and rapid abandonment. We also noted information concerning the vertical height of elevated residential locations. Table 2.1 lists both nominal and quantita-

Table 2.1 Height of Hills.

Nondefensive Explanations		Defensive Explanations	
Group	**Elevation**	**Group**	**Elevation**
Tzeltal	10 m	Dogon	300 m
Ashanti	low	Alor	100–150 m
Ganda	low	Hadramaut	60–100 m
Garo	low	Hopi	120 m
		Lau Fijan	250 m
		Maya	120 m
		Inca	high
		Iban	high
		Korea	high
		Pawnee	high
		Luo	high
		Garo	high

tive information on hill height, dividing the cases into nondefensive vs. defensive explanations. The hill height of defensive cases is from 60 to 305 m and is generally described as high. Three nondefensive cases are described as low, and a fourth is listed as 9 m high. All four of these cases were related to living on elevated locations to avoid wet conditions and flooding. (Note that for this comparison, the high Garo defensive sites and the low-hill Garo nondefensive settlements are separated.) Higher hills are preferred for defense, and lower hills may satisfy nondefensive concerns. In addition, the elevated settings of defensive locations have particular characteristics and include isolated hills, isolated ridges, small mountain spurs, locations next to narrow gorges, slopes with difficult approaches, platforms cut into the side of mountains, hilltops hidden by thick brush, and locations next to precipitous cliffs. All are clearly characteristics that enhance defensibility and limit access.

Settlement locations generally represent spatial compromises to facilitate access to environmental and social resources within particular ecological and cultural settings. In most cases, living in elevated locations serves to reduce access to many resources and external social interactions. During war this is advantageous; during peace it frequently is not. People apparently do not elect to live in elevated locations unless compelled to do so by circumstances that warrant the high transport costs of hill living. In contrast, it appears that many ritually related special use sites may involve a preference for hilltop locations. The patterns in our own society of some preference for elevated locations by the wealthy appears to be an artifact of modern conditions (including mechanized transportation) and cannot be expected to be analogous to traditional situations.

The analysis presented above points strongly to raiding and warfare as an explanation for residential use of isolated, elevated landforms. Are there other reasons to apply this explanation to Late Archaic cerros de trincheras in northwestern Chihuahua? The following sections of this chapter address this question.

Conditions Associated with Raiding and Warfare

There is growing recognition that raiding and warfare are not limited to societies with obvious social hierarchies. Several recent publications argue persuasively that anthropologists have long underestimated both the occurrence and importance of conflict in small-scale societies (Keeley 1996; Otterbein 2000), and in the past few years a number of books and articles have begun to reconsider the role of warfare in the prehistoric Southwest (Haas 1990; Haas and Creamer 1996; LeBlanc 1999; Lekson 2002; Rice and LeBlanc 2001; Schaafsma 2000; Wilcox and Haas 1994). Anthropologists have considered raiding and warfare from a wide range of perspectives, but for the purposes of this discussion our immediate concern is with the contexts that lead to these kinds of behavior. That is, what general social, economic, and technological conditions are commonly associated with raiding and warfare? Keeley (1996:117) summarizes empirical studies that have addressed the question. Surprisingly, he found that raiding and warfare are not strongly correlated with either high population densities or social hierarchies, as we might expect.

Keeley does specify four conditions associated with increased bellicosity: (1) rapid population growth, which increases economic demands and also stresses the capacity of social institutions; (2) development or introduction of new technologies of food production, transportation, and war; (3) the existence of frontier zones, such as zones of contact between complex and egalitarian societies, between pastoral nomads and village farmers, and between farmers and foragers; and (4) expectable but unpredictable disasters such as droughts, floods, and insect infestations.

Thirty-five hundred years ago agriculture was making its appearance in northwestern Chihuahua. This new technology opened a whole range of subsistence possibilities and at the same time imposed new constraints. People in different settings responded to agriculture in different ways. In northwestern Chihuahua we see a dramatic population increase, a strong emphasis on settlements in floodplain settings, increased sedentism, and population aggregation. These conditions must have required major changes in social institutions and, in our view, would have led to the kind of instability that Keeley describes. Instability would have been accentuated by fluctuations in agricultural production, which can result from a variety of causes. This is just the type of expectable but unpredictable disaster that Keeley found to be associated with increased raiding and warfare. Proximity to foraging people who continued a very different lifestyle in the Basin and Range province to the east implies that the early agricultural sites in northwestern Chihuahua were also a frontier zone, and this may also have been a factor that increased the intensity of conflict in the region.

In short, all of the conditions that Keeley identifies were present in northwestern Chihuahua 3,000 years ago, leading to a strong theoretical expectation of violent conflict during this period. Can we accept the residential occupation of cerros de trincheras as an empirical confirmation of this expectation? The next two sections of this chapter address this issue.

Settlement Pattern Criteria

Another approach to this issue is to consider the specific characteristics of the cerros de trincheras in northwestern Chihuahua. LeBlanc (1999) has developed a series of settlement pattern criteria that he uses to assess the prevalence of raiding and warfare in the prehistoric Southwest, and in this section we will evaluate the Late Archaic cerros de trincheras in northwestern Chihuahua against his criteria. The strength of this approach is that LeBlanc's criteria are not post hoc arguments developed to explain selected aspects of the cerros de trincheras. Instead they are general observations derived from a broad consideration of raiding and warfare, which appear particularly applicable to this situation.

One of LeBlanc's criteria, the location of sites on defensible landforms, is also a hallmark of the cerros de trincheras. Our own ethnographic review of hilltop occupations confirms an association with raiding and warfare and suggests that defensible postures are characterized by high (ca. 60–300 m), isolated locations with difficult access. Table 2.2 summarizes the four cerros de trincheras that we have tested or excavated. The lowest is Cerro los Torres, an 80-m-high hill, and the other three are on hills that rise between 120 and 160 m above the surrounding terrain. All of these hills have steep sides, and most of the constructed features can be reached only after climbing a steep slope. These sites all offer excellent views in 360 degrees. Detailed artifact distribution data from Cerro Juanaqueña indicate that residential occupation occurred on all sides of the hill, and it is likely that this is true of the other sites as well. The combination of excellent visibility and steep slopes ensures that the inhabitants of these hills could not be taken unaware. Any potential attacker could be seen from some distance, and attackers could not rush the settlement or even approach it rapidly.

Another of LeBlanc's criteria is evidence that sites were planned and laid out for defense. In the case of these four cerros de trincheras, perimeter berms are the most obvious evidence for planning and defensive layout. Although individual terraces are the basic features on these sites, the terraces are often contiguous, forming linear groups that we have termed macrofeatures. On the four cerros de trincheras discussed here, the macrofeatures defining the exterior boundaries of the sites are very large. At Cerro Juanaqueña the macrofeature that defines the northern, eastern, and southern perimeter of the site consists of 22 adjoined terraces forming a 400-m-long alignment. Where this macrofeature extends perpendicular to the slope, it resembles other macrofeatures composed of individual terraces, but on the northern and southern sides of the site, it follows the slope and takes the form of a large cobble berm rather than a terrace. This feature is also different from most other macrofeatures

Table 2.2 Four Cerros de Trincheras in Northwestern Chihuahua.

Site	Dist. to Floodplain (km)	Ht. of Hill (m)	Area (ha)	Total Terrace Length (m)	No. of Rock Rings	Period
Juanaqueña	.4	120	11.2	8,350	114	Late Archaic
Upper Complex			*6.0*	*4,980*	*100*	*Late Archaic*
Lower Complex			*5.2*	*3,370*	*14*	*Late Archaic*
Canelo*	1.9	160	5.8	3,900	50	Late Archaic
Torres	.9	80	5.2	2,300	8	Late Archaic
Vidal	.2	120	4.0	2,190	25	Late Archaic

Note: Lines in *italics* are subtotals.
* indicates some outlying features are excluded.

in that the cobble berm extends well above terrace surfaces in many places. A similar feature defines much of the exterior boundary of Cerro el Canelo, and Cerro los Torres is surrounded by a striking perimeter berm. Similarly, Cerro Vidal is enclosed by a perimeter berm on three sides, while the fourth side consists of a near vertical slope. These berms did not consist of freestanding masonry walls, which characterize later periods of Southwestern prehistory. However, they would have offered protection to defenders standing behind them, and because of their height and the insecure footing, they would have impeded attackers. Within the sites a maze of macrofeatures composed of adjacent terraces would have provided successive lines of defense.

LeBlanc argues that increasing site size is another line of evidence suggesting warfare, based on the simple principle that larger communities have a significant military advantage over smaller neighbors. We do not have good information about settlement sizes in the times preceding

1250 BC, but few prehistorians would expect any settlements approaching the scale of Cerro Juanaqueña. We have argued elsewhere that this one site may have included 200 to 300 inhabitants through much of the year (Roney and Hard 2002). The other three cerros de trincheras may have housed as few as 50 or as many as 150 inhabitants. This situation contrasts sharply with models of preagricultural times, when small populations of foragers are thought to have spent much of the year dispersed into individual nuclear family units. Response to raiding and warfare is one of several processes that can lead to population aggregation, but at least these observations are consistent with assumptions of prehistoric warfare.

LeBlanc points out that rapid construction is another characteristic of many defensive sites. He argues that when small, dispersed communities are abandoned due to the threat of attack, large defensive sites are often built immediately thereafter, using techniques particularly suited to rapid construction. One line of evidence suggests that the cerros de trincheras in northwestern Chihuahua were built rapidly, rather than growing slowly through accretion. The perimeter berms at the four sites described here suggest that large portions of these sites did not grow slowly through uncoordinated construction. Instead, the features appear to have been planned to accommodate specific needs and constructed in coordinated efforts.

Several of LeBlanc's expectations are either not met or cannot be addressed using data from northwestern Chihuahua. For example, none of the sites have protected domestic water supplies, a characteristic that is largely precluded by their hilltop location. However, all are adjacent to the floodplain of the Rio Casas Grandes, with relatively easy access to water.

LeBlanc also suggests that smaller sites needed more defensive capabilities than larger sites, hypothesizing that smaller sites are more likely to be located in highly defensible settings. We have found no evidence of this. Indeed, Cerro Juanaqueña is almost certainly the largest Late Archaic site in the region, and it is among the most defensible. LeBlanc does state that during intervals of extreme warfare, small sites may cease to exist. Instead, everyone resides in some form of larger, fortified community. Given the brief span of occupation at Cerro Juanaqueña, and the apparently synchronous use of cerros de trincheras in this region, this may well be the case during two distinct episodes in the Late Archaic period.

Other criteria that cannot be satisfactorily addressed on the basis of current information pertain to site distributions. During many periods of warfare in the Southwest, settlements tend to occur in distinct clusters separated by no-man's-land. Sites are clustered to provide mutual aid, and the empty zones between clusters are not exploited intensively, because they are not secure. The cerros de trincheras in northwestern Chihuahua form a distinct cluster as LeBlanc predicts, but settlement pattern data from the Late Archaic period are so incomplete that we are reluctant to stress this argument. Similarly, arguments related to the sequence of site abandonment within clusters and the sequence of cluster abandonment within a region simply cannot be evaluated at this time.

We do know that line-of-sight communication is possible between many of the cerros de trincheras in northwestern Chihuahua. Figure 2.3 shows all of the cerros de trincheras that we have documented, as well as the visual linkages among them. The 14 sites form three, or perhaps four, separate groups. Cerro Tascate in the north appears to be isolated, and three sites in the Rio Santa Maria drainage form a separate group. Seven sites in the Rio Casas Grandes drainage are definitely intervisible: Cerro Juanaqueña, Cerro la Virgen, Cerro el Canelo, Cerro la Angostura, Cerro la Fundición, Cerro los Torres, and Cerro la Cruz. Further south, Cerro la Boquilla de San Diego, Cerro Vidal, and Cerro Tinaja also form a definite group of visually interconnected sites. These two groups are connected by a line of sight between Cerro la Cruz and Cerro la Boquilla de San Diego.

Other Evidence

Several other observations have a bearing on the likelihood that the Late Archaic cerros de trincheras in northwestern Chihuahua reflect intensive episodes of raiding and warfare. First, LeBlanc and other authors often consider poorly treated human remains as evidence of warfare. These are human remains that did not receive the formal, highly standardized treatment typical in many prehistoric Southwestern societies. At Cerro Juanaqueña we excavated only 0.1 percent of the cultural deposits (37.8

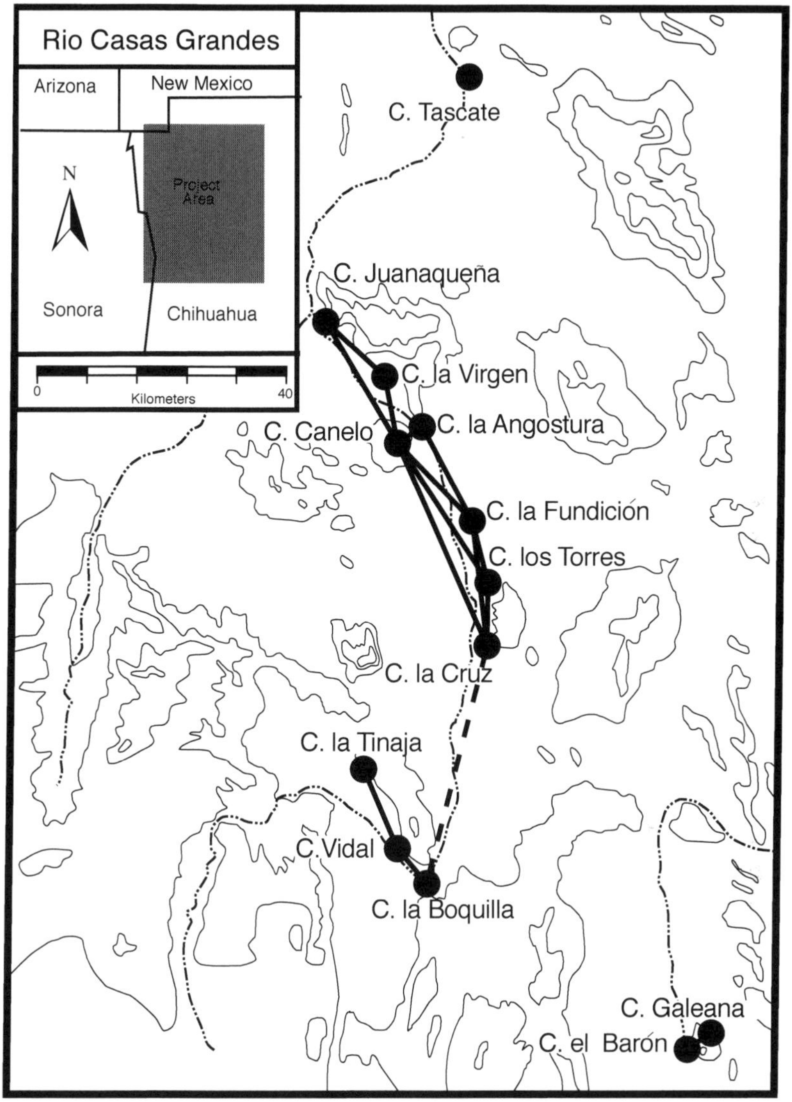

2.3 Line-of-sight relationships between Chihuahua cerros de trincheras locations.

m^3 excavated; 31,000 m^3 total), and we did not encounter any formal burials. However, three different proveniences on the site did yield 10 small fragments of human bone, and two of the human bone fragments from two different proveniences were burned (Schmidt and Nisengard 2000). It is possible that these bone fragments are derived from disturbed burials that we simply did not encounter in our test excavation units. Also, Late Archaic cremations are known from the Southwest Basin and Range province, and this behavior, or even accident, could account for the burned fragments of human bone. However, it is also possible that these observations reflect poorly treated human remains, another indicator of violence and warfare.

Second, a phenomenal number of projectile points have been recovered from Cerro Juanaqueña. This site has yielded more than 300 projectile points, and another 220 bifaces or biface fragments, most of which are also almost certainly from projectile points or preforms. This contrasts dramatically with artifact assemblages from many other Late Archaic sites in the Southwest. Based on size, most of these projectile points are dart points. They accompany a faunal assemblage that is strongly dominated by rabbits, a prey species most often taken by clubs, throwing sticks, and nets rather than by projectiles. These considerations raise the possibility that the artifact assemblage at Cerro Juanaqueña, and perhaps at some of the other cerros de trincheras as well, reflects raiding and defense.

Third, radiocarbon dates from four cerros de trincheras in northwestern Chihuahua suggest that use of these sites was brief and synchronous throughout the region. The 23 AMS radiocarbon dates from Cerro Juanaqueña indicate that its principal period of use was a brief interval around 1250 BC, with a second, more limited occupation around 300 BC. Four AMS radiocarbon dates from Cerro los Torres and Cerro el Canelo indicate that those sites were occupied at the same time as the principal occupation at Cerro Juanaqueña, about 1250 BC. Two AMS radiocarbon dates from Cerro Vidal show that it was occupied at the same time as the second occupation at Cerro Juanaqueña, around 300 BC. These data suggest that regional occupation of cerros de trincheras was synchronous during two episodes. These observations are difficult to reconcile with the "agriculture" and "display" models for cerros de trincheras.

Summary and Conclusion

Why did people live on hilltops in the Rio Casas Grandes valley 3,000 years ago? Three lines of argument, each substantiated with independent data, point to warfare. First, based on a global cross-cultural sample, people expend the additional energy to live on elevated landforms when defense is a key concern and when there is an absence of other places to live. The latter is certainly not a concern in the Rio Casas Grandes valley. The few other conditions of hilltop living include avoidance of flooding, access to agricultural fields, access to a wild resource (in one case), and symbolic reasons. In no case are hills residentially occupied for solely symbolic reasons. Agriculture is a common factor in hill living only when associated with conditions of limited options or unique circumstances. Low elevations suffice to avoid flooding. In contrast, special uses of hilltops are common and frequently relate to ritual activities. These findings strongly suggest, when linked with the other arguments, that raiding and warfare are the most likely explanation for residential use of the cerros de trincheras.

Second, Keeley's conditions that stimulate warfare were likely to have been present, including: rapid population growth that may have stressed resources, introduction of food production, a zone of contact between farmers and foragers, and unpredictable droughts and floods.

Third, the cerros de trincheras sites meet LeBlanc's predicted defensive characteristics, including: defensible land forms, defensive site layouts, rapid construction, large populations, and site intervisibility. Other data suggestive of warfare include two distinct but synchronous occupations among the four sites, and large numbers of projectile points at Cerro Juanaqueña. In summary, these sites are best understood as residential defensive settlements rather than any of the alternative models.

Acknowledgments

Our research in northwestern Chihuahua has been supported by the Instituto Nacional de Antropología e Historia in Mexico, D.F., and Ciudad Chihuahua. The work has been funded by the National Science Foundation (SBR-97086210, SBR-9809839, and SBR-0219185) and by the National Geographic Society. The University of Texas at San Antonio provided two UTSA Faculty Research Awards, among other support, and the U.S. Bureau of Land Management has supported our work.

One of us (RH) held a National Endowment for the Humanities University Teachers Fellowship while this chapter was being prepared for publication. Christiane Cunnar of Human Relations Area Files at Yale University generously provided access to eHRAF. Joe Davis and Larissa Galenes assisted with technical aspects of the research. The detailed comments of two anonymous reviewers improved the chapter.

Appendix 2.1 Ethnographic Data

Group	Country	Fieldwork Years	Limited Option	Defensive	Agri-cultural	Environ-mental	Sym-bolic	Nonresi-dential	Monu-mental	Hill Height
Akan (Ashanti)	Ghana	1941–1946				X	X	Agricul-tural, markets, army assembly grounds	X	Low

Akan (Ashanti) towns are centered on the palace of chief; some are situated on hills, but most are on the plains. Kumasi, capital of the Ashanti kingdom, in the eighteenth and nineteenth centuries was on a low rocky eminence above a permanently wet valley, suggesting why hill living was preferred at this location. A highly decorated, huge palace was encircled by a decorated wall, and both are considered monumental. Ashanti conducted wars of conquest with competing chiefdoms and fought the British. The British built a fort at Kumasi in the late nineteenth century, but prior to this there is no evidence that Kumasi hill location was defensive, although Hull (1976) suggested surrounding marsh was defensive. When the British abolished the office of the Ashanti priest-king and destroyed the symbolic fetish at Krobo Hill, the capital of Manya-Krobo state and residence of the priest-king, people abandoned Krobo Hill and settled at the foot of the hill, suggesting the hill location was tied to the symbolic value of location.

Group	Country	Fieldwork Years	Limited Option	Defensive	Agri-cultural	Environ-mental	Sym-bolic	Nonresi-dential	Monu-mental	Hill Height
Alor	Alor, Indonesia	1938–1939		X		X				100–150 m

Alor located villages on mountain spurs and ridges for safety during warfare prior to Dutch pacification in 1918, although water must be transported up. After pacification, the government insisted villages relocate to the valley floor, although the lower elevations are colder, causing discomfort.

Appendix 2.1 Continued

Group	Country	Fieldwork Years	Limited Option	Defensive	Agri-cultural	Environ-mental	Sym-bolic	Nonresi-dential	Monu-mental	Hill Height
Amhara	Ethiopia	1946–1970	X					Terrace agriculture, churches, markets, forts, grazing		
Amhara live on the deeply incised Shoan plateau that leaves only ridgetops for settlements and most other structures. Hilltops and hillsides are also preferred to avoid rainy season flooding. Substantial warfare, but no indications settlements were located for defense.										
Andamans	India	1906–1908		X				Lookouts		
Jarawa Andamans prefer to make camps on hills or ridges, clear vegetation, and post a look-out for enemies.										
Aymara	Bolivia	1937–1969	X		X			Herding, hills have named spirits, shrines of stones		
Aymara live in the steep Andes Mountains, and land suitable for farming is scarce. Scattered homes built on agricultural terraces are watered by mountain springs. Prehispanic hilltop fortified towns are not considered a case here, as they are not Aymara and not well understood.										

Basques	Spain	1976–1981	X		X		Herding, schools, churches, hermitages, foundries for wind, mountain fortifications

Basque farmsteads are scattered on mountainsides in Pyrenees and Cantabrian Mountains. Some communities are built on hillocks. Apparently there is limited bottomland, as two-thirds of the land is mountainous. Mountain herder huts are used. Special buildings are placed on hilltops. In 1936 Basque separatists fortified themselves on summit of Mt. Intxorta.

Buka	Bougainville	1929–1930	X[a]	X[b]		X[a]	

Buka living (a) on the coast, where raiding had ceased, utilized cliff top locations in order to watch for schools of bonito and/or when insufficient land was available along beach to escape very high waves. (b) In the interior, where raiding was still prevalent, hamlets are positioned on hilltops and hidden from sight by thick brush.

Copper Inuit	Canada	1908–1916		X		X	Hunting lookouts

Copper Inuit's numerous summer base camps, which Stefánsson visited, were placed on hills for fear of Indian attack, to watch for caribou, and to avoid mosquitoes. Tents were camouflaged for fear of attacks. All later visitors reported summer camps down low by rivers.

Appendix 2.1 Continued

Group	Country	Fieldwork Years	Limited Option	Defensive	Agri-cultural	Environ-mental	Sym-bolic	Nonresi-dential	Monu-mental	Hill Height
Dogon	Mali	1931–1989	X	X	X	X	X	Terrace agriculture, rituals, priest house, temple, lookouts		300 m
Dogon villages are sometimes walled, and many are located on plateaus behind narrow gorges and on mountain scree slopes for defense against slave raiding. Since British pacification in the late nineteenth and early twentieth centuries, many more villages were spread out on plains and plateaus; but mountain rims and slopes were still occupied. They provided access to water and agricultural fields, had symbolic value, and were used when other locations were filled. These scree and mountain rim villages now attract tourists (1980s). Elaborate priest's houses are isolated from villages high on hills, contain symbols of political alliance, and are loci of rituals.										
Eastern Toraja	Indonesia	1892–1932		X				Agriculture, spirits		
Eastern Toraja made extensive use of hilltop, fortified, defensive villages. However, people lived on farms and occupied fortified villages only during raids. Following Dutch intervention in 1905, Toraja moved their villages to valley bottoms.										

Ganda	Uganda	1900–1972	X			Agri-culture, ritual centers, shrines, temples, churches	X	Low

Ganda. Around Lake Victoria is swampland, leaving innumerable low, flat topped hills as dry land. Throughout the twentieth century, villages were constructed on hill slopes, as the hilltops were too rocky. The settlements consisted of scattered homesteads surrounded by fields. In early 1900s substantial warfare but appears unrelated to village locations or hilltop defense. At same time chiefly capitals or palaces were frequently relocated to various hills and encircled by reed fences several miles long. These classified as monumental here. Modern Kampala constructed on a series of hills.

Garo	India	1908; 1936–1983		X[a]	X[b]	Agri-culture, temples, altars, spirits		high[a]/ low[b]

Garo. (a) Prior to British pacification in 1876, Garo aggregated in large villages on high hills and participated in head hunting and raiding. Some villages were fortified with pointed bamboo stakes. (b) After pacification, Garo live in small villages on low hills to avoid soil moisture along drainages.

Appendix 2.1 Continued

Group	Country	Fieldwork Years	Limited Option	Defensive	Agri-cultural	Environ-mental	Sym-bolic	Nonresi-dential	Monu-mental	Hill Height
Hadramaut	South Yemen	1918–1951		X				Terrace agricul-ture, fortifi-cations, garrisons	X	60–100 m
Hadramaut have numerous hilltop settlements including fortified towns, cities, sultans' capitals, fortified sultans' residences, military fortifications, garrisons, and watchtowers. Many hilltop settlements were occupied in the early twentieth century. High-bastioned walls surround some settlements and are visible at a distance. Battlements, palaces, custom houses, and mosques are the most visible buildings. In some cases fortified sultans' palaces and/or military garrisons are on high hills with corresponding villages built below against slopes. Numerous hilltop ruins represent centuries of use. Conflicts involve competing chiefdoms, blood feuds, and caravan raids. Conflicts ceased by ca. 1950.										
Highland Scots	Scotland	1919–1959; 1981	X		X			Grazing huts, com-munity structures		
Highland Scots sometimes build houses and scattered farms on hills and hillslopes because the region is mountainous. Sometimes towns expand up moun-tain slopes.										

Hopi	USA	1890–1995	X	X	X	X	Terrace agriculture, shrines, spirits	120 m

Hopi settled on mesa tops for fear of Spanish revenge after pueblo revolt of 1680. Hopi pueblos have symbolic values and provide access to a range of agricultural strategies as well as springs. They are also ceremonial centers. Although many people have relocated to the base of the mesas, many others have remained on the mesa tops.

Iban	Borneo	1861; 1915	X				Agriculture	High

Iban, in 1861, retreated to a fortified settlement on the 3,000-ft summit of Sadok Mountain to resist British attempts to pacify Iban headhunting. There is a similar report from 1915. Iban normally built longhouse settlements on low terraces.

Ifugao	Philippines	1868–1941; 1961–1965		X			Terrace agriculture, rituals	

Ifugao rancherias are constructed on mountainside terraces to be close to irrigated, terraced fields that can rise thousands of feet up steep mountainsides. Extensive blood feuds and headhunting occurred until 1908, but settlement locations appear not to be defensive. Rice terraces are visually impressive. During WWII, Japanese built fortifications high in mountains of Ifugaoland, and families would also hide in mountains.

Appendix 2.1 Continued

Group	Country	Fieldwork Years	Limited Option	Defensive	Agri-cultural	Environ-mental	Sym-bolic	Nonresi-dential	Monu-mental	Hill Height
Inca	Peru	1532–1560; 1610; 1940s	X	X	X			Terrace agriculture, field houses, herding structures, shrines, temples, garrisons, observatories, roads	X	High
Inca of ca. 1500–1650 lived on extensive terraced fields, had mountain-top fortified cities and towns, and lived on hillsides to conserve level land for farming. Extensive ethnohistory and archaeological data.										
Iroquois	USA	1844–1859; 1933–1950		X				Cemeteries	X	
Iroquois constructed palisaded villages from ca. 1000–1700s that were frequently located on hilltops or elevated terraces away from major waterways. Council houses are considered monumental based on scale, labor investment, and visibility. By mid-to-late 1700s, many Iroquois (e.g., the Seneca) were no longer threatened by warfare and lived in unpalisaded, smaller villages along river flats.										

Khasi	India	Pre-1830s; 1872; 1910–1911; 1955–1958	X[b]	X[a]	X[b]	X[b]	Agri-culture, crema-toriums, ancient monu-ments, sacred groves, markets

Khasi. (a) Prior to British pacification in 1830s, there was substantial Khasi warfare, and settlements were located on hills with fortifications. (b) Late 1800s to present: villages located on hill slopes, as there is an apparent absence of flat land. Preferred locations were below summits for protection from wind. Hillsides around villages are farmed. Massive stone monuments and crematoriums built on hilltops as late as 1800s and probably for centuries before.

Appendix 2.1 Continued

Group	Country	Fieldwork Years	Limited Option	Defensive	Agri-cultural	Environ-mental	Sym-bolic	Nonresi-dential	Monu-mental	Hill Height
Korea	Korea	1883–1932; 1965		X				Terrace agricul-ture, ancient defensive refuges, fortified temples, shrines, graves	X	High
Korean case refers to ancient to nineteenth-century urban centers, including Seoul, Heizanchin, An-byong, Kaisong, and Hwang-ju, that are located on elevated hills surrounded by steep mountains and encircled with huge, fortified city walls. Gates are elaborate, decorated affairs and considered here to be monumental. Temples and palaces are also considered to be monumental. Elite offices and residences were built on hillslopes. Defensive constructions were built and used over centuries during Korean, Chinese, and Japanese conflicts ca. 1500s–1700s. Some of these locations were defensive refuges and occupied only during war. In contrast, Korean farming villages, from the late 1800s to the present, are located on valley bottoms and lower slopes of mountains providing protection from wind and access to fields. Lower slopes are used to a greater extent when valleys are very narrow. Hilltops and hillsides used extensively for shrines, graves, and temples.										
Kuna	Panama	1935–1936				X		Agri-culture, ceme-teries		30 ft
A Kuna riverside village is located on 30-ft-high bluff above river to escape danger of flooding river.										

Kurds	Iraq	1946–1957		X	Agriculture, shrines	X	

The Kurd case refers only to ancient fortified cities, capitals, and towns built on hilltops and cliffs, although many are still occupied. Examples include an immense palace complex that was built in 1748 on a rocky outcrop opposite Mt. Ararat, with domes, minarets, monumental gates, and multilevel courtyards that are considered monumental here. In addition the town of Rowanduz was built on a defensible bluff after it was destroyed in WWI. During Iran-Iraq war in 1980s 30–40-ft-high watchtowers were built on hill summits. Agricultural villages are also built on the lower part of steep slopes below springs. Summer temporary huts are built on terraced hillsides for coolness.

Lau Fijan	Fiji	1924–1934	X		Great temple located at hilltop fortress		840 ft

Lau Fijans abandoned fortified villages on peaks of hills and cliffs following European settlement and cessation of warfare in the middle of the nineteenth century. Hill settlements were then relocated to flats.

Luo	Uganda	1900	X		Rituals, ceremonial structures		High

Luo villages are built high up on the hillsides for protection against hostile clans.

Appendix 2.1 Continued

Group	Country	Fieldwork Years	Limited Option	Defensive	Agri-cultural	Environ-mental	Sym-bolic	Nonresi-dential	Monu-mental	Hill Height
Maori	New Zealand	1870–1920		X					X	
Maori built about 6,000 fortified hill villages between ca. fifteenth century AD and ca. 1850. Ethnohistorical and archaeological sources describe their use and construction. Many times hilltop fortified sites served as citadels for a dispersed and mobile settlement pattern. At times fortified sites were chiefly centers. Cases include occupation on a permanent basis as well as only in response to threats. Many include concentric palisades, terraces, ditches, firing platforms, gateways, and storage pits. Carved posts, as tall as 30 ft, with decorated images named after ancestors with defiant symbolism are classified as monumental here. Most fortified sites were abandoned shortly after European contact in late 1700s, but some continued to be used as late as ca. 1850 and involved Maori use of firearms and conflict with Europeans.										
Maya	Mexico	1932–1936		X				Agricul-ture		120 m
A Maya rebel group established headquarters on the bamboo palisaded hill of Icaiche ca. 1853 after other Maya formally submitted to Mexican government. Icaiche Maya resisted British expansion in the Yucatan in the late 1800s. The village was still occupied in 1889 but abandoned by 1932.										
Mbuti	Congo	1970–1973				X				
Mbuti temporary honey camps are located on steep hills.										

Miao	Thailand	1895; 1921–1941	X	X	X		Agri-culture, sacred trees, field houses	

Miao live in mountainous terrain with few level areas. However, in hostile regions of the mountains, they also selected defensible village positions, including slopes with a difficult approach, small mountain spurs, or platforms cut into side of mountains. Miao stated that they preferred the mountains to the lowlands. These Thai Miao had migrated from mountainous area of central China and settled in mountainous area of Thailand where lowlands were already occupied. Field houses were built on slopes in rice fields.

Okinawa	Okinawa	1951–1961	X[b,c]	X[a]	X[b,c]		Terrace agricul-ture, shrines, sacred groves, priestess' dwelling	X[a]

Okinawa has three contexts of hilltop residence: (a) In thirteenth to sixteenth centuries, with emergence of warring chiefdoms, fortified castles established on hilltops. These are considered monumental here as they were decorated with elaborate gates and lacquered fencing and are now ruins. (b) In 1724 increasing population of unemployed upper class were allowed to settle in unused hilly country. There they established villages, known as yaadui, on hilltops, apparently due to limited options. (c) In northern Okinawa, due to limited flat land, villages have been built on tops of low rolling hills for centuries.

Appendix 2.1 Continued

Group	Country	Fieldwork Years	Limited Option	Defensive	Agri-cultural	Environ-mental	Sym-bolic	Nonresi-dential	Monu-mental	Hill Height
Pawnee	USA	1928–1954		X		X		Cemeteries, home of sacred animals, lookouts, sacred bundles placed on hills		High

Some Pawnee villages were fortified with sod walls and constructed on high bluffs above rivers primarily in defense from Sioux during the first half of the nineteenth century. The evidence includes ethnohistoric, oral history, and archaeological sources. By mid-nineteenth century, Pawnee relocated to reservations. The fortifications were still visible in the early 1900s. Weltfish's (1965) informant from 1928–1936 on the Pawnee Reservation indicated living in hilltop villages was considered to be more healthful.

Group	Country	Fieldwork Years	Limited Option	Defensive	Agri-cultural	Environ-mental	Sym-bolic	Nonresi-dential	Monu-mental	Hill Height
Pomo	USA	1903–1918	X							

Pomo villages tend to be located on ridge slopes and crests as a product of deep canyons and little level land in the Sierra Nevada.

Rundi	Uganda; Rwanda; Burundi	1911–1925; 1949–1951	X		X	Terrace agriculture, royal cemeteries	

Rundi settlements tend to be on mountain ridges and higher slopes of valley because valley bottoms are swamps and lower slopes are steep.

Serbs	Yugoslavia	ca. 1914; 1922; ca. 1950			X	Agriculture, cemeteries, shrines	

Serb settlements in the 1920s are on hills and on river and high alluvial terraces that are dissected with river gorges in the Jassenica region. In the 1950s some elevated locations are abandoned in favor of settlements near valley-bottom roads to participate in commerce.

Shluh/ Berbers	Morocco	1920–1928		X		Mausoleums	

Shluh/Berbers' hamlets, villages, and leaders prefer to construct fortified settlements on hilltops. Also present are fortified communal storage structures.

Siwan	Egypt	1899–1927		X		Ancient tombs	X

Siwa, the principal town, was constructed on the summit of two limestone hills by an oasis. Siwa is fortified with a continuous wall that originally had only a single gate. Rooms constructed in "pueblo" fashion about 3 to 8 stories. Eight mosques with minarets are in town and are considered monumental. By early 1900s settlements were spreading out on adjacent plains. Now the city is at base of hill, and Siwa ruins on hilltop attract tourists. Some smaller fortified towns and villages were constructed on precipitous cliffs. The town of Aghurmi is built on a high, precipitous rock and is walled with a single gate.

Appendix 2.1 Continued

Group	Country	Fieldwork Years	Limited Option	Defensive	Agri-cultural	Environ-mental	Sym-bolic	Nonresi-dential	Monu-mental	Hill Height
Slovenes	Slovenia	1964–1965		X				Churches, old forti-fications	X	
Slovenes built castles and fortifications on hilltops (now in ruins) because they were involved in conflicts with invading Turks and warring city-states in the 1400s. However, old hilltop churches remain in use.										
Tanala	Madagascar	1926–1927		X				Rituals		
Tanala, 50–75 years ago (before 1926), lived in villages of 50–80 families in defensive positions, usually on hilltops, and fortified by 10–12-ft-high log palisades and deep ditches. The houses were built on 1.5–2.5-ft-high terraces or stone-faced platforms. The Tanala now live on the flats.										
Tarahumara	Mexico	1891–1998; 1930–1989	X		X	X		Agri-culture, herding, field houses		
Tarahumara construct rancherias in dissected canyon region on narrow ridgetops and farm hillsides due to absence of valley bottoms. In uplands, some winter houses are placed on ridgetops for better solar exposure and access to firewood.										
Tzeltal	Chiapas, Mexico	1925				X		Agri-culture, shrines, churches		Small
Tzeltal build scattered, isolated houses on small prominences in hilly pine country where slash and burn agriculture is practiced. Reasons given include drainage and being able to watch for strangers. Nearby prehispanic high terraced hills that form pyramids are not considered.										

Appendix 2.2 Bibliographic Sources for Appendix 2.1

Group	Sources
Akan (Ashanti)	Busia 1951; Fortes et al. 1947; Hull 1976; McLeod 1981; Meyerowitz 1974; Steel 1948
Alor	Du Bois 1944
Amhara	Buxton 1949; Hoben 1973; Messing and Bender 1985
Andamans	Radcliffe-Brown 1922
Aymara	Bouroncle Carreón 1964; Buechler and Buechler 1971; Carter 1965; La Barre 1948; Tschopik 1951
Basques	Milbrath 1986; Ott 1981; Turnbull 1981; Urla 1987; Zirakzadeh 1985; Zulaika 1988
Buka	Blackwood 1935
Copper Inuit	Jenness 1959; Stefánsson 1914
Dogon	Beek 1990; Cazes and Jacquard 1981; Griaule and Dieterlen 1986; Palau Marti 1957; Parin et al. 1963; Paulme 1940
Eastern Toraja	Adriani and Kruyt 1950; Downs 1956
Ganda	Apter 1967; Fallers 1964; Fallers 1960; Kagwa et al. 1934; Kiwanuka 1972; Mair 1934; Ray 1991; Richards 1966; Roscoe 1911
Garo	Burling 1963; Choudhury 1958; Khaleque 1988; Playfair 1909; Rongmuthu 1960; Sinha 1966
Hadramaut	Ingrams 1938; Meulen and Wissmann 1932; Sturler-Raemaekers 1953
Highland Scots	Darling 1955; Geddes 1955; Gregor and Crichton 1946; Moisley 1962; Stephenson 1984
Hopi	Clemmer 1995; Courlander 1982; Ellis 1974; Talayesva and Simmons 1942; Titiev 1971
Iban	Pringle 1968; Sandin 1967; Wagner 1972
Ifugao	Barton 1922, 1938; Beyer and Barton 1911; Conklin 1967; Dumia 1979; Kwiatkowski 1994; Lambrecht 1929, 1932, 1957; Villaverde and Case 1909
Inca	Cieza de Leon 1883; Cobo 1893; Rowe 1946; Vega 1871
Iroquois	Blau et al. 1978; Fenton and Tooker 1978; Morgan 1901; St. John 1981

Appendix 2.2 Continued

Group	**Sources**
Kashmir	Drew 1875
Khasi	Becker 1924; Department of Economics and Statistics, Assam, Shillong 1963; Godwin-Austen 1876; Gurdon 1907; McCormack 1964; Nakane 1967; Stegmiller 1921
Korea	Andrews 1919; Bishop 1898; Bonar 1883; Brandt 1971; Carles 1888; Clark 1932; Hulbert 1906; Lee 1936; Moose 1911
Kuna	McKim 1947
Kurds	Barth 1953; Hansen 1961; Izady 1992; Johnson 1940; Masters 1953; Roosevelt 1947
Lau Fijan	Bryan 1924; Thompson 1940
Luo	Roscoe 1915
Maori	Bellwood 1971; Best 1924; Davidson 1987; Firth 1959; Groube 1970; Smith 1990
Maya	Villa Rojas 1945
Mbuti	Turnbull 1962
Miao	Abadie 1924; Bernatzik 1970; Diguet 1908; Graham 1937; Ling and Ruey 1947; Robequain 1929; Wang 1948
Okinawa	Glacken 1953; Kerr 1958; Ladefoged and Pearson 2000; Lebra 1966; Pitts et al. 1955; Sakihara 1987; Tanaka 1974
Pawnee	Hyde 1974; Murie 1914; Wedel 1936; Weltfish 1965; Wishart 1979
Pomo	Barrett 1908; Kniffen; 1939; Kroeber 1953
Rundi	Maquet 1961; Meyer 1916; Pagès 1933; Smets 1946
Serbs	Drobnjaković 1973; Filipović 1954
Shluh/Berbers	Dupas 1929; Montagne 1930
Siwan	Belgrave 1923; Cline 1936; Stanley 1912; Steindorff 1904
Slovenes	Winner 1971
Tanala	Linton 1933
Tarahumara	Bennett and Zingg 1935; Hard and Merrill 1992; Kennedy 1978; Lumholtz 1902; Pennington 1963
Tzeltal	Blom and La Farge 1927

3

Tumamoc Hill and the Early Pioneer Period Occupation of the Tucson Basin

Henry D. Wallace, Paul R. Fish, and Suzanne K. Fish

The origin of this chapter lies in a deceptively simple question and a long-standing but friendly professional debate. The question is: why on earth would anyone want to live atop Tumamoc Hill? The dispute lies in the answer, with one of us (Wallace) asserting that warfare and the requirements of defense were the prime motivation for a move to the hilltop, and two of us (Fish and Fish), suggesting specialized functions other than defense. With the Fishes' recent and previous (Fish et al. 1986) excavations atop Tumamoc Hill providing critical dating and subsurface data, and Wallace and Lindeman's (2003) excavations at Valencia Vieja (a partially coeval riverine settlement not far to the south), the authors thought this an opportune time to reexamine our perspectives on Tumamoc and its role in Tucson Basin prehistory. In the process, we refine and clarify our views, and we come to a consensus on some points. Data from the recent excavations atop Tumamoc Hill are reported here for the first time.

Many researchers have favored a primarily defensive motivation for trincheras construction; others have posited single or combined residential, agricultural, ceremonial, and signaling functions (Downum et al. 1994; Fish et al. 1994; Fontana et al. 1959; Hard and Roney 1998; Hoover 1941; Larson 1972; McGuire et al. 1999; Sauer and Brand 1931; Stacy 1974; Wallace and Doelle 2001; Wilcox 1979). Many now acknowledge some combination of these functional designations for at least the larger more complex sites. Until recently, archaeologists have assumed that most Arizona trincheras sites postdated AD 1200. For some sites in the Tucson Basin, such as Linda Vista Hill and Cerro Prieto (Downum, this vol.; Downum et al. 1994), this assumption was backed up by evidence from surface collections and excavations. In most cases, however, the inference was built on a weak association with nearby villages and rare decorated sherds. Research over the past decade in northern Chihuahua (Hard and Roney 1998), the Altar Valley (McGuire and Villalpando 1993), along the Rio Magdalena (Fish and Fish, this vol.), Canador Peak (Roney 1999), and by two of us at Tumamoc Hill, have shattered the illusion of broader temporal uniformity. It is clear that hillslope and summit sites in the region are diverse not only in size and composition, but also in temporal placement. Well-dated trincheras components now range from 1200 BC to AD 1500. Within this range, it stands to reason that some sites may be multicomponent. Investigations on Tumamoc Hill support this assertion.

When Stacy (1974:210) conducted her detailed investigation of *cerros de trincheras* in the Baboquivari Valley west of Tucson nearly 30 years ago, she recognized that the sites she investigated needed to be placed in the context of the valley settlement system. A number of recent investigations underscore the interpretive value of placing trincheras sites within a contemporary local settlement pattern (e.g., Downum 1993; Fish et al. 1992a; Fish and Fish 1989). Steven LeBlanc (1999), David Wilcox and others (2001a), and Fish and Fish (this vol.) suggest that the scale of regional investigation must be much larger in at least some cases. We turn now to the regional and temporal context of Tumamoc Hill to better understand its cultural manifestations.

Tumamoc Hill Occupations

Tumamoc Hill is a flat-topped outlier of the Tucson Mountains on the western margin of the Santa Cruz River in central Tucson (fig. 1.3, Heisey, plate 4). The hill rises 228 m (700 ft) above the floodplain, and its fine-grained soils support a rich variety of Sonoran Desert upland vegetation, including saguaros and leguminous trees. Nearby, an igneous intrusion beneath the river maintained a nearly continuous surface flow historically (Betancourt and Turner 1990; McGinnies 1981; Schwalen and Shaw 1957). Abundant and reliable water combined with extensive alluvial river terraces made this a prime location for gravity irrigation in the Tucson Basin during both prehispanic and postcontact times.

A prominent Tucson landmark, Tumamoc has one of the most extensive, massive, and complex arrays of trincheras features in southern Arizona (fig. 3.1). The constructions are concentrated at the summit of

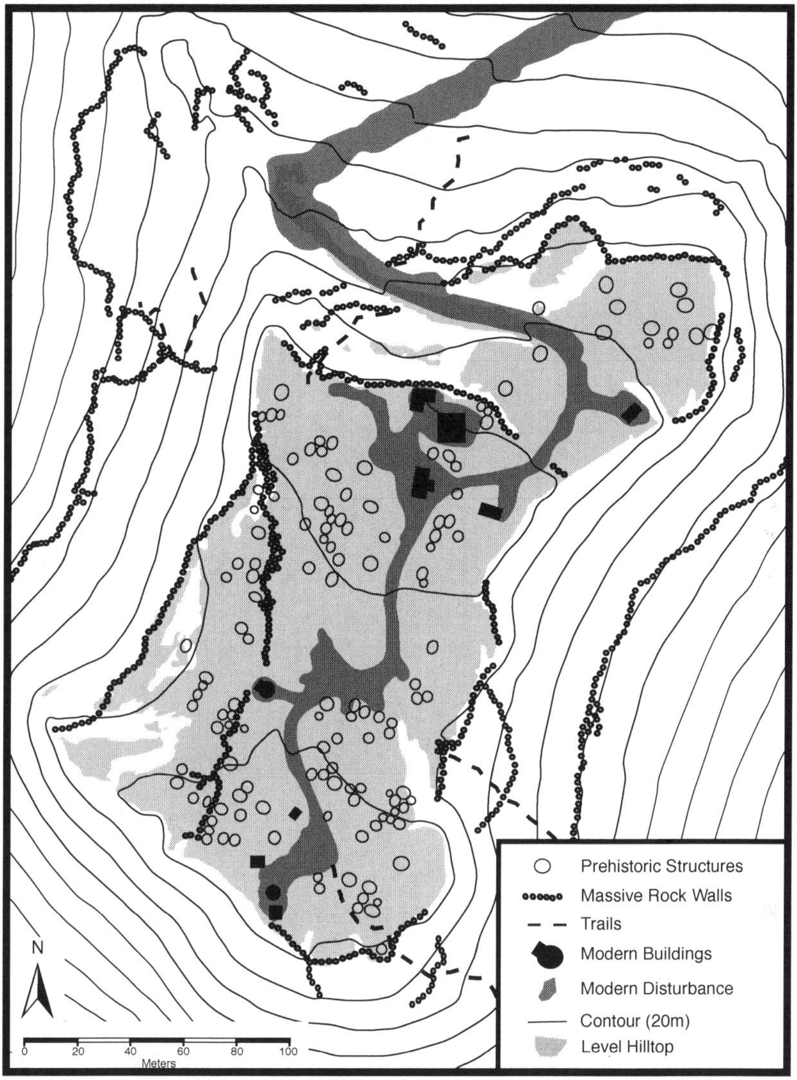

3.1 Distribution of structures and walls on the Tumamoc summit.

the hill and include massive encircling walls and terraces, an elaborate trail system, smaller terraces in residential areas, more than 125 stone outlines, large numbers of bedrock mortars and metates, and an extensive array of petroglyphs, as documented in an intensive 1970s survey by the Arizona Archaeological and Historical Society (Wilcox and

Larson 1979). Stone outlines range between 1.7 and 5.2 m on their longest axis. Shapes are predominantly rounded, but rectangular outlines are also present. They occur in clusters composed of two to ten outlines and frequently share common cleared areas and wall segments (Larson 1979:71–74).

Small-scale trench excavations were conducted by the Arizona State Museum in 1985 (Fish et al. 1986), and eight features were excavated in 1998—three stone-outlined pithouses, two pithouses not marked by stone outlines, and three small, stone-outlined terraces interpreted as activity areas or gardens (fig. 3.1). These excavations reveal that a major residential occupation took place during the Tortolita phase (ca. AD 550 to 650), following a residential presence of unknown magnitude in Early Agricultural (Cienega phase, ca. 800 BC to AD 50) times. The styles of numerous projectile points and other artifact types from the surface and the limited excavated remains suggest a substantial Early Agricultural occupation; radiocarbon dates (table 3.1) indicate that at least some of the major walls and terraces were in place by the Cienega phase. This dating of major construction rests on earlier (Fish et al. 1986) and more recent excavations into the fill behind Wall 1 (fig. 3.2) and radiocarbon determinations from an Early Agricultural pithouse, not marked by a surface outline, cut into it. The applicability of these localized findings to other Tumamoc terraces or walls requires additional confirmation. However, the discovery of trincheras sites of this age in northern Mexico (Hard and Roney 1998, this vol.) with similarly distinctive and massive encircling features and residential occupations lends credence to this likelihood.

A single Cienega phase feature has been excavated atop Tumamoc Hill, but 1998 excavations offer greater insight into the later Tortolita phase occupation. On excavation, seven of the previously mapped circular stone outlines proved to be three pithouses and three intentionally constructed nonresidential terraces of the same size range and shape (fig. 3.3). A fourth excavated Tortolita pithouse (Structure 7) that was not indicated by a visible stone outline further cautions that the number of mapped outlines cannot be directly projected as a number of houses. A fifth likely Tortolita pithouse reusing an existing depression is suggested by deposits of this age overlying the lower fill of the Early Agricultural pithouse behind Wall 1 (fig. 3.2). The fill of several Tortolita structures contained moderate amounts of secondary refuse, possibly indicating a sequence of occupation rather than a single momentary event. Recovered artifacts (table 3.2), demonstrate a full range of cultural activities typical of habitation on valley floor sites.

The sample of five houses and three activity areas was selected to test a variety of summit locations during a 10-day field season using crews from a University of Arizona field methods class. All excavated features fall in the lower size range for the 125 previously mapped stone outlines and below their average 3.3 m diameter (Larson 1979:72). The unique conditions of hilltop location contribute to the distinctive nature of Tumamoc architecture. Lower walls were built from dry-laid igneous cobbles available on the hill surface. Shallow bedrock constrained the depth of floors and the excavation of large, deep postholes. Neither hearths nor postholes were defined in any of the five excavated Tortolita phase structures. Combined with a probable bent-pole superstructure, the lack of internal features could be interpreted as indicating more ephemeral architecture than in other Tortolita phase sites. On the other hand, the floors appear to have been subject to extensive weathering, and none of the larger and potentially more substantial structures were excavated.

Early Ceramic/Pioneer Period Occupation of the Tucson Basin

For at least two millennia prior to the time of Christ, semisedentary farmers lived in small settlements in floodplain and low terrace settings along the Santa Cruz River in the Tucson Basin (Gregory 2001; Mabry 1998). Limited settlement also occurred on lower bajada alluvial fans (e.g., Fish et al. 1992a; Mabry 1998; Roth 1996) and in upland settings along major drainages and at the mouths of well-watered canyons and near springs along the front of the Santa Catalina and Tortolita mountains (Fish et al. 1992a, Huckell 1984; Roth 1996). The upland settings may have been seasonally occupied or for more extended intervals. Individual settlements typically consisted of no more than a dozen small circular structures, some used for habitation, and others for storage. At certain locations, such as at Las Capas and Santa Cruz Bend (Mabry 1998, 1999), larger settlements developed, perhaps twice the usual size.

Table 3.1 AMS Radiocarbon Dates from the Summit of Tumamoc Hill.

Context	Lab Sample Number	Conventional ^{14}C Age	Intercepts[1]	Calibrated 1-Sigma Range[1]	Calibrated 2-Sigma Range[1]	Wood/ Sample Species Dated	$^{13}C/^{12}C$ Ratio	Notes
Dates from 1998 Excavations								
PD 25, FS #2	AA45911	2078±44	90, 76, 59 BC	168–3 BC	201 BC–AD 22	*Zea mays*	−10.6	From fill of feature excavated into terrace behind Wall 1
PD 25, FS #1	AA45912	2244±52	351, 271, 261 BC	389–204 BC	400–172 BC	*Zea mays*	−10.4	From fill of feature excavated into terrace behind Wall 1
Structure 7, floor, PD 33, FS 10	AA45913	1511±48	AD 544, 549, 558	AD 475–617	AD 427–646[3]	*Phragmites*-type stem fragments	−23.8	Sample 1. Sample taken 45 cm below ground surface.
Structure 7, floor, PD 33, FS 10	AA45914	1578±49	AD 438, 453, 460, 520, 527	AD 421–541	AD 388–601[3]	*Prosopis* sp. seed	−22.9	Sample 2. Sample taken 45 cm below ground surface.

Dates from 1985 Excavations[2]

Terrace 1, behind Wall 1, Depth 60–65 cm	A2747	2110±90	161, 130, 120 BC	350–1 BC	388 BC–AD 76	*Cercidium floridium*
Terrace 1, behind Wall 1, Depth 50–70 cm	A3749	1130±270	AD 897, 922, 942	AD 652–1209	AD 397–1395	*Zea mays* cupules
Terrace 1, behind Wall 1, Depth 70–80 cm	A3750	2470±270	757, 695, 541 BC	896–206 BC	1286 BC–AD 75	*Zea mays* cupules
Terrace 1, behind Wall 1, Depth 70–80 cm	A3751	1630±270	AD 421	AD 86–662	201 BC–AD 979	*Zea mays* cupules

[1] Stuiver et al. (1998)

[2] Data from Fish et al. (1986:568). These are some of the first samples run on a new University of Arizona tandem mass spectrometry machine, and the results have sufficiently large standard deviations to make them suspect.

[3] The two dates from Structure 7 are statistically identical at the 95 percent level and can therefore be averaged. Averaged results are: 1 sigma: AD 435–561 (537); 2 sigma: AD 425–617.

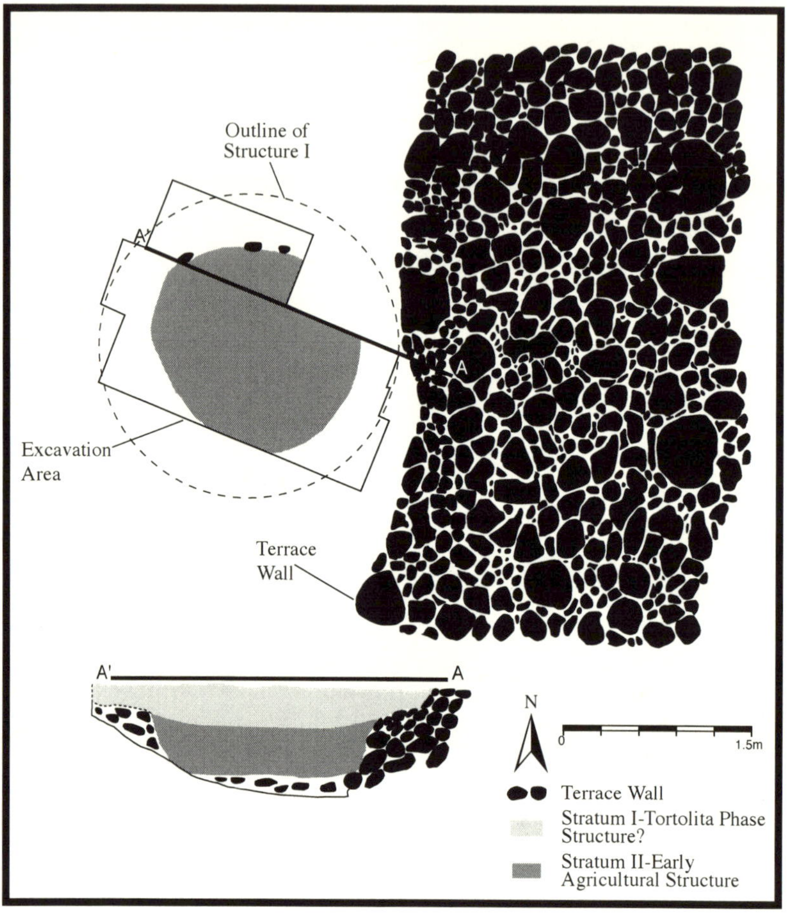

3.2 Profile and horizontal plan of excavations into terrace fill behind Wall 1.

Excavation data point to repeated reoccupation of these favored locations, resulting in very large numbers of concentrated archaeological features. Oversize round structures have been found at several sites (Mabry 1998), an indication of communal use and probable integrative function. Canal irrigation in the floodplain of the Santa Cruz River as early as 3200 BP has now been documented at multiple sites (e.g., Ezzo and Deaver 1998; Mabry 1999). There is a range of opinion on the permanence of local settlements in general, and particularly those of riverine irrigators. Some investigators suspect mobility or shifting settlements on a small scale within irrigation systems and also at larger scales as groups relocated near suitable farmland in response to shifting rainfall patterns and river conditions.

By AD 50, the pace of culture change began to accelerate. Although small, special-purpose fired clay containers had been used for several millennia, the beginning of the Early Ceramic period (AD 50 to 475—the Agua Caliente phase in the Tucson area) is marked by the first fully functional ceramic containers: seed jars or *tecomates*. Such containers were first produced in many areas across the southwest United States

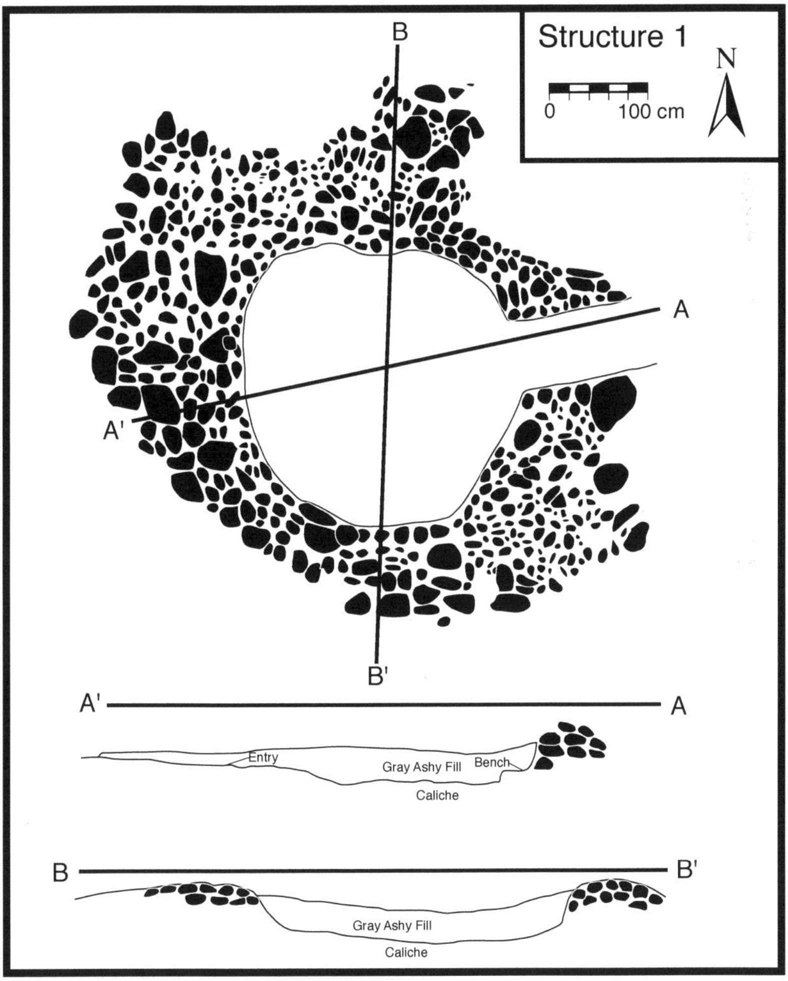

3.3 Example of an excavated Tortolita phase structure atop Tumamoc Hill.

Table 3.2 Artifact Summary from Excavated Features on Tumamoc Hill.

	Wall 1	Wall 1	Structure 1	Structure 2	Structure 3	Structure 4	Structure 5	Structure 6	Structure 7
Phase	Cienega	Tortolita	Tortolita	Tortolita	Tortolita	Tortolita	Tortolita	Tortolita	Tortolita
Feature type	Pithouse	Pithouse	Pithouse	Pithouse	Pithouse	Activity	Activity	Activity	Pithouse
Sample	Partial	Partial	Complete	Complete	Complete	Test trench	Test trench	Test trench	Complete
Ceramics									
Plainware > 1"	1	120	727	403	241	35	162	70	1,135
Redware > 1"		18	33	6	1	3	2	3	56
Flaked stone									
Debitage	8	4	333	217	18	96	25	18	182
Retouched flake	3	2	3	4		2	1		3
Core	1		4	11	3				3
Core tool	1	1							1

Hammerstone		I	I	I					
Projectile point	3	2	2	2		I			3
Biface	I		I						
Ground stone									
Pestle				I					
Informal mano	I		I	I					I
Formal mano		3	3	3					2
Slab metate			2	3				I	
Trough metate		I	I						I
Lapstone		I	I						
Other ground stone									
Shell		2							
Worked bone		2							

about the same time. Instead of being used for cooking, these vessels may have been for dry storage, perhaps of seed corn—an inference supported by a dramatic decrease in the number of storage pits (Heidke and Habicht-Mauche 1998). Particularly large structures, both round and later bean-shaped, have been documented at some sites, suggesting a continuation of the social patterns present in the Early Agricultural period. Exchange and production systems appear not to have changed much from earlier times during the Agua Caliente phase. Pottery was mostly locally made, and there are no indications of specialized production (Heidke 2003; Heidke and Habicht-Mauche 1998).

Changes during the Agua Caliente phase at about AD 400 presaged the advent of Hohokam culture. Rectangular structures replaced the traditional round (or occasionally bean-shaped) structures. Researchers have debated whether this marks an influx of migrants from the valleys to the east or is an in situ development (e.g., Cable and Doyel 1987; Wallace and Lindeman 2003; Wallace et al. 1995; Whittlesey 1995); regardless, it is noteworthy. Floor areas and residence locations in riverine settings did not change, based on evidence from the Stone Pipe site (Swartz and Lindeman 1997). A short time later, at ca. AD 475, the start of the Pioneer period, settlements along the major stream courses shifted from floodplain and lower terrace settings to second terrace locations overlooking prime farmland. This is the beginning of the Tortolita phase (AD 475 to 675/700) in the Tucson Basin sequence.[1]

Most sites with occupations that extended through the eighth and ninth centuries in the Tucson area were probably founded at this time. Those known to have Tortolita phase occupations are shown in figure 3.4. Most of these new settlements were probably fully sedentary. Some settlements were established in locations most suited to floodwater farming (such as the Triangle Road site and AZ AA:12:83); others were most likely focused on irrigation in the river floodplain (such as the Brickyard site complex, Hodges, and Valencia Vieja). Tortolita phase settlements appeared in virtually all settings occupied later in the sequence, including upland canyon mouth and spring locations. Many of the larger settlements established in the Tortolita phase became permanent villages occupied for 700 years or more thereafter.

The hallmarks of Tortolita phase occupation are the proliferation of artifact and architectural forms. The Papaguerian shell trade was initi-

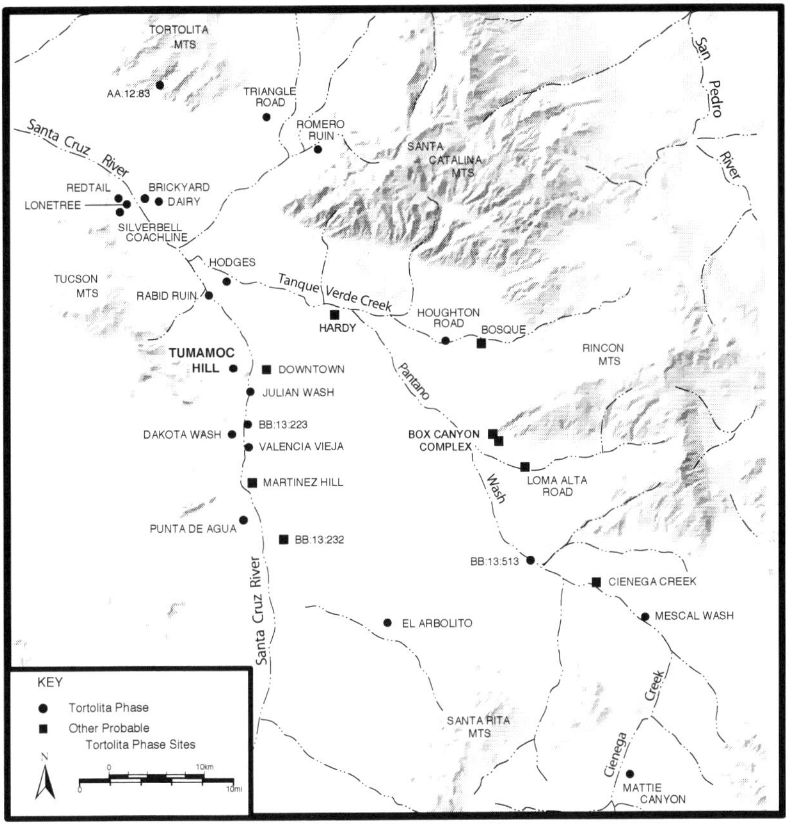

3.4 Distribution of Tortolita phase settlement in the Tucson Basin.

ated during this phase, and shell bracelets became commonplace. Ceramic vessel forms also proliferated, and pottery became more abundant, a trend most likely related to more intensively used and stable village locations. For the first time, pottery was used for cooking, and as a result, the number of pots per household increased dramatically. These trends have been interpreted as correlated with the introduction of floury Maiz de Ocho and the trough metate and mano (Adams 1994; Heidke and Habicht-Mauche 1998:82).

Partway through the Tortolita phase, based on the sequence observed at the Valencia Vieja site, population aggregation occurred. At Valencia Vieja, Wallace and Lindeman (2000, 2003) posit that at least five to ten families (or perhaps extended families) moved to the village, rapidly changing its character from a small settlement similar to the preceding small Agua Caliente farmsteads to a true village consisting of multiple lineages. Wallace and Lindeman (2000, 2003) have proposed that this process of settlement and aggregation may have correlated with intensification and expansion of agriculture in the river floodplain and floodplain margins, especially the expansion of existing canal systems and their related fields. A particularly important part of this process would have occurred near the beginning of the Tortolita phase (ca. AD 450 to 500), as new locations were settled, lineages banded together, and agricultural expansion took place; property rights and new systems of land tenure would have necessarily developed, ensuring the viability of the more permanent settlement locations.

Based on Lindeman's (2003) examination of architectural dating, developments along the lower Salt and middle Gila rivers were coeval with those documented in the Tucson area. The coincident timing of the inception of large-scale canal irrigation in the Phoenix area (Doyel 1991:247) with population aggregation and village formation points to the establishment of rigid systems of land tenure, a process that may well have stimulated similar events throughout southern and central Arizona wherever prime agricultural land was present.

Tortolita Phase Political and Economic Developments

The Tortolita phase was a time of cultural experimentation. With the advent of ceramic container cooking and a stable village location, utilitarian vessel forms achieved a level of diversity never again rivaled. It was as if every basic functional form had to be tried out before the most efficient varieties were identified and specific cultural preferences could be developed. A similar process is discernible with architecture. Tortolita phase architectural diversity is remarkable at large riverine settlements, possibly resulting from the rapid evolution of new leadership roles and community organization as a consequence of population aggregation and increased residential stability (Wallace and Lindeman 2000, 2003). At Valencia Vieja, part of the process of becoming a village was the establishment of a plaza, marking the focal point, and the construction of a series of oversize square structures around the plaza's perimeter. These structures are thought to be the residences of lineage leaders (Wallace and Lindeman 2000, 2003), as was proposed by Cable and Doyel (1987) for similar large houses in the middle Gila and lower Salt river valleys. Small residential courtyard groups at Valencia Vieja occur beyond this inner ring of higher-status residences and mark the locations of extended families. A nearly identical settlement structure is present at Snaketown (Wilcox et al. 1981) and is probably typical of large settlements of this period.

The Tortolita phase in the Tucson Basin can be viewed as a time of experimentation on political, economic, and social fronts. Politically, the shift accompanied population aggregation and the need for pooled labor to construct and maintain canal systems and fields in riverine settings. Decision making that had previously taken place within small corporate groups, with limited external interaction, now shifted to corporate groups. Competition between those groups may have led to formalized leadership roles, reflected in the appearance of the large square structures fronting the plazas at Snaketown and Valencia Vieja. The system was transitory, however, because the large square structures were replaced with smaller ones by the end of the Tortolita phase at Valencia Vieja and were gone by the start of the Gila Butte phase (ca. AD 750). This transition in community structure marks the evolution of political decision making from a segmentary lineage or corporate-group-based cooperative system to a more diffuse political system. The establishment of permanent ties to a particular point on the landscape and the development of a plaza fostered and encouraged this process. With long-term settlement in fixed locations, lineage leaders had the ability to legitimize their authority through ancestral ties and their successful participation in the development of an increasingly complex social and ritual landscape.

The plazas marked the corporate structure of the developing communities (see similar perspectives on plazas by Adler [1989], Hegmon [1989], and Rappaport [1968]). They signify a cohesive social unit composed of multiple extended families. The square structures probably were the residences of lineage leaders who cooperatively settled disputes and organized and scheduled communal agricultural projects. The reduced size of these domiciles over time suggests that the power and authority vested in their occupants diffused or shifted, perhaps due to developing social roles that crosscut lineage lines. The plaza, and the public secular and ritual activities that took place there, would have played an important role in this process. At Valencia Vieja and Snaketown, where these processes are most clearly documented, the period from AD 500 to 700 marks the point in the sequence when segmentary lineages develop, marked archaeologically by what have been called village segments (using the term as in Wallace [ed. 1995]; this differs from Howard [1990, 2000]).

Economically, the span of time marked by the Tortolita phase in the Tucson Basin and the Vahki, Estrella, and Sweetwater phases in the Phoenix area presaged the development of large-scale specialization in the production and distribution of utilitarian goods. The development of ceramic cooking technology and the appearance of flour corn and the grinding technology to go with it were cited earlier. Even with these innovations, there is no evidence for specialization in production of pottery during the period. With only one exception, most areas were producing their own pottery or acquiring it from a nearby source (Heidke 2003). Interestingly, shell and stone jewelry was being made by specialists and, for the first time in the sequence, was widely distributed in quantity (Eppley 1990:145; Vokes 2003). We suspect that valuable items were distributed differently from utilitarian goods and were most likely following social channels in place long before the Tortolita phase. The absence of village-level specialization in pottery, as was the case later in the sequence, is probably a sign that no formal intercommunity economic relationships had been established. It took the development of the ritual system marked by the construction of ball courts about AD 800 to facilitate these relationships and tie the region more closely together.

We mentioned one exception to the pattern of local production and distribution of pottery in the Tortolita phase. This is, interestingly enough, Tumamoc Hill. Based on James Heidke's analysis of the excavated sample from the 1998 excavations, Tumamoc pottery originated from many sources, contrasting with the emphasis on source(s) in the immediate vicinity at other sites (table 3.3). The implication is either that people from a number of different locations gathered at the site or that occupants were importing pottery from multiple sources (which also implies wide-ranging social contacts).

Table 3.3 Tortolita Phase Temper Provenance for Sherds Recovered from the 1998 Excavations on Tumamoc Hill.

Temper		Tortolita Red	Plainware
Volcanic sands	Beehive petrofacies	18.8	38.7
	Twin Hills petrofacies	—	15.1
	Indeterminate volcanic source	9.4	5.4
Granitic sands	Tortolita petrofacies	9.4	5.4
	Indeterminate granitic source	43.8	21.5
Metamorphic sands	Catalina petrofacies	—	2.2
	Indeterminate metamorphic source	—	1.1
Granitic or metamorphic sand		9.4	7.5
Indeterminate sand		9.4	2.2
Crushed gneiss/schist temper		—	1.1
Total vessels		32	93

Note: Numbers are column percentages of totals provided by ware. Analysis conducted by James Heidke. See Heidke (2003) for Tucson petrofacies locations.

The Role of Tumamoc in the Tortolita Phase

Although we recognize that Tumamoc Hill was repeatedly occupied, current data are limited for the pre-Tortolita-phase component(s). Our emphasis, therefore, is on the Tortolita phase occupation. Our interpretations rest on a series of key data sets (see summary in appendix 3.1) and on the strengths and weaknesses perceived in the interpretations drawn from them.

By any measure, recognition of the hilltop occupation of Tumamoc Hill in the Tortolita phase forces a serious consideration of regional settlement. Certain indisputable facts are involved in hilltop habitation. First, to build and live in a village, refuge, or fortress atop the 228-m-high hill required a considerable expenditure of energy. Although cobbles for lower wall construction were readily at hand, residents had to carry building materials—particularly wood, reeds or other thatching material—and water from the valley floor (probably from the floodplain of the Santa Cruz River). Substantial quantities of water would have been required both for the laborers and for mudding the superstructures, and no doubt many of the potsherds littering the main trails up the hill (Hartmann and Hartmann 1979) reflect mishaps in water transport. The 1998 excavations indicate that the structures were shallow pithouses rather than surface dwellings, requiring excavation into rocky soils and compact substrates. In many cases, retaining walls were built, and fill dirt and rock imported, to create enough level space for house construction and activity areas. Even without the summit-enclosing walls, the construction of these dwellings entailed considerable effort.

Wilcox (1979:29) estimated 700 person days for construction of the summit walls. We suspect a greater level of effort. The reported 1.75 km of walls would have required about 2,400 person days, or 6.5 person years, according to the experimental construction data generated by Hard and others (1999) at Cerro Juanaqueña, although this figure includes earth fill as well as rock construction.

It is important to keep in mind that Tumamoc is multicomponent and we do not currently know the extent of summit constructions during the Early Agricultural period. It is likely that some if not most of the massive encircling walls and terraces were built at that time, particularly in light of similar encircling constructions at even earlier trincheras sites in Chihuahua (Hard and Roney 1998). Tortolita residents may have added to them. Tortolita phase occupants also may have reused some existing clearings and rock enclosures to build their houses and extramural spaces. A sequence of this sort appears to be indicated by a Tortolita feature, identified by the excavators as a pithouse, excavated into the terrace behind Wall 1, which stratigraphically overlies and cuts into a previous pithouse of comparable size containing Early Agricultural period refuse.

Even if the Tortolita use of the Tumamoc summit entailed only the construction of houses, we do not think this was just another village; indeed, we know of no other Tortolita occupation on a hill. Although the hill supports abundant upland resources, and early spring crops in kitchen gardens and agave along terrace walls could have been grown to supplement the main summer harvests below, dietary staples would have come from irrigated fields on the adjacent valley floor. People would have had to tend to their lower fields if living atop the hill for any protracted time span; most food and water would have had to be carried from the valley floor. We propose two hypotheses to account for the Tortolita phase occupation on Tumamoc Hill. The first is a minor modification of an old idea: that settlement atop the hill was a response to the threat of warfare. The second is that the settlement served a special role in the regional settlement system. As will be seen in our conclusions, these ideas are not necessarily mutually exclusive.

Wallace: Tumamoc and Warfare, an Updated Perspective

The hypothesis that Tumamoc Hill is a defensive refuge has a long-standing history, but was most forcefully promoted by David Wilcox and his colleagues in the published results of the Tumamoc Hill Survey in 1979 (Wilcox 1979; Wilcox et al. 1979). It was the consensus of these researchers that the only hypothesis that adequately accounted for the construction of the walls encircling the summit was defense. Although Wilcox's interpretations suffer from the lack of excavated data and the mistaken belief that the fortifications dated to the Tanque Verde phase, his discussion of the walls themselves is sound. If anything, recent inspection of the summit suggests that Wilcox was conservative in his assessment of the magnitude of the encircling summit walls.

Excavations in features on the Tumamoc summit in the 1980s and 1990s led to very different perspectives on the significance of the walls. Given the likelihood that they date to the Early Agricultural period, they take on new meaning for that era as well as for later components on the hill. From Wallace's perspective, the reason for considerable soil buildup behind some of the walls becomes evident: prior to the Tortolita phase reoccupation, 700 or more years passed during which silting could occur. In particular, it is clear why Tortolita phase remains were found in the upper portion of the fill behind Wall 1. It is not clear whether these deposits were refuse or an actual pit structure. Refuse may well have washed down the slope from the structures immediately upslope. The underlying Early Agricultural period structure is situated in the basal fill immediately adjacent to the upslope side of Wall 1. This would seem to argue for some intentional fill behind the wall (but only about half of what we see today). Was this to provide a level space for housing? If so, the wall would have made the houses virtually invisible from the floodplain below. This would have also been the minimal fill necessary to make level footing for patrolling the wall and moving rapidly along it if there were the need for defense. P. Fish and S. Fish rely on their observations of homogeneous terrace fill lacking waterlain strata, concluding that the massive walls on Tumamoc such as the one discussed above—including the fill behind it—were built in a single operation, providing a suitable platform for Early Agricultural pithouses (and later ones), much as the terraces at Cerro Juanaqueña in Chihuahua were constructed and intentionally filled. However, the stratigraphy seen in figure 3.2 indicates that only half of the fill may have been added when the wall was built, and the remaining Tortolita phase deposit may be washed-down silt and refuse from the Tortolita phase occupation upslope. It should be noted that Wall 1 and the other walls that have fill behind them are all on slopes that are acting as catchments for runoff-carried silt. They are, however, in much the same position as some of their counterparts at Cerro Juanaqueña.

Fish and Fish conclude that if the summit perimeter walls are Early Agricultural period constructions, they cannot be directly linked to the motivation for settlement in the Tortolita phase. But can it be said that people never make use of fortifications from prior generations? The Tortolita phase inhabitants would not have overlooked the presence and defensive qualities of the massive walls atop Tumamoc Hill.

Regardless of when the Tumamoc walls were constructed, it is worth examining a few of the arguments and counterarguments concerning their function. Arguments against the walls being fortifications rest on two primary lines of reasoning: (1) that instead of revetments, they are retaining walls for agricultural terraces and structures; and (2) that they would have been inadequate to stop potential attackers. The first argument derives from the significant soil buildup on the uphill side of portions of the walls. This hypothesis received some credence from the 1998 excavations that uncovered a pithouse in the fill supported by Wall 1. However, the argument fails in three respects. First, Wallace proposes that the terrace-like sections on the Tumamoc summit and upper slope represent areas that were natural runoff catchments and that they silted in during the occupational hiatus between the Early Agricultural period and the Tortolita phase. There is no reason to think that the walls were built to *create* terraces. Had that been the case, the stratigraphic profile from Wall 1 (fig. 3.2) should have identified Early Agricultural period imported fill rather than the deep stratum of Early Agricultural refuse capped by Tortolita phase deposits. Second, in many cases atop Tumamoc Hill, the walls run vertically or at a significant angle up slopes in such a manner that they have no soil-retentive or water-guidance properties. These walls or portions of walls serve no purpose for agriculture or habitation. Third, for both agricultural and habitation purposes, there should be favored slopes, and one would therefore expect a concentration of terraces on these exposures. The north and northeast slopes are best for agriculture and habitation due to reduced solar radiation on summer afternoons and resulting greater soil moisture retention and reduced plant evapotranspiration (Katzer 1993:92). Contrary to these expectations, the Tumamoc walls completely encircle the hilltop. They are focused, as expected under the defense hypothesis, on points of access to the Tumamoc summit. One might expect, if the Tortolita occupation of the summit is a reoccupation and that defense was no longer an issue, that terraces would have been installed on the most favored slopes and that there would be only minimal use of the west slope. Surface sherd density mapping (Larson 1979:78), a proxy of the Tortolita phase use of the summit, shows equal use of west and east sides of the summit. There are no data available concerning the distribution of Early Agricultural period artifacts on the summit; however, the distribution of walls certainly does not correlate with optimal agricultural and habitation loci.

The argument that the Tumamoc walls might be inadequate for defense falters when one considers the nature of prehistoric and historic warfare. The weapons used during Tortolita phase times would have included clubs and arrows shot from bows. During the Early Agricultural period, weapons would have included atlatl darts and clubs. As Wilcox (1979:28) points out, those upslope have a significant advantage in combat. When one considers the difficulty of running up the loose rubble below the revetments while fending off arrows or darts shot from above, or from a rock-throwing, club-wielding defender stationed on stable footing above, it is clear that the fortifications could be effective. While it is true that downslope attackers can shoot arrows or darts at those above, they would be at a disadvantage because they would have little or no protection other than shields they might carry. Gravity would work against them for the range of their strikes, while it would be to the advantage of bowmen or atlatl-wielding defenders upslope. There would be a net benefit for the defenders resulting in the ability to strike before attackers could effectively return fire. Another advantage for defenders, noted by Wilcox, is the ability to rapidly move laterally on the slope in the cleared areas above the walls. Attackers attempting to scale the hill would not have the same freedom of lateral movement, due to the unstable rocky slope. Finally, areas with the gentlest slopes near the Tumamoc summit all have multiple walls, one above the other. Enemies who successfully scaled the slope to the top of the lowest revetment would be exposed in plain view until they could move to the next slope. Should attackers get past the first revetment, summit defenders would have successive defensible fallback positions.

Several other arguments have been made against a defensive function for Tumamoc. One is that the walls are too low to have served a useful defensive purpose. The walls presently average 38 cm above ground surface, but portions of some walls range up to 101 cm in height, and most average over 300 cm in width (Wilcox 1979:26). The loose nature of the rocks within the walls and the talus below them are evidence that their original height was greater than that observed today. How much so cannot be determined. However, on the gentlest approaches to the summit where the walls are most prevalent and most massive, it should be noted that it is the combination of the walls themselves plus the loose talus below them that confers a strong defensive advantage to those on the summit. It is literally impossible to move quickly over the loose rocks and boulders in the talus zones below the walls; to do so would be hazardous to limbs and life.

Another argument against a defensive function for the site (which assumes the walls are indeed effective defensive barriers) is that it would have been ineffective against a prolonged siege due to the lack of water atop the hill. While this is true if there were no water catchments on the hill, accounts of aboriginal warfare make it doubtful that this type of attack was commonplace. During a siege, attackers would be highly vulnerable if allied villages came to the rescue of those being attacked.

Rapid raids with quick retreats are more likely based on historic and ethnographic accounts of small-scale tribal warfare (Ember and Ember 1992; Keeley 1996; Kroeber and Fontana 1986; Russell 1975; Smith et al. 1966). Furthermore, sieges require a large attacking force, something that is unlikely given low population levels in the Tucson area during either of the two occupations of the summit. Also, as Fish and Fish discuss below, there might have been a prehistoric reservoir, eliminating the risk of being trapped atop the hill for an extended period.

If warfare was a primary concern of the Tumamoc occupants, one might expect more than the usual number of projectile points there. A comparison with other excavated Tortolita phase villages confirms that this is indeed the case. Eleven points were found in ceramic-bearing strata and contexts during excavations in 1985 and 1998 (fig. 3.5), which uncovered all or part of five Tortolita houses and three activity areas. The collection includes some dart points assigned to the Early Agricultural period as well as small triangular contracting stemmed arrow points that are new to the sequence in the Tortolita phase. The presence of both atlatl dart and arrow tip projectile points, which is common for Tortolita phase sites (e.g., Eppley 1990:130; Sliva 2003:243; Wellman 1999:28) suggests both the atlatl and bow and arrow may have been used during the phase. Some of the early dart point styles were probably still being made or were commonly picked up and reused during the phase. At Valencia Vieja, the nearest large Tortolita phase excavation, 13 projectile points were recovered from 86 excavated structures and many extramural contexts and areas. At Lonetree, there were four points from nine Tortolita phase houses and two ramadas (Bernard-Shaw 1990). Two dart points were found in the four structures most likely dating to the Tortolita phase (those containing redware) at the Triangle Road site (Wellman 1999:28). Points were lacking from the three structures and related Tortolita phase features at the Silverbell Coachline site (Hartmann 1997). The two Tortolita phase structures and two trash areas excavated at the eastern margin of the Hodges site (Swartz 1997) also failed to yield any projectile points. Clearly, the Tumamoc frequency stands out. This may also be the case for the Early Agricultural period component atop Tumamoc, based on the little known thus far. The single trench excavated behind Wall 1 in 1985 uncovered four broken dart points in the Early Agricultural stratum. In comparison, the excavations at Santa

3.5 Projectile points from the summit of Tumamoc Hill.

Cruz Bend (Mabry 1998:210; Sliva 1998:319) uncovered 63 Cienega phase structures and found only 20 projectile points. Numerous points have been recovered from the surface on the summit of Tumamoc Hill (Fish et al. 1986:565; Larson 1979:77), and visitors to the site over the years have collected many more. By any measure, there are or were many projectile points atop Tumamoc Hill, and they come from both primary occupations of the summit. What's more, Tumamoc Hill is not alone in this regard. The only other extensively excavated Early Agricultural period trincheras site, Cerro Juanaqueña, is reported to have very large numbers of dart points (Hard and Roney 1998:1661; Hard and Roney, this vol.).

The question must be raised at this point whether the summit walls on Tumamoc are relevant to the interpretation of the Tortolita phase use of the hilltop if the walls date many hundreds of years earlier. Perhaps the Tortolita phase occupants remodeled the hilltop to suit a different purpose, even if the original constructions were defensive. Such a possibility cannot be disproved, but there are several clues to indicate that the Tortolita phase occupation was not a typical village. There are no known community integrative facilities, as would be expected if it were a typical large village or a special communal gathering place for ritual purposes, and the ephemeral architecture suggests that those living atop the hill did not plan to stay very long.

Artifact data provide clues as to who may have resided on the Tumamoc summit and how long they stayed. Table 3.4 compares all Tucson-area Tortolita phase sites with available quantified data. As seen in this table, Tumamoc's Tortolita phase component bears similarities to Houghton Road and Triangle Road in having low frequencies of shell; it is similar to Houghton and Silverbell-Coachline in low frequencies of ground stone; and in flaked stone, it compares to Triangle Road. Overall, its greatest similarity is to the small, possibly seasonal sites in the sample, and most dissimilar to the large village site closest to it, Valencia Vieja, and other large riverine villages of Lonetree and Hodges. The implication is that Tumamoc may have been seasonally used, or used briefly or sporadically. It was not like the other villages, even though it may have been larger. Taken with the other artifact data, the diversity of pottery sources and the large size of the Tumamoc Tortolita phase settlement suggest a possible aggregation of diverse populations for short span(s)

Table 3.4 Comparison of Relative Artifact Frequencies from Tortolita Phase Sites.

	Tumamoc Hill	Triangle Road[1]	Valencia Vieja	AZ BB:13:223	Lonetree[2]	Silverbell Coachline	Hodges	Houghton
Sample	1999 Excavated contexts	All excavated contexts	Totals from 1997–98 excavations	Floor and floor fill in Features 1 and 4, and cache pits	All excavated contexts	All excavated contexts	Tortolita phase deposits	Features 5, 18, 139, 147, 148
Reference	This study	Wellman (1999)	Wallace and Lindeman (2003)	Downum and Dart (1986)	Bernard-Shaw (1990)	Hartmann (1997)	Heidke et al. (1996)	Ciolek-Torrello (1998); Arthur Vokes (personal communication 2002)
Counts								
Ceramics	2,877	2,525	15,989	112	6,392	271[3]	483	2,955
Flaked stone	934	779	9,680	152	3,365	37	207	1,405
Ground stone	30	221	430	12	152	4	49	38
Marine shell	2	5	154	4	30	0	5	1

Comparisons								
Ceramics/ Flaked stone	3.1	3.2	1.6	.7	1.9	7.3	.2	2.1
Flaked stone/ ground stone	31.1	3.5	22.5	12.7	22.1	9.2	4.2	37.0
Ceramics/ Ground stone	95.9	11.4	37.1	9.3	42.1	67.7	.9	77.8
Ceramics/ Shell	1,438.5	505.0	103.8	28.0	213.1	271.0	96.6	2,955

[1] Includes a probable Agua Caliente component.

[2] Includes some minor mixing with Middle Rincon.

[3] Count treats restorable vessels listed on p. 37 in Hartmann (1997) as single cases rather than as multiple sherds.

of time. This might be anticipated if a defensive posture was required. The presence of a high frequency of projectile points in the Tortolita phase contexts is also consistent with a defensive posture. Regardless of the nature of the settlement, the utility of the walls for defense (assuming their prior construction), would not have been lost on the Tortolita phase occupants of the valley.

Another concern has been a supposed lack of evidence for other defensive sites or fortifications coeval with the Tumamoc hilltop Tortolita phase occupation. This argument rests on weak footings. There may well be other fortified sites dating to the Tortolita phase. Black Mountain is a strong candidate, as it has similar walls and structures on the summit (Fontana et al. 1959). Rillito Peak at the north end of the Tucson Mountains is another possibility. When originally surveyed, it was thought to date to the Tanque Verde phase (Wallace 1983); a reexamination of the original data reveals significant parallels with Tumamoc. The assemblage of pottery was primarily plainware with some redware and only very rare decorated pottery from the Tanque Verde phase. When the site was originally surveyed, the Tortolita phase and its diagnostic pottery type, Tortolita Red, had not been defined. Rillito Peak lacks the massive revetment-like walls seen on Tumamoc, but that may make sense if the walls are an early phenomenon and the site is mainly Tortolita or mixed Tortolita and Tanque Verde. In the case of Rillito Peak, as is also true of Tumamoc, whether there are encircling walls or not, it is a defensive setting. Another site that bears strong similarities to Black Mountain and Tumamoc is the Blackstone Ruin (Tanner 1936). Contrary to Tanner's report, inspection of the site in 2002 revealed the presence of a series of walls on the only naturally unprotected slope facing to the north. An almost complete lack of artifacts limits the interpretive potential of the site, however. Modern mapping and testing are necessary.

No stockaded Tortolita phase villages have been documented, but up to now, no one has looked for a palisade wall at a Tortolita phase site (or at an Early Agricultural site, for that matter), and there have been too few excavations to know whether they are present. If a wooden stockade had been present at the most extensively excavated Tortolita phase village, Valencia Vieja, it probably would not have been seen, due to the lack of horizontal stripping outside the habitation perimeter. Postholes in extramural surfaces are often very difficult to see due to a lack of post-use trash fill. As will be seen below, palisade walls may not have been necessary if the threats of warfare were brief. As reported by Russell (1975:200–202), the absence of defensible site locations and fortifications does not necessarily signify peaceful times.

> In the relatively difficult to protect open setting of villages of the Gila River Pima during the nineteenth century, defensive measures included setting up sentries to guard field workers and villages and the establishment of intervillage cooperative war parties to repel Apache raiders (Russell 1975:201). These organizational responses would be archaeologically invisible, though the abandonment of outlying villages and aggregation into larger villages might be detectable (Wallace and Doelle 2001:243).

This passage indicates the variability in responses to the threat of raiding or warfare. It is worth noting that one of the most common responses to the threat of warfare is aggregation of populations, which is exactly what occurred near the beginning of the Tortolita phase at Valencia Vieja and probably at other newly founded Tortolita phase villages. Could this have been a response to warfare? Perhaps this was one of the motivations for agricultural intensification.

If the motivation for Tumamoc settlement was warfare, one must ask what the threat was. Wilcox's (1979) interpretations were based on the assumption that the site dated to the Tanque Verde phase, a time when many researchers have no trouble envisioning conflict. Now that we know the site dates much earlier, and that it is multicomponent, the question becomes: what is the social context of conflict in the Early Agricultural period, and if the Tortolita phase reoccupation was also defensively motivated, why would that point in the sequence also be a catalyst for such a drastic settlement response? With our limited knowledge of Early Agricultural period settlement and developmental sequences, and currently limited dating potential for the summit occupation of this period, it would be imprudent to draw conclusions about the contexts for warfare at that time. The fact that other sites appear to have similar summit walls in the region (Black Mountain, Blackstone, others farther west), and that there are other examples of potentially comparable sites in northwest Mexico (Hard and Roney 1998), indicates that Tumamoc may not be an isolated case. Instead, it is likely to be part of regional social processes.

For the Tortolita phase, current reconstructions predict the likelihood of conflict. The late fifth and early sixth centuries were a time of agricultural intensification and expansion and of aggregation of increasingly sedentary population in second terrace settings. The process of establishing permanent residences and staking claims to large sections of the best arable land probably occurred very rapidly across the southern Southwest. Without a rapid response to this process, one was likely to be left out in the cold with second-rate farmland or no land at all. The system of land tenure that developed would have built on an earlier, less rigid system that had been in place for at least a millennium, originating with the earliest floodplain irrigation systems. Unlike these earlier systems, the early Pioneer period irrigation systems underwent rapid and, in some areas, massive expansion, opening up a tremendous amount of new irrigable land. The pooled labor required to build these larger systems represents social alliances that would have served to both develop and protect the resources they developed. Two primary sources of potential Tortolita phase conflict are envisioned. The first could have originated from those who failed to acquire suitable farmland. As an internecine affair, I think, such conflicts would have been unlikely to develop to the point of full-scale hostilities, due to social relationships already in effect among riverine communities and the long relationship of corporate groups to certain portions of the floodplain.

A more likely source of conflict is one seen repeatedly in historic times: outlying nonriverine areas would have been threatened by the aggregation of populations into villages along the river that may have further restricted access to riverine resources and accentuated a riverine/hinterland dichotomy. It is easy to imagine a number of scenarios involving conflict between local farming communities and more nomadic groups in the surrounding areas—just as happened between postcontact farmers such as the Pueblos and O'Odham and the Navajo, Apache, and Yavapai. Small-scale raiding may have occurred, inducing a retreat of riverine populations to the Tumamoc summit at the worst of times early in the Tortolita phase. I would envision a relatively short-term occupation until the threat abated. The diversity in ceramic sources supports the idea that Tumamoc may have been settled by multiple, spatially separated populations who temporarily aggregated atop the hill for defensive purposes. It would be more difficult to believe that pottery was being imported from a wide array of sources if the site was tied to just one village at the base of the hill, given that some of the region's best clay (that was extensively used later in the sequence) was located near the St. Mary's site at the foot of Sentinel Peak, also known as "A" Mountain (Diehl 1996).

Whether repeated occupation of the Tumamoc summit occurred cannot be predicted, due to the idiosyncratic nature of such low-level tribal conflict. No evidence of remodeling was discovered in the structures excavated, but more work would be needed to test this possibility. What we can expect for Tumamoc is that hilltop habitation would not replicate a riverine village. Indeed, if multiple settlements briefly coalesced atop Tumamoc, it should not look like a riverine settlement at all. Also, those building atop the hill would, no doubt, expect that their stay would be short-term (until the threat of violence diminished). Therefore, flimsy construction techniques (as seen in the excavated sample) would be sufficient. The general artifact data offer significant support for the contention that occupation was limited. Defense does not preclude the utilization of the Tumamoc summit for other purposes, however. Some of those purposes are considered below.

Fish and Fish: A Special Village, an Updated Perspective

The Tortolita settlement on Tumamoc Hill, like all other trincheras occupations, is undeniably on a hill, by definition a "defensible" location. For some regional scholars, this perception of trincheras sites appears to overshadow all other considerations, placing a greater burden of proof on any alternative interpretation. It is also true that where we can confidently account for motivations in our own and more recent societies, there are instances of hill residence in which defense has no bearing, even in a historical sense. Should we assume the past to have been qualitatively different than the present in this regard? Significantly, archaeologists working in highland Mexico and its northern boundaries (Kowalewski, this vol.; Nelson, this vol.) are not reluctant to entertain nondefensive motivations for prehispanic occupations on hills.

Nowhere has a defensive assumption been more resolutely applied than to Tumamoc Hill, throughout the history of research and in the face of dramatically changing perceptions of its temporal and cultural affiliation. The noted geographer Ellsworth Huntington (1904, 1914) visited the southern Southwest early in the twentieth century and pronounced Tumamoc a fortress due to its encircling terraces and walls, in contrast to his vineyard comparison for the 900 tall, more formal terraces at Cerro de Trincheras in northern Sonora. David Wilcox (1979:31–34) proposed a defensive scenario involving the Tumamoc terraces and walls as a response to the threat of armed intervention by tribute-seeking chiefdoms along the Salt and Gila rivers during the Hohokam Late Sedentary and Early Classic periods. Although acknowledging the likelihood that at least some of the main walls date centuries earlier, our coauthor Henry Wallace likewise attributes a defensive posture to the later Tortolita village. No matter what the chronological or societal context, the only acceptable motivation for some scholars is defense.

Admittedly, the linear stone constructions on Tumamoc Hill surround the residential area on the summit, making them a stronger argument for defense than can be cited for three other southern Arizona trincheras sites of possible pre-Hohokam date, where encircling layouts are lacking. The variable nature of the Tumamoc walls is paradoxical, however. Along the "walls" are extensive terrace-like stretches with relatively deep fill that is even with the top of retaining walls. In other stretches, the rocks extend above the surface, but there are also segments in which the walls consist of no more than a single line of cobbles on the ground. A pithouse excavated into the fill of the massive upper east terrace or wall (Wall 1) demonstrates that it served more than Wilcox's (1979) proposed purpose of providing stable footing for defenders. In fact, the presence of houses might hinder defensive mobility to some degree. As there were no surface indications of the pithouse, its chance discovery in a trench suggests the likelihood of additional terrace structures.

The average above-ground height of only 38 cm for Tumamoc's outer walls (Wilcox 1979:25), along with occasional wall segments no more than one or a few cobbles high, seems less than ideal for defense. There is unquestionably an advantage in a position uphill from attackers, but that advantage should increase with wall height, particularly for protection against attackers shooting arrows from below. Why, then, did Tumamoc builders not value wall height, at least to the extent of duplicating the 80- to 120-cm above-ground height reported for the discontinuous wall segments at nearby Black Mountain (Fontana et al. 1959:43)? Wilcox (1979:28) mentions several other anomalous situations for defense, including a gap in one wall and several that end in unprotected areas.

Today as in the past, Tumamoc's walls/terraces are highly visible and impressive edifices, often incorporating boulders too large for one or two persons to carry. It is unlikely that they were casual social boundaries, but this observation does not rule out the possibility that their construction conveyed a strong message of communal investment and shared commitment other than, or in addition to, defense. In their massive construction style and encircling layout, the walls resemble those of Canador Peak, Cerro Juanaqueña, and other Chihuahuan sites of Early Agricultural times, rather than the discontinuous and less sizeable stoneworks of later Tucson Basin Hohokam trincheras locations (also often attributed to defense). Whatever the function of the massive encircling walls, this widespread and chronologically discrete mode of construction suggests broad regional intercommunication during these early times and what could be regarded as a corresponding trincheras "horizon style."

In light of the substantial investment in Tumamoc walls and the extensive leveling of hilltop space for residence, it can be questioned whether this sort of village settlement represents the most efficient alternative for defense. Given that inhabitants must have regularly obtained water and tilled irrigated fields below, the effort for a nonpermanent refuge would have been considerable. Even without the investment in walls and houses, the hill alone would have offered a secure location for crop storage and a highly defendable momentary retreat if stocked with water. Conversely, even small parties of enemies hovering near the base during conflicts could have intercepted residents on critical trips for water and or tending and salvaging crops.

By the Tortolita phase and undoubtedly even earlier, Tucson farmers were exploiting the agricultural zones utilized by their Hohokam successors. A longstanding concern with land tenure is probable during the prior millennium of canal networks, but Tortolita population may have reached new thresholds. Aggregation into larger sites is apparent, but, with the sole exception of Tumamoc Hill, there is no indication in Tortolita settlement patterns for defensive locations in response to conflict over arable land or threats to agricultural stores. Settlements were dispersed across the basin in approachable locales, houses were not tightly clustered within sites, and defensive measures such as stockades are unknown. Stockade-like defenses have been repeatedly identified during this general time span in the northern Southwest (e.g., Fuller and Morris 1991; McNamee 1992; McNamee and Hammack 1992; Rohn 1974) and the adjacent Mogollon regions (e.g., Di Peso 1958, 1974; Tuthill 1947); if present in southern Arizona, the typical broad mechanical stripping of local investigations should have fostered their discovery. In most regions where archaeologists ascribe hilltop settlement to conditions of pervasive threat, such locations are repetitive elements of settlement pattern rather than isolated or unusual instances.

As previously noted, some or all of Tumamoc's large encircling walls predate the Tortolita village. Assuming the walls are defensive, the Tortolita reoccupation might or might not reflect a response to similar conditions. At the very least, preceding construction would suggest conflict among appreciably earlier agriculturalists that was not contingent on Tortolita phase processes and events.

The size and substantial character of the Tumamoc village, in conjunction with a hilltop location, appears unique among Tortolita phase settlements in the Tucson Basin. If the site is primarily defensive, it is noteworthy that other populations with prime river lands did not feel the same need to build and inhabit a retreat of this sort. There are no possible trincheras villages of similarly extensive scale near the Tortolita occupations north along the Santa Cruz, even at the end of the Tucson Mountains where a later Hohokam trincheras site was built. The sole candidate is Rillito Peak (Wallace 1983), with many fewer features, no encircling walls, and strong evidence for a Tanque Verde phase occupation in addition to any Tortolita presence. Some of the earliest known canals occur in this part of the basin, documenting more than a millennium of irrigated farming by Tortolita times. Significantly, all trincheras sites are confined to the volcanic Tucson Mountains on the western side of the basin, without counterparts on granitic hills near Tortolita settlements to the east.

Among two other possibilities for Tortolita trincheras sites, Black

Mountain south of Tumamoc, along the river to the south, has discontinuous wall segments and about 30 stone outlines no larger in diameter than the smallest Tumamoc structures. Collections of the relatively sparse ceramics do little to confirm a Tortolita occupation, due to the absence of redwares and the predominance of Classic period Hohokam diagnostic types (Fontana et al. 1959:47; Hartmann and Hartmann 1979:62). The Blackstone Ruin, outside the Tucson Basin and 30 miles to the west in the Avra Valley, consists of 114 stone outlines, with a few much larger than any at Tumamoc (Tanner 1936). If its occupation dates primarily to the Tortolita phase or any other ceramic interval, it appears to have been ephemeral; full excavation and testing of 40 structures produced only a few sherds in two cases. Should future investigation prove Rillito Peak, Black Mountain, or Blackstone Ruin to be of Tortolita age, they nevertheless represent much less substantial and sustained occupations.

Tumamoc's attractant qualities should be considered. Although uphill, the 1.5-km distance to Tumamoc from permanent water at the river is minimal, especially in view of the very restricted locations of perennial sources within the basin as a whole. Canals coming off the river in the direction of the hill would have carried water closer still. Tumamoc overlooks some of the most desirable irrigable land along the Santa Cruz. In unusual proximity to such fields, the villagers also would have had rights to the abundant upland resources covering the hill, including dense saguaros and other cacti. These concentrated and convenient resources would have lured gathering parties to the hill both before and long after Tortolita times.

Tumamoc Hill is subject to significant microclimate effects. Inversion and cold air drainage create as much as a 20° F difference in temperatures between the summit and the floodplain below on winter nights. Over five years of measurement, there were 38 freezing winter nights on the upper slope, compared to 263 along the river. The annual interval between first and last freezes during these same years averaged 36 days above and 157 days below (Hastings and Turner 1965:17). Warmer hill temperatures may have appealed to winter residents.

Related to the amelioration of winter temperatures was an opportunity to take advantage of winter rains to grow small terrace crops in the spring. At that time of the year, stored supplies from the main summer harvests would be at a low. This kind of seasonally specialized spring production was practiced ethnographically by the Hopi, who constructed terraces to capitalize on similar microclimate effects that permitted corn to mature in July, well before their major harvests. Early season terrace crops were particularly valuable to the Hopi, because they were necessary to supply feasts and observances mandated at this time by the ceremonial calendar (Hack 1942:30). Spring terrace crops on Tumamoc may have begun by the Early Agricultural occupation. In a sample of 130 pieces of charred corn from the pithouse of this date behind Wall 1, 125 instances were cob fragments, suggesting that cobs as well as the more easily transported shelled kernels were routinely present (Fish et al. 1986:565–566).

Additional indications of a sustained occupation during which crops might have been planted were recovered from the Early Agricultural feature. When encountered in a 1985 trench, the fill of this feature was mistakenly interpreted as a stratum beneath a much later terrace (Fish et al. 1986). An extension of the trench and horizontal excavations to either side in 1998 revealed the Early Agricultural deposits to be within a circular depression with a flattened bottom, with a diameter of 1.75 m, and an area of 2.41 m (fig. 3.2), a floor area in the lower range for Early Agricultural period structures (Gregory 2001:261). The feature strongly conforms to criteria for a pithouse. With a maximum depth of 0.75 m, it appears to have been cut slightly deeper into terrace fill than the Tortolita pithouses cut into bedrock elsewhere on the summit. Diverse resources identified by flotation and pollen span spring through fall seasons. Structural and fuel wood was dominated by valley floor species (Fish et al. 1986:566–567). The artifact assemblage included cores, flakes, points, and groundstone. Burned daub suggests a substantial superstructure. A spouted stone tray fragment, polished stone cruciform, and clay figurine are Early Agricultural diagnostics in Tumamoc surface collections that further denote ritual activities and more than a casual presence.

Arrangements indicating a village layout are evident in the Tortolita phase settlement. Although some of the stone outlines could date to the immediately preceding Agua Caliente phase (because, in surface collections, Agua Caliente assemblages are largely distinguished from those of Tortolita times by the absence of redwares), the excavated sample of houses from varied locations points to an exclusively Tortolita occupation. The clustering of stone outlines into definable groupings (Larson 1979:74–75) may be analogous to Tortolita phase household and village relationships. Excavations in 1998 also disclosed outlined features and terraces serving as gardens or activity areas within these groupings.

Important aspects of village layout may be obscured by extensive modern disturbance. A paved road from below gives access to bladed roads and parking lots on the approximately 6.4 ha (16 acre) summit. In dispersed locations across the top are two astronomical observatories, a fire lookout tower, eight television and microwave towers with related buildings, miscellaneous smaller structures, and utility lines that service these facilities. The most extensively disturbed zones occur in the central and most level portions of the village. These conditions make it difficult to fully compare Tumamoc village structure with that of other large Tortolita settlements.

As noted by Wallace and Lindeman (2000, 2004), the appearance of aggregated sites such as Valencia Vieja, organized around a plaza, marks a new level of differentiation in Tortolita phase settlement pattern. Plazas present opportunities to interact with outsiders as well as to integrate residents through public activities. Tumamoc's summit disturbance makes it difficult to confirm the presence or absence of a plaza. A tantalizing but inconclusive description of the summit prior to modern building was published in the *Arizona Daily Star* ([Wolf] 1919) following visits by a University of Nebraska archaeologist, Robert F. Gilder, and Byron Cummings from the University of Arizona: "The houses were probably one-room affairs and were erected about a central plaza, streets radiating from the central point like the spokes of a wheel. What appears to have been a large reservoir is also discernable." The mention of a reservoir is as intriguing as a plaza and could indicate some kind of subsequently obliterated water catchments or large stone enclosure. Gilder also estimated 250 "room" outlines.

Gilder's attention to the hill was initially attracted by noticing "at a distance of a couple of miles what appeared to be a paved road leading toward the mountain top." This north slope main trail and a variety of others were studied as part of the 1970s survey. Well-preserved segments of the carefully cleared main trail are 1 to 3 m wide and bounded on each side by piled boulders up to 1 m high in some places. Offering easy, rapid travel, it enters the summit area through a large break in the uppermost encircling wall and can be traced to the village center (Hartmann and Hartmann 1979:41). Additional formal and informal trails facilitate summit access and pass through gaps in the encircling walls, primarily on the east and south sides of the hill. The earlier trail investigators believed that the frequently curving paths of entry through the low walls could have served a defensive function. However, the elaborate trail system also would have facilitated travel by Tumamoc residents and visitors to their village. The breadth, formality, labor-intensive construction, and high visibility of the main north trail to the village center, and possibly the upper segments of a few others, seem particularly compatible with ceremonial processions.

The greater diversity of pottery sources in Tumamoc assemblages than at contemporary analyzed sites reflects more than the inconveniences of pottery manufacture on the hill. If Tumamoc villagers had acquired most of their pottery from the nearest floodplain inhabitants, or if they made it themselves near their fields below (perhaps during stays in fieldhouses), their assemblage would exhibit the same local-source emphases as at other Tortolita phase sites. The greater diversity in temper sources also may reflect more widespread or intensive interactions, such as visitors taking food containers, serving vessels, or gifts and trade items to Tumamoc for special events. This possibility is buttressed by turquoise, shell, quartz crystal, obsidian, and other exotic chipped stone in Tumamoc surface (Larson 1979:77) and excavated collections.

Comparison of excavated Tumamoc artifacts with those from other Tortolita sites must take sample contexts and categories into consideration. A total of 10 projectile points from five houses at Tumamoc may represent a higher ratio than elsewhere, but only three small points are of a style known to have been manufactured during this phase. The remaining seven points are larger and commensurate with Early Agricultural or even older occupations and most likely represent discovery and reuse during Tortolita times. The ready availability of these larger points is reflected by their abundance in surface collections (as is the case at Cerro Juanaqueña) and by the recovery of seven in the brief 1985 investigations (Fish et al. 1986:563). Significantly, the only small, diagnostic Tortolita phase points from Tumamoc Hill are the three recovered from two of the structures excavated in 1998; none has been found on the surface. The other Tortolita phase sites in table 3.4 lack comparable preceding occupations as local sources of older points.

In a similar vein, it may be misleading to compare artifact frequencies from five small houses and trenches through three activity areas at Tumamoc with frequencies compiled from numerous houses of all sizes, from burials, and from a host of other features, as at Valencia Vieja. Although ratios of some artifact categories vary between Tumamoc and other individual Tortolita phase sites, the limited Tumamoc sample nevertheless produced a similar diversity of artifacts in ratios that generally overlap those of other Tortolita settlements. Tumamoc manos and metates were frequently heavily worn; more than 80 recorded bedrock mortars further document intense food processing at the site. Limited recovery of shell jewelry is in keeping with the lack of artifacts from burials and larger houses.

The foregoing discussion has addressed the practical motivations that archaeologists emphasize when interpreting settlement patterns. These dimensions clearly do not exhaust the reasons why prehistoric inhabitants chose to live on hills (e.g., Nelson, this vol.). Tumamoc Hill offers an unparalleled panoramic view of the entire Tucson Basin, and its summit is likewise prominently visible from most vantage points below. The nearly universal tendency to associate enhanced status with elevated situations is evident in the extra effort (such as gouging out roads and homesites and pumping water uphill) that today's regional residents expend to live in foothill locations in the Tucson Mountains (actually coinciding with one Hohokam trincheras site!) or on Phoenix's Camelback Mountain. It is not improbable that past societies held similar concepts of special or elevated place.

Who established the Tortolita phase village on Tumamoc Hill? As claimants to the basin's most productive riverine land and most reliable domestic water, the future residents of Tumamoc Hill were positioned for negotiating prominent roles in the increasingly differentiated Tortolita phase settlement system. Ready access to a maximum diversity of elevational resources may have been an added inducement for residents with social or ritual aspirations. Dense hillslope saguaros would have generously supplied hosts for pivotal observances involving saguaro wine, as in O'odham rituals. As occupants of an enduring landmark, village leaders also may have manipulated social memory to their advantage. As a portentous location of much earlier times, Tumamoc may have been the key to exclusive ritual formats grounded in founders and commemoration. Responses to ceremonial activities might have further encouraged seasonally extended or permanent residence. Auspicious moments in ritual cycles could have been effectively signaled from Tumamoc's summit. Calendric officiants could prominently observe astronomical configurations and mark horizon points without restriction in scheduling critical agricultural and ceremonial events. We suspect that the effort expended in the impressive and highly visible main trail on the north slope is related to specialized and integrative performances centered on Tumamoc Hill.

The many positive nondefensive aspects of Tumamoc living are not necessarily incompatible with defense. However, in a Tortolita world with few other archaeological indicators of persistent or overriding conflict, the uniqueness of this hilltop village is best understood through multiple motivations, any or none of which may have been a paramount factor. If we focus too narrowly on prime movers, we may miss the full complexity and meaning of this singular site in Tucson Basin prehistory.

In many respects, the most significant aspect of Tumamoc Hill may be as the location of the earliest public architecture in the Tucson Basin and perhaps in southern Arizona, in the sense of large-scale construction undertaken with coordinated, communal labor. The canals of early farmers likely foreshadow these shared efforts but do not join members of agricultural societies in the same way. The massive walls erected on Tumamoc Hill exhibit the same enduringly visible qualities as later ball courts and platform mounds, undoubtedly holding the attention of subsequent prehistoric peoples as much as that of archaeologists, and they retain the ability to impress to this day.

Conclusion

Excavations of modest scale in 1985 and 1998 have forced a reappraisal of the role of Tumamoc Hill in Tucson Basin prehistory. Rather than a Hohokam site, as had been assumed, two unexpectedly ancient and apparently discrete occupations were identified. The earlier, probably responsible for the construction of the walls encircling the summit and probably a set of structures as well, dates to the Cienega phase (800 BC to AD 50) of the Early Agricultural period (still earlier components are also possible). A later occupation, securely dated to the Tortolita phase (AD 475 to 675/700), appears to have witnessed the construction of numerous pit dwellings on the Tumamoc summit and generated much of the visible refuse.

At the present time, that is what we *think* we know. The reality, however, is that the excavations atop Tumamoc Hill revealed how little we do know. For example, the single "terrace" cross-section trench (behind Wall 1), cut in 1985 and reopened and expanded in 1998, does not provide a construction date that can be automatically projected to all the other massive alignments. To do so will require additional cuts that extend through the walls and unequivocally establish their relationship to the associated strata. Similar cuts are required through other perimeter alignments that retain soil and residential terraces to establish whether there are Cienega phase structures as well as Tortolita phase ones, and how many. Perhaps the greatest need is for a detailed map of the summit and upper slopes, showing all walls, cleared areas, summit structures, and related features, along with natural features of the landscape (such as cliffs and bedrock outcrops) incorporated in the wall system. Management concerns mandate mapping of all classes of material culture, including mortars, cupules, grinding slicks, petroglyphs, and portable artifacts, in addition to the more visible rock structures. Once a complete map is created, additional excavations could target a limited set of structures, selected to sample the full range of size, setting, and function categories. This is necessary to determine whether the current sample is representative, and whether Cienega phase, or even possibly Agua Caliente phase, structures are present. This would also conclusively determine whether Tortolita phase inhabitants reused Cienega clearings and perhaps built atop earlier structure foundations.

Discoveries atop Tumamoc have a direct bearing on the interpretation of other cerros de trincheras in the region. The similarities in summit perimeter walls/terraces among Tumamoc, Black Mountain, and to a lesser extent, Blackstone (as well as other sites in Papagueria) lead us to suspect (or at least consider) a common origin and intent in their construction. As noted by P. Fish and S. Fish, massive encircling walls may mark a horizon style of hilltop masonry construction. Studies in the Tucson area should target the summit walls on Blackstone and Black Mountain to assess dating, and test excavations of structures and trash deposits with dating in mind should be conducted on Black Mountain, Rillito Peak, and Blackstone.

Two things became very apparent to each of us as we worked to put this chapter together: (1) there were no simple answers to the question, "Why were people living atop Tumamoc Hill?"; and (2) the perspectives we brought to the table were not mutually exclusive. The multicomponent nature of the site complicates interpretations. Assuming that the summit-encircling walls/terraces were constructed in the Cienega phase, later occupants of the hill may have added most of the rock enclosures. We also must wonder if many of the rock circles were originally constructed in the Cienega phase and then reused by the Tortolita phase inhabitants. The apparent secondary refuse in the fill of some excavated structures may demonstrate a repeated sequence of construction and abandonment, suggesting that not all structures were contemporaneous throughout the occupational span. The limited set of excavated structures, biased toward smaller stone outlines, makes any interpretation based on architecture somewhat speculative. As artifacts and botanical remains from the 1998 excavations are further analyzed, additional clues may be obtained.

In previous publications we staked out rather polarized positions regarding the motivation for building cerros de trincheras sites in the Tucson area (e.g., Fish et al. 1984; Fish and Fish 1989; Wallace [ed.] 1995; Wallace and Doelle 2001; see also Downum 1986, 1995; Downum et al. 1993, 1994; Katzer 1985, 1993). The careful reader of some of these publications will note, however, that both defensive and nondefensive qualities of the sites have always been recognized—the trick is to understand which activities were involved, and how much weight we should assign to each. We agree that the summit of Tumamoc Hill is a special place on the landscape and that the hill is a regional landmark. The fact that Tumamoc Hill was a Tucson landmark prehistorically is attested by artifacts and extensive rock art virtually spanning the local sequence. The abundance and breadth of such evidence is not replicated at other hilltop locations along the Santa Cruz or elsewhere in the Tucson Basin. Furthermore, the massive cobble and boulder features on the summit are still impressive long after the well-plastered houses of contemporary basin settlements have disappeared. Tortolita phase villagers and their leaders who decided to occupy the hill and undertake summit construction must have been mindful of these enduring qualities, the more so if earlier walls were already in place.

Perhaps the most important conclusion we share is that no matter what interpretation we choose, it has important implications for the understanding of prehistoric settlement in the region. If warfare was the primary motivation for occupying the hill, the impacts of war on the prehistoric sequence must be considered. If the site was a gathering place for rituals, or if it represented a village with a unique social role, we must revise our models of regional settlement. Almost any role we can reasonably assign to the site results in important implications. The exact implications cannot yet be specified, but future research will narrow the alternatives and perhaps inspire new ones.

Note

1. The Tortolita phase was originally included in the Early Ceramic period by Wallace and others (1995). Given accumulated evidence that the Tortolita phase is analogous to the Vahki phase in the Middle Gila, and that both phases include the origins of the Hohokam culture, Wallace (2003:22) moved the phase from the Early Ceramic period to the Pioneer period.

Appendix 3.1 Key Data for Interpreting the Tortolita Phase Occupation of Tumamoc Hill

Setting	Tumamoc Hill is one of the most striking natural landmarks in the Tucson Basin. It is adjacent to one of the best areas in the region for irrigation agriculture, and the immediate vicinity of the hill was occupied throughout prehistory. From the hill summit one has a clear view of most of the Tucson Basin.
Dating	The excavated ceramic assemblage dates one occupation of the hill to the Tortolita phase due to the presence of plain utilitarian vessels of many shapes and sizes plus a redware identified as Tortolita Red. This is confirmed by ^{14}C dates (1511 ± 48 and 1578 ± 49 BP) and small contracting stemmed projectile points (see Sliva 2003:243). An Early Agricultural period component is indicated by a variety of pre-Tortolita projectile point styles and ^{14}C dates (2078 ± 44 and 2244 ± 52 BP). Petroglyphs and decorated pottery document continuing intermittent use through the Hohokam sequence.
Type and span of occupation	The Tortolita phase use of the hill summit included a residential component. People were actually living on the summit for enough time to generate a continuous surface scatter of household refuse. Some houses contain trash, possibly indicating a sequence of occupation. The assemblages, typical of Tortolita phase sites (see table 3.2), include formal manos and trough metates, sometimes worn beyond use. The limited sample of smaller structures excavated to date at Tumamoc are not elaborate like some of those at Valencia Vieja or other excavated sites along the Santa Cruz, and they lack formal hearths. On the other hand, extra effort was expended in creating a level surface for building and a stone foundation. Standardized artifact counts from the sampled range of smaller Tumamoc structures compare best with structures at other Tortolita phase small sites.
Magnitude of occupation	Larson (1979:71) reports on 125 rock structures atop Tumamoc Hill. Our investigations revealed many more. There are also many more structures on the hill summit than can be counted by the rock enclosures, because not all pit structures were encircled by stones. Conversely, some "structures" marked by

	rock enclosures may have been activity areas and garden plots rather than loci of habitation. We suspect the actual number of structures atop the hill to be at least double that recorded by Larson. Some of the structures probably date to the Early Agricultural period, although they may have been reused in the Tortolita phase.
Method of structure construction	The five excavated structures were small (< 3 m in diameter), informal, round to oval pit dwellings lacking postholes and formal hearths. In most cases wall bases consisted of one to several courses of basalt cobbles and boulders with an average height of 30 cm for the stone portion. Burned daub in the fill indicated a mudded superstructure. The lack of postholes suggests a curved, bent-pole construction technique rather than the more typical post-and-beam center-ridged construction of excavated Tortolita phase riverine sites. However, structure outlines are highly variable in shape and size (1.8 m to 5.1 m in length) as is typical of Tortolita phase settlements, and only small ones were excavated. Some structures or activity areas were constructed on the hill summit by building terrace walls and importing soil to provide a level surface. Others were also excavated into the underlying substrate to create a level surface, or fill was imported into the structure interior to level it.
Site organization	Small, courtyard-sized areas have been cleared and bordered with structures and walls on the summit, which may relate to particular extended families. Clusters of dwellings may indicate particular corporate groups. Along with the apparent substantial population for this time, there is a central area without structures suggestive of a community-wide integrative structure in the form of a plaza. (A historic account by archaeologists Byron Cummings and Robert Gilder indicates one was present when they visited the summit in 1919.) This arrangement may indicate some sort of formal village structure as seen at Snaketown and Valencia Vieja, taking into account the limitations of the terrain. Historic impacts to the summit may have obscured further key evidence, however.

Appendix 3.1 Continued

Resources	There are no known sources of water or reservoirs atop Tumamoc Hill (although a historic account suggests there might have been a reservoir); water was likely obtained from canals nearest the base or the river itself. An attractive resource during all periods would have been the dense stands of saguaro, paloverde, and other upland species next to prime bottomlands. The more than 70 formal bedrock mortars may have been used to process paloverde beans, although mesquite beans may have been imported and have been recovered from flotation.
Pottery sourcing	The pottery recovered from excavations on the hill summit originated from widely dispersed sources (table 3.3), suggesting aggregation by diverse groups or social contacts with diverse groups. This is very different from other known Tortolita phase sites, all of which have pottery from nearby or local sources (Heidke 2003). The assemblage is similar in diversity to the Agua Caliente phase ceramic assemblage from the Stone Pipe site (there are no analyzed ceramic collections from Tortolita phase contexts at St. Mary's or any other sites between Tumamoc and Hodges, so we are unable to compare Tumamoc's pottery with contemporaneous assemblages along this stretch of the Santa Cruz River).
Projectile points	Large numbers of projectile points were recovered from both Tortolita phase and Early Agricultural period contexts on Tumamoc, relative to coeval sites in the Tucson area (see text); however, the number of excavated contexts is small.
Walls/Terraces	Some of the walls documented by Wilcox (1979) are more extensive than he reported; they even continue across the top of the bedrock outcrops. As reported by Wilcox (1979), the walls retain soil to form terracelike settings suitable for habitation and agriculture in some areas, but do not in many others. Where construction was more terracelike, tops of walls are often flush with the uphill fill they retain. Where walls are freestanding, average height above surface is less than 50 centimeters. The walls, when taken with cliffs and bedrock outcrops, completely encircle the hill summit. More walls occur on gentle slopes than on steep slopes. A few wall

	segments connect to bedrock outcrops by running upslope, precluding use for habitation or agriculture. None of the walls is or was likely to have been carefully stacked masonry. They are, instead, piles of rubble consisting of loose cobble to boulder-sized basalt rocks.
Agriculture	Areas of significant soil depth upslope from the long walls and numerous smaller terraces would have been well-suited for agriculture, benefiting from upslope runoff. Spring crops could have been planted with winter rains, as the soil atop Tumamoc retains moisture and cold air inversion greatly diminishes the threat of frost. At least one long wall (Wall 1) had sufficient soil depth at the time of Early Agricultural–period occupation to permit the construction of a pithouse. Whether the soil in this terrace was imported or naturally deposited is unknown. There are no terraces/walls on the lower slopes of Tumamoc Hill. Dry farming field systems on the lower slopes and adjacent Tucson Mountain bajada probably post-date the use of the summit (Masse 1979).
St. Mary's Ruin	Although reported to be a primarily Rillito and Rincon phase site, St. Mary's Ruin, a large settlement at the foot of Tumamoc Hill, was joined to the hill summit with a trail and is likely to have been first settled in the Tortolita phase, based on evidence from other similar sites in the region.

4

Cerros de Trincheras in Southern Arizona

Review and Current Status of the Debate

Christian E. Downum

Trincheras sites have received a surprisingly slight amount of research attention until about the past two decades, even though they are perhaps the most visually prominent and enduring archaeological features in the Sonoran Desert. The first field research at trincheras sites came in the late nineteenth and early twentieth centuries. Among the pioneers, cultural geographer Ellsworth Huntington wrote most extensively about the function and importance of trincheras sites. Huntington was an ardent environmental determinist who wove his interpretations of trincheras sites into treatises on the role of environmental change in setting the patterns of human settlement in the southwest United States and northwest Mexico (Huntington 1913, 1914). Huntington proposed that trincheras sites were used primarily for habitation, but also envisioned that some of the terraces could have been used for agriculture during episodes of ameliorated climate.

Archaeologists and geographers of the 1920s through the 1950s offered additional interpretations of trincheras sites (e.g., Fontana et al. 1959; Tanner 1936; Gabel 1931; Johnson 1960; Sauer and Brand 1931). Few of these viewpoints were informed by excavation or anything other than brief reconnaissance visits. Only two sites were excavated in southern Arizona and one in Sonora. One of the Arizona sites was Cerro Prieto (Heisey, plate 9; AZ AA:7:11 ASM), where Byron Cummings and a group of students from the University of Arizona exposed a single masonry structure during a weekend outing. This work was never reported, and it survived only in the memory of one of the participants, Emil Haury, who recalled this work during an interview I conducted in the 1980s (Downum 1993). The only other excavated Arizona site was the Blackstone Ruin, excavated by Clara Lee (Fraps) Tanner, who reported her findings in a brief article (Tanner 1936). In Sonora, Alfred Johnson (1960:40–52) tested trincheras features on a slope adjacent to the La Playa site.

The lack of excavation data did not inhibit archaeologists from forming opinions about the function of trincheras sites. Normative concepts of culture and a tendency to view cultural phenomena in terms of "influences" and trait diffusion encouraged interpretations emphasizing a single dominant function. The most popular interpretation of trincheras sites, buttressed by early historical reports of their use by Native American groups (Burrus 1971; Smith et al. 1966), was that they served as some sort of defensive retreat, usually characterized as being of a short-term or emergency nature (Farmer 1957; Fontana et al. 1959; Hoover 1941; Huntington 1914; Johnson 1960; Sauer and Brand 1931; Walters 1926). Other interpretations included use of trincheras sites as habitations (Bowen 1972; Huntington 1914; Sauer and Brand 1931; Tanner 1936), refuges from floodwaters (Gabel 1931), agricultural areas (Huntington 1914), signaling stations (Fontana et al. 1959; Sauer and Brand 1931), and vineyards(!) (Huntington 1914).

Archaeologists renewed their interest in trincheras sites during the 1970s. The most significant projects of this era were the dissertation research of V. K. Pheriba Stacy (1974, 1977), who conducted a comparative study of trincheras sites in southwestern Arizona; the 1974–1976 Tumamoc Hill project (Hartmann and Hartmann 1979; Wilcox and Larson 1979), which focused on a single site (Tumamoc Hill) but also involved surface survey and collections at a few other sites in the Tucson Basin; and the 1979–1980 Rillito Peak field project in the northern Tucson Basin by Henry Wallace and James Holmlund. None of these projects involved excavation, so researchers were unable to obtain independent chronological data. Functional assessments were based on surface architecture, features, and artifacts. Nonetheless, each of these projects contributed significant new information on trincheras sites and offered hypotheses framed in contemporary archaeological methods and theory. Stacy's dissertation work anticipated more recent trends in southwestern archaeology by considering trincheras sites as components of larger communities. The work by Wallace and Holmlund (Wallace 1983) produced detailed documentation of the various features of Rillito Peak and offered suggestions about trincheras features such as petroglyphs, terraces, mortars, and an enigmatic class of pecked bedrock or boulder features known as "cupules." The Tumamoc Hill project applied modern techniques of survey, artifact collection, and site mapping to a large number and variety of trincheras features. David Wilcox (1979) contributed noteworthy interpretations from this project, proposing that the terrace features at Tumamoc Hill were used as defensive platforms. He also presented a regional culture-historical scenario to explain why such conflict might have existed.

Research of the 1980s and Early 1990s

Late in 1979 Paul Fish and Suzanne Fish began planning archaeological investigations to explore multiple hypotheses about trincheras sites in and around the Tucson Basin (see fig. 1.3). They were interested in agricultural systems of the ancient Southwest, and were intrigued by the idea that some trincheras terraces might have been used for cultivation. It was apparent to them that new data, including excavation data, were needed to move previous debates beyond what been a predominantly speculative period of trincheras archaeology. There had been no large-scale excavations at a trincheras site in Arizona since the 1930s, and interpretations of trincheras sites were based almost exclusively on logical arguments regarding surface artifacts and the surface appearance of features and their potential performance characteristics. Only slight attention (e.g., Stacy 1974, 1977; Wilcox 1979) had been paid to the role of trincheras sites within larger systems of settlement. However, due to a lack of systematic archaeological survey, very little was known about the nature and distributions of sites surrounding *cerros de trincheras*. The large-scale surveys of the Tucson Basin and surrounding areas, fostered by the Central Arizona Project, were yet to come (see discussion below, and Downum 1993 and Fish et al.1989, 1990, 1992b for additional history of these projects).

Linda Vista Hill

A large development project brought the opportunity to conduct new field research at a Tucson Basin trincheras site. In 1980 the University of Arizona received financial support from developer Lew S. McGinnis to conduct archaeological explorations at the floodplain village of Los Morteros (Wallace 1995:20, 30–31). McGinnis was planning a large residential community. Aware of the importance of the Los Morteros site, he was seeking a means to facilitate the development while satisfying preservation concerns (Lange and Deaver 1989:xi). McGinnis donated 32 acres of Los Morteros to the University of Arizona Foundation and made a donation to fund test excavations at the site. Paul Fish and Suzanne Fish of the Arizona State Museum headed the studies.

Near Los Morteros was a cerro de trincheras known as the Rattlesnake Pass site (Hartmann and Hartmann 1979), later renamed Linda Vista Hill (Downum 1986). The side-by-side presence of a floodplain village and a trincheras site provided an opportunity to study interactions between the two components and to test the Fishes' ideas regarding a possible agricultural use of trincheras terraces. As part of the Los Morteros research project, they obtained permission from private landowners to conduct research on Linda Vista Hill. In 1980–1981, and again in 1987, the Fishes and several collaborators carried out a program of mapping, surface collection, and excavation (Downum 1986, 1993, 1995; Fish et al. 1984).

Linda Vista Hill is a rugged, 100-m-tall andesitic peak at the northern end of the Tucson Mountains. The hill itself is a distinctive topographic feature, one of numerous peaks within the mountain chain. It supports a lush paloverde-saguaro vegetation community. The site of Linda Vista is about 2.3 km west of the Santa Cruz River, next to the Tucson Basin Hohokam site of Los Morteros. The latter is considered to have been one of a small number of core villages in the Tucson Basin, primarily because of its large size, exceptionally long occupation (Late Pioneer through early Classic periods of the Tucson Basin Hohokam cultural sequence), and the presence of a ball court (Wallace 1995). Archaeological features on Linda Vista Hill are spread over the eastern and northern slopes, facing Los Morteros. Masonry features extend from the hill's base to its summit, with no appreciable break in distribution.

The research at Linda Vista Hill was conducted in multiple stages. The first effort used aerial photography to create a site-wide map of terraces, masonry foundations, and other visible construction on the hillside (fig. 4.1). This resulted in the documentation of more than 250 individual features, all of dry-laid, naturally occurring boulders. Based on size, shape, and orientation to slope, the rock features were sorted into three categories: Type I, a broad, semicircular platform type, oriented

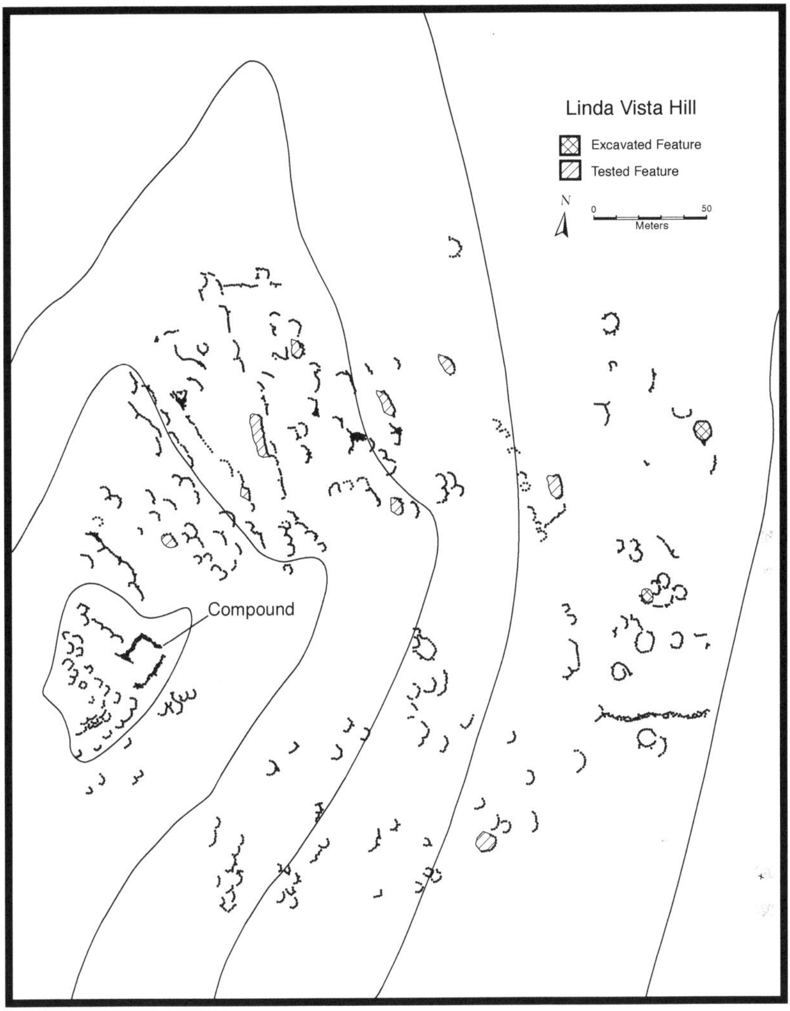

4.1 Map of the Linda Vista Hill trincheras site.

perpendicular to slope; Type II, a narrow, linear, "terrace" type, oriented perpendicular to slope; and Type III, a miscellaneous group, including a compound or stone-walled enclosure at the summit, alignments paralleling the slope, rock piles, small rock circles, and zigzag alignments. When features had been numbered and plotted on a map, artifacts resting on their interior surfaces were collected. More than 5,000 potsherds and 144 lithic artifacts were recovered.

Following mapping and surface collection, a sample of features was selected for test excavation. The sample was drawn to ensure coverage of a variety of feature sizes and types, as well as various areas of the hill. Nine Type I features, seven Type II features, and two Type III features (including the hilltop compound) were tested. Based on test excavations, six Type I features were selected for complete excavation.

The mapping program established that the Linda Vista trincheras site was a substantial hillside construction with a great deal of formal variation among its features (Downum 1986, 1995). Type I features, apparently representing the foundations of structures, were distributed rather evenly over the southeast and northeast slopes. Type II features, more terrace-like in appearance, were mostly on the middle and upper portions of the northeastern slope. Type III features, relatively few in number, were concentrated mostly on the northern edge of the northeastern slope and at the base of the hill. A major Type III feature, consisting of a boulder wall running directly uphill, divided the site into two distinct components (one to the north of the wall, and one to the south).

Surface collections documented an average of approximately 20 artifacts per feature. Typical of Hohokam habitation sites, ceramic artifacts far outnumbered lithic items. Sherds that could be typed document a predominantly early Classic Hohokam component. Most sherds (n = 67) that could be typed were the Early Classic type Tanque Verde Red-on-Brown, with only one sherd each of Rillito Red-on-brown (late Colonial period) and Rincon Red-on-brown (Sedentary period). Almost all the lithic artifacts were flakes, but scrapers, drills, tabular knife fragments, hammerstones, cores, polishing stones, pigments, a stone ax, ground stone, and three large, unmodified cobbles were also collected. Projectile points accounted for only two of the 144 lithic artifacts recovered.

Excavation of the Type II (terrace-like) features revealed important aspects of terrace construction (Downum 1995; Fish et al. 1984). Trenches through these features showed that they were built by piling boulders to form a retaining well, then scraping hillside sediments behind the wall to fill the space with cobbles, soil, and boulders. The excavated terraces generally disclosed a sequence consisting of a layer of fine-grained fill near the surface, grading into fill with abundant cobbles and boulders.

In some of the features, a use or occupation surface could be identified by compaction of sediments or the presence of flat-lying artifacts. In other features, artifacts were mixed throughout the fill. All of this evidence suggested that Type II features were terraces built and used during the Hohokam period of occupation, probably during the later Classic period. Pollen samples taken from some of the Type II features revealed the presence of corn and yucca or sotol pollen. These samples also had elevated frequencies of agricultural weeds, suggesting that at least some of the terraces had been cultivated (Fish et al. 1984).

Excavation of Type I features revealed that most were probably masonry-outlined pithouses and adjacent surface enclosures outlined with masonry (figs. 4.2 and 4.3; Heisey, plate 6; Downum 1986, 1995). Three of the pithouses were formal structures with clay-plastered floors and formal, clay-lined hearths near the structure's center. Two pithouses were burned and contained rich assemblages of floor artifacts, including reconstruct-ible vessels (plain and decorated bowls and jars), a ceramic scoop, formal ground stone, hammerstones, polishing stones, a charred basket, cores, tabular knives, lithic debris, a projectile point, an argillite nose plug, a bone tube (pipe or cloud blower?), and other artifacts associated with domestic life and possibly household-level rituals. Adjacent masonry-outlined surface rooms also included floor assemblages, suggesting that they were specialized open-air activity spaces serving as adjuncts to the more formal houses. The recovery of tabular knives, a stalk of yucca or agave, large stone "anvils," steep-edged scrapers, and other tools sug-gested the importance of fiber working.

A burned desert willow beam from of one of the houses produced a radiocarbon date of approximately 600 BP ± 80 (A-2746; uncalibrated one-sigma). The same structure's hearth yielded an archaeomagnetic date of 1040–1110 (95 percent confidence) (Downum 1986:223). The hearth of an adjacent house gave an archaeomagnetic date of 1000–1160 (95 percent confidence). These dates, though somewhat disparate, bracket the Early Classic period (AD 1150–1300) ceramic assemblages found in the houses.

Excavations at the summit of the hill revealed a roughly rectangular compound enclosure outlined with massive stone walls (Downum 1995:1174–1177). The inside of this compound included one or more post-reinforced adobe structures that had burned (fig. 4.4). A few

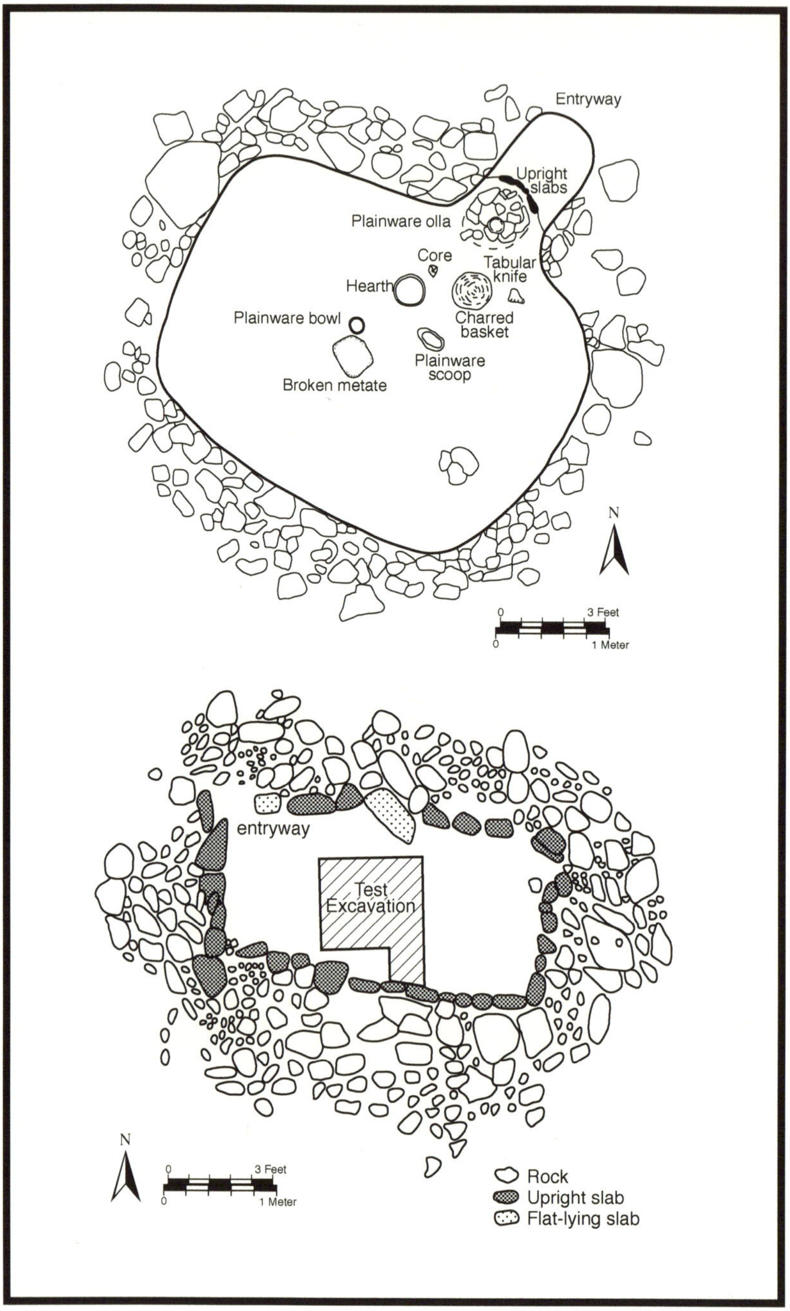

4.2 Plan view of selected excavated structures at Cerro Prieto (bottom) and Linda Vista Hill (top).

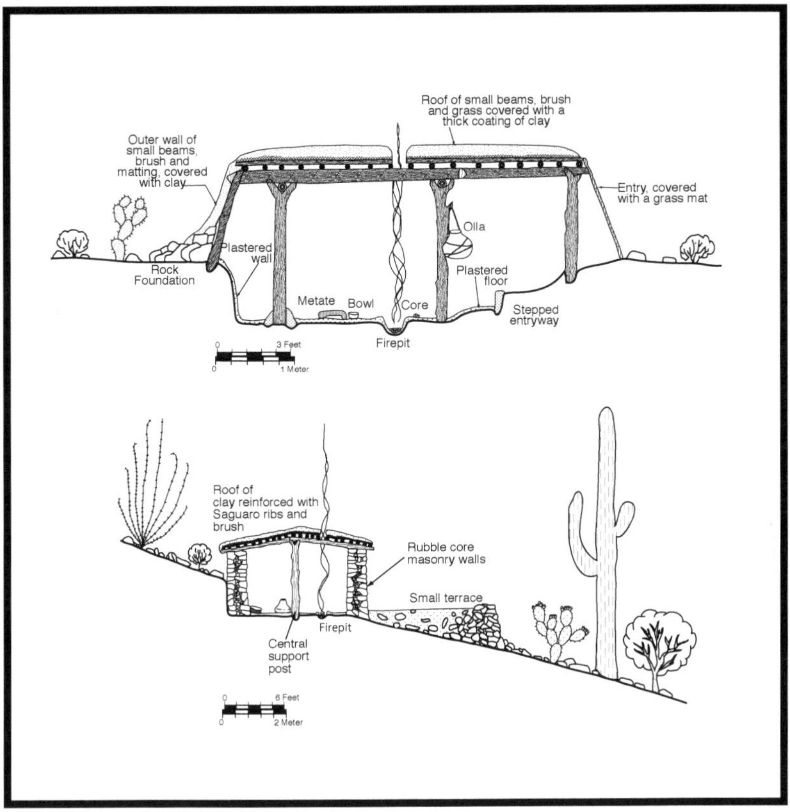

4.3 Artist's conception of profile views of domestic structures at Cerro Prieto (bottom) and Linda Vista Hill (top).

artifacts were recovered, two of which are of special interest. These are a large, cylindrical pestle, embellished by carving to resemble a human phallus, and an accompanying small, carved stone bowl (Lange and Deaver 1989:314). This set of artifacts suggests that the compound was the scene of ritual or ceremonial activities. The compound at the summit of Linda Vista Hill was roughly comparable in size to the surface of the contemporaneous Marana platform mound, hinting that activities of a comparable social scale took place in both locations.

Cerro Prieto

Closely following the work at Linda Vista Hill, Douglas Craig, John Douglas, and I began a program of mapping and test excavation at the

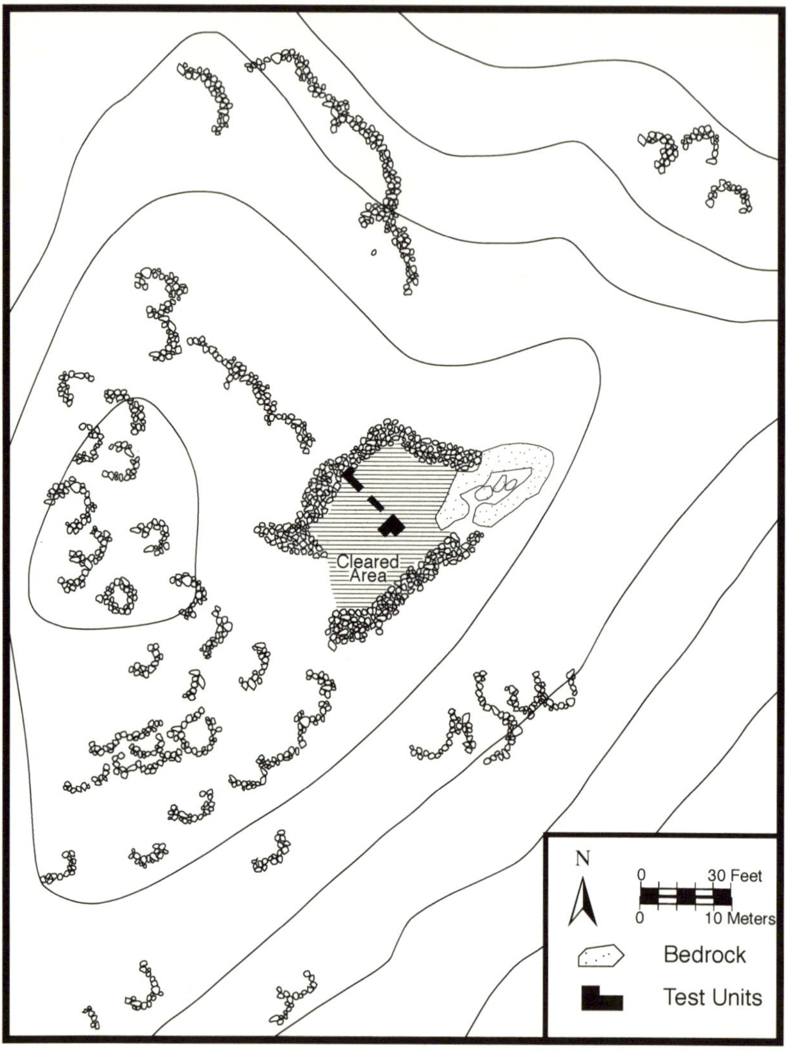

4.4 Stone walled compound at the summit of the Linda Vista Hill trincheras site.

site of Cerro Prieto, north of the Tucson Basin. Henry Wallace and James Holmlund, who had conducted rock art research at the adjacent multisite complex of Pan Quemado, introduced me to this important cerro de trincheras. In 1981, as an adjunct to UA/ASM work at Los Morteros, Wallace conducted test excavations within a masonry structure and large terrace at Cerro Prieto. From 1983 until 1991, Craig, Douglas, and I mapped Cerro Prieto using photogrammetry and total station mapping techniques (Downum et al. 1985, 1993).

Cerro Prieto is a 244-m-high hill that forms the northernmost and highest extension of the Samaniego Hills, a low, igneous range that straddles the Pima-Pinal county line about 60 km north of Tucson. Vegetation is virtually identical to that of Linda Vista Hill. Most archaeological features at Cerro Prieto rest on the lower slopes of the hill, where the gradient averages about 23 percent. Another, smaller concentration of features lies at the summit of Cerro Prieto, which forms a relatively flat surface.

Archaeological efforts at Cerro Prieto consisted of test excavations in two features (an apparent masonry structure [fig. 4.2] and a large terrace), and extensive mapping and recording of surface features. We recorded each feature at Cerro Prieto on a standard field recording form that noted size, orientation, and details of construction. We then transferred individual feature maps onto a topographic map based on aerial photography and photogrammetry. This resulted in an overall site map covering a rectangular area of about 500 by 700 m (fig. 4.5).

We recorded in detail more than 300 features, including 11 stone-outlined compounds (fig. 4.5), more than 230 structure foundations, six large terraces, 30 smaller terraces, and dozens of rockpiles, talus pits, petroglyphs, trails, waffle gardens, and other features. Temporally diagnostic artifacts at Cerro Prieto indicate a limited period of occupation, encompassing only the Early Classic period from about AD 1150 to 1300.

When mapping was completed we used formal attributes to define two broad categories of structures: those with rectilinear shape and those with circular or oval outline. Both types exhibited attributes consistent with a residential use, including sufficiently large size, careful masonry construction (with dry-laid, rubble core walls), and obvious doorways and threshold steps. Testing of a rectilinear foundation (fig. 4.2) confirmed that it had been a house. The house yielded numerous artifacts, including tabular knives, lithic debitage, a hammerstone, a mano, plain and decorated sherds, a bone awl, a shell bracelet fragment, and burned adobe fragments.

Houses were clustered into discrete sets that apparently were used by

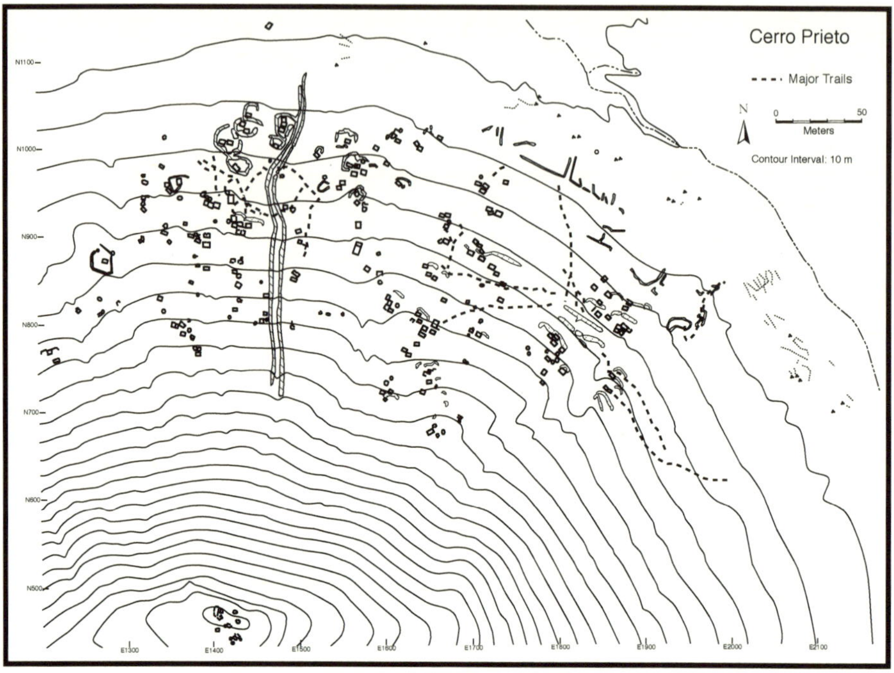

4.5 Map of the Cerro Prieto trincheras site.

corporate groups, perhaps one or more households. Nearly 75 percent of all structures at Cerro Prieto fell within 46 clusters, which could be further subdivided into small clusters (comprising two to five structures) and large clusters (six to nine structures). When we compared the attributes of houses in large versus small clusters, we found that the larger clusters contained the largest and most carefully built structures at the site (as measured in terms of overall floor area and the frequency of carefully fitted, plane-faced walls). This suggested that some social groups at Cerro Prieto were wealthier and enjoyed greater social power and prestige than other groups (Downum et al. 1993).

Structures at Cerro Prieto show some remarkable similarities to structures at the Fortified Hill site, a contemporaneous hillside occupation near Gila Bend, Arizona. Specific details of house shape and construction techniques (doorways, threshold steps, wall construction) are nearly identical in many cases, and the layouts of groups of structures are quite similar (see Downum et al. 1993: fig. 4.19). The Fortified Hill site contained Tanque Verde Red-on-brown pottery as the dominant decorated type. This is an anomaly for a site so far removed from the Tucson Basin but provides another similarity with Cerro Prieto.

The large and small terraces at Cerro Prieto represent the largest such features in and around the Tucson Basin. They also are the farthest north extension of such features in the desert Southwest. Terraces at Cerro Prieto can be seen from a distance of several kilometers and provide the lower slopes of the hillside with a stepped appearance. Excavations into one of the terraces revealed that it had been filled with trash deposits rich in sherds, flaked stone, and other habitation debris. Dense concentrations of trash on the surfaces of unexcavated terraces suggest that they were filled in a similar fashion.

The walled compounds at Cerro Prieto are fascinating and seemingly unique, consisting of roughly rectangular areas enclosed by massive masonry walls. In some cases, soil and subsurface caliche deposits of the hillslope were cut away in order to level the surfaces of the compounds. Collapsed rubble and surviving wall footings suggest that walls more than 2 m high surrounded the compounds. These walls were carefully laid, with stones arranged so that their smooth faces formed a flat vertical plane. Although often large in surface area (up to 28 by 32 m), the compounds contain few structures. One of the compounds has no apparent surface structures. All of the compounds except one have clearly visible entryways, and the single exception may also have a doorway. Compounds cluster on the northwestern side of the site, away from the large terraces on the northeastern flank of the hill. Terraces and compounds, all dating within the Early Classic period, thus form mutually exclusive distributions, suggesting that different areas of the site were reserved for different functions or social groups. Like Linda Vista Hill, Cerro Prieto is bisected by a massive rock feature, in this case a natural channel that had been cleared, with large boulders stacked on either side.

Cerro Prieto exhibits numerous prehistoric trails that connected features and facilitated access across the site. Trails are formed by clearing pathways of rock and stacking boulders along either side of the cleared areas. Some trails lead from the base of the hill into areas containing concentrations of structures. Waffle gardens and contour terraces outlined in stone lie at the base of the hill. A set of walls and cleared areas upslope of these features appears to have been a water-harvesting system, designed to funnel runoff from the hillslope into particular garden plots.

Contextual Studies

Large-scale surveys also contributed to our understanding of trincheras sites in southern Arizona. From the mid-1980s through the early 1990s, impressive full-coverage surveys established the community contexts of Tucson Basin trincheras sites. The areas surrounding Linda Vista Hill and Cerro Prieto were intensively surveyed as part of the Fishes' Tucson Basin and platform mound survey projects (funded by the U.S. Bureau of Reclamation, Arizona State Parks, and the Arizona State Land Department). Individual communities were identified that were centered around the Marana and Los Robles platform mounds, and Linda Vista Hill and Cerro Prieto were recognized as specialized components of a larger system of settlements and limited activity sites (Downum 1993; Fish et al. 1992c).

Interpretation of Linda Vista Hill and Cerro Prieto

The excavations and surveys of Linda Vista Hill and Cerro Prieto led to new interpretations for these sites. In my opinion, and in the view of the Fishes as well, neither site could any longer be interpreted as a short-term, emergency defensive refuge. In a series of publications reporting the new work (e.g., Downum 1986, 1993, 1995; Fish et al. 1994; Fish et al. 1992c), we offered a view of Tucson Basin trincheras sites that rejected prior notions that these sites were short-term defensive refuges.

From mapping, survey, and excavation data, we proposed that Linda Vista Hill and Cerro Prieto were devoted to long-term habitation, not short-term defense. Each is laid out with distinct clusters of houses and adjacent terraces, some interconnected with trails. The amount and type of refuse are not consistent with short-term use, but instead, with extended habitation. Clusters of structures, particularly those at Cerro Prieto, were designed without apparent regard for defense. Groups of houses frequently had no enclosing walls, and doorways of houses and openings for terraces almost always opened downslope, toward potential attackers, with no attempt made to strengthen or fortify such weak points. At least some Type II terraces at Linda Vista and several of the terraces at Cerro Prieto, representing a form previously interpreted at other sites as "defensive walls" (see Wilcox 1979), appear to have been used for cultivation. Others seem to have provided level spaces adjacent to hillside structures, that is, functioned as domestic activity areas. Furthermore, a network of trails and cleared corridors provided easy access into the heart of Cerro Prieto, a definite design flaw for a defensive refuge. These trails and corridors would have been highly visible from a distance, and easily known to any potential attackers conducting reconnaissance of the village. The most easily defended portions of Cerro Prieto (the upper talus slopes and the flat-topped summit) showed no rock constructions (e.g., "defensive platforms") that could be interpreted as defensive features.

Full-coverage survey of the communities affiliated with Linda Vista Hill and Cerro Prieto also allowed us to point out additional flaws in a defensive interpretation for these cerros de trincheras. To provide one example, most of the Tanque Verde phase floodplain settlements in the Los Robles Community surrounding Cerro Prieto, as well as the Marana Community associated with Linda Vista, were located several kilometers distant from their supposed defensive refuges (Downum 1993; Fish and Fish 1989; Fish et al. 1992c). Thus, the majority of the population within each community (including presumed community leaders living on or near platform mounds) would have been isolated from their supposed emergency refuges. Also, the surface areas of the built portions of Cerro Prieto and Linda Vista do not seem sufficient to have protected all members of their respective communities. There was ample reason from both ceramic and radiocarbon evidence to conclude that both Los Robles and Marana were fully populated and functioning communities at the peak of their occupations, when Linda Vista and Cerro Prieto were constructed and occupied, so the latter sites seem inadequate (both in terms of geographical isolation and scale of construction) to have served community needs for defense. In the case of Cerro Prieto, another hill (Pan Quemado) was closer to the majority of floodplain-dwelling populations in the Los Robles Community and would have been ideal for defensive use. Pan Quemado, however, was never developed into a cerro de trincheras with "defensive platforms" and other supposedly defensive features (Downum et al. 1993).

In addition, I noted (Downum 1993) that no natural source or storage structure for drinking water existed in the vicinity of Cerro Prieto. This would have been a major problem for Cerro Prieto's residents if attackers wished to engage the village in prolonged combat. However, at Pan Quemado there is a presumed prehistoric reservoir in an area surrounded by defensible slopes. There is no evidence that this reservoir or any part of this hill was ever fortified. It is not clear why a community interested in defense would fail to develop the hillside closest to its center into an emergency refuge, given that it had an important source of drinking water.

Based on all these considerations, both Linda Vista Hill and Cerro Prieto were viewed as large habitation villages within larger, articulated sets of settlements making up discrete Early Classic communities.

Tumamoc Hill: A Puzzling Anomaly

Perhaps the most surprising and puzzling finding of the 1980s trincheras research program came during 1985 excavations at Tumamoc Hill. Here, the Fishes excavated a single test trench within a terrace on the east side of the hill summit (Fish et al. 1986). The excavations were designed to examine terrace construction techniques and to assess the agricultural potential of the terrace by recovering soil and pollen samples. The results were unexpected. Rather than yielding just soil and rock, the terrace fill also produced abundant pieces of charcoal, including carbonized corn. Excavators also recovered numerous lithic artifacts, including Late Archaic–style projectile points, and architectural daub. Subsequent radiocarbon analyses of burned corn samples revealed an early date, placing the corn in the first millennium BC (Fish et al. 1986). This date was consistent with the presence of Late Archaic projectile points.

To my knowledge, this was the first hint that some trincheras features might have considerable antiquity, and the Tumamoc discoveries were among the earliest at that time pointing to cultivation of corn in the San Pedro stage of the Cochise culture. At the time, it was simply not clear what should be made of an (unexpected) discovery of Archaic projectile points and burned corn within a supposedly Hohokam-age trincheras feature. All other available evidence seemed to indicate that trincheras sites were a late prehistoric phenomenon (Downum et al.

1994; Hartmann and Hartmann 1979: 60–65). There was no cognitive framework for assimilating the idea that trincheras features might date as early as the Archaic period, which in southern Arizona was thought at the time to be certainly preceramic and mostly likely pre-agricultural (Berry 1982; Downum 1986; Huckell and Huckell 1984; LeBlanc 1982).

Recent Research: Late 1990s and Beyond

Since the mid-1990s there have been remarkably productive new research programs, abundant new data, and creative interpretations involving trincheras sites in northern Mexico and southern Arizona. One especially important project has been the mapping and excavation of the "type site" of Cerro de Trincheras in Sonora by Randall McGuire and Elisa Villalpando (McGuire et al. 1999; McGuire and Villalpando, this vol.). Their multiyear project involved detailed mapping of the distribution and form of masonry constructions at the site, followed by excavation of a large sample of features. The work by McGuire and Villalpando established beyond any reasonable doubt that Cerro de Trincheras was a large and complex habitation site, dating primarily to the late prehistoric period. Survey of areas surrounding Cerro de Trincheras (Fish and Fish 2003, this vol.) helped to place Cerro de Trincheras in local and regional contexts, and firmly established that this community was one that had no regional equal (in terms of size and structural complexity) during its period of occupation.

In 1997, Robert Hard and John Roney (1998, 1999, this vol.; Hard et al. 1999) conducted excavations at the site of Cerro Juanaqueña in northwestern Chihuahua. Their excavations have revolutionized our understanding of the time depth and very early complexity of the trincheras phenomenon. Cerro Juanaqueña is a large, terraced hillside complex containing nearly 8 linear km of rock features, comprising numerous terraces spread over an area of about 10 ha (Hard and Roney 1998). AMS radiocarbon dates on maize and squash remains from Cerro Juanaqueña produced the stunning result that the site's rock features, representing some 16 person years of effort to construct (Hard and Roney 1998, 1999; Hard et al. 1999), were built at least 1,000 years before the Christian Era. As Hard and Roney (1998) correctly note, this discovery has important implications for a host of issues in southwestern archaeology, especially models concerning the origins of agriculture and the nature of social organization during the Archaic period.

Meanwhile, back in the Tucson Basin, in the late 1990s Paul and Suzanne Fish excavated numerous additional features on the lower slopes of Linda Vista Hill. During this work they identified additional habitation structures largely similar to the houses I excavated in the 1980s. From their 1998 excavations, the Fishes obtained radiocarbon dates that fixed these features in the Hohokam Early Classic period. Dates obtained so far are AD 1014–1282 (A10035, from Feature 105; two-sigma calibrated range, date obtained from beans) and AD 965–1283 (A 10036, from Feature 117; two-sigma calibrated range, date obtained from agave).

The Fishes opened additional structures and terraces at Tumamoc Hill (Wallace et al., this vol.). They obtained further artifactual evidence of an Archaic occupation of it. In fact, based on the latest round of excavations, it appears that at least some of the large terraces at Tumamoc Hill supported Archaic age structures. The new excavations document a substantial Pioneer period presence as well. Numerous houses were excavated, indicating a residential function on the hill dating to the Tortolita phase (ca. AD 475 to 675/700). These findings reveal that the bulk of Tumamoc Hill's use and occupation, as measured by hilltop structures, dates to the Late Archaic/Early Agricultural and Pioneer (Tortolita phase) periods, not the Hohokam late Colonial, Sedentary, and Early Classic periods, as previously proposed (cf. Downum et al. 1994; Hartmann and Hartmann 1979:53–56).

New Data, New Interpretations, New Critique

The interpretation of trincheras sites as defensive features has recently been renewed in the context of an emerging debate about the role of warfare in southwestern prehistory. In the 1990s, a number of researchers began to assert a new model of conflict and warfare for the prehistoric Southwest (Haas and Creamer 1993, 1996, 1997; LeBlanc 1999; Wilcox and Haas 1994). Among its adherents, the status of this model now occupies an explanatory status somewhere between ruling theory (Chamberlin 1890, 1897; Tweney et al. 1981) and paradigm (Hoyningen-Huene

1993; Kuhn 1962). For want of a better term, and because some may object to application of the term *paradigm* to this school of thought, I will refer to it as the "warfare model." In brief, the warfare model of southwestern prehistory holds that organized conflict was a potent determinant of ancient southwestern cultural patterns and changes, explaining a multitude of phenomena: massive population relocations, changes in social structure, patterns of exchange, political alliances, technological change, choices of settlement location, architectural patterns, and even extinction of some cultural groups (see for example LeBlanc 1999; LeBlanc and Rice 2001; Lekson 2002). Below, I review two of the major critiques of the 1980s Tucson Basin trincheras work that are rooted in the warfare model, one offered by Steven LeBlanc (1999) and the other by Henry Wallace and William Doelle (2001).

LeBlanc (1999:132–133, 256–264) briefly reviews trincheras sites in his synthetic book on southwestern warfare. Rather than using excavated evidence from trincheras sites to evaluate the warfare model of southwestern prehistory, LeBlanc instead uses the model itself to assign a defensive function to trincheras sites. LeBlanc (1999:258) is unimpressed by the multiple seasons of excavation work conducted by McGuire and Villalpando at Cerro de Trincheras. He notes that McGuire and Villalpando (1993) "do not seem to accept a defensive explanation" for what the latter argue from excavation data are residential and multifunctional terraces at the site. LeBlanc dismisses their interpretations in favor of the arguments of Sauer and Brand (1931), who on the basis of surface evidence "make an excellent argument for these Sonoran trincheras being defensive." LeBlanc (1999:258) also reviews and then summarily discounts the 1980s and 1990s excavation results from Tucson Basin trincheras sites (Downum 1986, 1993; Downum et al. 1993; Fish et al. 1984). He concludes his assessment of the trincheras phenomenon with the following summary: "The trincheras sites I have visited were certainly capable of providing defense, and given what is known about changes in warfare over the entire Southwest at the time they begin to appear, I believe the case for their being defensive is the stronger one" (LeBlanc 1999:258).

Wallace and Doelle (2001:248–249) provide a much more detailed critique of the Tucson Basin trincheras work. In a volume titled *Deadly Landscapes: Case Studies in Prehistoric Southwestern Warfare* (LeBlanc and Rice 2001), Wallace and Doelle take issue with the interpretations put forth by Downum, Fish, and Fish in the 1980s and 1990s. The latter authors' interpretations are characterized as promoting "alternative explanations centered on agricultural diversification . . . and ceremonialism." In challenging these ideas, Wallace and Doelle offer a detailed discussion of Tucson Basin trincheras sites and relate them to "a larger scale temporal and settlement pattern framework" (Wallace and Doelle 2001:252). Warfare and disruption of settlement patterns, including construction of "fortified villages" at Linda Vista, Rillito Peak, and Cerro Prieto, are related to deteriorating social conditions. The reasons for this putative social upheaval are unknown but are attributed to a proposed "significant decline in environmental conditions" (Wallace and Doelle 2001:257). No specific time period for this decline and no environmental evidence are adduced, except to refer to work by Dean et al. (1994) regarding a decline in streamflow in the Salt and Verde rivers and to mention a "serious drought" that affected "northern and central Arizona" ca. AD 1275 (Wallace and Doelle 2001:283).

A major criticism by Wallace and Doelle concerns what they (2001:248) refer to as the "agricultural hypothesis." This concerns results published by the Fishes, the late Keith Katzer, other colleagues, and me (Downum 1986, 1995; Downum et al. 1993, 1994; Fish and Fish 1989; Katzer 1985, 1993). Wallace and Doelle (2001:247–248) assert that the agricultural hypothesis was proposed to counter "the hypothesis that warfare was the motivation for wall and village construction at the hillslope and summit sites" of the Tucson Basin. Under the heading "Peaceful Walls?" they claim that, according to the supposed agricultural hypothesis, agriculture has been proposed as the "prime motivation" for constructing trincheras sites and features (Wallace and Doelle 2001:248). They then challenge the so-called agricultural hypothesis on several bases. First, terraces and other features are not all oriented to the north, northeast, or northwest. This is perceived to be a problem because "if agriculture was a prime motivation, then all sites should be oriented in the optimal manner" (Wallace and Doelle 2001:248). Second, "one would expect construction of such sites on the best climatically suitable slopes that can be readily reached." This is proposed as a logical flaw because "in the Linda Vista/Rillito Peak area there is a well-suited north-facing gentle-sloped hill ideal for terracing. . . . however, it was never used" (Wallace and Doelle 2001:248–249).

Wallace and Doelle (2001:248–251) discuss what they term an "overlooked" wall in a saddle between Linda Vista Hill and the next volcanic peak to the north. This wall is viewed as a vital piece of evidence in establishing that trincheras features at Linda Vista Hill were built for defensive reasons: "The massive wall at Linda Vista that blocks the only ready access from the west was also overlooked by these researchers [Downum, S. Fish, and P. Fish] and was shown for the first time in Wallace (1995:814–817). . . . We doubt that anyone could interpret the Linda Vista wall as anything but an intentional barrier." A nearly identical argument is made by Wallace (1985:814), who writes that "this wall, not discussed in previous publications, is difficult to explain through anything other than a defensive motivation."

Wallace and Doelle further propose that Cerro Prieto, a residential settlement with houses connected by numerous trails, was actually a fortified village. In doing so, they challenge the previous interpretations of Downum (1993) and Downum et al. (1993). Wallace and Doelle (2001:247) acknowledge that the terraces at Cerro Prieto "were used for residential and probable agricultural and mortuary purposes," and that the slope upon which the village was built "is a gentle one." They argue, however, that the settlement as a whole was defensive by design: "rapid vertical access is limited because of the boulder-strewn surface. Without an intimate knowledge of the trail system, one cannot move rapidly in any direction within the village. Access to the community is further restricted by the very large terraces and compound walls" (Wallace and Doelle 2001:247).

Finally, Wallace and Doelle (2001:251) question what they consider to be a second single-function hypothesis, that trincheras sites could have been constructed for ideological, political, or symbolic reasons (Downum 1993:119–122; Downum et al. 1994:292). Wallace and Doelle (2001:251) summarize the proposition as follows: "[Downum and others have hypothesized that] all or many of the sites in question were constructed as a result of new ideological and ritual belief systems initiated in the Early Classic period as part of a reorganization on the heels of the retraction from the ball-court system." They criticize this argument as "particularly weak" for three reasons: (1) "Some ritual use of the mountains . . . is expected whether warfare was involved or not"; (2) "if the sites were purely ritually focused, repeated ritual behavior should be observed"; and (3) the abandonment of the ballcourt system and construction of trincheras sites are events "significantly apart from one another, on the order of at least 150 years" (Wallace and Doelle 2001:251).

Response

My response to the critiques reviewed above is structured by three considerations: (1) theoretical bias, (2) logical structure of arguments, and (3) empirical content.

Theoretical Bias

For some researchers, warfare as an explanatory factor in southwestern archaeology has become an exceptionally powerful and illuminating interpretive framework. This viewpoint is so deeply held that for adherents of the warfare model of southwestern prehistory, few if any major events or processes in southwestern prehistory can be understood without reference to warfare. This raises an old and fundamental question in the pursuit of scientific understanding, namely, whether deeply held convictions about a theoretical viewpoint can inordinately color consideration of alternative explanations (Chamberlin 1890, 1897; Derry 1999). Below, I explore the nature of theoretical bias within the warfare model and briefly consider how this may have skewed recent interpretations of trincheras sites.

In recent revivals of the defensive interpretation for trincheras features, theoretical bias favoring the southwestern warfare model is overtly and clearly stated with no hint of discomfiture. Whether this is epistemic flaw or virtue I will leave the reader to decide, but an abiding affection for the warfare model rings with clarity throughout many of these works. LeBlanc (1999:ix), for example, writes of his deeply held commitment to the warfare model in the preface of his book on southwestern warfare: "It had become clear to me since beginning research in the area in 1972 that I could never explain the events in the El Morro Valley, near Zuni, New Mexico, except by warfare. *How* it explained them, *I had no idea*, and that is where things remained for more than twenty years" (emphasis added). He further remarks that, after considering the work by Haas and Creamer on putative warfare among the Kayenta Anasazi, he awoke to the realization that warfare could explain events not just at El Morro, but throughout the Southwest: "For the first time, I had an explanatory model and a way of looking at warfare. *I was then committed* to working out the larger picture" (LeBlanc 1999:x, emphasis added). The personal depth of theoretical commitment is underscored by such statements as "I did not set out to study warfare; *it found me*" (LeBlanc 1999:6, emphasis added), and ". . . we must remember that the truth, once understood, is always more interesting than fantasy" (LeBlanc 1999:320).

Devoted adherents of the warfare model also have alleged psychological weakness in those failing to see warfare as a driving force in southwestern prehistory. Again, whether or not this reveals an unacceptably jaundiced research bias I will leave the reader to decide. Nevertheless, the rhetoric does imply that doubters of the warfare model might do well to search their souls, if not hasten to book a counseling session. For example, LeBlanc (1999:6) writes that "the archaeological community simply has not come to grips with warfare," which is characterized as an "acute" failing. Another example is as follows: "We cannot wish away the unpleasant aspects of the human condition if we are ever to understand that condition" (LeBlanc 1999:320). Similarly, LeBlanc and Rice (2001:1) adopt exhortative tones more commonly sounded in the pages of advice columns than in archaeological literature when they write: "War is not a pleasant topic. Few people want to dwell on warfare or its consequences, and archaeologists are no exception. Yet in spite of our desire to wish intersocietal conflict away, it is clear that warfare is a common aspect of human behavior and that it has played a role in shaping social systems. . . . If we have failed to recognize warfare in the Southwest—where it turns out to be commonplace and important—then what must be the situation elsewhere in the world?"

Work by Wallace and Doelle (2001) reveals an equally strong and morally laden advocacy for the warfare model of southwestern prehistory. For example, as an antidote to what they perceive as a socially and historically rooted bias against warfare in the Southwest, they warn readers against accepting unspecified "myths of warfare our own society promotes" (Wallace and Doelle 2001:286). Like LeBlanc, they advocate acceptance of the model for reasons that seem more based on emotional appeal than intellectual rigor: "It is time to face the dark side of the past and learn from its most painful lessons" (Wallace and Doelle 2001:286).

All of these statements suggest that the warfare model, at least in the relatively early stages of development that it now represents, comes bundled with potentially significant bias. For now, I argue two points. First, the claim that archaeologists have systematically ignored ancient warfare in the Southwest is not entirely supported. The inclination among Southwest scholars to ignore or suppress evidence of warfare is probably not now, nor was it in the past, as widespread as some warfare-model advocates have proposed. Throughout the history of southwestern archaeology, there has been significant literature and thought about the importance of warfare, presented by some of the most significant scholars in the field. To name just a few such sources, the classic works by A. V. Kidder (1962:336–339), Harold Colton (1936, 1937), and Julian Steward (1937, 1955)—hardly marginal figures in the discipline's development—embed or highlight explanations of southwestern prehistory based on the existence and consequences of conflict. Some contemporary works (e.g., Stone and Downum 1999) also assign a central role to conflict in the development of southwestern archaeological theory, independent of the warfare model advocated above.

Second and much more important, strongly held bias can be counterproductive to reliable understanding of the past. Adherents of the current warfare model of southwestern prehistory sometimes offer advocacy that well transcends empirical or logical content. Legitimate concerns can therefore be raised about the objectivity of some warfare-based interpretations, including those involving trincheras sites. Given the degree of theoretical bias and moral admonishment reviewed above, it seems reasonable to ask whether researchers so deeply committed to the warfare model can have fairly considered the possibility that some archaeological cases (such as trincheras sites) might *not* represent the effects of prehistoric warfare.

Trincheras sites may, or they may not, represent evidence of warfare and its consequences. This is a matter for empirical and logical evaluation, rather than a priori theoretical advocacy. The real challenge for any researcher (myself included) is not to utterly eliminate bias (an impossibility), and neither is it to replace one form of bias with another. It is instead to acknowledge, understand, and compensate for biases in a search for the most robust interpretation among competing ideas. In my view, recent literature on trincheras sites, written from the perspective of the warfare model, does not entirely meet this challenge. As the debate over the role of warfare in the Southwest matures, it is my hope that consideration of the trincheras phenomenon can be successfully decoupled from highly charged theoretical imperatives.

Logical Structure

The hypothesis that trincheras sites were designed and used primarily as defensive refuges has proven resilient and adaptable. Through several decades, this idea has undergone considerable changes in terms of the proposed dates of conflict, the proposed attackers, and the proposed nature of defensive use. What has remained stubbornly constant is the idea that trincheras features *must* have been used for defense in some fashion because they *look* defensive.

Much of this argument has been, and still is, based on the formal attributes of masonry structures. Such reasoning uses a "performance characteristics" approach, in which aspects of particular features (usually walls and terrace platforms) are assessed for how they might have performed with respect to hypothesized activities. Early use of this logic asserted that because terraces are today level and mostly free of rock, they would have provided more secure footing for a defender (Wilcox 1979:27–28). Therefore, the terraces were designed and built for defense. Similarly, because walls could have provided protection from arrows and other missiles, such walls must have been built for protection against such missiles (Wilcox 1979:28).

More recent interpretations of cerros de trincheras (e.g., LeBlanc 1999) use a nearly identical form of argument. Again, the idea is that trincheras features and sites *must* have been used for defense because they *could* have been: "The trincheras I have visited were certainly capable of providing defense, and given what is known about changes in warfare over the entire Southwest at the time they begin to appear, I believe the case for their being defensive is the stronger one" (LeBlanc 1999:258).

Unfortunately, this type of argument is a logical fallacy that leads to unreliable conclusions. Specifically, it is known as the "fallacy of affirming the consequent" (Barker 1974:93), or the "fallacy of the undistributed middle term" (Derry 1999:100). The fallacy is illustrated with the following example: "All stop signs are red. This bird is red. Therefore, this bird is a stop sign." In the case of trincheras features, such reasoning is as follows: "All defensively oriented features give an advantage to the defender. This trincheras feature would have given an advantage to the defender. Therefore, this trincheras feature is a defensively oriented feature."

Such reasoning could be applied to a host of built features. For example, it could be argued that because the roofs of houses provide an elevated platform that would give advantage to a defender, house roofs are therefore evidence of warfare. Or it could be reasoned that because Italian vineyard terraces provided excellent positions for German Army machine guns during World War II, the terraces must have been designed and built as defensive platforms.

This is not to say that all arguments about all archaeological phenomena or even the more limited domain of potentially defensive sites or features can be reduced to simple analysis of logical propositions. Far from it. I do claim, however, that consideration of multiple alternative hypotheses and a more complete knowledge of the form, arrangement, landscape context, chronology, and contents of individual features (gained through detailed mapping of features, examination of surface artifacts, landscape analysis, and archaeological excavation) are far superior to speculation and logically fallacious reasoning. A superb example of how multiple lines of evidence can be used to strongly support a defensive interpretation of rock features (in this case, Coast Salish fortifications of the Lower Fraser River Canyon of British Columbia) is provided by Schaepe (2006).

Empirical Content

Recent defensive interpretations of trincheras sites entail several major empirical problems. First is the often cursory and incomplete nature of the review itself. In some formulations, there is no sustained empirical argument for why trincheras sites should be viewed as defensive, other than repeated assertion. For example, LeBlanc (1999) does not elaborate on why the superficial 1930s conclusions of Sauer and Brand, based on surface characteristics, are to be preferred over the detailed mapping and excavation data obtained by McGuire and Villalpando. He comments (1999:258) that "in Sonora, at least, some trincheras sites were habitation sites according to McGuire and Villalpando (1993)," but dismisses these results by persisting without elaboration that "Sauer and Brand (1931) make an excellent argument for these Sonoran trincheras as being defensive." There is no mention of the cerros de trincheras of Linda Vista Hill and Cerro Prieto, where evidence for hillside residences on stone platforms has been well published and unequivocal (Downum 1986, 1993). LeBlanc (1999:258) notes only that "many of these [trincheras] sites had terrace walls which were higher than needed to form farming terraces," which therefore "would have actually impeded farming access." The implication is that if an unspecified "many" trincheras features at unspecified sites have an unspecified wall height "higher than needed" for farming, then a defensive motivation for the construction of trincheras sites must be a superior general explanation for their construction.

In the current era, however, assigning a single function to trincheras sites—whether that function is defense or anything else—can no longer be supported. Based on detailed mapping and excavation data, local researchers have advocated since the early 1980s that there are actually multiple formal categories of trincheras features with different functions. Some trincheras are known to have served as house platforms (Downum 1986, 1993; Downum et al. 1981; Hard and Roney, this vol.; McGuire and Villalpando, this vol.); some apparently functioned as garden plots (Downum et al. 1981; Fish et al. 1984; McGuire et al. 1999, this vol.); some were used for ceremonial or ritual purposes (Downum 1995; Fish and Fish 2004, this vol.; McGuire and Villalpando, this vol.); some were extramural activity areas (Downum 1995; McGuire and Villalpando, this vol.); and some had functions that have not yet been discerned or, indeed, may have been defensive in nature (e.g., the Type III walls at Linda Vista Hill). The inferred complexity of trincheras sites and features, however, is ignored in the following quotations: "The argument that Southwestern trincheras were built not for defense but for agricultural purposes is considered in chapter 6" (LeBlanc 1999:132); and "Dave Wilcox (1979) persuasively argues for their having been defensive, but S. Fish et al. (1984) and Downum (1986, 1993) argue they were agricultural" (LeBlanc 1999:258). Neither I nor the Fishes ever have argued that trincheras sites were used solely for agriculture or for any other single purpose. We have instead inferred from mapping, surface collection, survey, and excavation data that the multiple categories of rock platforms, terraces, and walls traditionally glossed under the term *trincheras* served multiple functions (see especially Downum 1986 and Downum et al. 1993).

Another empirical problem with recent interpretations of trincheras sites is an oversimplification of the impressive temporal variability that we now know characterizes trincheras sites. This empirical complexity does not serve well the broad and, in my view, overly simple generalizations favored by various warfare-driven reconstructions of prehistoric events. To cite one example, LeBlanc (1999:259) writes that during the 200- to 300-year "Late Period" of the Hohokam area, "there is little doubt that people outside the core area were living in a state of significant warfare" (LeBlanc 1999:259). Trincheras features are supposedly explained by "what is known about changes in warfare over the entire Southwest at the time they begin to appear" (LeBlanc 1999:258). Unfortunately for this explanation, however, the totality of trincheras sites and their various features are now known to have been built at many different times over a period of approximately three millennia, beginning in the Archaic. This is hardly evidence of convincing temporal correlation between "changes in warfare" and cerros de trincheras. Even when we confine analysis to the later end of the time scale (i.e., the millennium or more that is encompassed by the Hohokam ceramic period), the examples in this volume demonstrate that major cerros de trincheras were decidedly not built and occupied at anywhere near the same time (even if, to be generous, we conflate two or three centuries, as LeBlanc has done).

It is also possible to question on empirical grounds some of the more detailed arguments that have been presented by Wallace and Doelle (2001). Much of their discussion relies on an oversimplification of the 1980s and early 1990s literature on Tucson Basin trincheras sites. For example, I can find no justification for the claim that my colleagues and I have proposed that all trincheras features were used exclusively for agriculture or for any other single purpose (cf. Wallace and Doelle 2001:248). Instead, we have taken great pains to point out that so-called trincheras features surely served multiple functions. In 1986, I proposed that the trincheras features at Linda Vista Hill should be grouped into multiple formal categories representing divergent functions. I even proposed that conflict might have been one of the motivating factors behind the movement of features onto the Linda Vista hill slope (Downum 1986)! Consideration of a diversity of feature types and functions, and multiple hypotheses concerning function and use of the features, has been a consistent aspect of our work. A quote from Fish, Fish, and Downum (1984:55), now more than 20 years old, illustrates our perspective: "The absence of detailed information concerning individual features has undoubtedly strengthened a tendency to assign trincheras sites a unitary function rather than to regard them as complexes of associated features with diversified functions."

To turn to a specific case, I must dispute the notion that the Fishes, Katzer, and I proposed that small garden plots were the principal motivation for constructing the habitation villages of Cerro Prieto and Linda Vista Hill. This inaccurate claim is clearly stated: "But can one justify placing a village in such a setting for these small kitchen gardens? . . . By all measures, agriculture is unlikely to be the motivation for building these sites" (Wallace and Doelle 2001:250). The reality of our published interpretations is far from this. In a detailed discussion of the possible use of trincheras features for agricultural purposes, we argued for a complex set of pressures and incentives, including warfare: "As less accessible, dispersed, and defensible targets, terrace crops also might have survived intentional destruction during conflict" (Fish et al. 1984:70). In the same article, we also considered how demographic pressure, existing land tenure systems, and individual ownership of small plots might have functioned to encourage use of hillside terraces in some times and places: "*Some* trincheras features *may* have originated under such conditions of tenure and incentive. . . . A *number of possible roles* for hillside terraces . . . [have] been discussed" (S. Fish et al. 1984:70–71, emphasis added). Thus, Wallace and Doelle's (2001:250) stance that we proposed that entire villages were founded on hillsides to take advantage of "kitchen gardens" does not accurately reflect our position.

Rather than proposing hillside occupation to have been motivated by agricultural pursuits or any other single factor, other colleagues and I have proposed something quite different, that is, that the people who designed and built the Linda Vista Hill and Cerro Prieto hillside settlements were driven by complex mix of ideological, social, environmental, economic, and political concerns (Downum 1993:119–122; Downum et al. 1993; Downum et al. 1994). The supposed "agricultural hypothesis" of hillside village construction thus seems to be a foil to support the alternative (and, in my view, equally simplistic) single-function hypothesis that Tucson Basin trincheras sites and features (glossed as "fortified villages"; see Wallace and Doelle 2001:256) were spawned by warfare.

Turning to the supposedly "massive wall" at Linda Vista Hill that was "overlooked" by previous researchers, I have two comments. First, I became aware of the wall during the initial mapping work at Linda Vista Hill. However, it fell outside the aerial photograph used to map the site and so was not included on subsequent site maps. Second, at the time of the early fieldwork at Linda Vista Hill, it was unclear whether the wall was unequivocally prehistoric. Previous landowners had indicated that the area surrounding Linda Vista Hill had been fenced and used for grazing sheep. It was my view that the wall was possibly a modern construction used to keep sheep away from a steep precipice and confine them to the lower slopes of Linda Vista Hill. In any case, this wall is not a lynchpin in a defensive argument regarding Linda Vista Hill; it is merely one of numerous "Type III" surface constructions (usually, isolated low walls lacking significant fill behind them) having an unclear function. As noted, a defensive use for these types of walls cannot be definitively ruled out, but the totality of evidence from Linda Vista Hill does not strongly support a defensive interpretation for them.

As my colleagues and I have argued at length elsewhere (Downum et al. 1993), the proposition that Cerro Prieto can be termed a "fortified village" (Wallace and Doelle 2001: 258–259) cannot be supported by a review of the evidence. For Cerro Prieto, a "boulder strewn surface" is supposedly a hindrance to the movements of attackers. However, Cerro Prieto is laced with a trail system that provides ready access up and across the inhabited hillslopes. An "intimate knowledge of the trail system" (Wallace and Doelle 2001:247) would certainly not have been necessary for attackers, because the trail system is visually evident from a distance even today. During prehistoric times, the trails would have been even more obvious, because vegetation in the village would have been greatly diminished. In any event, attackers could have quickly learned trail patterns merely by observing the hillslopes and watching residents' movements. Terraces and compound walls would have provided some impediment to movement on the slopes, but these features occupy a very small proportion of the hillslopes and therefore would not have provided protection to the great majority of Cerro Prieto's occupants. Multiple, nondefensive functions of the terraces and compounds, which are distributed at opposite ends of the site and thus are removed from the main concentrations of residences, are more likely and have been partially documented by excavation (Downum et al. 1993).

The critique of the idea that some trincheras features were used for ceremonial or ritual purposes has also excessively simplified our arguments. Wallace and Doelle (2001:251) write: "If sites were purely ritually focused, repeated ritual behavior should be observed. No such consistency in behavior is noted for the sites in question." This criticism is irrelevant, because nowhere have we claimed that Linda Vista Hill, Cerro Prieto, or any other trincheras site was "purely ritually focused." Further, the term "consistency" remains undefined, either in formal terms or by example.

Given the difficulties involved in finding material traces of ritual behavior in the archaeological record (Walker 1995), there is remarkably convincing evidence of ritual activities associated with some of the trincheras features at Cerro Prieto and Linda Vista Hill, Cerro de Trincheras, Tumamoc Hill, and other sites. Ritual activities involving volcanic hills may even be a generalized late prehistoric cultural phenomenon (Fish and Fish, this vol.), extending to sites such as the excavated and roughly contemporaneous central Arizona hilltop site of AZ T:4:8 that contained a conch shell trumpet (Spoerl and Gumerman 1984), at the northern periphery of Hohokam territory. The slopes and summits of each of these sites show architectural forms, artifacts, petroglyphs, or some combination of these that strongly suggest ritual behavior (see review presented by Downum et al. 1994, and McGuire and Villalpando, this vol.). Rather than showing inconsistency, the evidence for ritual behavior at late prehistoric hillside and hilltop locations in southern and central Arizona and in northern Sonora is far more consistent than the material evidence for warfare. Wallace and Doelle (2001) claim, for example, that projectile points at several sites in the San Pedro River valley and in the Tucson Basin provide supporting evidence of warfare. However, they make no mention of the meager number of projectile points from surface collections and excavations at the supposedly defensive sites of Linda Vista Hill and Cerro Prieto. Only two projectile points were found at Linda Vista Hill, and only one was observed at Cerro Prieto, a site of considerably more surface area and subsurface exposure.

A final unsupported critique is that "a central problem of the previous research related to so-called trincheras in the Tucson Basin is that researchers have not adequately considered the variability between and within these sites" (Wallace and Doelle 2001:251). On the contrary, the Fishes and I have long written that the trincheras phenomenon encompassed multiple functions, "including use as residences, agricultural plots, and ceremonial compounds" (Downum et al. 1994:292). This conclusion has not been presented as a matter of belief or opinion, but has been repeatedly supported by empirical evidence gained through detailed mapping, surface survey, excavation, and artifact analysis.

Lessons Learned

The study of trincheras sites has obviously entered a new and fruitful period of field research and analysis. Debates about the function and role of trincheras sites in larger social systems continue with renewed vigor. Here I offer some conclusions that I believe are warranted from consideration of both the old and new work.

First, our previous estimates about the general age of trincheras sites were wrong. In fact, they were very, very wrong. We now know that characterizing all trincheras sites as a primarily late prehistoric phenomenon (e.g., Downum et al. 1994; Wilcox et al. 1979) missed the mark by about three millennia. These sites are now known to span a very long period of time, from the second millennium BC to at least the terminal prehistoric period. Many factors lay behind our erroneous conclusions, but in most instances we were persuaded by surface evidence from potsherds regarding the apparent dates of trincheras site use. Nothing better illustrates the danger of relying too heavily on surface remains, and, therefore, the value of excavation data.

We were also wrong about the pervasiveness of a particular orientation of trincheras sites. We were not necessarily incorrect in inferring an agricultural use for some terraces, but terraces at many sites are not predominantly oriented to the north and east. In hindsight, the sample used by Keith Katzer to draw conclusions about general trends in the orientations of trincheras features was far too small. From today's perspective, informed by a large increase in the sample of known trincheras features from Sonora and Chihuahua, trincheras features may be oriented mostly to face rivers and major corridors of travel. That is, irrespective of compass bearing, the majority of trincheras features may have been situated to overlook major drainages and travel routes. If so, this points to the importance of social, rather than environmental, factors in determining the locations of some trincheras features and sites.

Defensive interpretation of trincheras sites is obviously a complicated issue and one that does not lend itself to simplistic characterizations. It should be apparent that any unitary interpretation of all trincheras sites is untenable. Trincheras sites are too structurally complex, formally variable, and chronologically diverse to be explained by any single factor. There were undoubtedly many factors that determined the design and use of so-called trincheras features across a vast geographic area and an impressive sweep of time. There is indeed a role for conflict and warfare in the interpretation of southwestern prehistory. Viewing trincheras sites as complex constructions with complex motivations does not require the rejection of conflict and warfare. However, the stubborn biases evident in previous glossings of all trincheras sites as "defensive" or "fortified" sites do not serve us well.

As an alternative to the rather simple interpretation of cerros de trincheras as defensive refuges, I suggest that it is possible to consider some of these sites as relevant to the issues of prehistoric competition and conflict without classifying them as a single category such as fortifications. Past interpretations of cerros de trincheras as fortifications or defensive refuges have cast them in a decidedly passive light; that is, the hillsides and their associated features were built in response to the fear of conflict. Constructing a cerro de trincheras thus is viewed as a reactive measure, a response to an overt or implied threat from other social groups. In this scenario, the intent in building such a site is to provide a place of last resort, a platform upon which to make a final stand. Overall, this implies an asymmetry of forces or tactics, with the group building the trincheras features believing that they need the advantage provided to them by the hillside features to successfully counter threats.

I suggest an alternative view, one that proposes that the larger cerros de trincheras such as Linda Vista and Cerro Prieto may have been rather aggressive political and symbolic statements, designed to send a message to other groups regarding territorial control and political power. In this view, large cerros de trincheras were never built with the intent of using them as hiding places or retreats of last resort, they were instead built as highly visible monuments commemorating the power (and implied threat of resistance or retaliation) represented by a cooperating village unit or other population aggregate. This suggestion follows a model of tribal political development recently proposed with colleague Glenn Stone to explain developments in a prehistoric competitive frontier setting in northern Arizona (Stone and Downum 1999). In this model, hilltop villages and multistory structures are interpreted as "monumental pueblos," designed to assert dominance over particular territories by particular groups. Following ethnographic analogy with similar frontier situations in West Africa, we have proposed that actual conflicts were rare, because they were seldom necessary to enforce territorial claims. Instead, dominance and the jockeying for power by one group over another was expressed in multiple ways, including strategic placement of villages at geographical crossroads, construction of highly visible settlements designed to impart a sense of territorial control, and marking of the landscape with "hypervisible" features such as stone alignments. Ethnographically, many features such as elaborate field boundaries cannot be explained with reference to any functional performance. Instead, they serve as highly visible markers placed on the landscape, designed to be seen by any who would entertain thoughts of appropriating particular territories or resources.

Given the spectacularly visible nature of many trincheras constructions, and the presence of numerous other potential territorial markers on the Hohokam cultural landscape (e.g., clusters of petroglyphs), it may be that cerros de trincheras were in fact the opposite of a defensive refuge. Rather than presenting a stylized venue for conflict, they may have been built to effectively discourage such conflict. Physically and symbolically, it must be admitted that terraced cerros de trincheras loom above the landscape. As artificial terraced hillsides, they offer powerful visual evidence for the organization of hearts, minds, and hands, organization that may have been understood to be at the ready in case of threat or territorial transgression.

Finally, of all the recent discoveries regarding trincheras sites and features, I find the results from Cerro Juanaqueña (Hard and Roney 1998) to be the most fascinating. These findings are also inspirational, because they show again the potential of the archaeological record to surprise us. In 1994, when with the Fishes and I wrote a review of the status of trincheras research (Downum et al. 1994), none of us imagined that any of the known trincheras sites could have had a substantial Archaic age component, much less an Archaic occupation of the magnitude now known for Cerro Juanaqueña. It now appears increasingly likely that the large terraces at Tumamoc Hill were constructed in those early times. Recent work by the Fishes (Wallace et al., this vol.) shows that at least some of the large terraces at Tumamoc Hill contained Archaic age structures. Thus, they may have been built largely as house platforms, just as the terraces at Cerro Juanaqueña were.

The implications of these findings at a regional scale are largely unexplored by the greater community of Southwest and borderlands scholars (but see Hard and Roney 1998). I suggest, however, that in addition to a defensive interpretation, more analysis should be devoted to the potential symbolic and organizational implications of Archaic age trincheras sites. The presumably low population densities of the Early Agricultural period landscape do not intuitively support the idea that organized warfare was a motivating factor in constructing a site like Cerro Juanaqueña. Further, the type of incipient monumental construction that appears to be represented at Cerro Juanaqueña and possibly at Tumamoc Hill and others is not without precedent in the ancient New World or Old World archaeological records (for example, the earthworks of Poverty Point [Kidder 2002; Sassaman 2005] and the enigmatic tower of PPNA Jericho [Kenyon 1960; Moore 1978] come to mind) and therefore may have important theoretical implications for our perception and understanding of the range of organizational possibilities expressed by preagricultural and early agricultural societies. Much has been written by advocates of the warfare model regarding how biases against warfare have clouded our vision of the southwestern past. I would urge us not to be similarly blinded by the biases of the emerging warfare model of southwestern prehistory, to the point that we might overlook some fascinating possible instances of precocious organizational complexity in a time and place and under circumstances few if any expected to find them (three millennia ago, in the southern deserts, during a transition to an agricultural lifeway).

Conclusion

Clearly our understanding of the trincheras phenomenon has advanced remarkably in the past decade or so, with the greatest acceleration coming in just the past few years. Two major lessons drawn from the recent work are that (a) simplicity in our understanding of this phenomenon and unitary interpretations of trincheras are no longer supportable, and (b) excavation is a powerful tool for advancing our knowledge, far superior to mere surface observation and speculation based thereon. In this chapter, I have summarized the results of excavation-based studies at two trincheras sites in and near the Tucson Basin, and I have reiterated and defended conclusions regarding these sites. In doing so, I hope that I have contributed to our understanding of this complex phenomenon, at least at the basic level of understanding functions of particular sites and features and the diversity that they represent. The hardest but surely most rewarding task lies ahead: understanding the meaning and implications of trincheras sites in the context of long-term cultural history and processes of culture change in the southern Southwest and the northern frontier of Mesoamerica.

5

Excavations at Cerro de Trincheras

Randall H. McGuire and M. Elisa Villalpando

Dark, isolated, volcanic hills dot the deserts of Sonora, Mexico, and southern Arizona. The prehistoric inhabitants of the deserts constructed terraces up the sides of many of these hills and built rooms, compounds, and other edifices on their summits. The resulting *cerros de trincheras* are among the most prominent archaeological sites in the region, but, paradoxically, among the least well known. In 1895 W. J. McGee (1898:xl) described the largest such site, Cerro de Trincheras (fig. 1.3; Heisey, plate 7), as "the most elaborate prehistoric works known to exist in northwestern Mexico." Over a hundred years of archaeological research in the Sonoran desert have confirmed his assertion and have shown the site of Cerro de Trincheras to be one of the most distinctive, striking, and substantial archaeological sites in the Northwest/Southwest. Despite more than a century of investigation, archaeologists still puzzle over the question of why people would choose to invest so much time and labor to build terraces and other structures on the steep, cobble-strewn slopes of an isolated volcanic hill. Observers have speculated that Cerro de Trincheras was a massive terraced agricultural field, a rude village, a signal station, or a refuge fort. The last explanation, with its image of terrified women and children fleeing to the safety of the hill while their men fought a rear-guard action against enemy raiders has been the most popular and enduring interpretation.

The vast majority of these speculations have been just that: guesswork based on superficial and even casual observations. Our research at Cerro de Trincheras in the spring of 1995 and 1996 was the first systematic excavation at the site, and based on this fieldwork we have developed a more informed and nuanced interpretation of the site. We have found evidence for all of the functions that other researchers have advanced to explain why people choose to live on these isolated hills, including agriculture, ritual, and defense. Each of these functions is too simple an answer by itself, however, given the complex site we have excavated. This complexity suggests to us that Cerro de Trincheras was a major prehispanic town and a regional center in its own right. Future research on this site and others like it should focus on the lived experience of being a resident of a town on a hill and on the dynamic relationship between this experience and the realities of warfare, religion, economy, and society in the region (Fish and Fish, this vol.; O'Donovan 2004). In this chapter, meanwhile, we summarize our excavations and interpretations to demonstrate the complex nature of life in the town of Cerro de Trincheras. Our discussions will pay special attention to defense and the interpretation of the site as a refuge fort.

Past Research and Interpretations of Cerro de Trincheras

Although the earliest written account of Cerro de Trincheras dates to the end of the seventeenth century (Mange 1926), no archaeologists conducted intensive investigations at the site until the 1990s. Many archaeologists have visited the site in the last hundred years, but none tarried there for more than a few days (Ekholm 1939; Huntington 1913, 1914; Johnson 1960; McGee 1895; Noguera 1958; Sauer and Brand 1931). Some did not even take the time to climb the hill the site occupies before concocting their speculations (Lumholtz 1912; Sandomingo 1954; Wasley 1968).

These archaeologists entered Sonora from either the north or the south to answer questions posed outside of the region, and they interpreted the archaeology of the region in terms of processes emanating from afar. They tended to explain cultural developments in Sonora based on one of two models: either that these developments were the southern fringes of the Hohokam or Mogollon traditions of the southwest United States (Haury 1976), or that they resulted from the expansion of Mesoamerican polities and processes into the Northwest/Southwest (Di Peso 1979, 1983; Di Peso et al. 1974a). Research over the last decade and a half has challenged this external perspective (Braniff C. 1992; Carpenter 1997; McGuire and Villalpando 1989, 1993, 1994; McGuire et al. 1993). More research and knowledge has encouraged archaeologists to interpret the archaeology of northern Sonora in terms of local developments and relationships.

Numerous propositions have been advanced to account for Cerro de Trincheras. Two of these, the idea the site was a refuge fort (McGee 1898), or that it was a massive terraced agricultural field (Huntington 1913, 1914), had been rejected prior to our excavations based on recent research in southern Arizona (Downum 1993), and at Cerro de Trincheras (O'Donovan 1997, 2004). It is clear that the site was a terraced town. Four other hypotheses remained open questions that we sought to answer with our excavations.

One of the most common artifact types at the site is shell-jewelry manufacture waste. The prevalence of this material inspired external models that interpret Cerro de Trincheras as a trade outpost that specialized in the manufacture and exchange of shell jewelry. The external model takes two forms: (1) that Cerro de Trincheras was a shell-jewelry production site, at the southern periphery of a Hohokam regional system (Brand 1935a, 1938; McGuire and Howard 1987; Robles 1973; Sauer and Brand 1931; Tower 1945; Woodward 1936), or (2) that Cerro de Trincheras was a fortified village established by Mesoamerican merchants to protect their shell manufactory at the nearby site of La Playa (Di Peso 1979, 1983). In both of these hypotheses, Cerro de Trincheras developed as a result of far-flung economic relations and the expansion of foreign cultures or polities.

Two other models base the founding and growth of Cerro de Trincheras in local processes. The first of these questions that the site was a major center and instead views it as a rustic village of the desert branch of the Hohokam; that is, as a provincial adaptation of the Hohokam culture to the local environment (Haury 1976; Johnson 1960). The second model posits that Cerro de Trincheras was an indigenous center for a late prehistoric polity in the Río Magdalena drainage (Braniff C. 1992; McGuire and Villalpando 1989, 1993). Our research results tend to favor the latter of these two interpretations.

Since we completed our excavations, LeBlanc (1999) has invoked cerros de trincheras in general and the site of Cerro de Trincheras as evidence for widespread warfare in the prehispanic Northwest/Southwest. His interpretation that the site of Cerro de Trincheras was simply a refuge fort or sanctuary does not adequately account for the complex site that we excavated. Nonetheless, the defensive nature of terraced towns and their relationship to warfare remains a question worthy of further consideration

The Trincheras Tradition and the Site of Cerro de Trincheras

Cerro de Trincheras lies in the Trincheras tradition of northern Sonora (fig. 1.1). The term *trincheras* can be somewhat confusing, because archaeologists have used the name to refer to ceramic types (Trincheras Purple-on-red and Trincheras Polychrome) (Brand 1935b), to an archaeological tradition (fig. 1.3) (Bowen 1976a), to agricultural terraces in and along streambeds in Chihuahua (Howard and Griffiths 1966), to a type of site (cerros de trincheras) (Sauer and Brand 1931), and to a specific site (Cerro de Trincheras) (Mange 1926). The ceramic types were manufactured in northern Sonora and define the Trincheras tradition. Cerros de trincheras sites consist of terraces, rooms, and walls built on isolated, usually volcanic hills. These sites are most common in the Trincheras tradition but also occur among the Hohokam (Downum et al. 1994), in the Río Sonora (Doolittle 1988), and east into the Casas Grandes region of Chihuahua, Mexico (Hard and Roney 1998, this vol.). The largest example of this type of site is Cerro de Trincheras.

The Trincheras tradition extends from the international border on the north, south to Desemboque, and from the Gulf of California east to the Rio San Miguel (fig. 1.3). Bowen (1976a) divided the chronology of the tradition into four numbered phases. The earliest of these phases (? to AD 200) is a Late Archaic complex much like the Cochise tradition of southern Arizona, with agriculture appearing by 500 BC (Villalpando et al. 1999:160). Purple-on-red ceramics appear in Phase 2 (AD 200 to 800). During Phase 3 (AD 800 to 1300), these developments continue, with larger pithouse villages, cremation burial, and the appearance of cerros de trincheras. By Phase 4 (AD 1300 to 1450), the tradition changed dramatically. The production of painted pottery ceased, the geographical range of the tradition contracted, and Trincheras people built the site of Cerro de Trincheras. By the time of the first reliable Spanish reports, in the 1600s, O'odham (Pima and Papago) peoples, who are probable descendants of the Trincheras tradition people, inhabited the region.

The site of Cerro de Trincheras covers a large, isolated, volcanic hill south of the modern town of Trincheras, in the Rio Magdalena drainage (fig. 1.3). The Rio Magdalena drainage lies in the Sonoran Desert. Before arroyo cutting and large-scale water pumping in the late nineteenth century, the river surfaced year round, wide and marshy in front of Cerro de Trincheras. Today it is dry most of the year. Precipitation comes primarily in the form of summer cloudbursts, with lesser amounts of rain falling from extensive winter fronts. Temperatures between the months of June and September routinely exceed 40° C. Rainfall is insufficient to support corn agriculture without the use of irrigation. Creosote bush, ironwood, mesquite, and cholla cactus cover the plains. Columnar cacti (saguaro, cardón, garambullo, and organ pipe) thrive on the lower slopes of the hill, along with palo verde and other cacti. The floodplains of the river are wooded with mesquite.

Cerro de Trincheras is visually monumental and can be seen across the plain from more than 40 km away. The hill covers approximately 100 ha and rises 156 m above the surrounding flat desert floor. The most obvious features at the site are the 902 terraces, located primarily on the north slope of the hill. Some of these terraces extend for 100 m or more, but most are 15 to 30 m. They range in height from tens of centimeters at the base of the hill to slightly over 3 m at the summit. The hill is dotted with hundreds of quadrangular and circular rooms with dry-laid rock walls that stand up to a meter in height. Two structures stand out from the rest of the architecture on the site. La Cancha (the court) is a 75 by 15 m rectangle with rounded corners, near the base of the hill's north face (fig. 5.1). The Plaza del Caracol sits on the crest of the hill, toward the east end (fig. 5.2; Heisey, plate 11). El Caracol (snail shell) itself is built of dry-laid cobbles, with walls standing to a height of 1.6 m. In plan view these walls form a 13 by 8 m spiral that looks like a snail shell cut in half.

Since 1991, we have conducted research at Cerro de Trincheras working under permits from the Instituto Nacional de Antropología y Historia (INAH) of Mexico. Binghamton University (Binghamton, New York) and the Centro INAH Sonora (Hermosillo, Sonora) cosponsored the projects, with substantial help from the Arizona State Museum and

5.1 La Cancha, Cerro de Trincheras.

Geo Map Inc. (both Tucson, Arizona). In 1991, the National Geographic Society (Grant # 4454–91) funded surface survey and aerial photography needed to produce a map of Cerro de Trincheras (fig. 5.3) (O'Donovan 1997, 2002). We returned in 1995 and 1996 to excavate the site, with a grant from the National Science Foundation (SBR930224). Analysis of the results of these excavations is complete, and the write-up of a multivolume final report is ongoing in Binghamton and Hermosillo. In 1998, we cooperated with Paul Fish and Suzanne Fish of the Arizona State Museum in a National Geographic Society–funded (Grant # 5856–97) survey of the environs of Cerro de Trincheras (Fish 1999; Fish and Fish 2004; Fish and Fish, this vol.).

Cerro de Trincheras Excavation 1995 and 1996

Our excavations at Cerro de Trincheras lasted eight months, divided evenly between two field seasons in the spring of 1995 and 1996. Each season's excavation crew included six archaeologists from the United States and six from Mexico. The project employed up to 50 local residents as excavators, cooks, and artifact washers. We set up a field laboratory in Trincheras to do preliminary cleaning, sorting, and analyses. At the end of the field season all ceramics, chipped stone, ground stone, and shell were returned to the Centro INAH Sonora in Hermosillo for further analysis and curation. Samples for specialized analyses (pollen, flotation, faunal, and chronometric) were brought to the United States.

5.2 El Caracol, Cerro de Trincheras. Aerial photograph © Adriel Heisey.

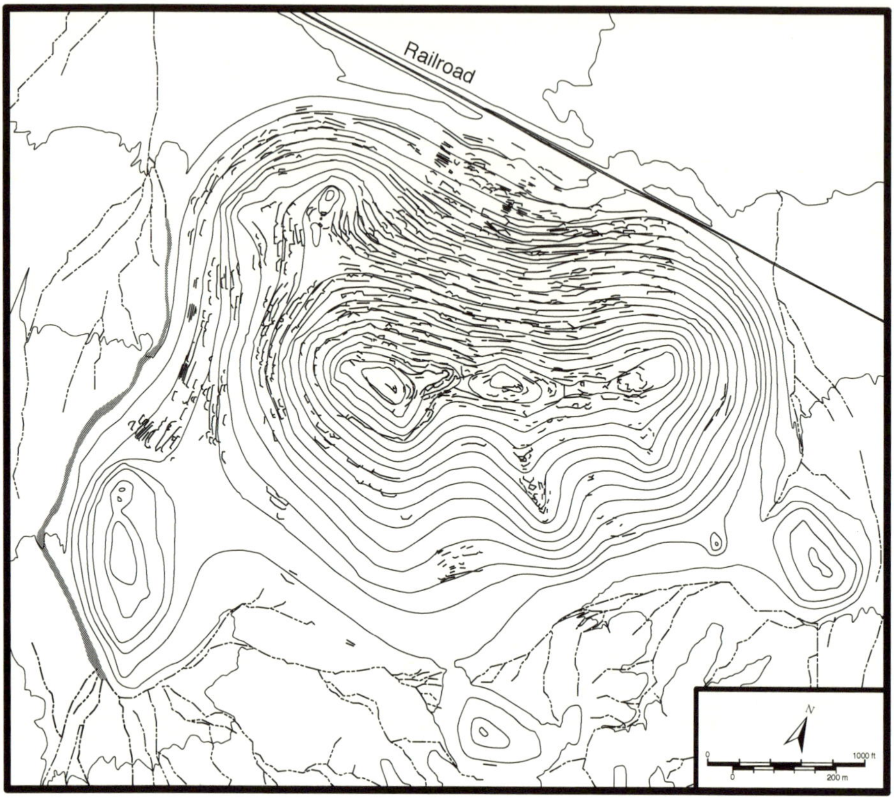

5.3 Map of Cerro de Trincheras. Mapping and computer cartography by Geo-Map, Tucson, Arizona.

Provenience Control

Given Cerro de Trincheras's size and extreme topography, we did not maintain a single grid or elevation control over the entire site. Instead, during mapping of the site in 1991, we assigned each terrace a unique number. We also divided the hill into a series of areas designated by letters, A–E (O'Donovan 1997, 2002). The top of the hill was Area A. The north face of the hill (with most of the terraces) was Area B. The south face of the hill was Area C, and the west face of the hill was Area D. We found a concentration of artifacts on the plain behind the hill and designated that Area E. During excavation, loci were designated by the area letter and by a number within these areas (A.1, B.1, B.3, B.4, etc.). We established a separate grid and elevation datum in each locus. At the end of the project, Geo Map Inc. of Tucson surveyed in the locus datum and grids and added them to the site map. The field crews excavated 13 loci distributed in all of the areas, except Area C, which has few terraces and a mostly empty slope. The basic provenience control unit on the terraces in Areas A and B was a 1-m square. In Areas D and E, which are off the hill and where excavations were more extensive, we used 2-m squares.

General Excavation Procedures

The excavation sample was judgmental based on feature types and areas defined in the mapping project. By sampling different feature types, we were able to infer different activity units, and by sampling within and between areas we were able to discuss the distribution and chronology of these units across the site. This approach allowed us to estimate parameters such as the number of houses per residential terrace and, in turn, to make inferences about population and labor investment. The broad-based sample gave us chronometric data from all portions of the site and information on activity structure across the site.

During the 1995 excavation season, we focused our efforts on Areas B, D, and E. In Area B we worked in a location where the 1991 survey had revealed large amounts of shell (O'Donovan 1997). In 1996 we dug in area A (the top of the hill) and in other portions of Area B.

The physical remains, topography, and soil conditions varied enough among features and loci that no single excavation method could be used over the entire site. Crews followed certain general procedures in all areas. All excavations were done by hand. Archaeologists drew stratigraphic profiles when appropriate, and (as much as was possible) artifacts were collected by natural and cultural levels. With the exception of exploratory trenching, excavators passed all fill through 1/4-inch or 1/2-cm screens to increase artifact recovery. When field crews encountered buried features, they excavated, collected, mapped, and photographed them in their entirety. We plotted all excavations and features on the site map generated by the 1991 mapping project.

Dating Samples

In order to derive chronometric dates, the archaeologists collected ^{14}C and archaeomagnetic samples. We recovered ^{14}C samples only from features and gave priority to collecting burned annual material (for example, reeds, matting, seeds, and twigs) from good context. Unfortunately, we encountered very little such material in situ. Consequently, most of our ^{14}C dates were derived from burned corn from flotation samples. When possible, archaeologists collected multiple samples from the same context. We also took archaeomagnetic samples from in situ burned features. We submitted 20 ^{14}C samples to Beta Analytical in Miami, Florida, for analysis, and eight archaeomagnetic samples to the Colorado State University archaeomagnetic laboratory in Fort Collins, Colorado. The ^{14}C samples yielded excellent results, but none of the archaeomagnetic samples yielded dates, because of the magnetic characteristics of the hill.

Biological Materials

The project collected pollen, faunal, and flotation samples. The collection techniques were developed in cooperation with the three specialists who analyzed the materials (Peter Stahl, faunal analysis; Charles Miksicek, flotation; and Suzanne Fish, pollen analysis). The specialists also reviewed the protocols for laboratory processing, storage, and shipment of samples. Archaeologists collected pollen samples from fresh exposures, whether from profiles or surfaces, to avoid contamination by modern airborne pollen. The laboratory director took pollen washes from intact ceramic vessels, and from metates from primary contexts. The field crews collected animal bone in the course of general excavations. All flotation samples were searched under a magnifying glass in the field lab for small bone elements. We standardized flotation samples at four liters per sample. Preferred sampling locations included the floors and roof fall areas of burned structures, hearths, or roasting pits, and any kind of stratified trash with visible ash, charcoal, bone, or shell.

The research design for this project did not call for the excavation of human burials. The 1991 survey located a prehistoric cremation cemetery in the site, but we did not excavate in this area. Field crews did encounter 11 semiflexed inhumations in terraces, most in features. These burials contained few if any grave goods. Archaeologists dug each of these burials in their entirety, collected them, recorded them, and photographed them. Penny Dufoe Minturn and Lorrie Lincoln-Babb analyzed these remains (Minturn and Lincoln-Babb 1995). With the clear evidence for cremation at Cerro de Trincheras, it was puzzling to find scattered burials. During the Protohistoric and Historic periods the O'odham buried their dead in a semiflexed position within rock cairns on hillslopes (Underhill 1946). Most or all of the 11 burials from Cerro de Trincheras may be O'odham.

Excavation Areas

Excavations on 21 terraces uncovered 124 features, including seven jacales, nine pithouses, four quadrangular stone structures, 25 circular stone structures, La Cancha, and El Caracol (Zavala 1998). We recovered in excess of a million artifacts, with sherds weighing in excess of three metric tons. The total excavated area was over 12,000 m^2, yielding almost 1,300 m^3 of fill. Our work sampled 2.3 percent of the terraces on the site but less than 1 percent of the total site area.

Archaeological deposits at Cerro de Trincheras tend to be shallow, usually 10 to 20 cm. Our excavation units averaged 12 cm in depth. The fill in the terraces was also very fine, seemingly the consistency of talcum powder. Shallow deposits in fine silt meant that the preservation of materials was generally quite bad. Organic materials were present only if charred, and bone, both animal and human, was usually in poor condition. Features fared only slightly better. Houses (both surface jacales and pithouses) usually showed much evidence of disturbance. Artifacts also suffered damage as a consequence of the shallowness of the site. For example, potsherds tended to be quite small, averaging only 3.2 g by weight and about 2 cm in diameter (Langer 1997). A second consequence of the shallowness of deposits is that an unknown but clearly large amount of material had been removed from the surface of the site. In 1895, McGee (2000:60–61) reported that metates and mortars littered the surface of the hill. Residents of Trincheras frequently spoke to us of items such as metates, pots, and skulls that they knew had been picked up from the surface of the ruin. Older residents said that much more material was once visible on the surface, but that it had been collected over the years. Most of this material was sold to U.S. collectors, who visit Trincheras fairly regularly.

Zavala (1998) divided the 124 features at Cerro de Trincheras into 15 types. The most common of these types consisted of 42 pits of various forms (hearths, roasting pits, puddling pits, ash pits, and trash-filled pits). We encountered four different kinds of structures. Jacales were insubstantial structures made from ocotillo branches attached to a frame of posts, then packed with mud. Pithouses resembled similar structures from the Hohokam region, with plastered floors excavated 10 to 30 cm into the ground, and slightly ramped entryways. The most visible structures were circular and quadrangular stone structures. These had dry-laid stone walls of unshaped andesite cobbles. The walls formed a base for a perishable, jacal-like superstructure. We also found ramadas, occupation surfaces, petroglyphs, middens, stairs, and the 11 burials.

Each area (A, B, D, and E) had its own distinctive group of features. We were able to define a clear pattern for habitation on the terraces of Area B based on data from the 1995 and 1996 excavation seasons. We consistently find four kinds of structures on these terraces, circular rock structures, quadrangular stone structures, jacales, and ramadas. Some subset of these features seems to make up a household. We found these patterns on terraces in loci B.1, B.2, B.3, B.4, B.6, B.7, B.9, and B.11. Areas A, D, and E were each unique in their feature patterning.

Area A. Area A includes several discrete loci defined by three peaks (the highest being El Pico de los Zopilotes) and two saddles. El Caracol (Locus A.1) sits in the eastern saddle (El Abra Este). In plan view it consists of a spiral wall that makes the structure look like a snail's shell cut in half (Gallaga 2001). The structure measures 12.6 by 7.7 m, and the walls still stand to a height of 1.5 m. The feature is part of a complex that we have called La Plaza del Caracol: a flat plaza to the west of the feature and a group of terraces and round rooms to the east and west of the spiral and its plaza. We excavated El Caracol and 16 circular stone structures in the plaza and stripped a portion of the plaza surface. Given the location of the features and the situation on top of the hill, activities in this complex were secluded and presumably private.

Several things made Locus A.1 unique over and above its location on top of the hill. The very thin layer soil was a natural reddish color, not the cultural gray of the deposits in the other areas. The artifact density was low (38,818 sherds, or 3.72 percent of the site total, 1,072 sherds per m^3), and the proportion of lithics to ceramics the highest of any excavated area.

Area B. Area B contains the highest number of terraces of all of the areas. It therefore received most of our attention. We defined and excavated 11 loci in Area B.

Locus B.1 consisted of two terraces (Price 2000). Terrace 347 was immediately upslope from Terrace 351. Terrace 351 was constructed first as a single unit. The wall of the terrace is 1 m high on its downslope face and 3 m wide at its base. The wall is in reality two walls with loose rubble fill between them. Each of these two walls is approximately 1 m high by 1 m wide and was built directly on bedrock. The inhabitants filled the terrace with cobbles and trash. In many cases we could identify discrete dumping episodes of ash, trash, and charcoal in the terrace fill. The wall of Terrace 347 is much less substantial; it varies in height on its downhill face from 30 to 60 cm, and varies in width from 50 cm to 1 m. The wall was not carefully laid coursed stone but consists of large, roughly piled-up stones. In several spots the rocks had been laid over the fill of Terrace 351, indicating that Terrace 347 was built after Terrace 351. The fill of the terrace is primarily cobbles and trash.

Both terraces yielded high numbers and densities of artifacts, but only two features. Locus B.1 accounted for 23 percent of the sherds recovered from the site (2,869 sherds per m^3). Other artifacts included metates, manos, shell manufacture waste, and chipped stone. Jacal 1 and Storage Platform 1 were both found on Terrace 347. Jacal 1 was an oval concentration of cobbles that measured roughly 4 by 3 m. Storage Platform 1 was a flat stone floor about 1.5 m in diameter and flush with the surface of the terrace. It may have been a base for a basketry and/or an adobe granary similar to those preserved in the caves of the Sierra Madre (Lister 1958). We found no evidence for houses or features on Terrace 351, which appears to have been an activity surface associated with Terrace 347.

Locus B.2 consisted of a single terrace, 370. The front wall of this terrace was substantial (1.5 m tall and 1.5 m wide). The wall was not rubble-filled like the wall of Terrace 351; rather, it consisted of a mass of coursed cobbles and boulders. The terrace was filled with cobbles and trash, but the density of trash appeared to be less than in locus B.1. The builders of the terrace included a ramp on the front of the wall that allows access from the terrace below. We encountered a hard-packed surface over much of the terrace that may be a prehispanic occupation surface. This surface was quite shallow over the terrace, ranging in depth from 5 to 10 cm. We uncovered three features in Locus B.2. The largest, Jacal 2, contained a concentration of domestic artifacts, including an olla that had been buried in the terrace fill with its neck protruding. The other two features were a pit of unknown function and a burial. Artifact densities were moderate compared with the rest of the site (1,895 sherds per m^3).

Loci B.3 and B.4 consisted of two terraces, 330 and 313. These two terraces were constructed behind two different walls but appear to represent a single occupation. The front wall of Terrace 330 consisted of a double row of coursed cobbles, laid on bedrock. It was 50 to 65 cm high and 35 to 50 cm wide. The site's inhabitants had filled the terrace with cobbles and trash. The density of trash was lower than in Locus B.1 but higher than in B.2 (B.3, 1,530 sherds per m^3; B.4, 2,735 per m^3). We excavated four features associated with the terrace. The first, Circular Stone Structure 17, had an identifiable floor. The second, at the front of the terrace, was a smaller terrace that we initially identified as a ramp for access to Terrace 330. The third was a set of two steps that provided access from Terrace 229 to 330. The fourth was a group of lines that had been incised in the bedrock at the west edge of Terrace 330.

The front wall of Terrace 313 consisted of two walls of coursed cobbles with rubble fill between. The downslope face of the wall ranged in height from 1 to 1.2 m. The top of the wall ranged in width from 1.3 to 2 m. The terrace fill consisted of cobbles and trash, with a density of artifacts comparable to that of Terrace 330. We found a single jacal on Terrace 313.

La Cancha (Locus B.5) is a prominent feature at the base of the north face of the hill (Martínez 2001a). It is a large (13 × 51 m internal dimensions), flat platform with a circular stone structure at its center. La Cancha is visible from almost every terrace on the north face of the hill. We dug two stratigraphic trenches through it and stripped 639 m^2 of its surface. The excavations revealed that the platform had been carefully constructed, with a much higher proportion of earthen fill to rocks than in other terraces, and with an almost perfectly flat surface. We also discovered that someone had driven a bulldozer through it, punching holes in the west and east ends and leaving tracks on its floor. Excavations revealed no evidence that La Cancha was roofed. Given this fact, and because it was visible from almost all of the terraces on the north face of the hill, whatever activities occurred in La Cancha would have been very public. Given the central location, its size, and the special care taken in its construction, these activities were probably ritual performances or games. La Cancha was probably not a ball court, because the circular structure at its center would have interfered with the game. This area yielded the lowest artifact density on the hill (307 sherds per m^3). Cremated bone and charcoal were scattered through the fill of the feature, suggesting that it was a locus for cremation-related ceremonies. (A lack of ash, charcoal, and burned soil suggests that it was not a crematorium.)

Locus B.6 consisted of three terraces (593, 594, and 576) built upslope from La Cancha (Martínez 2001b). These terraces had a series of three circular stone structures attached to the faces of their walls and one quadrangular stone structure built into one of the walls. Adjacent to these structures and below the walls were three platforms. We think that the people of Cerro de Trincheras used the platforms as open-air work areas. Platform 2 had five broken ceramic vessels on its occupation surface. The artifact density of this locus was low compared to that of other terraces and Locus A.1 (1,320 sherds per m^3). A single jacal suggests that Locus B.6 included dwellings as well as work areas.

Locus B.7 was a residential terrace (211) two-thirds of the distance up the north face of the hill. This terrace included what we call an ancillary terrace (210) (O'Donovan 1997, 2002; Zavala 1998). Ancillary terraces are small, usually rock-filled, terraces built on the backs (the uphill ends) of larger terraces. Ancillary terraces occur primarily on terraces at the higher elevations of the north slope. The field crews excavated one jacal on this terrace. The presence of the jacal as well as the mix of ceramics, flaked stone, ground stone, and shell artifacts suggest that this was a residential terrace. The terrace was filled with cobbles, soil, and trash. This terrace had the second highest artifact density of any area excavated on the site (4,358 sherds per m^3).

El Mirador (Loci B.8, B.9, and B.10) is roughly at the center of the north face of the hill, and about four-fifths of the way up the hill. It consists of three terraces, one above the other. These are the tallest and most impressive terraces on the north face of the hill. The lowest (Terrace 280, Locus B.8) had a small ancillary terrace (350) but lacked other features. This terrace yielded a very high proportion of Chihuahuan trade pottery, ceramic pipes, and other special items. A ramp connected the lower terrace to the middle terrace (Locus B.9, Terrace 277). The middle terrace supported a quadrangular stone structure, a jacal, and a burial. This terrace appears to be a habitation space with a household. The uppermost terrace (Locus B.10, Terrace 226) was rock-filled, with virtually no soil. It lacked features and yielded few artifacts. The artifact densities decreased from the lowest terrace to the highest (B.8, 4,960 sherds per m^3; B.9, 2,626 sherds per m^3; B.10, 2,264 per m^3). What is most striking about these terraces is their prominent position. They are the only points from which virtually all of the terraces on the north face of the site can be viewed.

Locus B.11 was at the eastern edge of the north slope. It consisted of a single terrace (553) with an ancillary terrace (554) and a circular stone structure (25) built into its wall. We found very few artifacts on this terrace (1,297 sherds per m^3) and no features. The fill of the terrace was cobbles and soil, with little trash.

Area D. Excavations in Area D concentrated on two separate types of features, quadrangular stone structures and terraces. Area D was distinct in having a large number of quadrangular stone structures, and our excavations focused on these structures. Area D also contained residential and narrow terraces. The density of artifacts in this area was noticeably less than in other excavated areas (225 sherds per m^3).

We excavated three features that the survey had identified as quadrangular stone structures (O'Donovan 1997). From the surface all of these features had earth fill inside square or rectangular rock alignments. This led us to interpret them as rooms. Two features turned out not to be rooms, but platforms of cobbles with a slight depression in the center. One feature did turn out to be a quadrangular stone structure.

Excavations in Terraces 3, 9, 11, 13, 15, and 17 examined the relationship between residential terraces and narrow terraces. Terraces 3, 9, and 11 were broad, relatively low, long terraces with sufficient surface area to have been used for residences. The retaining walls of each were not made of coursed stone, but rather with long, linear piles of cobbles.

The widths of these terraces ranged from 10 to 19 m. They ranged in height from 50 to 75 cm on the downslope side, and in width at their bases from 2 to 4 m. We located five small pits, as well as a burial excavated into Terrace 9. The fill of these terraces was cobbles, with very few artifacts and little earth. Terraces 13, 15, and 17 were narrow terraces. In each of these the terrace walls were a single layer of cobbles, about 1 m wide, with the terrace surfaces ranging in width from 1.5 to 2.3 m. These three terraces would not have been wide enough to support residential structures (jacales, quadrangular stone structures, or circular stone structures). The fill of the three terraces was an even mix of cobbles and soil. They resembled contour terraces in southern Arizona that have been interpreted as used for the cultivation of agave (Fish et al. 1992b).

The field crew excavated two structures associated with Terraces 9 and 11. Quadrangular Stone Structure 3 was a square room built at the back of Terrace 11 so that the room and the terrace shared a wall. El Caracolito was a feature built into the wall of Terrace 9. As the name suggests, in plan view it resembled the cross section of a snail shell. We recovered a concentration of *Conus* shell rings from this feature. Neither of these rooms had prepared floors or floor features.

Area E. Area E was a pithouse village .5 km south of the base of the hill (McGregor 1998). All nine pithouses located by the project were in this area. Unlike the rest of the site, where the fill was cobbles with some dirt mixed in, the fill of Area E was fine, sandy silt. We also encountered deeper deposits in Area E than in other areas, with features occurring at depths from 10 to 60 cm. Despite this depth, preservation of pithouses was generally poor, reflecting both the insubstantial nature of the houses and the fine, highly permeable fill. We stripped a zone of 667 m^2, or 22 percent of Area E.

Fully 42 percent of the features that we excavated at Cerro de Trincheras were in Area E (52 of 124). We located evidence for nine pithouses and two possible house floors clustered in the northwest portion of the excavated area. Only five of these pithouses were complete; all were round to oval, with short ramp entryways. Diameters ranged from 2.3 to 5 m. In no case could we define the pit walls, but based on the change in elevation on the ramps they appear to have been 10 to 30 cm deep.

Evidence for the other four consisted of short ramp entries or fragments of burned floor. In most of these cases the ramp entries had been plastered and then intentionally burned. These pithouses were much less substantial and more irregular in form than Hohokam pithouses. Middens and extramural pits formed an arc around the houses from north to east to south. South of these features we found the north edge of a cremation cemetery, but we did not excavate any cremations in Area E. The layout of the area resembles that of a Hohokam hamlet: a courtyard group surrounded by activity areas used for resource processing, storage, and waste disposal (McGregor 1998:161). The adjacent cremation cemetery is also consistent with the Hohokam pattern.

Artifacts and biological samples indicate that Area E was an agricultural settlement, contemporaneous with the occupation of the terraced hill. The 1998 survey of the environs of Cerro de Trincheras located numerous other such hamlets in the region (Fish 1999; Fish and Fish 2004; Fish and Fish, this vol.). The artifact density of Area E (76 sherds per m^3) was considerably below that of the terraces on the hill. Macrobotanical remains suggest that the occupants of Area E cultivated corn, squash, beans, and cotton and used a variety of wild resources, including cholla buds, mesquite, and grass seeds. Animal bones included jackrabbit and deer. The range of artifacts varied little in either style or function from the artifact assemblages on the terraces. The seven ^{14}C samples processed from Area E had a two-sigma range of AD 1250 to AD 1450.

Artifacts

Our excavations recovered more than 1,118,000 artifacts, over 974,000 of which were sherds. The next most common category of artifacts was flaked stone (over 135,000), followed by shell (6,793) and ground stone (764).

The vast majority of the ceramics were locally made plainwares. The most common of these is the Trincheras tradition type Lisa 3 (a thin coil and scrape plainware), which made up over 65 percent of the total sherds. Thirty-four percent of the sherds were Lisa Tardía. Lisa Tardía is a thicker paddle-and-anvil plainware that may correspond to Sells Plain in southern Arizona and is found in the Altar Valley of Sonora. Forms included bowls, jars, seed jars (*tecomates*), and plates. The only locally made painted wares were a handful of Trincheras Purple-on-red sherds. Painted wares made up only 0.15 percent of the total sherds (less than 1,500 sherds). Most were from Chihuahua (58 percent), with Gila and Santa Cruz polychromes making up 26 percent, and local Trincheras types 11 percent. We recovered no Hohokam types from the excavation (Gallaga 1997, 2002).

The flaked stone artifacts represented an expedient technology with few formal tools (Contreras 1998). Almost all of the flaked stone artifacts (98 percent) were unmodified flakes. The assemblage suggests uses including cutting, scraping, pounding, and drilling. The vast majority of these artifacts were made from locally available stone.

The shell assemblage includes evidence for shell jewelry production, as well as finished pieces and unworked shell (Vargas 1997). These shells represented 52 marine shell genera and 69 species, all from the Panamic shell province in the Gulf of California. The most common genus was *Glycymeris* (54 percent), with *Conus* the next most common (26 percent). The most common types of jewelry were beads (21.6 percent), bracelets (17 percent), and rings (20 percent). The inhabitants of Cerro de Trincheras did produce a large quantity of shell jewelry, but most of this production was for local consumption. There is little evidence for interregional trade of shell from the site (McGuire et al. 1999).

The ground stone assemblage at Cerro de Trincheras was in many ways different from those of other Sonoran Desert archaeological traditions (Greenwald 1997). Metates included one basin metate similar to those found elsewhere in the Southwest/Northwest. Concave metates were a specialized form suitable for grinding corn and other seeds. These metates were used with long manos (two handed) but differed in cross section from the trough metates found in southern Arizona. We recovered one narrow metate that would have been used with a mano longer than the width of the metate. We found similar *metates delgados* in the Altar Valley (McGuire and Villalpando 1991, 1993). The most common ground stone tools were small slab metates and grinding slicks that may have been used in shell jewelry production. Field crews recovered these artifacts primarily from areas with high concentrations of shell manufacture waste and the wear patterns on them are the right size and form for grinding and polishing marine shells.

The Town of Cerro de Trincheras

The four models that we sought to evaluate using our excavation data can be divided into two sets of two models each. The external models postulate that the site was built as a specialized outpost to produce shell jewelry for faraway groups. The internal models explain the existence of the site in terms of local processes.

The external models differ in terms of the distant groups identified as the builders of Cerro de Trincheras. Either the site produced shell for a Hohokam exchange network based in Arizona (Brand 1935b, 1938; McGuire and Howard 1987; Robles 1973; Sauer and Brand 1931; Tower 1945; Woodward 1936), or Mesoamerican merchants built it as a fort to protect their shell manufactory at the nearby site of La Playa (Di Peso 1979, 1983). If these models were correct, we would expect to find evidence of jewelry production for exchange, and artifacts and/or styles that reflect the contact with the faraway culture of both.

The results of our excavations do not support these external models. Cerro de Trincheras was not a Hohokam site (Haury 1976; Johnson 1960); neither does it appear to have been part of a Hohokam or southern Arizona exchange network (McGuire and Howard 1987; Woodward 1936). The architecture and ceramics at the site differ significantly from those of southern Arizona. We found no Hohokam artifacts, and the common, contemporary, southern Arizona ceramic type Tanque Verde Red-on-brown is conspicuous by its absence at Cerro de Trincheras. The shell analysis indicates that most of the production was for local consumption (Vargas 1997). There is little evidence of trade that links the site to the north. Neither was Cerro de Trincheras a fortified village established by Mesoamerican merchants to protect shell production at the nearby site of La Playa (Di Peso 1979, 1983). Large-scale shell production La Playa predates the occupation of Cerro de Trincheras, and La Playa was probably abandoned before Cerro de Trincheras was built (Villalpando et al. 1999). Finally, we found no artifacts that originated from Mesoamerica or that were stylistically Mesoamerican.

The internal models differ in their interpretation of the size and complexity of Cerro de Trincheras. Johnson (1960) and Haury (1976) proposed that the site was a rustic village of the desert branch of the Hohokam, with an economy based primarily on hunting and gathering. We have proposed that Cerro de Trincheras was an indigenous town of the Trincheras tradition.

Our excavation data show that Cerro de Trincheras was an agricultural town, and a regional center, rather than a rustic village. Of the 20 ^{14}C samples, 19 had two-sigma ranges within the span of AD 1250 to 1450, and the twentieth overlapped this range. These dates are consistent with the dating of the late prehispanic decorated ceramic types from the site (including Ramos Polychrome, Babícora Polychrome, Santa Cruz Polychrome, and Gila Polychrome [Gallaga 1997]). The town had a complex internal structure, with each precinct serving a distinct function or purpose. The people of the town also manufactured shell jewelry and engaged in limited trade of shell jewelry with other prehispanic peoples to the east, but apparently not to the north.

Agriculture

Pollen and macrobotanical remains indicate that the people of Cerro de Trincheras cultivated corn, squash, and cotton, and the frequency of occurrence of these cultigens in flotation samples is comparable to those from riverine Hohokam sites. They also cultivated agave, which was an important plant for food, fiber, and basketry. The natural range for agave starts about 300 m higher than Cerro de Trincheras, but it can be cultivated at lower altitudes. In southern Arizona, prehispanic peoples used contour terraces similar to our narrow terraces to grow agave at elevations comparable to Cerro de Trincheras (Fish et al. 1992b). Cerro de Trincheras flotation samples yielded agave spines that presumably would have been removed from wild agave gathered from higher elevations and transported to the town. The lithic sample also included large tabular knives that archaeologist often interpret as agave knives.

Settlement Structure

La Cancha and El Caracol both appear to have been specialized ritual structures, but each was designed for very different audiences. La Cancha lies near the base of the hill and was not roofed. The rest of the site rises above La Cancha like a gigantic amphitheater, so that virtually everyone who lived in the town could have seen the ceremonies held there. El Caracol is on the crest of the hill, in a walled plaza where only a few people could have viewed ceremonies.

The vast majority of the terraces on the hill created platforms where families lived. Each household included at least one brush and mud house, a ramada, and sometimes a round (or quadrangular) room with rock foundations and a brush or jacal superstructure. Households may have occupied one or more terraces (Price 2000). None of the structures on these terraces were massive or durable. Paradoxically, the terraces that supported them are substantial and have stood for over 500 years.

High on the north face of the hill, one group of three terraces stands out from the rest with the highest terrace walls in the town. We called this group of terraces El Mirador (the lookout). They occupy the only spot from which someone could have viewed all of the other household terraces on the north slope of the hill. We suspect that this complex was the home of the site's ruling household. There could have been a reception area below, a domestic area in the middle, and a platform above from which proclamations were made or ceremonies conducted in view of the town's population.

There seems to be a pattern to the terraces on the north face of the hill. The lowest terraces, below La Cancha, appear to have been used for specialized activities, such as agave fields. The next group of terraces, between La Cancha and El Mirador, were primarily for domestic use. The terraces, the structures, and the artifacts seem to become more elaborate with greater elevation. A cluster of households (Loci B.1–B.4) on the east end of Area B specialized in shell work. The terraces from El Mirador to the crest do not appear to have been habitation terraces, because they lacked domestic structures and domestic artifacts. The soil in these terraces was a natural red, not the gray that resulted from the deposition of ash, charcoal, and organic trash. The highest terrace in El Mirador is one of a series of terraces and walls that circles the entire hill and blocks access to the crest. This barrier is broken only at El Mirador and along a trail up the west side of the hill. This pattern of walls and trails suggests that access to the crest of the hill was limited and controlled.

The crest of the hill would have been an administrative and ceremonial precinct accessible only to a few of the site's inhabitants or only at special times. This precinct included the Plaza El Caracol at its east end and the highest peak of the hill at the west end. The only feature on the peak of the hill is a V-shaped wall that points to the rising of the sun on the winter solstice. A little lower down on the north face of the peak, another V-shaped wall points to the rising of the sun on the summer solstice.

Population and Labor Investment

How does Cerro de Trincheras compare in size, population, and labor investment to other major prehistoric Northwestern/Southwestern towns? Comparison of the site to major pithouse villages, such as Snaketown, or to large pueblos, such as Pueblo Bonito, is difficult, because these sites differ in terms of features, construction, layout, and topographic position. Nonetheless, detailed maps and data on terraces allow us to estimate the population at Cerro de Trincheras and the labor investment involved in building the town. These estimates can be compared to similar ones for other Northwestern/Southwestern sites. This is a highly speculative procedure, but the analysis does give us a preliminary basis for such comparison.

The provisional population estimate for Cerro de Trincheras is based on our inference that the majority of the terraces were residential in nature. A maximum estimate is obtained if we assume that all residential terraces were occupied at the same time. Based on ethnographic accounts, Hohokam archaeologists frequently assume that each pithouse housed five people (Haury 1976; Wilcox et al. 1981). If we assume that each residential terrace supported one house, we can count terraces to estimate the number of houses. We can estimate the number of residential terraces in two ways. A maximum estimate is obtained if we consider every terrace with a width greater than 2 m to be a residential terrace (710). A minimum estimate is obtained if we use the 15 by 2 m dimension of residential terraces at Cerro Prieto (Downum et al. 1993) (420). Based on these parameters, the high estimate would be 3,550 people, and the low estimate 2,100 people. We hesitate to accept either of these numbers. We do not know how many houses or households may have been present on each terrace, if households may have used more than one terrace, and the assumption that all terraces would have been in use at one time is almost certainly incorrect. This rough estimation does, however, suggest that the maximum population of the site was in excess of a thousand people.

A town with more than a thousand individuals was a large place by Northwestern/Southwestern standards. The highest estimate for the peak population of the largest Sedentary period Hohokam town, Snaketown, is 2,000 (Haury 1976), while the lowest is just over 1,000 (Wilcox et al. 1981). Early Spanish sources report the largest pueblos in the Rio Grande Valley had populations of 2,000 to 3,000, and these estimates may be inflated (Simmons 1979). High-end estimates for the population of Arroyo Hondo, a 1,000-room pueblo near Santa Fe, New Mexico, do not exceed 1,500 people (Wetterstrom 1986). Lekson (1986:272) estimates the population of the 8 km^2 area around Pueblo Bonito in Chaco Canyon at 2,100 to 2,700 people.

We can also make comparisons based on the amount of labor that went into the construction of Cerro de Trincheras versus other major towns. The mapping and measurement of all surface features at Cerro de Trincheras gives us good data on the volume of masonry standing on the hill, and the volume of fill behind the terraces (O'Donovan 1997). Our estimates of masonry and fill volume, and any labor estimates derived from them, are minimum approximations, because they do not include buried masonry and non-masonry construction at the site. We estimate the total volume of masonry in terraces, walls, and rooms as 27,882 m^3. We estimate the volume of fill behind the terraces at 35,504 m^3.

Lekson (1986) provides a series of parameters for estimating labor investment at Chaco Canyon. These parameters are useful, because they allow us to compare labor estimates for Chaco pueblos and Cerro de Trincheras using the same assumptions. Therefore, even if the estimates do not accurately assess the actual number of hours that went into the construction of these prehistoric edifices, they still give us a rough relative comparison for the two areas. Not all of Lekson's parameters apply in the case of Cerro de Trincheras. Masonry at the Cerro was dry-laid, so no estimation is needed for making mortar, and since the materials were directly available, there are little or no transportation costs. Lekson (1986:278) estimates the labor to lay masonry as 13.25 person hours per cubic meter, the labor to procure stone as 7.1 person hours per cubic meter, and the labor to excavate fill as 1.9 person hours per cubic meter (Lekson 1986:285). Multiplying the estimates for stone procurement and laying masonry by the masonry volume from the Cerro (27,882 m^3) yields an estimate for masonry construction of 567,398 person hours.

Multiplying the estimate for fill excavation by the fill volume (35,504 m^3) yields a labor estimate of 67,457 person hours for fill. Totaling these two figures gives an estimate of 634,856 person hours for construction of the whole site. This estimate assumes that all materials (rocks and fill) were available next to the terraces, and it would be increased if transportation cost were added to the equations.

It appears that the labor involved in the site is about 18 percent of the total labor that went into the construction of all nine of the great houses in Chaco Canyon. Lekson does not give a total for all the labor involved in the construction of these houses, but his summary statistics (Lekson 1986: table 5.1) would indicate that about 3,400,000 to 3,500,000 person hours went into the construction of all nine great houses. The labor involved in building the terraces at Cerro de Trincheras may have been comparable to the labor invested in the construction of Pueblo Bonito. In sum, our analysis suggests that the labor cost of building the masonry features at Cerro de Trincheras was at least as much as the labor cost of a 600- to 700-room pueblo.

From these tentative estimates of population and labor investment for Cerro de Trincheras we conclude that the town was a major place in Northwestern/Southwestern prehistory. It is similar in physical complexity, size, and population to the largest towns in the Northwest/Southwest.

Cerro de Trincheras Defense and Warfare

It appears that Cerro de Trincheras was a town with agricultural features, craft barrios, elite residences, ceremonial structures, astronomical observatories, a ritual precinct, plazas, and a population in excess of 1,000 people. But why build such a town on top of a steep, rock-strewn, volcanic hill? For many archaeologists the obvious explanation is defense. Cerro de Trincheras was certainly located in a defensible position, and defense may have been one consideration in locating the town on the hill.

LeBlanc (1999: 132–33, 258, 265) interprets cerros de trincheras (including Cerro de Trincheras) as fortified sites and as evidence for widespread warfare in the prehispanic Southwest/Northwest. Specifically, he resurrects the old idea that such sites were refuge forts that were occupied as sanctuaries during times of attack or danger. This notion of refuge forts springs from superficial examinations of such sites that fail to identify the true extent and variability of the archaeological remains on the hills. The superficial nature of such analysis is shown by LeBlanc's (1999:259) assertion, upon examination of a photo, that the site of Cerro de Trincheras is covered with concentric walls. This is simply not the case. The features that from a distance (or in a photo) appear to be concentric walls are the over 900 individual terraces that cover the north and west sides of the hill (O'Donovan 1997). Furthermore, the south slope of the hill (Area C) has only a few isolated clusters of terraces. The results of our excavations clearly demonstrate that Cerro de Trincheras was not solely a refuge fort.

Indeed, every excavation done on a cerro de trincheras in Arizona, Sonora, and Chihuahua has located habitation structures and a suite of artifacts and other features normally associated with agricultural villages (Downum 1986, 1993; Tanner 1936). This includes the most ancient of known cerros de trincheras sites, Cerro Juanaqueña, in Chihuahua (Hard and Roney 1998). Every detailed study of cerros de trincheras indicates that they were villages and towns, not simply refuge forts as suggested by Wallace (1995:818).

As agricultural settlements these sites had a multitude of functions and activities. Their location on steep rock- and cactus-strewn hills made them defensible, and archaeologists have recorded apparent defensive features on many (but not all) cerros de trincheras. These features include curtain walls, restricted entrances, walled access trails, and zigzagged gates. In contrast, Downum et al. (1994) point out that many aspects of cerros de trincheras are not defensive and would in fact compromise the defense of these hills, but Wallace (1995:817–818) disagrees. The debate is not particularly illuminating, because each side frames it as an either/or question: either cerros de trincheras are defensive, or they are not.

At Cerro de Trincheras the hill is steep and difficult to climb, but ramps and stairs on the north slope (Area B) make that effort easier—until, that is, just below the crest of the hill, where terraces and curtain walls close off access on all sides. Only two paths that pass though several zigzagged gates break this barrier. Is the restricted access to the crest of the hill a ritual barrier to keep out the uninitiated and unworthy, or a hilltop castle to repel attackers? It could function as either or as both. Cerro de Trincheras was a town with a complex internal structure that accommodated a variety of functions and activities. We concede that defense was clearly a concern at the site and an important factor in the siting of this town. However, simply labeling the sites as defensive does not give us a sufficient understanding of it or of its role in regional settlement systems. Defense may be a necessary part of an explanation for why the site was constructed, but it is not a sufficient explanation for the complexity of the site structure and the range of feature types on the hill.

Other factors may have also encouraged the construction of terraced towns. O'Donovan (1997, 2002) has noted that Cerro de Trincheras presents us with a paradox. The site is visually monumental, due to the hundreds of terraces that cover a prominent hill. The work involved in terracing the hill may have been comparable to that required to build Pueblo Bonito in Chaco Canyon, New Mexico. But the structures that the Trincheras people built on these terraces were flimsy, involving a minimum of labor investment.

This paradox may be one of several keys to understanding why the Trincheras people constructed their grand town on a hill. They built their homes in an open, breezy, insubstantial style that works well in the hot, dry Sonoran Desert. They used the position of households on the hill, rather than the substance of their homes, to communicate the social positions of families. By terracing the hill, the Trincheras folk transformed a prominent natural feature into a human creation that expressed their social organization and religious beliefs. They achieved a degree of monumentality and distinction that stacking the same rocks into a pueblo or mound could never have achieved (O'Donovan 1997, 2002).

Conclusion

Cerro de Trincheras still occupies its dark, isolated volcanic hill and fascinates modern observers. Our analysis of the 1995 and 1996 excavations has examined the internal structure of the site in greater detail than this brief summary allows. We are struggling to develop an explanation for the site that captures all of the site's variability and does not reduce it to a simplistic functional label. To do this we have abandoned the either/or logic of simple functional labels (O'Donovan 2004). People did not build Cerro de Trincheras solely for defense, or for monumental effect, or to grow agave, or to make shell jewelry, or to perform rituals, or to build houses on. They built it to do all of these things, and the mix of these activities may have changed over time. People lived on Cerro de Trincheras and did all of the things that implies. We are focusing on the lived experience of being a resident or visitor to this town and upon the dynamic relationship between this experience and the realities of warfare, economy, religion, and society in northwestern Sonora. We hope that this analysis will yield a much more sophisticated and nuanced answer to why people built a town on a hill, and a better understanding of the place of Cerro de Trincheras in the ancient history of the Northwest/Southwest.

Plate 1. Key attributes of most borderlands trincheras sites are broad visibility within their basins and intervisibility among one another. The view from the late prehistoric trincheras site in the foreground includes Cerro de Trincheras and two smaller trincheras hills in northwest Sonora. Aerial photograph © Adriel Heisey.

Plate 2. Cerro Juanaqueña, a preceramic (1250 to 300 B.C.) trincheras site in northwest Chihuahua, has 8 km of terrace walls and covers more than 11 ha. The straight line crossing the hill is a fenceline that separates the heavily grazed section on the left from the better-vegetated slopes on the right. Aerial photograph © Adriel Heisey.

Plate 3. Cerro Vidal, another early northwest Chihuahua trincheras site, has perimeter walls or terraces on three sides of the hill, while the fourth side has a steep, near-vertical face. The combined length of all terraces and walls is less than one quarter of the total at Cerro Juanaqueña. Aerial photograph © Adriel Heisey.

Plate 4. Visible in the foreground, walls and terraces of the Early Agricultural period encircle the summit of Tumamoc Hill overlooking downtown Tucson, Arizona. Aerial photograph © Adriel Heisey.

Plate 5. Canador Peak, an early Ceramic period trincheras site in southwest New Mexico, has massive encircling walls resembling those of Cerro Juanaqueña and other early hill sites in northwest Chihuahua and Tumamoc Hill in Tucson, Arizona. Aerial photograph © Adriel Heisey.

Plate 6. Houses at late prehistoric Cerro Prieto north of Tucson, Arizona, cluster in discrete groups, each likely including one or more households. Aerial photograph © Adriel Heisey.

Plate 7. Late prehistoric Cerro de Trincheras in northwest Sonora is the largest and most elaborately constructed trincheras site. An impressive series of 900 terraces climbs the amphitheater-shaped north face of the hill in step-like fashion. Aerial photograph © Adriel Heisey.

Plate 8. A circular stone "corral" tops a late prehistoric trincheras site along the Rio Magdalena in northwest Sonora. Aerial photograph © Adriel Heisey.

Plate 9. The Cerro Prieto village is bisected by a massive walled drainage that was formed by stacking boulders to either side of a natural cleft. Aerial photograph © Adriel Heisey.

Plate 10. Rock walls ring the summit of a late prehistoric trincheras site on a low hill along the Río Magdalena. The aerial view adds a landscape perspective to the layout of cobble features mapped at the site (*right*). Aerial photograph © Adriel Heisey.

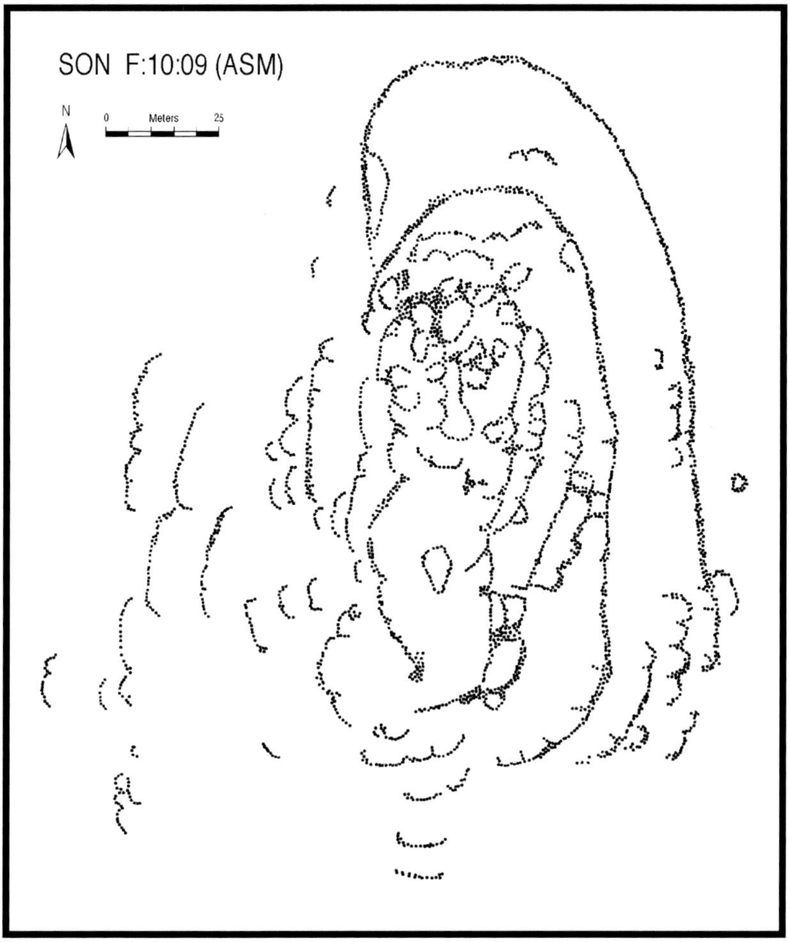

SON F:10:09 (ASM)
N
0
Meters
25

Plate 11. The outline of El Caracol, a cobble enclosure in the ritual precinct atop Cerro de Trincheras, resembles the cross-section of a snail shell. Its walls are 1.6 m high. Aerial photograph © Adriel Heisey.

6

Regional Heartlands and Transregional Trends

Suzanne K. Fish and Paul R. Fish

We examine the roles of trincheras sites in the settlement systems and societies of two sectors of the Northwest Mexico/Southwest U.S. region. We designate these two areas "trincheras heartlands" in the sense that hill sites in each exhibit distinctive modes and are patterned components of settlement patterns emanating from a recognized cultural tradition. One heartland is centered on the basin of the Rio Magdalena in northwest Sonora, and the other is centered on the Tucson Basin in south-central Arizona (fig. 1.3). We view trincheras sites in the two heartlands as elements of constructed landscapes, embodying concepts about both natural features and symbolic architectural forms (Ashmore and Knapp 1999). We argue that trincheras sites established after the initial plainware horizon in these regional sectors represent variations on an ideologically influenced theme of hilltop settings and features. A constellation of trincheras concepts and its archaeological manifestations appeared first in the Trincheras culture sequence of Sonora and subsequently were incorporated by the Tucson Basin Hohokam, modified according to the tenets of their own tradition. We outline trincheras developments in the Sonoran heartland and Hohokam variants after AD 1200 and discuss these configurations against the backdrop of transregional trends during late prehispanic times.

Postcontact beliefs provide insights into a rich conceptual heritage surrounding hills. In the ethnography of northwest Mexico and the southern Southwest, elevated hill settings carry a variety of spiritual values, serving as highly visible territorial markers, homes of supernatural beings, locations of shrines, hiding or storage places for sacred objects, cemeteries, and starting points for dream journeys (e.g., Bahr 1994; Bowen 1976b; Garcia et al. 2002; Hinton and Watahomigie 1984; Lumholtz 1902; Russell 1908; Schaefer and Furst 1996). Concomitantly, hills are the prescribed locations for a variety of rituals. Specific to a trincheras site, local residents warned the Spanish explorer Mange (1926:276) that interference with features on Martinez Hill in Tucson would result in a tempest. Prehispanic ideology concerning hills was set within a broader Mesoamerican-influenced sphere that encompassed the terraced hills of societies farther south in Mexico as well as those in the trincheras heartlands of Sonora and Arizona (see Nelson, this vol.).

Without exception, the chronologically and culturally variable hilltop remains that archaeologists of the Northwest/Southwest term "trincheras sites" fall outside the range of ordinary occupations when compared with local settlements of similar age and affiliation. We suspect that threads of symbolic continuity underlie the widely recurring selection of visually prominent low peaks over time (Heisey, plate 1), but our ability to understand the roles of particular trincheras sites in their own societies is dependent on placing them in a meaningful contemporary context. New dimensions emerge when we view such sites as elements of comprehensive settlement patterns within culturally defined landscapes. Moreover, this framework provides sound bases for discriminating among alternative interpretations. We adopt this approach in interpreting and comparing trincheras sites in the settlement systems of two adjoining heartlands.

The Sonora and Arizona heartlands are situated in strikingly similar basin and range environments, giving rise to parallels in the distributions of the settlements of prehispanic farmers. Annual rainfall near 300 mm in both areas is bimodal rather than restricted to one main season (Brown 1994:200–202). As a result, a rich and zonally varied Sonoran Desert vegetation, marked by columnar cacti and leguminous trees, provided abundant wild resources in each basin. Intermittently flowing desert rivers, the Rio Magdalena to the south and the Santa Cruz River to the north, and their tributaries supported a similar pre-Columbian combination of mid-scale riverine irrigation on basin bottoms and floodwater farming on basin slopes (Fish 1995; Fish and Fish 2004).

Comparison of trincheras sites as elements of settlement patterns in the two heartlands is made possible by the cumulative findings of investigations over the last two decades. In northwest Sonora, the largest and most elaborately terraced of all trincheras sites, Cerro de Trincheras

(Heisey, plate 7), was surface-collected, mapped in detail, and thoroughly tested by excavation (McGuire et al. 1999; McGuire and Villalpando, this vol.; O'Donovan 2002). A full-coverage survey block of approximately 75 km^2 surrounds this preeminent regional center (Fish and Fish 2004), and a systematic transect survey inventoried the Altar Valley to the west (McGuire and Villalpando 1993). The Tucson Basin is a particularly well-studied sector of southern Arizona. Comprehensive mapping and excavated samples provide detailed information for three Hohokam trincheras locations (Downum 1993; Downum et al. 1994; Fish et al. 1984; Fish et al. 1992c; Wallace 1983). Full-coverage blocks within an extensive survey of over 1,200 km^2 clearly reveal the spatial and territorial relationships of these three sites in the northern Tucson Basin. Survey coverage in other parts of the basin provides settlement backgrounds for additional trincheras sites (e.g., Doelle et al. 1985).

The Rio Magdalena Basin Heartland

Hill sites of the Trincheras Culture sequence in the Rio Magdalena heartland are assigned to two inclusive ceramic periods and one more precisely defined late phase because stratigraphic and chronological controls are as yet insufficient for finer divisions. Plainwares of an initial interval of the Early Ceramic period, characterized by prevalent seed jar or *tecomate* shapes, can be distinguished from the following plainwares of this period, which are associated with painted pottery. Painted types with specular red paint (Trincheras Purple-on-red/brown) of the Early Ceramic period appear to largely coincide with the Hohokam Preclassic period, when Red-on-buff or brown painted styles also were common in southern Arizona. This correspondence rests largely on occasional finds of intrusive Trincheras painted sherds in the southernmost Hohokam sites. Trincheras Purple-on-red/brown ceramics may have persisted somewhat beyond the end of the Hohokam Preclassic period, into the beginning of the Early Classic period Tanque Verde phase of the Tucson Basin Hohokam. The manufacture of painted wares had already ceased in the Sonoran heartland by approximately AD 1300, however, during the main occupation of Cerro de Trincheras. Radiocarbon dates from Cerro de Trincheras place the El Cerro phase of the Late Ceramic period

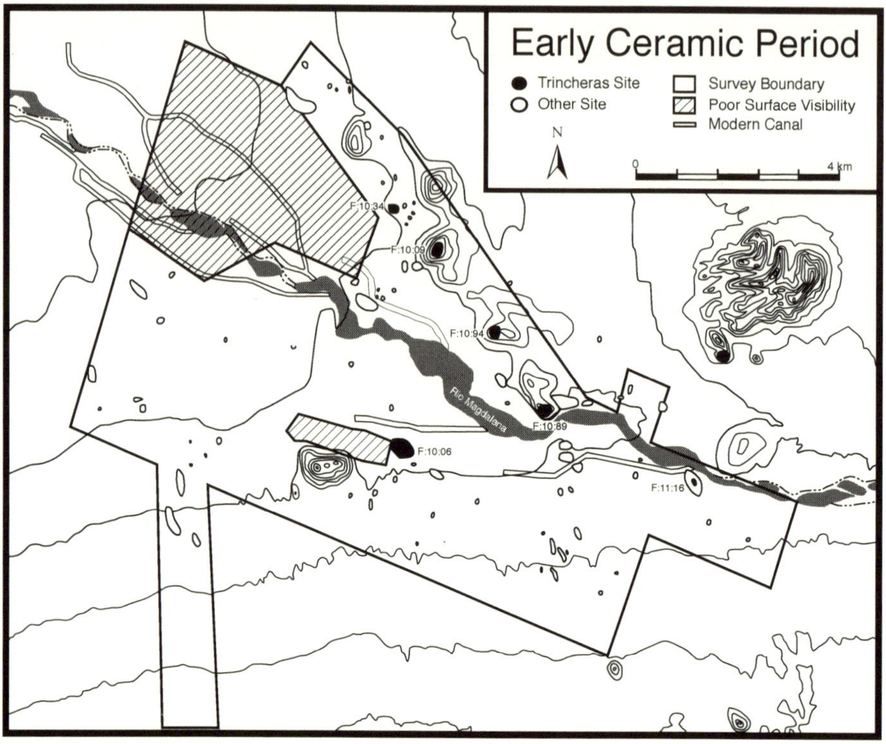

6.1 Early Ceramic period trincheras sites in the Rio Magdalena survey area.

between AD 1300 and 1450 (McGuire and Villalpando, this vol.). Infrequent Chihuahuan polychromes occur among the local plainwares of the El Cerro phase.

To investigate the developmental history of Cerro de Trincheras and its settlement system and to clarify the role of the many smaller or secondary trincheras sites within territorial organization, archaeologists from the Arizona State Museum and the Instituto Nacional de Antropología e Historia conducted a 75-km^2 full-coverage survey around this impressive center, and systematic reconnaissance for additional secondary sites within 5 km beyond the full-coverage boundaries (figs. 6.1 and 6.2). Riverine irrigation and floodwater farming supported an extended ceramic sequence (Fish and Fish 2004). Numbers of sites and the total area of residential sites rose dramatically over Early Ceramic period levels during the AD 1300–1500 El Cerro phase occupation at Cerro de Trincheras. These developments also included an increase from seven secondary trincheras occupations in the survey and surrounding 5-km reconnaissance area during the Early Ceramic period (fig. 6.1) to an El Cerro phase maximum of 14 (table 6.1, figs. 6.1 and 6.2).

Trincheras sites of the Rio Magdalena heartland are variable in extent, architecture, and principal occupational functions. In contrast to the dense residence and spatially differentiated precincts of Cerro de Trincheras, site layouts and the density and diversity of surface artifacts suggest that other trincheras sites were inhabited less intensively, and that some lacked any substantial residential population. Numbers of terraces at secondary trincheras sites also are modest. Compared to the 1-km^2 terraced habitation area of Cerro de Trincheras, that of the largest secondary site, El Cerro phase SON F:10:9, covers a much smaller

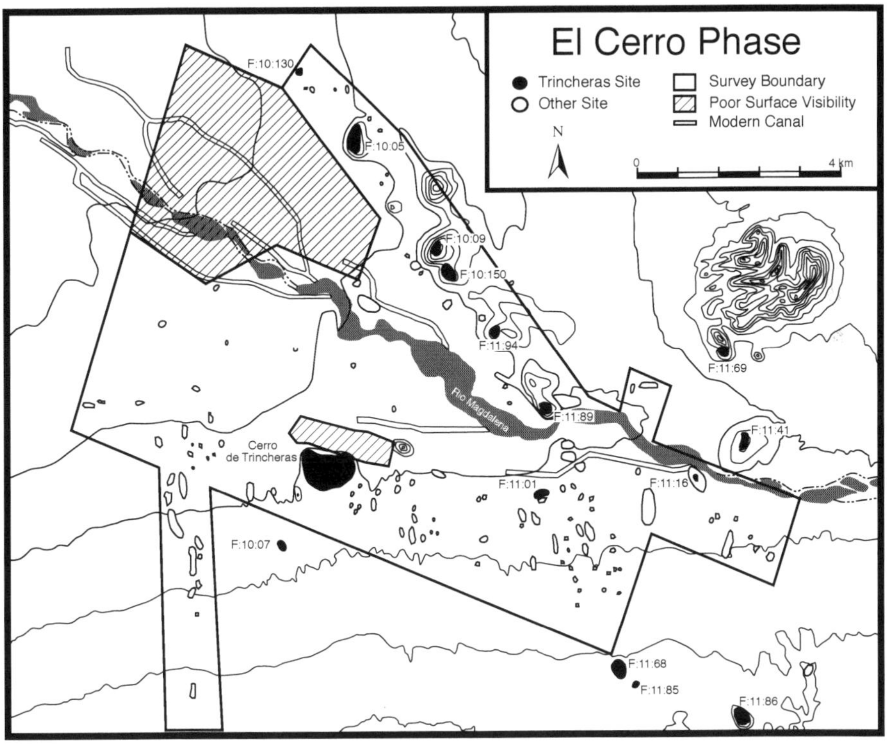

6.2 El Cerro phase trincheras sites in the Rio Magdalena survey area.

Table 6.1 Selected Characteristics of Secondary Trincheras Sites.

Site #	Chronology[2]	Site Size (m^2)	Corral/ Size	Attach-ment to Corral	Rock Rings	Artifact Abundance[1]
F:10:05	El Cerro phase	43,000	(1) 21 m dia. (2) 15 m dia. (3) 13 × 17 m (oval)	Yes	Yes	Moderate
F:10:07[3]	El Cerro phase	6,000	No	No	Yes	Low
F:10:130	El Cerro phase	16,900	20 × 15 m (oval)	Yes	Yes	Low
F:11:01	El Cerro phase	40,600	(1) 21 m dia. (2) 15 × 30 m (quad)	Yes	Yes	Abundant
F:11:41	El Cerro phase	?	?, > 10 m	?	Yes	Low
F:11:68	El Cerro phase	45,000	22 m dia.	Yes	Yes	Moderate
F:11:85	El Cerro phase	7,100	Clearing[4]	No	Yes	Moderate to Low
F:11:86	El Cerro phase	35,700	24 m dia.	Yes	Yes	Abundant
F:10:150	El Cerro phase	43,000	13 m dia.	No	Yes	Moderate
F:10:09[5]	El Cerro phase/Early Ceramic	57,000	No	No	Yes	Abundant
F:11:88[6]	El Cerro phase/Early Ceramic	45,000	20 m dia.	No	No	Abundant

Table 6.1 Continued

Site #	Chronology[2]	Site Size (m^2)	Corral/ Size	Attachment to Corral	Rock Rings	Artifact Abundance[1]
F:11:16	El Cerro phase=Early Ceramic	23,800	Disturbed?	Disturbed?	Disturbed?	Abundant
F:11:89	El Cerro phase/Early Ceramic	41,100	15 m quadrangle	No	?	Abundant
F:11:69	Early Ceramic/El Cerro phase	11,500	8 m dia.	No	Yes	Abundant to Moderate
F:11:94	Early Ceramic/El Cerro phase	26,900	Clearing[4]	No	Yes	Low
F:10:06	Early Ceramic	42,500	Disturbed?	No	Yes	Abundant
F:10:34	Early Plainware	17,000	No	No	Yes	Moderate

[1] Based on field estimates of surface artifact abundance. Abundant = 1000s sherds, 10s ground stone, 10s shell. Abundant-Moderate = 1000s sherds, 10s ground stone, no shell. Moderate = 100s sherds, multiple ground stone, multiple shell. Moderate to Low = 100s of sherds, no ground stone, multiple shell. Low = 10s sherds, no more than 1 piece of ground stone, no shell.

[2] Dominant temporal category is listed first; = indicates that Early Ceramic and El Cerro phase proportions appear roughly equivalent.

[3] On a small hill 2 km south of Cerro de Trincheras, SON F:10:7 has only a few terraces and rock rings and may be an ancillary location closely related to the regional center.

[4] No corrals with standing walls but cleared areas at summit. SON F:11:85—28 m diameter and rock alignments on two sides; SON F:11:94—20 × 30 m (oval) with stone outline.

[5] The entire site is recorded as encompassing 700,000 m^2, including extensive agricultural fields with contour terraces and grids. The 57,000 m^2 in this table corresponds to the habitation area.

[6] SON F:11:88 is located more than 5 km east of full-coverage survey boundaries. It is therefore not included in summary statistics other than modal size of corrals.

57,000 m^2 (although extensive agricultural features on lower hillslopes expand its total area to 700,000 m^2; table 6.1). Early Ceramic sites such as SON F:10:6 also are among the larger and unquestionably residential trincheras occupations, as are other Early Ceramic sites in the adjoining Altar Valley (McGuire and Villalpando 1993).

Small rock rings, circular stone outlines no more than a few courses high and typically 2 to 5 m in diameter, consistently occur on the summits of trincheras sites in the Magdalena Basin. In many instances, the rings are accompanied by a larger summit corral (Heisey, plate 8). Corrals (a functionally misleading term retained in this chapter because of widespread usage in trincheras literature) are apparently unroofed, dry-laid stone enclosures with walls rising higher than those of rock rings, usually rounded in shape but occasionally quadrangular. Wall heights are variable, from 40 cm to more than 1.5 m; maximum diameters are 13 to 24 m (mean = 18.7 m for 11 corrals with well-documented dimensions in the study area, excluding an outlier at SON F:11:69 with an 8 m diameter; table 6.1). An average corral size near 20 m also has been noted for Sonoran trincheras sites away from the Rio Magdalena (Bowen 1972, 1976a; Braniff C. 1992; Hinton 1955:5; McGuire and Villalpando 1993). The low height of some corral walls is incompatible with any uniformly defensive purpose. Given similarities in form and positioning, corrals and rock rings at secondary trincheras sites probably are conceptually related to specialized features in a formal precinct with restricted access atop Cerro de Trincheras (McGuire et al. 1999: 140–141; McGuire and Villalpando, this vol.). We suggest that the relatively standardized sizes of corrals and rock rings and their placement on flat areas of summits conform to ideological prescriptions and ritual practice.

Trincheras Sites in Magdalena Basin Settlement Patterns

A single low hill (SON F:10:34) in the survey area is a convincing candidate for an earliest trincheras location. A few rock rings occur in conjunction with small numbers of irregularly placed stone walls and rudimentary terraces surrounding a large central cleared area on the summit. Among hundreds of early plainwares, including tecomate or seed jar shapes, sherds of the ensuing Trincheras Purple-on-red/brown painted types are absent. In contrast, painted pottery is present at each of seven other trincheras sites with Early Ceramic period components. SON F:10:34 likely was no longer in use by the time the painted wares at the other sites were manufactured. Early plainware components at additional sites could be obscured in mixed assemblages containing the painted types of subsequent Early Ceramic period occupations. Other instances of trincheras sites affiliated with the initial plainware horizon of the Northwest/Southwest are reported in southwestern New Mexico at Canador Peak (Heisey, plate 5; Roney 1999), and in southern Arizona at Tumamoc Hill (Wallace et al., this vol.). A chronological hiatus may separate SON F:10:34 from Early Ceramic trincheras sites of the following part of the sequence marked by Trincheras Purple-on-red/brown styles.

Six trincheras sites with Early Ceramic period painted wares within the main survey area (a seventh in table 6.1, SON F:10:88, is more than 5 km from the full-coverage area and thus excluded from distributional consideration) are distributed in a more limited zone around the river (fig. 6.1) than those with later El Cerro phase components (fig. 6.2). The even spacing of Early Ceramic trincheras sites, despite the localized occurrence of suitable hills, is noteworthy. Each is 2.5 to 4 km from its nearest neighbor, with the exception of SON F:10:34. Its closer spacing to a neighboring trincheras site (SON F:10:9) is not surprising, given its assignment to the initial plainware horizon and probable abandonment prior to the appearance of painted types. Regularity of spacing is even more apparent for those Early Ceramic sites with assemblages indicating concentrated residence (fig. 6.1, table 6.1). Less abundant and diverse assemblages occur at only one site (SON F:11:94), suggesting that most Early Ceramic occupations were multifunctional and residential. As a caveat, it is often difficult to evaluate the contribution of early versus late components to assemblages spanning extended occupations. All Early Ceramic trincheras sites other than SON F:10:34 of the initial plainware horizon and SON F:10:6 continued in use during the succeeding El Cerro phase, indicating continuity in the significance of these specialized hilltop locations.

Rock rings at SON F:10:34 and at most other Rio Magdalena trincheras sites apparently represent the earliest, most common, and most persistent kind of summit feature. The chronological parameters of the typical form of corral are not well delimited by present data, because the dating of these features is uncertain at multicomponent sites (table 6.1). Of seven Early Ceramic occupations with Trincheras Purple-on-red/brown pottery, only one (SON F:10:6) is of solely Early Ceramic age. Two (SON F:10:9 and SON F:10:6) unequivocally lack a corral, and summit disturbance at one other (SON F:10:16) is too great for determination. A 20-x-30-m stone-outlined clearing at the fourth such site, SON F:11:94, resembles a corral in size and summit placement. It and an unusually small enclosure of only 8 m diameter at the fifth Early Ceramic site (SON F:11:69) may represent early versions of corrals, which then became more standardized with time. Corrals of modal 13- to 24-m size occur at the remaining two trincheras sites (SON F:11:88 and F:11:89) with Trincheras painted ceramics, but in conjunction with later El Cerro phase components. Limited artifacts with an isolated Altar Valley corral include no later diagnostic ceramics (McGuire and Villalpando 1993:144–145), tentatively supporting the appearance of this kind of summit feature before the end of the Early Ceramic period.

Patterns from nine single-component El Cerro phase occupations leave little doubt as to the key nature of corrals at later trincheras sites (table 6.1; Heisey, plate 10). Seven have these enclosures. The two exceptions apparently are special cases: SON F:11:85 has a 28-m diameter, stone-outlined summit clearing and is locationally paired with another hill site containing a corral; SON F:10:7 is a small hill with few features, close to Cerro de Trincheras, perhaps serving a limited ancillary function for that center. The size of corrals at the single-component El Cerro phase sites bespeaks a widely held template for such facilities. Five of the six corrals with precise measurements have maximum dimensions between 20 and 24 m.

Beginning in Early Ceramic times, some sort of integrative role based on communally shared observances can be posited for trincheras sites, in view of their unusual elevated settings, summit features, and regular spacing among ordinary basin settlements. Although the extent of survey is insufficient to provide complete data on settlements surrounding all trincheras sites, an examination of recorded distributions is nevertheless instructive. Concentric circles at a distance of 2 km from Early Ceramic trincheras sites identify a practicable range for frequent communication and participation in hilltop activities by daily round-trip travel

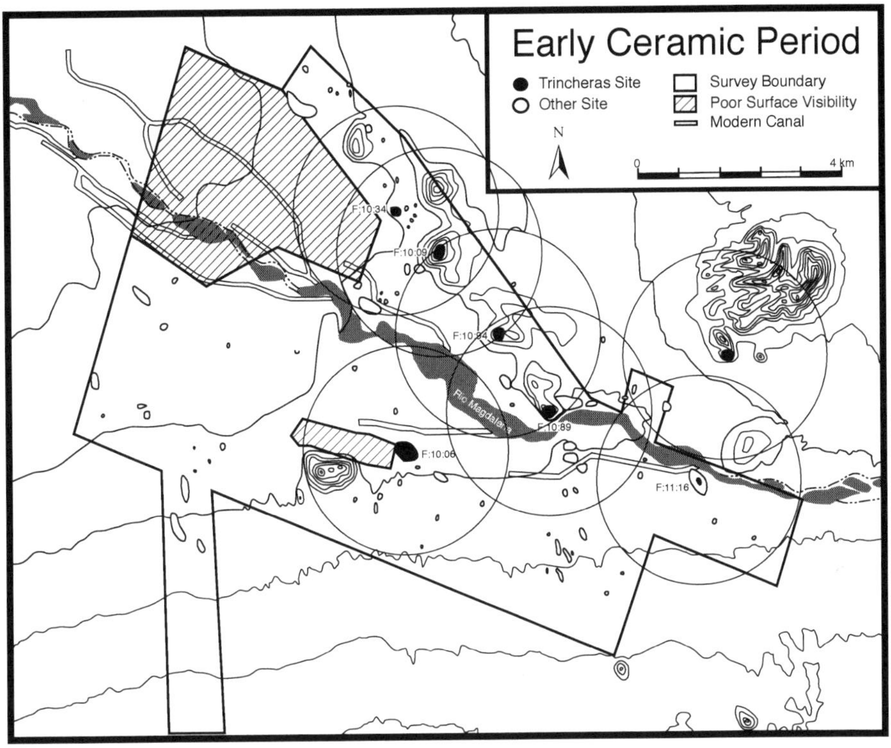

6.3 Radii of 2 km drawn about Early Ceramic period trincheras sites in survey area.

(fig. 6.3). The great majority of dispersed Early Ceramic settlements are encompassed within this distance from one of the evenly spaced trincheras sites.

Early Ceramic settlements more than 2 km from any trincheras "node" occur in the northwest sector of the survey area beyond SON F:10:9 (assuming SON F:10:34, the initial plainware site, was no longer in use), in a broad western sector beyond SON F:10:6, and in a southern sector beyond the conjoined 2-km circles about SON F:10:6, F:11:89, and F:11:16 (fig. 6.3). In the southern sector, it can be questioned whether basin settlements south of the Rio Magdalena were effectively integrated within the 2-km sphere of SON F:11:89, given that they were separated from it by the river, a natural boundary for the irrigation systems of basin farmers. It is precisely in the three areas of more distant Early Ce-

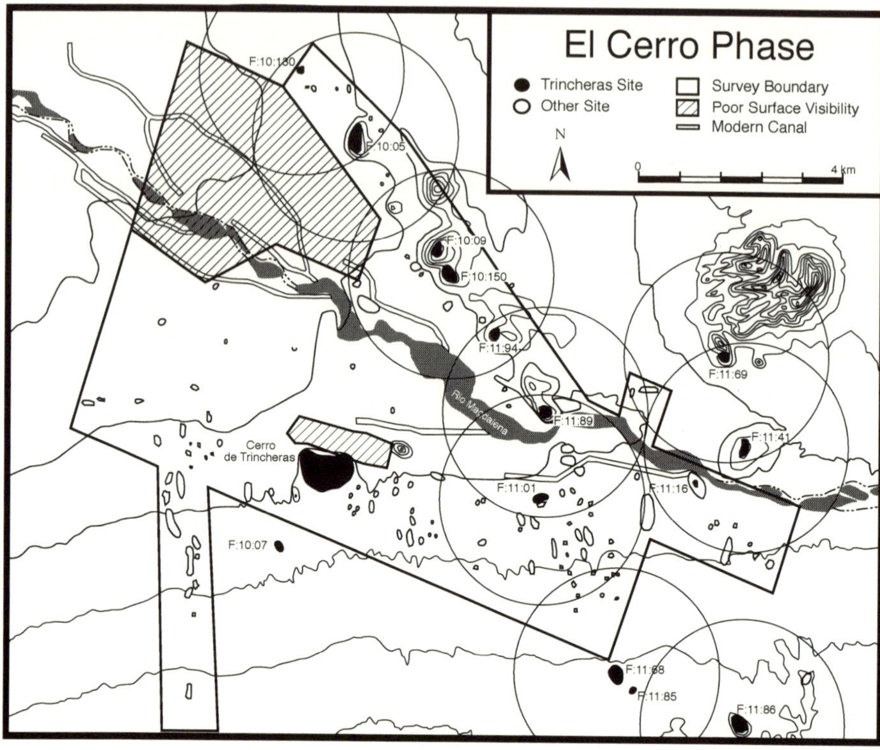

6.4 Radii of 2 km drawn about El Cerro phase trincheras sites with corrals in survey area.

ramic settlements that new trincheras sites appeared in the following El Cerro phase (fig. 6.4). SON F:10:13 and F:10:5 were established in the northwest sector, and SON F:11:68, F:11:85, and F:11:1 were established in the southern sector. The new SON F:11:1 most likely served settlements across the river from SON F:11:80.

For the Early Ceramic settlements more than 2 km distant from a trincheras site in the survey's western sector, SON F:10:6 was closest (fig. 6.4). Although heavily disturbed by modern activity, the terraces at SON F:10:6 are unusually well built. The site is further distinguished by greater artifact densities, more shell, and higher proportions of painted wares than any other Early Ceramic hill site. The El Cerro phase rise of the regional center at nearby Cerro de Trincheras coincided with the abandonment of SON F:10:6, the only instance in which a trincheras site of the local painted sequence failed to persist into later times. SON F:10:6 was the probable precursor to Cerro de Trincheras in a trend toward increasing settlement system primacy. It apparently was eclipsed and replaced as that emerging regional center consolidated its primate position.

Cerro de Trincheras stood out dramatically as the preeminent town in the Magdalena Basin and beyond. To put its primate status into perspective with regard to residential scale, Cerro de Trincheras covered 1 km^2, more than twice the combined 444,000-m^2 habitation areas of all 14 El Cerro phase secondary trincheras sites within the survey and reconnaissance boundaries. Cerro de Trincheras was further distinguished by its spatially and architecturally differentiated layout, with a formal, restricted summit precinct and other divisions of public and residential structures (McGuire and Villalpando 1999:140–141, this vol.).

Cerro de Trincheras is 1.5 km west of SON F:10:6 and closer to the numerous and previously remote settlements of that sector (fig. 6.4). The new regional center was well positioned to serve western settlements established during the Early Ceramic period, including those previously associated with SON F:10:6, along with the new settlements that proliferated on the surrounding valley slopes during the El Cerro phase. Cerro de Trincheras's central position amid the western settlements suggests that it provided specialized hilltop functions for an appreciably larger hinterland than did other late trincheras sites.

Activities associated with corrals at the El Cerro phase secondary trincheras sites likely were related in some manner to higher-level enactments at the similarly constructed, but more elaborately shaped enclosure on the plazalike summit of Cerro de Trincheras. This enclosure is known as the Caracol for its outline resembling the cross section of a snail shell (McGuire and Villalpando, this vol.). Like the Caracol, most corrals at El Cerro phase secondary sites were accompanied by smaller rock rings. In at least five instances, additional circular outlines much like the rock rings were attached to the inside or outside of the corral wall (see figs. 6.5 and 6.6 for examples). A rock ring also is located within the interior of La Cancha, an open, courtlike public facility in the midst of residential terraces on the flanks of Cerro de Trincheras (McGuire et al. 1999:140).

Outside the greater reach of Cerro de Trincheras among surround-

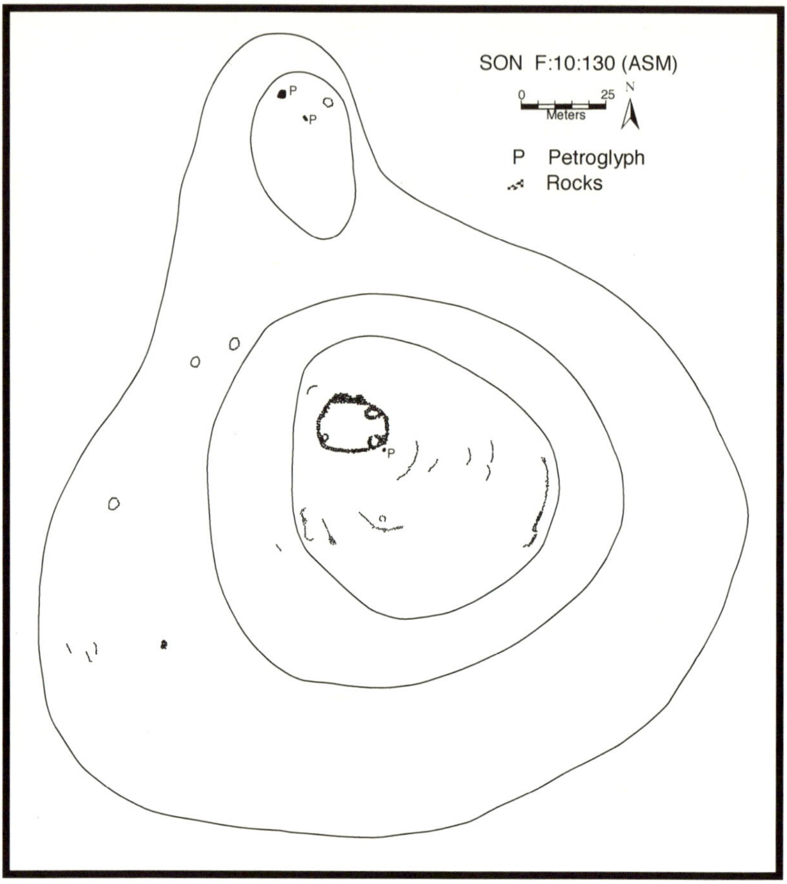

6.5 SON F:10:130, a typical El Cerro phase secondary trincheras site.

ing settlements, the spacing of the six El Cerro phase secondary trincheras sites with abundant artifacts indicating substantial residential occupations is fairly even. The Rio Magdalena probably divided the settlements associated with each of the two closest of these sites, SON F:11:89 and F:11:1, which were on opposite sides of the river. Significantly, however, five of the nine secondary El Cerro phase trincheras sites with documented corrals did not produce evidence for sustained residence (table 6.1, fig. 6.4)

Summit functions involving corrals were largely divorced from residence in a large proportion of the trincheras sites with El Cerro phase components. Two sites with corrals in the northwest study area (SON

F:10:5 and F:10:130) are marked by modest artifact densities (fig. 6.2 and table 6.1). In the eastern study area, another new site with a corral (SON F:11:41), across the river from the more clearly residential SON F:11:16, also yielded relatively low densities. At SON F:10:9, a substantial residential site in the central survey area, occupation continued from the Early Ceramic period into the El Cerro phase. A corral was never built within the habitation area at this site, but an El Cerro phase feature was placed on an adjacent and conjoined lower peak. The lower peak, separately designated SON F:10:150, has only moderate artifact densities. In two other instances of locationally paired El Cerro phase trincheras sites, one of the two is a smaller site on a low hill; only a few small terraces were recorded on SON F:10:7, just south of Cerro de Trincheras, and SON F:11:85, close to SON F:11:68, also lacks a corral.

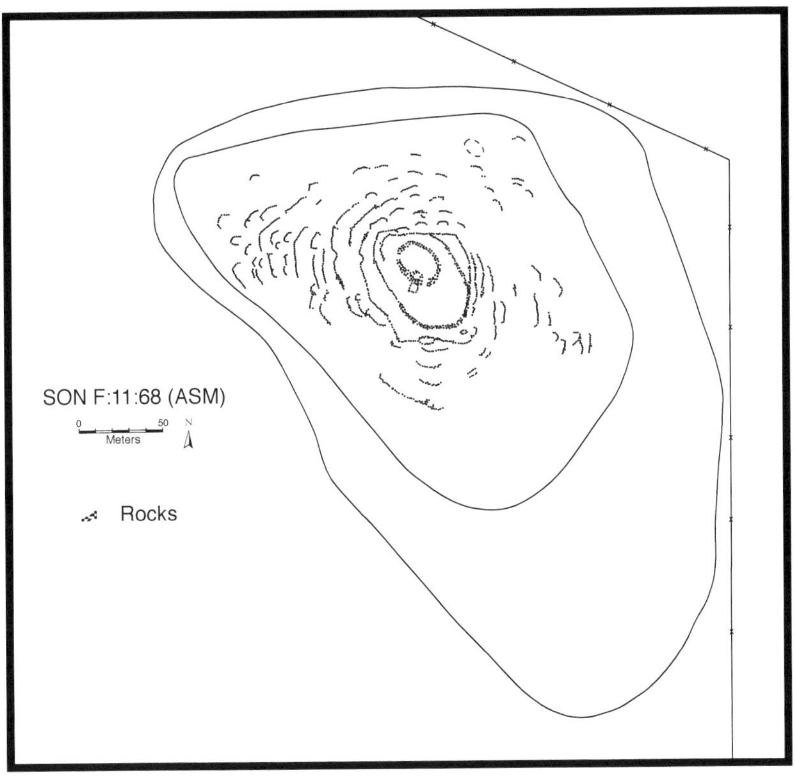

6.6 SON F:11:68, a typical El Cerro phase secondary trincheras site.

Because corrals are presumed to have been facilities for communal observances at El Cerro phase trincheras sites, we drew circles with 2-km radii about them to examine settlement integration related to their use during this time (fig. 6.6). The circles about secondary trincheras sites with corrals encompass almost all recorded El Cerro phase settlements outside the more expansive array surrounding Cerro de Trincheras. (We are inclined to consider SON F:11:16 as being among El Cerro phase sites with corrals in view of its high artifact densities, remnants of large terraces, and location at the intake of the survey area's major canals, even though the construction of hacienda headquarters on the summit precludes confirmation. A circle about this site would include the remaining settlements within a 2-km radius.)

El Cerro phase trincheras sites in the survey area are both more numerous and more widespread outside a settlement core along the Rio Magdalena than their Early Ceramic predecessors. The geographic expansion of later trincheras sites with corrals, and the standardized form of these features after AD 1300, implies the replication and institutionalization of specialized functions. During a time of population growth and aggregation, the regional center at Cerro de Trincheras emerged in tandem with this heightened emphasis on communal events at secondary trincheras sites (Fish and Fish 2004). The network of integrative trincheras nodes increasingly interlinked populations of the Sonoran heartland during the El Cerro phase.

Heartland Connections

One or perhaps a few initial plainware sites were in use near the beginning of the ceramic sequence in both heartlands. Thereafter, concepts shaping the later order of trincheras configurations appear to have emerged in Sonora. A comparatively large number of Sonoran trincheras sites with Early Ceramic period painted ceramics precede the fewer and later Tucson instances of the Tanque Verde phase. These Hohokam sites appeared just before or during the early years of an El Cerro phase proliferation of trincheras sites to the south. The geographic proximity of the two heartlands is sufficient to have fostered the broad sharing of concepts regarding hill site form and function. The linear distance between Cerro de Trincheras and today's central Tucson is about 225 km, only slightly farther than the 200 km from Tucson to the center of Phoenix, in the cultural core of the Hohokam domain.

Resemblances between Trincheras and Hohokam cultural expressions have been noted in ceramic technology and in pottery and rock art designs, especially in terms of Hohokam variants in southern Arizona and Papaguería (e.g., Braniff C. 1992; Haury 1976; Johnson 1960, 1963; Lindauer and Zaslow 1994; McGuire 1991; Sauer and Brand 1931). Occasional Trincheras painted pottery types occur in Hohokam sites of the Preclassic period, but ceramic evidence is thereafter lacking for direct exchange in either direction (McGuire et al. 1999:143; McGuire and Villalpando, this vol.). Small numbers of El Cerro phase intrusives, limited to plainwares, might not be readily recognized in Hohokam assemblages, but none of the rare Red-on-brown sherds from Rio Magdalena sites are attributed to Tanque Verde tradewares from southern Arizona.

The lack of identifiable trade items coincident with Tucson Classic period trincheras sites notwithstanding, communication between the Sonora and Arizona heartlands could have taken fairly direct routes. The Rio Magdalena originates to the north of Cerro de Trincheras, and its valley provides an immediate corridor leading toward the upper reaches of the Santa Cruz River, which flows north into Arizona and through the Tucson Basin. The Altar Valley of Sonora, just west of Cerro de Trincheras, gives easy entry into the Avra Valley of Arizona, which parallels the Tucson Basin along its western boundary with Papaguería. In the area between the two heartlands, trincheras sites occur along both routes.

The distribution of late prehistoric trincheras sites between the two heartlands further strengthens an inference of broad conceptual sharing. Sonoran trincheras sites dating to the timespan of the Hohokam Classic period are present on the upper reaches of the Santa Cruz River before it turns north and reenters Arizona (Sauer and Brand 1931: 68). West of the Tucson Basin, trincheras sites of the Avra Valley and Papaguería in Arizona (Stacy 1974) are largely continuous in distribution with those of the Altar Valley in Sonora (McGuire and Villalpando 1993); collections at many of these sites document El Cerro or Tanque Verde phase occupations. On the east, several late prehistoric trincheras sites occur along the San Pedro River in Arizona (Jeffery Clark, personal communication 2002) and hill sites with corrals overlook the Rio Sonora in Mexico (Doolittle 1988:29–32).

The Tucson Basin Heartland

Tumamoc Hill (and possibly one or two other trincheras sites in the Tucson Basin proper) was occupied in the Cienega phase (800 BC–AD 1) and during the plain-and-redware Tortolita phase, AD 475–675/700 (see Wallace et al., this vol.). After the Tortolita phase, small numbers of surface ceramics of the Hohokam Preclassic period show that basin residents occasionally visited both Tumamoc Hill and future Classic period trincheras locations (e.g., Hartmann and Hartmann 1979:62–63). However, there were no further occupations during the long interval leading up to the Tanque Verde phase of the Early Classic period (ca. AD 1200–1350), when sites were once again constructed on Tucson hills.

Information on trincheras sites as elements of settlement systems during the Tanque Verde phase of the Early Classic period is largely the result of extensive regional survey designed to delimit the multisite Hohokam territorial entities called "communities" (Fish and Fish 1994, 2000a). Clusters of settlements surrounded Classic period community centers containing public architecture in the form of earthen platform mounds. Two well-studied trincheras sites that were multifaceted villages, Linda Vista Hill and Cerro Prieto (fig. 1.3), occur within the boundaries of the Marana (Fish et al. 1992c) and Robles (Downum 1993) communities, respectively. Three other trincheras sites appear to have Tanque Verde phase or, in one case, probable Late Classic period components. Rock rings like those in Sonora occur at all the Tucson sites. Features closely resembling Sonoran corrals also are present on the summits of two sites (Linda Vista Hill and Martinez Hill) and what may be distinctive variants occur at a third (Cerro Prieto).

Linda Vista Hill (also known as Los Morteros or Rattlesnake Pass) is part of the 146-km^2 Marana Community (fig. 6.7) in the northern Tucson Basin. With an abundance of Tanque Verde pottery, but without the Salado Polychromes of the mid-1300s, this trincheras site appears to have been contemporary with the other Tanque Verde settlements

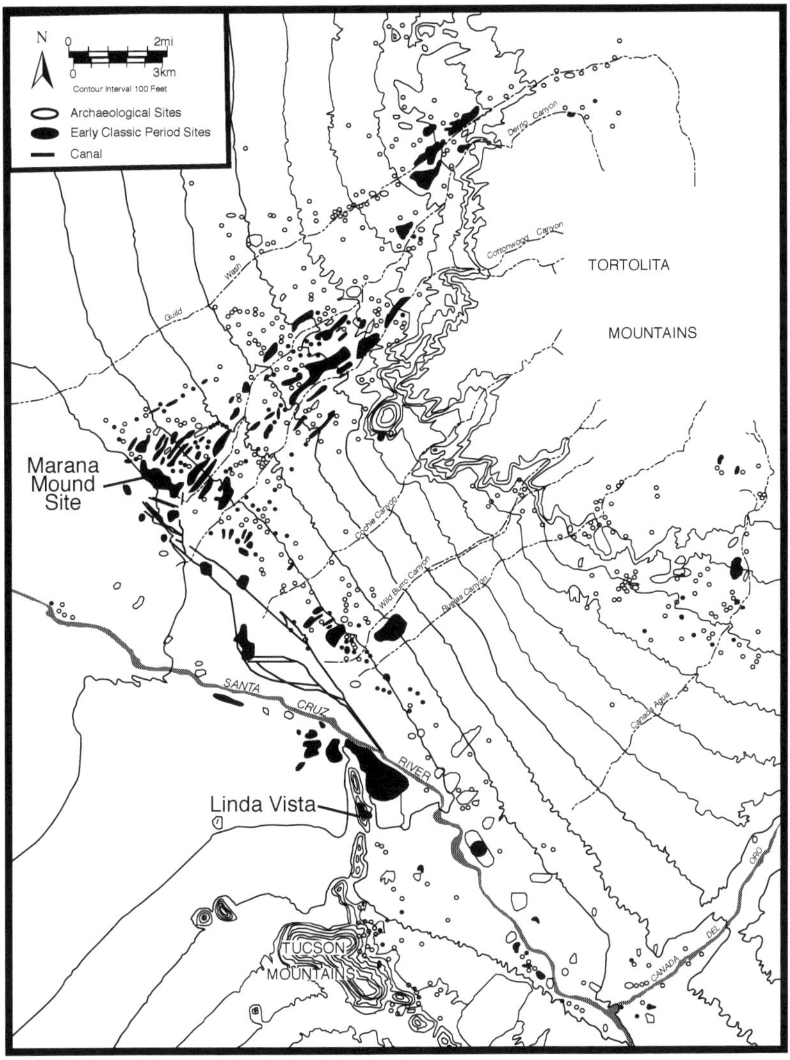

6.7 Location of Linda Vista Hill in the Marana Community.

that were abandoned in general synchroneity throughout the Marana Community at the end of the Early Classic period (Fish et al. 1992c). More recent chronometric evidence (see Downum, this vol.) outweighs previous interpretations that Linda Vista Hill (Wallace 1995:814–818;

Wallace and Doelle 2001:255–256) was the final defensive retreat of the Marana Community, occupied after inferred conflict had caused the other community settlements to be abandoned.

The Linda Vista trincheras site covers the summit and the north and east slopes of a peak at the north end of the Tucson Mountains, a low range at the basin edge (fig. 6.7, also fig. 4.1). The informal cobble walls of more than 215 terraces were built to provide level spaces for houses, extramural activity areas, and garden plots (Downum 1986, 1993, 1995; Fish et al. 1984). Based on 13 excavated pithouses, the rounded walls of individual residential terraces are often coterminous with the walls of the dwellings they contain. About 80 terraces are sufficiently wide to have accommodated typical houses and the remaining 135 appear to have supported terrace agriculture and other outdoor activities (Fish et al. 1984). The arrangement of terraces suggests groupings of households within the village (Downum 1986).

Houses are variable in size, form, and preservation, but some have plastered floors and walls and formal hearths. Many have diverse assemblages of domestic artifacts, including deeply worn trough metates. Aside from accessible stone for building and other contingencies of a hill location, these houses and their assemblages differ little from counterparts on the valley floor. Charred pine structural wood shows that timbers from mountains across the basin sometimes were used as main supports, as was the case in the adobe rooms at the Marana Community's center (Fish and Fish 2000).

A stone-outlined enclosure on the Linda Vista summit has been termed a "compound" in keeping with Hohokam nomenclature for Classic period adobe enclosures (fig. 4.4). The Linda Vista enclosure is highly reminiscent of Sonoran corrals in its size (21 × 14 m) and its roughly quadrangular shape that fits within El Cerro phase variation. A test trench inside the enclosure or compound revealed post-reinforced adobe walls unlike the pithouse architecture on residential terraces. The same trench encountered an unusual small stone bowl and pestle and a very large phallus-effigy pestle. A set of rock rings on the summit outside the compound are 1.5 to 2 m in diameter. Excavation of one of these features revealed no discernible floor above bedrock but numerous Tanque Verde sherds in shallow fill (Downum 1995:1174–1177, 1180–1181).

Linda Vista Hill is just above and adjacent to a Tanque Verde phase settlement stretching along the Santa Cruz floodplain at the base of the Tucson Mountains. Less than 3 km north in the Tucson Mountains and also adjacent to contemporary riverine settlement is Rillito Peak, a diffuse array of 90 residential and agricultural terraces. Several rock rings are clustered at the site, but not in a well-defined summit space (Wallace 1983). A reassessment of evidence for Rillito Peak chronology suggests an early plainware horizon presence at the site and raises questions about the extent of its Tanque Verde component (Wallace et al., this vol.). Regardless of its unresolved size during the Tanque Verde phase and relationship to nearby Linda Vista Hill, Rillito Peak clearly was of more limited residential scope and shared virtually the same position within the Marana Community.

Cerro Prieto is on an isolated peak of the Samaniego Hills (Downum 1993, this vol.). It is part of the 136-km^2 Robles Community, about 20 km northwest of the Marana Community (fig. 6.8). Cerro Prieto is larger and differs from Linda Vista Hill in terms of architecture and layout (fig. 4.5). Abundant surface pottery in hillside residential areas and the sole excavated structure indicate a Tanque Verde occupation. The village terraces cover the middle to lower northern slope, supporting about 250 stone structures. Of these, 232 are quadrangular houses, often with full-height stone walls, and the remainder consists of smaller circular to oval outlines more like the Linda Vista terrace pithouses.

Compared to Linda Vista Hill, the Cerro Prieto village layout exhibits a more pronounced demarcation of house groups and precincts. In addition to dispersed house clusters, 12 stone-walled compounds or enclosures, each containing only one to several structures, are concentrated in an upper central portion of the residential area. Like the stone compound on the Linda Vista summit, the Cerro Prieto village compounds fall within the range of Sonoran corrals in their circular to oval shapes, average diameters near 20 m, wall heights from 50 cm to 1.5 m., and in the frequent attachment of ancillary features to the perimeter wall (Downum 1993:62, 75). On the other hand, the 12 Cerro Prieto village compounds outnumber corrals at Sonoran trincheras sites, where the maximum is three; rather than rock rings as in Sonora, larger rooms with higher walls (of predominantly quadrangular shape) are attached to the Cerro Prieto enclosure walls.

Among terraces at Hohokam sites, five massive and visually impres-

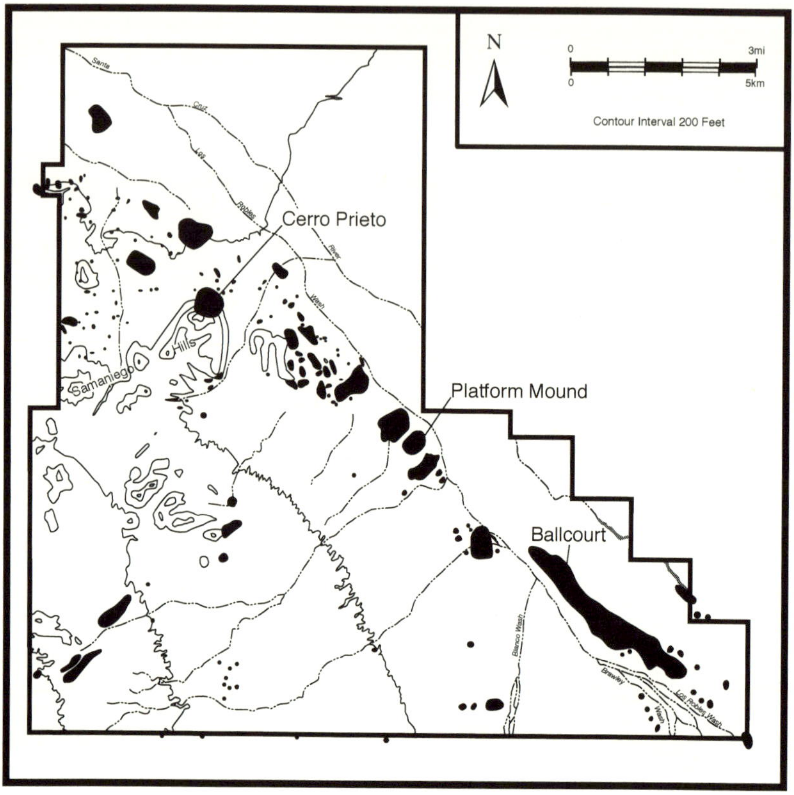

6.8 Location of Cerro Prieto in the Los Robles Community.

sive, stone-faced features at Cerro Prieto stand out for their formal, straight-faced masonry walls that most closely approach the massive style of Cerro de Trincheras in Sonora. The walls of these five terraces, up to 4 m high and 60 m long, are arranged in steplike fashion on the lower east slopes of the village (Downum 1993:77). An agricultural complex of low terraces, linear borders, and check dams near the base of the hill below the village receives runoff from upper slope catchments, as is the case with one of the Rio Magdalena trincheras sites (table 6.1).

Features atop the massive hill are separated from the village by steep upper slopes. A channel lined by stone walls on both sides descends from a cleared summit area overlooking the village, dividing the residential zone below. Approximately 30 stone features in the summit precinct include small rock rings, free-standing quadrangular structures with walls up to 75 cm high, and four quadrangular structures with attached wall segments of varying height. Sherds and other artifacts are rare. Downum (1993:68) deemed summit features nonresidential because of the generally smaller size of structures than in the village area, their less formal construction, and the lack of domestic debris.

Several authors have identified Linda Vista Hill and Cerro Prieto as refuges by virtue of their locations on hills and have cited them as evidence for Classic period warfare (e.g., Doelle and Wallace 1991; LeBlanc 1999; Rice 2001; Wallace and Doelle 2001). These two trincheras sites and all others are located in the volcanic mountains on the west side of the Tucson Basin. They are absent from Tanque Verde phase communities near the granitic peaks on the east side of the basin, although eastern populations also should have been at risk in a Classic period landscape shaped by endemic warfare. In the respective Marana and Robles communities of Linda Vista Hill (and nearby Rillito Peak) and Cerro Prieto, most of the population lived in open, unprotected settlements at a distance from these supposed refuges (figs. 6.7 and 6.8). Linda Vista Hill is 10 km distant from the central platform mound site of its community, and Cerro Prieto is 6 km distant from its community center, offering little effective protection to community leaders (or fleeing families with young children and the aged) without lengthy advance notice. There were no outer walls at the two trincheras sites, and dispersed residences on the lower slopes of both villages were readily accessible. Even if Linda Vista Hill and Cerro Prieto were occupied partly for local rather than community-wide defense, they were at the same time populous residential settlements, with differentiated summit precincts, terrace gardens, and confirmed burials at Cerro Prieto.

Two additional hills are potential Classic period trincheras sites. Black Mountain in the southernmost part of the Tucson Basin has about 30 small rock rings (Fontana et al. 1959:43) and stretches of massive walls that may correspond with a Late Archaic/early plainware occupation (Wallace et al., this vol.). As at Rillito Peak, small numbers of Tanque Verde phase sherds among generally sparse artifacts may indicate a Classic period component, related in an uncertain manner to these features. Martinez Hill, too, is in the southern part of the Tucson Basin (fig. 1.3) and adjoins the mound center of its community (Gabel 1931). As at Linda Vista Hill, there is a stone enclosure or compound on the summit. The Martinez Hill compound is identical to roughly quadrangular Sonoran corrals and is likewise accompanied by a set of rock rings. Small round outlines or rock rings are attached to the wall of the Martinez Hill enclosure (Stacy 1974:175), as they frequently are to Sonoran corrals of the El Cerro phase, a pattern not evident at the other Tucson trincheras sites of the Tanque Verde phase. The community center at the base of Martinez Hill was occupied beyond the Tanque Verde phase into the Late Classic period, suggesting that the summit compound with attached features may have been built, as well as used, after AD 1350, coincident with the mostly post–Tanque Verde phase time span of the El Cerro phase in Sonora.

Trincheras Sites in Tucson Basin Settlement Patterns

Tanque Verde phase trincheras sites of the Tucson Basin heartland can be considered a specialized settlement type on several grounds. They are set apart by hill locations. They are the only habitation sites other than platform mound centers with precincts that are spatially and architecturally differentiated from ordinary residences. Moreover, the kinds of features in summit precincts are not duplicated in the other settlements of their communities.

Well-developed villages of the Early Classic period are thoroughly documented on the slopes of Linda Vista Hill and Cerro Prieto. In both cases, summit precincts are segregated from ordinary residences, the more so by intervening upper slopes at the latter site. Martinez Hill departs from the pattern of these two trincheras sites in that the associated village is not on the hill itself, but adjacent below, and is the mound center of its community. Quite likely a Late Classic period trincheras site on the basis of the dating of the adjacent center, Martinez Hill may reflect the El Cerro phase trend in Sonora toward frequent isolation of corrals from residential environs.

The Tucson Basin trincheras sites occur in multiple, but not all, communities. The communities containing the five confirmed and suspected Classic period occupations are at the northern and southern edges of the basin, where residents may have had greater contact with followers of concepts originating in Sonora, as witnessed by the many hill sites in Papaguería and in areas beyond Hohokam boundaries to the south. Tucson trincheras sites plausibly might have been built by ethnically distinct groups among Hohokam populations (Downum 1993:121; Downum et al. 1994). Tellingly, however, trincheras assemblages are not marked by intrusive ceramic or other artifact styles, the indicators for proposed northern migrants in Classic period sites at the eastern edge of the basin (e.g., Slaughter and Roberts 1996).

The distribution of Classic period trincheras sites in Tucson Basin settlement patterns differs sharply from distributions in the Magdalena heartland, particularly in terms of the more numerous El Cerro phase sites. Tucson trincheras sites are singular elements rather than regularly spaced constituents of settlement systems. The Hohokam incorporated hill-related ideology from the south into the mound-centered organization of their communities. Just as existing communal observances were strongly centralized at platform mound centers, summit observances at trincheras sites also were narrowly focused within Hohokam communities rather than more widely dispersed among basin settlements as in Sonora.

A Closer Look at Summit Features

We have identified ideologically charged summit features as linkages to definitive trincheras concepts embodied in the sites of Sonora and Arizona heartlands. Thus, the ideological significance of these features and the observances associated with them are key issues. The simple morphology of rock rings and corrals, known largely from durable surface remains, undoubtedly glosses original variation and meaningful detail. Moreover, regional ethnography offers multiple plausible frameworks for developing and testing interpretations.

Rock rings are the most consistent features of late prehistoric trincheras sites in the two heartlands and beyond. Archaeologists sometimes have assumed that they are the results of moving cobbles on rocky surfaces to create clearings or "sleeping circles." Although the persistence of rock rings from the Late Preceramic/initial plainware horizon into late prehispanic times could be seen as indicative of long-term continuity or conscious conservatism in the architecture of later hill sites, it is unlikely that all these features are functional or symbolic equivalents. On the basis of occasional floor features and excavated assemblages from the earliest trincheras sites of Chihuahua and Arizona, rock rings of this era primarily represent domestic structures with lower walls of stone, and they typically occur in residential settings (e.g., Hard and Roney 2004:281; Roney 1999:176; Wallace et al., this vol.). As a cautionary tale, three of six excavated rock rings in the Early Ceramic period village at Tumamoc Hill proved to be shallow pithouses, but the other three were formally outlined terraces for house gardens or outdoor domestic activities. Only in one early plainware site in Sonora (SON F:10:34, table 6.1) does an isolated rock ring in an area elevated above the rest of the site presage the usual situation of later summit features.

Evidence from the few instances of excavated rock rings on the summits of later trincheras occupations is enigmatic. Those in the formal summit precinct of Cerro de Trincheras are judged of specialized use, yielding much lower artifact densities than other round-to-oval habitation structures in residential areas (Zavala 1998:111, 113). All such features at this site lack well-defined floors and are interpreted as having low rock walls that supported perishable superstructures (Zavala 1998:43, 48). A single excavated rock ring outside the compound or enclosure atop Linda Vista Hill in Tucson produced appreciable ceramics but, again, no definable floor (Downum 1995:1180–1183). Just east of the Rio Magdalena heartland, isolated rock rings on seven hills along the Rio Sonora revealed only burned earth, fulfilling the excavators' expectations for their use as fire-signaling facilities in a long-distance network among intervisible hills (Doolitttle 1988:32). This interpretation follows Di Peso's (1974: 360–365) proposal for signaling networks among late prehistoric hill sites or *atalayas* in northwest Chihuahua, many of which also contain rock rings (Swanson 1997, 2003:758–759).

Corrals are commonly described as enclosures. Corrals with rock rings attached on the interior indicate an open design accommodating internal structures, as was confirmed for the Linda Vista Hill summit feature by the walls of an adobe room in a test trench (see Downum, this vol.). At ca. 13 m in diameter, the excavated Caracol at Cerro de Trincheras barely overlaps the minimum corral size at surrounding secondary sites; it lacks a definable floor or roof indications (Zavala 1998:106). Although roof spans for Rio Magdalena corrals approaching the average 18.7-m diameter would have been great, the need for full-length beams could have been mitigated by internal supports. Excavations in corrals are too limited to rule out the possibility of roofs or superstructures in some instances, and, if so, large postholes eventually should be encountered.

The ethnography of the Northwest/Southwest offers intriguing models for ritual structures that would have archaeological signatures like rock rings and corrals. The Seri sought hilltops for spiritual purposes, awaiting visions in stone-outlined circles the size of rock rings (Bowen 1976b:40–41). The Huichol built small circular or quadrangular "god-houses" in ritual complexes on hills and other elevated landforms (Lumholtz 1902 2:53–54, 145, 147–148). Remains of their low stone walls beneath conical roofs of perishable thatch would resemble rock rings. Low hills served as ritual dance spaces for such widely separated groups as the Pima of southern Arizona (Russell 1908:205) and the Cora of Sinaloa (Lumholtz 1902 1:516–519). Lumholtz (1902 1:517) pictures a stone-outlined Cora dance clearing on a hill in the larger size range of corrals.

Arrangements of ritual spaces for calendrically organized events suggest ways in which small and large features analogous to rock rings and corrals might be related. Round, stone-walled Huichol "temples," facilities as large as 13 m in diameter for gatherings and dances, are typically accompanied on promontories by several smaller god-houses dedicated to particular spiritual entities (Lumholtz 1902 2:27–29, 147–149). These smaller structures also temporarily shelter officiants and their families during active intervals of ceremonial cycles (Lumholtz 1902 2:53, 151). The complexes of temples and god-houses usually are not situated in villages (Lumholtz 1902 2:53), recalling El Cerro phase trincheras sites in which summit precincts do not co-occur with sustained residence. The Cora (Lumholtz 1902 1:516–519) and Tepehuan (Lumholtz 1902 1:461–462), too, build small adjoining structures at the edges of their dance clearings for related paraphernalia and activities.

The Vikita ceremony of Piman groups, although not held on hills, offers an alternative but somewhat similar model for relationships among structures and places that figure in ritual cycles. Round, open enclosures of perishable materials generally mirror the sizes of rock rings and corrals (the large Vikita enclosures are 10–30 m in diameter) of trincheras sites (Chesky 1942:3; Davis 1920:166; Hayden and Steen 1937: 269). Positioned next to the large, high-walled enclosure for dances and oratory, the smaller enclosures provide storage for paraphernalia and secluded spaces where dancers prepare and musicians perform. The nine-day ceremonial sequence among related villages progresses from initial observances in the lesser Vikita structures of smaller settlements to culminating ceremonies at the major village, raising the interesting possibility of hierarchical scheduling among Rio Magdalena trincheras sites.

Beyond the presence per se of rock rings and corrals, for which current data are most systematic on a broad geographic scale, layouts and additional attributes of trincheras summits hold great promise for reconstructing ideological themes and ritual practice. Numbers and combinations of the two feature types at Sonoran secondary sites vary widely, from isolated instances of each to as many as three corrals and as a many as a dozen rock rings at a single location. Exclusivity is indicated by restricted access and controlled entrance to the summit precinct of Cerro de Trincheras (McGuire et al. 1999; O'Donovan 2004:40). At many Sonoran secondary sites, perimeter terraces, walls, and entryways also channel access and circulation. The orientations of entrances and passages often appear to guide the directionality of approaches to summit precincts and to particular features. Rock art is abundant and widespread at some trincheras sites (a high proportion of Sonoran hills), but occasional or absent at others (e.g., Linda Vista Hill and Cerro Prieto); petroglyphs sometimes occur on boulders incorporated into Sonoran corral walls. Features with astronomical and calendric correlates are documented only for Cerro de Trincheras (McGuire et al. 1999:141) and Shaw Butte, a hilltop site near Phoenix with trincheras-like features (Bostwick 2001:47–50), but may await discovery at other sites. Finally, excavated artifact assemblages, as from Linda Vista Hill, and more intensive collection of summit precincts may shed further light on ritual activities.

Transregional Trends

We have gained new insights into the trincheras sites of two cultural traditions by viewing them as elements of settlement systems. Comparison of late trincheras configurations and chronologies of the Magdalena and Tucson basins brings developments in each into focus as separate yet intertwined processes. Just as the Rio Magdalena sequence has relevance for the timing and form of Tucson trincheras sites, so too does a wider frame of reference add perspective to still broader trends. Hill sites that have received a "trincheras" designation (admittedly an imprecise term and a nonexhaustive inventory) also occur beyond the two heartlands in transitional and culturally distinct spheres to the east, west, south, and, more tentatively, the north.

If late prehispanic trincheras sites of the two heartlands and surrounding regional sectors represent a unitary phenomenon at some fundamental level, locally contingent formulations were sources of variability across space and cultural traditions. At the core of shared concepts were the portentous qualities of hills as natural features, tangibly expressed in the widespread preference for relatively low volcanic peaks with high intrabasin visibility. Differential selectivity may be inherent in trincheras hill profiles ranging from flat-topped to conical, but variability is most readily registered in locational and constructed parameters. Specialized summit features in Rio Magdalena sites, for example, occur both within and apart from residential occupations. Magdalena and Tucson hill sites contrast in regularly occurring versus more occasional locations among other settlements. The distribution of quadrangular corrals encompasses individual instances in the Altar, Magdalena, and Tucson basins, but all reported cases on the Rio Sonora (Doolittle 1988:33). On the other hand, corrals are not present in trincheras sites recorded in Papaguería (Stacy 1974). Such overlapping but non-isomorphic attributes and arrangements present a major obstacle to a precise definition fitting only and all trincheras sites. At the same time, geographic and temporal patterns constitute optimal avenues for future analysis.

The proliferation of hill sites with masonry features across vast tracts of the Northwest/Southwest is a hallmark of the post–AD 1200 era. Sites on hills are not absent prior to this time, but their ubiquity in the following decades is striking. Although regional archaeologists view these sites from disparate vantages, they repeatedly have acknowledged the scale of the phenomenon by treating expansive arrays as closely related members of a single classificatory set. Among these inclusive categories, binational "trincheras sites" are a foremost case. "Atalayas" that span northwest Chihuahua (also cited in northeast Sonora) are another, and "hilltop sites" in central Arizona (see Wilcox et al., this vol.) are a third.

The relational properties of these categories are based on loose commonalities in material remains, intervisibility, and inferred functions.

The intensification of regional conflict is a comprehensive and unified explanatory framework for the proliferation of hill sites (e.g., Di Peso 1974; LeBlanc 1999; Swanson 2003; Wilcox and Haas 1994). According to this construct, intervisibility corroborates coordinated positioning for vigilance and communicating imminent threats. The relevance of intervisibility and communication is not limited to conflict, however. Highly visible hilltop settings might just as convincingly celebrate spiritual qualities of these landforms, reify elevated spiritual status vis-à-vis lower basin settlements, ensure locational exclusivity in ritual practice, and enhance dramatic communication of calendrics or momentous ceremonial events (Heisey, plate 1).

Along with a growing number of archaeologists who have examined a critical role for ideology in late prehistoric hill sites (e.g., Bostwick 2001; Downum 1993; Downum et al. 1994; Fish and Fish 2004; McGuire et al. 1999; McGuire and Villalpando, this vol.; O'Donovan 2002, 2004), we hope to have demonstrated that this is an equally valid and vital framework for understanding trincheras sites and addressing the larger transregional patterns of which they are a part. We believe that this alternative (but not mutually exclusive) framework gains credibility against the backdrop of other encompassing ideological trends that emanated from the south during these times, as in the spread of the katsina cult and the transcendence of polychrome iconography (e.g., Adams 1991; Crown 1994). These transregional phenomena conveyed a core of concepts that the peoples of the Northwest/Southwest widely but variably incorporated to enrich their own evolving traditions.

7

Delineating Hilltop Settlement Systems in West-Central Arizona, AD 1100–1400

David R. Wilcox, Judith Rowe Taylor, Joseph Vogel, and J. Scott Wood

I will lift up mine eyes unto the hills; from whence cometh my help?[1]

Among the earliest sites to receive archaeological notice in the North American Southwest were those on hilltops, where the walled enclosures were sometimes called "corrals" and otherwise were thought to be defensive facilities or places of religious worship (Burrus 1971; Forman 1941). In southern Arizona and northern Sonora, the term *cerros de trincheras* was colloquially used for them (Bandelier 1892; Brand 1943; Sauer and Brand 1931). The class of sites currently called *cerros de trincheras* is by no means homogeneous if we compare their defining attributes. Many of these hilltop sites have low walls parallel to the contours, but some have well-built, high vertical walls (Sauer and Brand 1931), while others are dry-laid and are, indeed, little more than revetment rock arrays formed when areas upslope were cleared of rock (Wilcox 1979).[2] In the Sierra Madre Occidental, parallel arrays of vertical walls that cascade down drainages, capturing soil behind them, are clearly agricultural features—yet they, too, are called "trincheras" (Herold 1965; personal observation). In other cases arc-shaped rock walls mark the downslope edges of residential terraces and are only incidentally contiguous along certain contours (as at Linda Vista Hill). On Martinez Hill, large contiguous areas are enclosed by walls, a variation not found at other Tucson Basin sites (Stacy 1974; personal observation). Black Mountain is a fortified hilltop but not a trincheras site. Sauer and Brand (1931:81 n. 17) say of the Black Mountain site: "We are inclined to consider it as something apart in design, period, and people from the Trincheras sites."

Given such diversity, it is little wonder that there has been considerable controversy about the anthropological interpretation of trincheras sites (see Wilcox 1979 for a review of early discussion, and Wilcox et al.

2001a for later debate; see also Wallace and Doelle 2001:250–251) on the variability of trincheras sites. The debate was again joined at the advanced seminar held at the Amerind Foundation, January 9–10, 2002. We readily agreed that the Las Trincheras site in Sonora is a town (but see Wilcox 2004), but it may have been a fortified town, just as Linda Vista Hill and Cerro Prieto may represent fortified villages (Wallace and Doelle 2001). The Fishes (this vol.) appear to have made a good case for the ceremonial purposes of the so-called *corrals* in the Magdalena Valley, Sonora. Some of those sites have no "curtain walls" that encircle the hills with corrals, while others do: why is there this difference? We continue to think the walls on Tumamoc Hill were built as defensive walls, fronting on residential terraces only in rare cases. It is interesting to look back on the observations of Robert Fletcher Gilder (1856–1940), an avocational archaeologist from Nebraska (see Wolf 1975) who made a study of Tumamoc Hill in 1918: "Upon all sides of the mountain where it is possible to reach the summit without scaling a perpendicular wall there are three well constructed lines of fortifications. These are not in a straight line surrounding the mountain, but are laid out with a knowledge of the military value of the salient and they zigzag around, offering to those on the inside of the fort the opportunity of an enfilading fire against an attacking foe" (*Arizona Daily Star* 1919). Well said! No doubt this debate will continue.

Now that it has been shown that some of these sites have great time depth, dating back to the Early Agricultural period (Hard and Roney, this vol.; Wallace et al., this vol.), the controversy has taken on new dimensions. In light of this, it is interesting to revisit Brand's (1943:137) argument pertaining to sites in the Corralitos, Chihuahua, area: "No potsherds were found on the cerro, but such a result was to be expected as these cerros de trincheras in Northwestern Chihuahua were apparently used only as watch towers and as citadels in cases of extreme need." We now would wonder if they are preceramic sites. So, too, in Sonora, where Bandelier (1892:491–493) makes a similar argument about the Batonapa site, though he also cites local tradition for the defensive-refuge hypothesis, and Doolittle (1988) supports this interpretation. However, the fact that they have been features on the archaeological landscape since then also invites questions about their possible reuse, perhaps in different ways than those for which they were first created. On Tumamoc Hill, for example, which is now known to have been occupied in the early centuries AD (Wallace et al., this vol.), Tanque Verde Red-on-brown pottery has been found (Wilcox and Larson 1979:6). Clearly, a normative (monothetic) logic by which we label a site as a trincheras site and then assume on that basis that a fixed set of attributes were present is unwise. A different approach to their understanding is needed.

At the advanced seminar it was often remarked that multiple "functions" were indicated at trincheras sites. That is no doubt true, but it in no way is evidence against the inference that a primary motivation for locating a village, town, or refuge on a hilltop was defense (see also Wallace and Doelle 2001). Tumamoc Hill may have initially been a fortified village with habitations in the numerous stone circles on top (see Larson 1979), and, much later, a defensive refuge, a place to which the residents of the St. Mary's site—connected to it by a trail (Hartmann and Hartmann 1979)—and others resorted in time of danger. More controlled excavations are needed to address these alternatives.

Our suggestion is that a value-neutral, nonfunctional term be substituted. When a functionally loaded label is applied, bias is immediately introduced, and the difference between description and explanation may be compromised. We thus propose grouping all the sites that have been labeled *cerros de trincheras* as part of the larger class of "hilltop sites," whose only defining attribute is that they are archaeological sites located on the tops or upper sides of hills, ridges, or mountains. A new classification of hilltop sites is needed based on the comparison of cases. In that way, the confusion about what can meaningfully be called *cerros de trincheras*—if we are to keep this term at all—can be scientifically reevaluated.

In west-central Arizona, hilltop sites are a prominent part of the archaeological record, often having high-standing walls, room blocks, and numerous artifacts. Questions about the interpretation of these sites have led to hypotheses that implicate other hilltop locations that have much less impressive remains—or in some cases, no architecture or even any artifacts at all! The scientific study of these sites has been a process of intellectual interaction and discovery that periodically requires us to step back and systematically reassess what has been learned. From this point of view, earlier efforts can be seen as a successive series of approximations to which we bring our own, latest conceptions. By being respectful, but critical, of the work of our predecessors, we can begin with a large corpus of data that we can add to, refine, and reconfigure as we seek to construct more parsimonious and comprehensive theories about the past.

In this way, we advocate that old concepts give way to new ones. We use the concept of a "settlement system" as a basic unit of analysis. By a "settlement system," we mean a set of sites whose populations interacted in a series of economically and socially significant activities that were replicated on multiple intra-annual cycles that reproduced a group identity. Interaction can be shown on the basis of the structure of such systems, by establishing interdependency of functions, and by transactional relationships, such as material exchanges of pottery, lithic resources, etc., and ritual reciprocity. All previously collected site data can be reevaluated in terms of this organizational concept, and the establishment of settlement system constructs can then be used to examine intergroup scales of interaction. This chapter tentatively delineates a series of such settlement systems—and the larger social system of which they may have been parts—in west-central Arizona. These data and methodological perspectives can then be used in comparative studies of hilltop settlement systems to the south, and in other world areas.

Hilltop Sites in West-Central Arizona

Since 1997 we have collaborated in the conduct of a "hilltop survey" in west-central Arizona. We take this study area to be the domain bounded by the Mogollon Rim or Interstate 40 on the north, the Big Sandy River on the west, the crests of the mountains east of the Verde River on the east, and the edge of the Phoenix Basin on the south. Previous surveys, beginning with that of Amiel Whipple in 1854 (Forman 1941), and especially the work of Spoerl and Gumerman (1984) and Austin (2000) in the 1970s and 1980s, documented a rich corpus of these sites, distributed throughout most parts of this vast area. Spoerl (in Spoerl and Gumerman 1984) proposed a four-part functional classification of these sites into hilltop forts, retreats, habitations, and centers (see also van Waarden 1984). She agreed with Austin that smoke-signaling or the use of fire at night was an important function performed at these sites. Austin (2000) accordingly and quite systematically recorded line-of-sight relationships among his set of hilltop sites.

Although Spoerl's is a functionally "loaded" classification in the labels chosen, comparison of cases supports her partitions. The so-called forts are small sites, with only a wall across the easiest access, or a small walled enclosure. Austin regarded such sites as "lookouts," and he was led to consider some hilltop sites with only a few sherds and lithics (or even no artifacts) as members of this class. We have not included sites with no artifacts or architecture on our maps, feeling that for now we will stick with "marked" sites that have what are presumably protective walls before we will include them as "lookouts." The "retreats" are larger walled enclosures with only one or two rooms and few artifacts. The habitation sites can also have walled enclosures but have more than two rooms and numerous artifacts. The "centers" are large habitation sites with 70 to 80 rooms in them, such as the Tip Top site (AZ T:4:8[PC]), and Brazaletes (NA13,577) (Spoerl and Gumerman 1984; Valehrach and Valehrach 1971; van Waarden 1984).

Starting with Austin's sketch maps and site cards, we have done the following: (1) edited and published a paper of his (Austin 2000) that sets forth his model for what these data may mean; (2) compiled and published an accurate distribution map of Austin's hilltop sites (Austin 2000); and (3) mapped several hilltop sites and assembled more comprehensive distribution maps of hilltop sites throughout west-central Arizona (Wilcox et al. 2000; Wilcox et al. 1999, 2001a, 2001b). We also, in the latter maps and their associated data tables, applied Spoerl's classification to Austin's data.

Independent of these efforts, one of us (Wood), working on behalf of the Tonto National Forest, collaborated with the Bureau of Land Management (BLM) in nominating the little-known settlement system of fourteenth-century pueblos on Perry Mesa to the National Register of Historic Places as a district (Stone 2000). Further efforts by the BLM to protect these sites led to the promulgation of the Agua Fria National Monument, a process we supported, but which included only part of the Perry Mesa settlement system in the monument (Wood and Wilcox 2001).

Following a field trip to see some of these sites, Wood entered into a collaboration with Wilcox and Gerald Robertson, Jr., to investigate what we perceived to be the military implications of the Perry Mesa system. Robertson was a former military officer in Vietnam and an avocational archaeologist. He suggested that the Perry Mesa population was the aggressor, and that they had cooperatively deployed their settlements on Perry Mesa to resist expected retaliation (Wilcox et al. 1999, 2001a). To pursue this hypothesis, we wanted to know who were the neighbors of the Perry Mesa population (who were friends and who enemies), and what were the antecedent defensive systems in west-central Arizona. Robertson also insisted that early warning is essential for an effective defense, so we began looking for hilltop sites that could have served as lookouts. Thus, the relationship of hilltop sites to non-hilltop sites was inferred to be a key structural feature of the settlement system as a whole.

These events led the Museum of Northern Arizona (MNA) to initiate a "hilltop survey" and to reach out in an ever-widening series of collaborative relationships to accomplish it. We wanted to visit the sites indicated on the maps we were creating, so that fresh observations could be made, and we hoped to locate and record new hilltop sites so that the region-wide networks of communication via smoke signals and fire that we suspected had been used could be documented. And we wanted to do this on a macroregional scale, because we suspected that the nature of the social interactions that may account for the structure of settlement systems in west-central Arizona cannot be understood short of that. Wood's (1987) concept of a Central Arizona Tradition in part encouraged us to approach the problem in this way.

We began by postulating where "missing nodes" in the communication network should be and finding that they were there (Wilcox et al. 1999, 2001a). Hearing of our work, Judith Rowe Taylor, an Arizona Site Steward who then lived in Bumble Bee, took us to see sites she was watching west of Perry Mesa that opened our eyes to the possibility of a hilltop communication network prior to the fourteenth century that linked the New River area to the south with the greater Prescott region to the northwest. This was the key insight that informed our study of the antecedents to the Perry Mesa system (Wilcox et al. 2001b). Taylor then introduced Wilcox to Joseph Vogel, a Site Steward in Prescott who owns two small planes and was glad to collaborate in this inquiry. Suddenly we had a way to find new hilltop sites whose architecture is visible from above. Having found new sites, we could organize field trips to hike in and record these sites.

Wilcox also cooperated with Sharlot Hall Museum in Prescott, giving a talk on the hilltop survey, and this led to his meeting other Site Stewards who have now contributed significantly to the project. Finally, others have also shared what they know and have led us on hikes to see many more hilltop sites. In this way, it has been possible to carry out a most unusual archaeological survey on a macroregional scale to investigate the relationships of hilltop sites to one another and to lower-lying settlement systems. A trip report was written after each flight and field trip, and new sites were recorded into Museum of Northern Arizona's "NA" site system. This volume (like the symposium that gave rise to it) is an excellent comparative context in which to present our preliminary findings. To do so, we divide our data into five spatial groupings that arguably are parts of distinct settlement systems.

The Perry Mesa and Bloody Basin Settlement Systems

In our initial model of the Perry Mesa defensive system, we argued that the Phoenix Basin Hohokam were the enemy, and we showed that early warning of an approach up the Agua Fria was indicated (Wilcox et al. 1999, 2001a). The relationships of a site called Point Extreme (NA12,560), from which one can look out on the junction of Squaw Creek with the Agua Fria and then can turn and see a walled enclosure (AR 03-12-01-1364; NA26,702) upstream that in turn has line of sight with Squaw Creek Ruin (NA12,555), are seen as evidence for this claim. However, as we looked more carefully at the 1:100,000 maps of this region, we saw that Cave Creek also afforded a pedestrian pathway from the Phoenix Basin to Perry Mesa. Cave Creek heads in an area where Squaw Creek also heads, as does Lime Creek (which flows into the Verde). Holmes Canyon comes south into this same area and then turns northward as Roundtree Canyon to flow into Bloody Basin. Was there early warning for Perry Mesa (and Bloody Basin) from this direction?

In a series of flights with Vogel, we discovered two hilltop sites, the Rosalie Lookout (NA25,989) and the Six Bar Lookout (NA26,001), and three previously unrecorded pueblos that confirm the hypothesis of early warning (table 7.1). Fort Metate (NA26,007) is a 70-room pueblo perched on a basalt cliff above upper Squaw Creek, and it has an enclosing wall on the other two sides. From it there is line of sight to Six Bar Lookout, which has line of sight to both Squaw Creek Ruin and Rosalie Lookout. Rosalie also has line of sight to Squaw Creek Ruin, and from it one can monitor movement along the route of today's Bloody Basin Road. In January 2005 David Gregory (personal communication 2005) took the UTMs of the line-of-sight relationships discussed in the text and used Terrain Navigator to test the claims: all were confirmed.

Cottonwood Springs Ruin (NA26,008), a site previously known to the Tonto Forest, is a 50- to 60-room pueblo on a hilltop just north of the headwaters of Cave Creek that has line of sight to Holmes Canyon Ruin (NA26,009), another 50- to 60-room pueblo on a high ridge with a panoramic view of Bloody Basin that Vogel spotted from the air. In between is Doorway Ruin (NA26,015), a 40-room pueblo that occupies the whole top of a small butte in Holmes Canyon. Whereas Forest Road 24 today runs north from Carefree and down Roundtree Canyon into the Bloody Basin, Roundtree is narrow, and it appears to us that the best pedestrian route aboriginally would have been up Holmes Canyon, thus from Cottonwood Springs past Doorway, Holmes Canyon, and South Fork ruins into Bloody Basin. Wood and Wilcox visited Mud Springs (NA1720), Lookout (NA1721), and Dugan (NA1722) in Bloody Basin but found that none of them were intervisible. Neither did any of them appear to have line-of-sight relationships with other known sites. More work on the latter issue is needed.

North of Perry Mesa is a hilltop site called Estler Peak (NA25,978), from which we predicted there should be a hilltop site in the Cordes Junction area. Site Stewards Judi and Rollie Myers found it: Horseshoe Butte (NA25,985) is a walled enclosure that one can easily see from Squaw Creek Ruin and that has lines of sight to all the pueblos both in the northern part of Perry Mesa and on Black Mesa along the west side of the Agua Fria. Horseshoe Butte and Rosalie are *not* intervisible; neither, apparently, are Estler and Rosalie, but Estler and Horseshoe are. Thus, while it seems that Perry Mesa was provided with a hilltop network of early warning on all sides, and Bloody Basin had one on the south, we have not found a link (or "relay") of comparable sites between the two. This is surprising if the hypothesis of a Verde Confederacy (see

Table 7.1 New Data on Selected Sites in the Perry Mesa and Bloody Basin Settlement Systems.

MNA Site No.	Other No.	No. of Rooms	Type	Record	Comments
25,985		5	Fort/ Lookout	V; PA	Horseshoe Butte
26,090		5	Fort/ Lookout	V; PA	Fort Silver
5423	N:16:6 (ASM)	30–40	Pueblo	V	Richinbar; racetrack
13,310	N:16:6 (ASU)	ca. 50	Pueblo	V; PA	Badger Springs; plaza; racetrack
—	12-01-1364	none	Fort/ Lookout	PA	Squaw Creek Fort; walled enclosure
25,989		none	Fort/ Lookout	V; PA	Rosalie Look-out; walled enclosure
26,001		5	Fort/ Lookout	V; PA	Six-Bar Look-out
26,007		70	Pueblo	V; PA	Fort Metate; enclosing wall; plaza
26,015		40	Pueblo	V; PA	Doorway; on butte
26,009		50–60	Pueblo	V; PA	Holmes Canyon; on high ridge
1720	12-01-64	50–60	Pueblo	V; PA	Mud Springs
1721	12-01-01	ca. 50	Pueblo	V	Lookout; great-kiva-like room; defensive
1722	12-01-02	ca. 50	Pueblo	V	Dugan; possible plaza

Record key: V = visited; PA = photographed from the air

below) is correct. It also shows that just because a site is on a hilltop, one cannot automatically see all other hilltop sites.

The Verde Confederacy

One of our principal findings when we mapped out the distribution of Perry Mesa's fourteenth-century neighbors was how continuous they were from Perry Mesa to Polles Mesa, and from Perkinsville to Davenport Wash (fig. 7.1). We postulated the concept of a Verde Confederacy, a political relationship among six or seven more or less distinct settlement systems that shared in a conflict relationship with the Phoenix Basin Hohokam, and perhaps with other neighboring groups (Wilcox et al. 1999, 2001a). Thus far, one of the principal facts supporting the confederacy model is that highly defendable sites are concentrated on the perimeter of this macro-settlement system, while those "inside" it are often in poorly defendable locations (see Wallace and Doelle 2001:272 for a similar case of this pattern in the San Pedro Valley). Our new findings (above) about the southern approach to Bloody Basin strengthen the evidence for this pattern.

What we have not yet found are linkages in line-of-sight networks that connect one subsystem within our inferred Verde Confederacy with one another. The absence of a link to Fort Metate has been mentioned above. In our earlier study (Wilcox et al. 2001a) we tried to find a link between the upper and middle Verde subsystems and did not find one. Similarly, we have looked for a connection between Estler Peak and the middle Verde with mixed success. Tom Wright took us to the Gap Creek Pueblo (NA25,993) dating to the AD 1150–1250 period. It sits on a "peninsula" with sheer walls above a trail across the Black Hills. It does look down into the middle Verde—but we have yet to identify any sites there that are intervisible with it. On the west, a ridge intervenes between it and Estler Peak. However, we have now found a walled-enclosure site (NA26,045) near Dugas, and so we conclude that more work needs to be done in this area.

More generally, we are aware of the theoretical importance of recording where sites are not, as well as where they are—something Wilcox advocated 25 years ago. Bandelier (1892:24), too, understood this point: "It is just as necessary to trace out where remains do not exist, as to

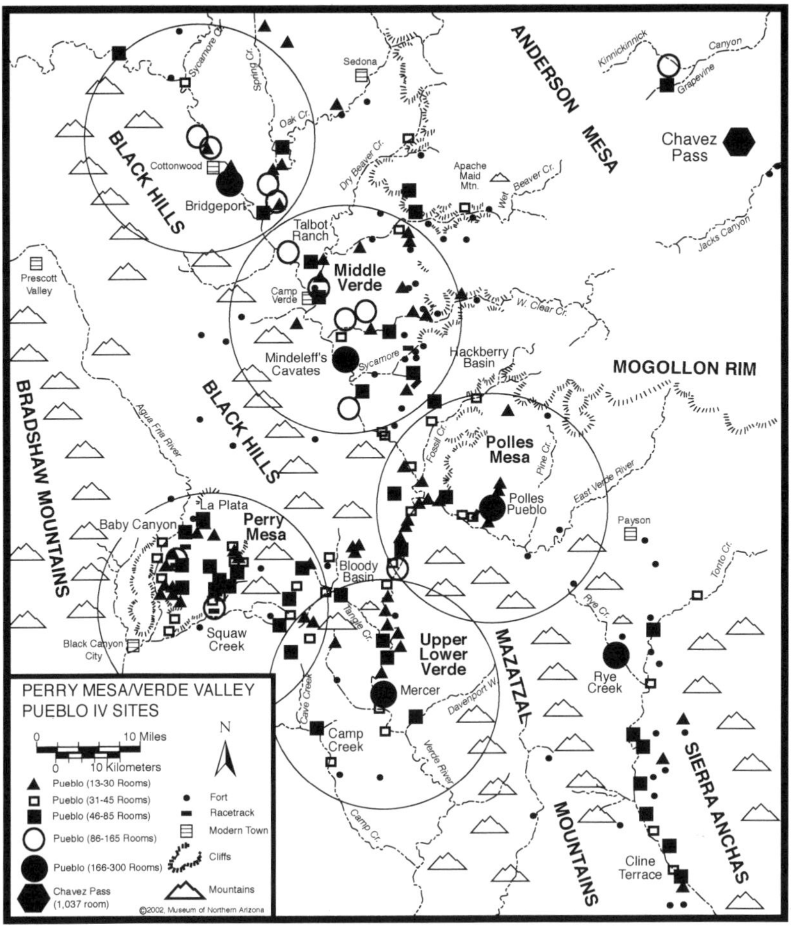

7.1 Map of fourteenth-century pueblos in west central Arizona.

determine where they are." We have been seeing hilltops without any sites on them, but have yet to attempt a *systematic* recording of such locations.

In the course of visiting a series of large pueblos along the upper and middle Verde (including Perkinsville, Limestone/Iron Rock, Big Cornville, Oak Creek, Walker Basin Fort, Calloway No. 2, John Heath, Wingfield Mesa, Fort Jawbone, Doran Castle, and Brown Springs [see table 7.2]), Wilcox brought out the MNA survey collections from these sites and discovered a previously unnoticed pattern: from Montezuma

Table 7.2 New Data on Selected Sites in the Middle Verde Valley.

MNA Site No.	Other No.	No. of Rooms	Type	Record	Comments
26,073	12-04-589	30+	Fortified pueblo	PA	Cedar Bench
5348A	09-015-201	100+	Fortified pueblo	V	Brown Springs
5348B		?	Compound	V	Brown Springs Compound
26,072		2+	Fort/ Lookout	PA	(across from Brown Springs)
3604	04-01-100	60-75	Fortified pueblo	V	Doran Castle
3605		12	Fort/ Lookout	V	Doran Fort
5705		None	Racetrack	V	Hackberry Racetrack
26,061	04-01-560	3	Fort/ Lookout	V	Fort Jawbone
25,993		8–10+	Fortified pueblo	V	Gap Creek Pueblo
26,016		8	Fortified pueblo	V	Walker Basin Fort; series of walls blocking access
4093		65–100	Fortified pueblo	V	Calloway No. 2; great-kiva-like room; plaza
6662		12–15	Pueblo	V	Salt Mine Pueblo; on hill
1500	04-06-41	c. 50	Pueblo	V	Oak Creek
1268, 1768	04-06-43	70–100	Fortified pueblo	V	Big Cornville (aka Chandler)

Table 7.2 Continued

MNA Site No.	Other No.	No. of Rooms	Type	Record	Comments
4645A, 5223	04-06-87, 04-06-392	75–140	Fortified pueblo	V	Limestone
4645B	04-06-83	16	Pueblo	V	Iron Rock; plaza
1259	O:5:175 (ASM)	13	Pueblo	V	Wood's Pueblo
2440, 9469	N:4:2 (ASU)	ca. 85	Fortified pueblo	V	Perkinsville; enclosed plaza

Record key: V = visited; PA = photographed from the air

Castle northward to Perkinsville most of the Pueblo IV sites (with collections) have late (Jeddito) Black-on-yellow pottery, and two have tree-ring dates after AD 1385. Those sites are Tuzigoot, with a 1386vv date, and Perkinsville, with a 1387r date. There is Tonto Polychrome from Montezuma Castle. In contrast, southward from the Mindeleff cavates to Doran Castle and Brown Springs, the pottery cross-dating indicates abandonment by the middle 1300s.

We agree with Peter Pilles that the "center" of the middle Verde settlement system during early Pueblo IV was probably Clear Creek Ruin (NA2806)—as the circle on fig. 7.1 suggests. Quite a bit of yellow-ware is in the MNA collections from this site, including true Jeddito Black-on-yellow. Interestingly, if one considers the distance from there that one could go and come back in a day (which statistic we take to be 11 miles), the perimeter defined by an 11-mile radius from Clear Creek Ruin takes in the area from Talbot Ranch to Verde Hot Springs. In our earlier study (Wilcox et al. 2001a) we found no line-of-sight connection between Talbot Ranch and sites farther upstream. On the other hand, the line of "forts/lookouts" along Sycamore Canyon north of the Hackberry Basin—to which we can now add Fort Jawbone, NA26,061—might mark a systemic boundary (Wilcox et al. 2001a). Once the Mindeleff cavates, Brown Springs and the Hackberry Basin sites dropped out, two very defendable sites, Clear Creek Ruin and John Heath, were on a southern boundary. Yet on the west side of the Verde also lay the peculiar Wingfield Mesa site (AR 03-04-01-67), which Jerry Robertson regarded as highly vulnerable to attack! North of it lay the Verde salt mines (Morris 1928). Clearly, much more fine-grained chronological analyses of the history of these sites and their relationships are needed, which we have now begun to do (see Wilcox and Holmlund 2007).

The bottom line is that the proposed Verde Confederacy apparently broke apart by the middle 1300s and a 12-mile (19 km) buffer zone opened up in the middle Verde, separating the upper Verde settlement systems from those south of Verde Hot Springs (where late 1300s pottery is found). The famous Verde salt mines (Morris 1928) are just north of this buffer zone.

Wilcox, Robertson, and Wood (2001a) already realized the possibility of this boundary, and recent work by North, Senior, and Foster (2003) further confirms its presence. North of it there is very little (but some) Salado Polychrome; south of it there are "racetracks"; in the middle, however, in Hackberry Basin, there is also a racetrack as well as a large "community room," a feature repeatedly found at middle Verde sites. Scott Wood also has pointed out that the Towel Creek trail, which runs east-west south of Hackberry Basin, connects with a probably Fossil Creek trail, which in turn was probably an aboriginal trail link to Polles Mesa to the south (Wilcox and Holmlund 2007). Immediately below Brown Springs, where the Towel Creek Trail comes out, there is a ford in the Verde. These relationships are a current focus of continuing research reported by Wilcox and Holmlund (2007).

This significant change within the Verde Confederacy may have been linked to changing relationships on a larger scale. Long-distance exchange linked the upper Verde system with the Hopi Mesas via Chavez Pass and the Homol'ovi cluster (Byrkit 1988; Wilcox and Holmlund 2007), bringing Hopi yellowwares to the Verde Valley and probably sending cotton textiles, copper minerals, obsidian, and salt to Hopi. Conflict may have erupted over the control of this exchange system. Within a generation or two, however, abandonment of the Homol'ovis (perhaps due to massive floods in the 1380s that presumably wiped out their irrigation systems [Lyons 2001]) apparently resulted in a domino effect of abandonment at Chavez Pass and in the upper Verde. These possibilities, if true, would go a long way toward explaining why such environmentally excellent places as the upper and middle Verde ever were depopulated.

More recent studies in connection with the La Plata Mapping Project (Wilcox and Holmlund 2007) have further documented the cultural boundary in the Brown Springs–Doran Castle region. The presence of Sityatki Polychrome at Perry Mesa and Verde Valley sites, and Jeddito Stippled at Big Cornville Ruin (in ASM collections) and a site on Oak Creek (seen by Jerry Ehrhardt at the National Museum of the American Indian [personal communication 2004]), could mean that sites in the northern part of what we still posit was part of a Verde Confederacy persisted to at least AD 1400 and possibly a little later.

Foothills North of the Phoenix Basin

From Boulder Creek north of Lake Pleasant (on the Agua Fria) eastward past New River, Cave Creek, and Carefree to the Verde River, a linear array of hilltop sites is present in the saguaro-rich foothills that bound the north edge of the Phoenix Basin (Wilcox et al. 2001b; fig. 7.2). Frank Hamilton Cushing visited several sites in this region in 1887 (Hinsley and Wilcox 2002; Wilcox et al. 2001b), and Jesse Walter Fewkes (1912) reported several sites on the lower Agua Fria below Boulder Creek, including one cerro de trincheras site (AZ T:7:34 [ASU]) with parallel walls that follow the contours.[3] Later studies (Holliday 1974; Spoerl and Gumerman 1984; Valehrach and Valehrach 1971; van Waarden 1984) have made many of these sites relatively well known, and unpublished work by Simmons (n.d.), Raymond (1952), and Tonto National Forest surveys add valuable information. Diagnostic pottery and carbon-14 dating suggest that these sites date to the period AD 1100 to 1250 (Wilcox et al. 2001b).

We have flown over many of these sites to photograph them from the air, and have hiked in to see Indian Mesa (AZ T:4:1[PC]) and Pepsi Cap (AZ T:4:5[PC]) at the west end, and Sears-Kay, Blue Mountain, Brazeletes, and Citadel on the east end. We also recorded the Table Mesa Ruin (AZ T:4:44 [ASM]) and discovered and recorded a set of sites north of Rover Peak that we call the Claret Cup sites (table 7.3).

As a result, it is now possible to define the following network, west

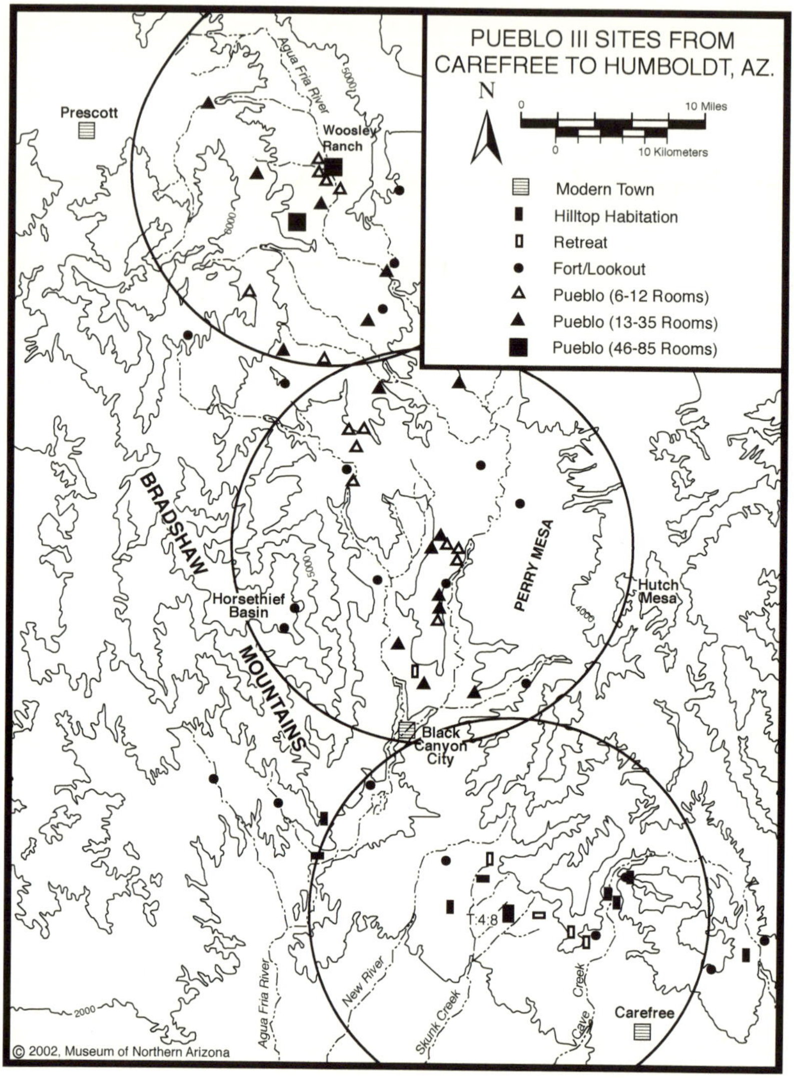

7.2 Map of the hilltop settlement system in the foothills north of Phoenix, AD 1100–1250.

Table 7.3 New Data on Selected Sites in the Foothills North of the Phoenix Basin.

MNA Site No.	Other No.	No. of Rooms	Type	Record	Comments
15,754	T:4:1 (PC)	17+	Hilltop habitation	V; PA	Indian Mesa (aka Dobyns); petroglyphs adjacent to site
—	T:4:2 (PC)	7	Hilltop habitation	PA	Boulder Creek; courtyards
25,990		1	Hilltop retreat	V; PA	Agua Fria; walled enclosure; entry
—	AZ T:4:44 [ASM]	30+	Hilltop habitation	V; PA	Table Mountain; 3 interlocked compounds; courtyards
T:4:5 (PC)	12-01-375	5	Hilltop retreat	V; PA	Pepsi Cap; petroglyphs near top of butte
—	T:4:8 (PC)	87	Hilltop habitation center	PA	Tip Top
9835	12-01-09; U:1:10 (ASU)	26	Hilltop habitation & fort	PA	Skull Mesa Fort; walled enclosure
	S 84; U:1:20 (ASU)		Fort	PA; V*	Elephant Butte; no ceramics
26,060		none	Ceremonial	PA; V*	oval enclosure
26,080	12-01-74; U:1:1 (ASU)	ca. 40	Hilltop habitation	V; PA	Sears-Kay Site

Table 7.3 Continued

MNA Site No.	Other No.	No. of Rooms	Type	Record	Comments
26,077	B:1:3(GP); 12-01-65	21	Hilltop habitation	V; PA	Blue Mountain; defensive wall; courtyards; redware
26,081		?	Fort/look-out	PA	Kentuck Mtn. Fort; circular; peepholes
26,078		ca. 10	Hilltop habitation	PA	Dos Cerros
13,577	U:2:1 (ASM)	100+	Hilltop habitation center	V	Brazaletes site
26,079		2	Fort/look-out	PA, V*	St. Clair Peak Fort; Rectangular walled enclosure
26,082	12-01-188	30+	Hilltop habitation	V; PA	Citadel
26,083	12-01-187	none	Ceremonial	PA	Dance Circle; oval enclosure; entry; petroglyphs
3509	12-01-04	225–300	Pueblo	PA	Mercer; 5 plazas; platform mound?
26,084	12-01-640	75–87	Pueblo	V; PA	Davenport Wash; plaza
26,073		several	Hilltop habitation	PA	Sunset Mtn.
—	12-01-642; O:14:152 (ASU)	none	Ceremonial	PA	Tangle Top; oval enclosure; entry

Table 7.3 Continued

MNA Site No.	Other No.	No. of Rooms	Type	Record	Comments
26,023		none	Fort/look-out	V; PA	Upper Claret Cup; 1 petro-glyph
26,026		ca. 10	Hilltop habitation	V; PA	Magnum Claret; walled enclosure; courtyard

Record key: V = visited; PA = photographed from the air; V* = visited at our request

to east, of line-of-sight connections: Boulder Creek (AZ T:4:2[PC]) to Pepsi Cap to Tip Top[4] to Room-with-a-View (AZ T:4:7[PC]) to Elephant Butte (AZ U:1:20 [ASU]), and then from Skull Mesa (NA9835) to Magnum Claret (NA26,026; fig. 7.3) and Upper Claret Cup (NA26,023) to Sunset Mountain (NA26,050). The last site has not yet been visited, but it was reported to us by archaeologist Tom Wright, and Vogel has photographed it from the air. From it, apparently, one can see the whole of present-day Horseshoe Reservoir and probably to Brazeletes. The area below Horseshoe Dam can also be seen from Upper Claret Cup (NA26,022). We are still looking for a linkage from Elephant Butte to Skull Mesa. What is surprising, and anomalous, is that Indian Mesa does not appear to have a line-of-sight connection to this network, nor does the Agua Fria Fort (NA25,990). However, Pepsi Cap does have line of sight with the Henrie site (NA11,646; fig. 7.4) and probably the Flyby site (NA26,056; see below), both on southern tips of Black Mesa. Between these sites there are very few known sites, and there may be a 10-mile-wide (16 km) buffer zone in this area, defining a boundary between two different settlement systems. Rock Springs lies in this zone, and we note as an alternative that the apparent absence of sites is due to lack of survey which the prevalence of private land in this area inhibits.

Another indication that the hilltop sites and associated lowland sites (Holliday 1974; Spoerl and Gumerman 1984; van Waarden 1984) from Boulder Creek eastward to the Verde were part of a single settlement sys-

7.3 Looking to Skull Mesa Fort, NA9835, from Magnum Claret, NA26,026. Left to right: Shelley Rasmussen, Lila Elam, Judy Taylor, and Trudy Mertens (seated).

tem is the presence of the east-west Table Mesa Road (Forest Road 41), which connects the Table Mesa area to the 24 Road three miles (5 km) north of Seven Springs. Some sites are known along the west and east ends of this route where it runs between New River Mesa and the New River Mountains, but much of the route has not yet been intensively surveyed. We suggest that this route may have been an ancient trail. From Seven Springs eastward, Site Steward Lila Elam postulates a route for this putative trail all the way to the Verde (a hypothesis now under investigation). Sites are known along that segment of the route.

In February 2002, Wilcox accompanied Lila Elam and others to investigate this putative trail. From a tank, what is now an old cow trail follows the contours from Deer Flat down to a flat with a site above Buck Basin, and then continues down toward another site. There is an excellent rock art site near the tank at Deer Flat with four rows of dancing figures holding hands. Wood suspects there is a trail from Buck Basin down to the Citadel site, but this has yet to be followed out. Just how to authenticate a prehistoric trail in this area is still a puzzle.

While more work clearly needs to be done, we view these data as supporting the inference of a conflict relationship of raiding between this region and the Phoenix Basin Hohokam (Wilcox et al. 2001b). The so-called northern periphery between the two areas had become a buffer zone by about AD 1100, and many of the latest houses in Hohokam settlements in that zone prior to 1100 were burned (David Abbott, personal communication 2001; North 2001). A more complex hypothesis would be to infer that this east-west line of hilltop sites and related settlements down below them were a series of dispersed communities confederated into a defensive system. Line-of-sight relationships are usually tightest within local areas, and the distances between New River and Cave Creek, and between Cave Creek and Carefree, are such that it is unlikely that help could have been sent to one another very quickly. This problem was solved by the redeployment of those populations onto Perry Mesa (Wilcox et al. 2001a).

Three sites in this region constitute a distinct morphological class of oval rock-walled enclosures (table 7.3). They do not appear to be particularly defensive, and like the corrals in the Trincheras area of north-

7.4 Henrie site, NA11,646, with Pepsi Cap, AZ T:4:5 (PC) in background, visible over Shelley Rasmussen's head.

ern Sonora (see Fish and Fish, this vol.), they may be ceremonial sites. Wilcox has seen a site along the Colorado River north of Laughlin that is a circle on a hilltop, said by local avocational archaeologists to have been used historically for puberty ceremonies. Much more focused examination of this class of sites and new comparative studies of them are needed.

Middle Agua Fria

Stretching from the south end of Black Mesa on the south to the high East and South Forts (NA 15,345 and NA15,344) in Horsethief Basin on the west, and from the Agua Fria on the east northward to the Mayer area and the Poague walled enclosure (NA13,597) on the northwest, a settlement system of small pueblos located on defendable hilltops can be postulated that dates in the AD 1100 to 1250 time period (fig. 7.5). Our investigations from the air have photo-documented many sites in this poorly known region, and we have discovered and documented new sites on Townsend Butte (NA25,992), Horseshoe Butte, Arcosanti (NA26,017), the south tip of Black Mesa (the Flyby site, NA26,056), and a hilltop south of the confluence of Squaw Creek and the Agua Fria (NA26,000) (see table 7.4). We have visited many sites, including Henrie, Euler (NA15,752), Spanish Hill (NA25,975), East Fort (NA15,345) and South Fort (NA15,344), Horseshoe Butte, Fort Silver (NA26,090), Townsend Butte, Arcosanti, Nash (NA25,954), Jagged Tooth (NA4634; see Schroeder 1954), Copper Mountain South (NA25,979), and Myers Fort (NA25,973). Fort Silver is a massive wall across a mesa tip that overlooks the northwest edge of Perry Mesa, west of La Plata Ruin. Inside the wall are five or six boulder circles and a ceramic assemblage of brownware, Wingfield Plain, and only one late redware sherd. Like part of Point Extreme on the southwest of Perry Mesa (NA11,640), the Three-Dog site (NA11,595), and two other sites along the north rim of Squaw Creek (NA13,466 and 26,701), this site may be part of the middle Agua Fria settlement system during Pueblo III times.

From East Fort all of both Black and Perry mesas are clearly visible, as is the whole Bumble Bee area. Similarly, from Copper Mountain one has a panoramic view in all directions, with lines of sight to Myers Fort,

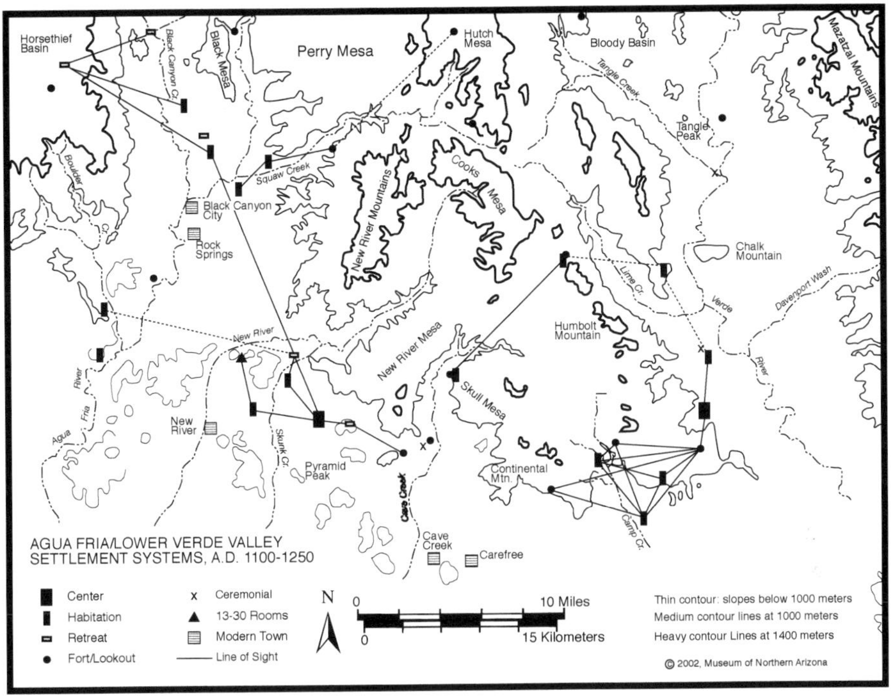

7.5 Map of the middle and upper Agua Fria settlement systems, AD 1100–1250.

Boulder Maze (NA25,994; see below), Estler Peak, Arcosanti, Horseshoe Butte, and other sites. Whereas most of the habitation sites in the northern Phoenix Basin foothills are compounds of various kinds, usually with curvilinear walls, the habitation sites in the middle Agua Fria system are pueblo room blocks. The plainware pottery in the former area is predominantly phylite-tempered Wingfield Plain, whereas in the latter area it is a sand-tempered brownware that has yet to be formally described. While tentative, these findings appear to support the hypothesis of distinct settlement systems. They still may have been loosely allied in a confederacy against the Phoenix Basin Hohokam, however (Wilcox et al. 2001b). This may mean that they all spoke dialects of the same language but were politically distinct in ways comparable to the subgroupings seen historically among the Yavapai (Gifford 1936) and Western Apache (Goodwin 1942). If so, the later "Verde Confederacy" would

Table 7.4 New Data on Selected Sites in the Middle and Upper Agua Fria Settlement Systems.

MNA Site No.	Other No.	No. of Rooms	Type	Record	Comments
26,000		13	Hilltop habitation	V	Wall across ridge on south end
11,646	N:16: (PC)	c. 22	Fortified pueblo	V; PA	Henrie; courtyard
26,056			Fort/ lookout	PA; V*	Flyby; walled enclosure
15,752		20	Fortified pueblo	V; PA	Euler
25,975		2	Hilltop retreat	V; PA	Spanish Hill; walled enclosure
15,345	09-02-02	1	Hilltop retreat	V; PA	East Fort; walled enclosure
15,344	09-02-01		Fort/ lookout	V; PA	South Fort; walled mesa tip
5856		20–30	Pueblo	V; PA	Running Deer
25,981		30	Fortified pueblo	V	Alkali Canyon
25,982		18	Pueblo	V	Quadruped
25,978		4	Fort/ lookout	V	Estler Peak
26,017		32	Fortified pueblo	V; PA	Arcosanti
25,045		?	Fort/ lookout	PA	Dugas
26,088		3+	Pueblo	PA	(east of Dugas)
25,992		None	Fort/ lookout	V	Townsend Butte

Table 7.4 Continued

MNA Site No.	Other No.	No. of Rooms	Type	Record	Comments
25,979		None	Fort/look-out	V	Copper Mountain South
25,977		14+	Fortified pueblo	PA	Earl Cline
4634		23–30	Fortified pueblo	V; PA	Jagged Tooth
25,954	09-02-08?	c. 15	Fortified pueblo	V; PA	Nash
13,597		None	Fort/look-out	V	Poague Lookout
1510, 2411, 4637		c. 50	Fortified pueblo	V; PA	Humboldt; plaza
25,974	N:12:9 (ASM)	18	Fortified pueblo	V	McMahon; compound wall; courtyard
25,994		5	Hilltop habitation	V; PA	Boulder Maze; walled enclosure
4363	N:8:1 (ASM)	80+	Pueblo	V; PA	Woolsey Ranch
14,180		7	Hilltop habitation	V	Nordwall
11,358, 13,405		20+	Fortified pueblo	V; PA	Stansell; enclosing wall; courtyard
3810, 6654, 14,549		20+	Fortified pueblo	V; PA	Coyote; courtyard
38, 14,548		8–15	Fortified pueblo	V; PA	Aiken; compound wall; courtyard

Table 7.4 Continued

MNA Site No.	Other No.	No. of Rooms	Type	Record	Comments
3639		38	Pueblo	V	Stillman Windmill; on low ridge
3339, 4031		53+	Fortified pueblo	V	Fitzmaurice; burned

Record key: V = visited; PA = photographed from the air; V* = visited at our request

represent a more aggregated and reorganized version of this congeries of populations, who were redeployed during the middle 1200s into a smaller net area where new defensive systems could be established.

Upper Agua Fria

Centered in Lonesome Valley and the Humboldt area, this region exhibits a mixture of small pueblos and compounds with room blocks that are connected by a line-of-sight network. The pottery is similar to that in the middle Agua Fria and contrasts with the Prescott Gray ware found in the woodlands to the west. Tentatively, we suggest that the sites in the period AD 1100–1250 in this region constituted a distinct settlement system, though we see no strong evidence of a southern boundary with the middle Agua Fria system to the south. Only a few sherd types diagnostic of the 1200s are reported from sites in this set. St. Johns Polychrome was found at Fitzmaurice Ruin (Barnett 1974), and we found a piece of Tusayan Polychrome at the Jagged Tooth site. Some of these sites might have lasted for some time past AD 1250, but not past 1300 (Wilcox et al. 2001b; see also Wilcox et al. 2007).

We have visited or photo-documented from the air the following sites (table 7.4): Aiken (NA3809), Coyote Ruin (NA3810), Stansell (NA11,358), Nordwall (NA14,180), Fitzmaurice (NA4031), Woolsey Ranch (NA4363), McMahon (NA25,974), and Humboldt Ruin (NA1510, 2411, and 4637). Simmons (n.d.) apparently regarded his Stillman Windmill (aka Piedra Roja) site (NA3639) as part of this settlement system. It is on Granite Creek close to the Del Rio argillite source. We have visited it and suspect it goes with the pueblo sites in the Del Rio area and along the upper Verde, though it is some distance south of them. Recent analyses of the ceramic collection made from it now at the MNA include Kiet Siel Polychrome and Tuwiuca Black-on-orange, both pointing to a date at least as late as AD 1275 (Wilcox et al. 2007). Humboldt Ruin is a pueblo of about 50 rooms perched on a granite dyke (much like Jagged Tooth), with a plaza marked by stone alignments that may have anchored a wooden palisade. Discovery of this site from the air and recording it served to clear up numerous errors in the MNA site files that regrettably were reported in an earlier article (Wilcox et al. 2001b).[5] It has line of sight to both Nordwall to the north and Myers Fort to the south.

The largest site in this settlement system is the centrally located Woolsey Ranch site, which we estimate had about 80 ground-floor rooms. It was thus comparable in size to the hilltop centers of Tip Top or Brazeletes farther south, but with more tightly packed rooms.

East of Woolsey Ranch, along the Cherry Road route to the Verde Valley, there are also other hilltop sites. The Boulder Maze site (NA25,994) was seen by Vogel from the air and then recorded. We also visited the Smith site (NA5338), and Site Stewards Tom and Sue Weiss have visited Ash Creek Fort, NA7284. Tom Weiss (personal communication, 2002) reports that the Ash Creek Fort has lines of sight to Boulder Maze, Copper Mountain North and South, and Horseshoe Butte, but not to Smith or Estler Peak. These sites thus appear to be part of the middle Agua Fria settlement system. We are still looking for another "relay" that will tie the Cherry Road/Ash Creek sites to the upper Agua Fria system, but at this writing we have not found it. Much more work needs to be done on the chronology of all these sites.

Greater Prescott Area Settlement Systems

There are reasons for thinking that the greater Prescott area, from the Mogollon Rim and Interstate 40 on the north, to the upper Verde on the northeast, the Big Sandy on the west, and the Hassayampa below Wagner on the south, is either one huge interactive settlement system or a congeries of smaller ones that may have been confederated (fig. 7.6). Ceramically, there appears to be a continuum of variation (Euler and Dobyns 1962; but see Christenson 2000). The Groom Creek figurine

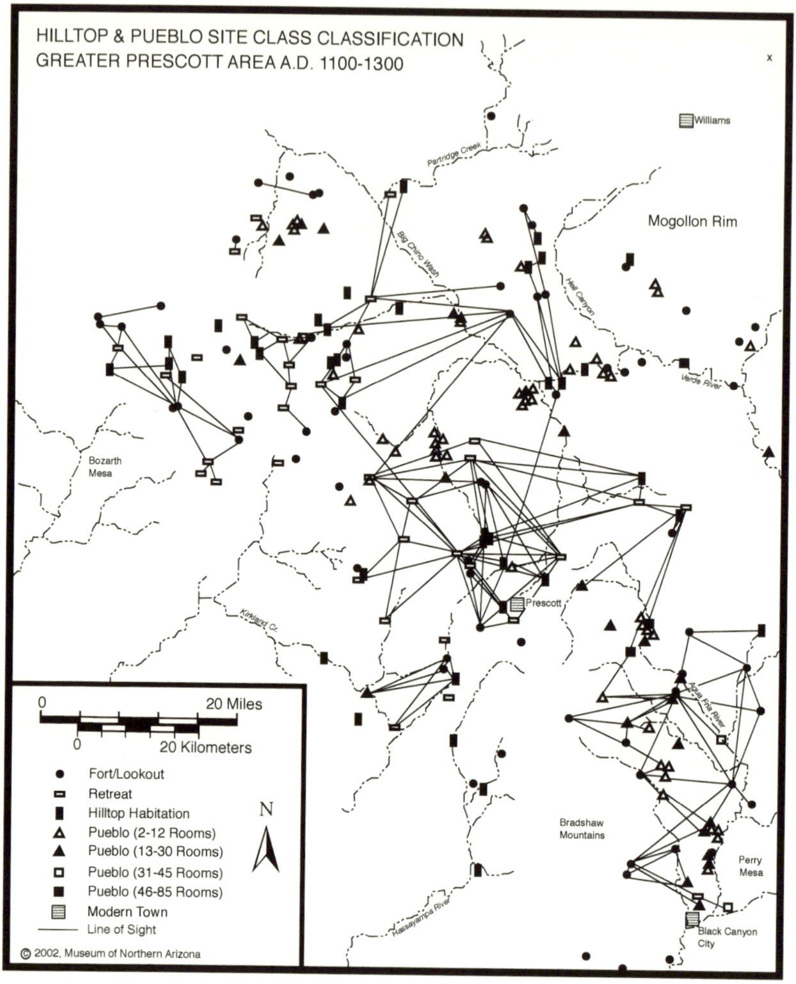

7.6 Map of hilltop sites in the Greater Prescott area, AD 1100–1300.

complex, however, points toward a distinct subculture (Motsinger 2000), and Austin (2000) perceived a boundary between the woodland populations and those in the grasslands to the east (see also Wilcox et al. 2000). Austin's (2000) premise that the people in the woodlands were "Mountain Patayan" implies linguistic ties to Hokan-speaking populations along the Colorado River, an idea also subscribed to by Colton (1939). Alternatively, these populations might all have spoken one or more languages of Uto-Aztecan, like their neighbors in the Verde Valley, as is implied by the latter's classification as "Southern Sinagua" (see Downum 1992; Pilles 1981).

If the populations of west-central Arizona were Uto-Aztecan speakers, this would imply a continuous dialect chain of connectivity from the Hohokam (presumably proto-Tepiman speakers: Wilcox 1986; Shaul and Hill 1999) and the Hopi via the Cohonina and Sinagua—both of whom are thought to be Uto-Aztecan speakers (Colton 1946; Wilcox 1989). The differences seen between modern Hopi and Tepiman, therefore, could be in large part due to the disappearance of these intermediate populations 600 years ago (see Miller 1984; Cortina-Borja and Valiñas 1989; and Hill 2001 for current debate about Uto-Aztecan).

We have visited or photo-documented from the air several sites in this vast region (table 7.5), including Hunt's Twins (NA14,894), Hunt's Knoll (NA13,203), Milligan (NA1899), Indian Peak (NA13,205), Fiero (NA13,195), and Olsen (NA14,250) in the Walnut Creek settlement system; Cheryl (NA13,183), Molly G (NA13,236), Morgan (NA13,237), and Wells (NA14,530) in the upper Verde settlement system; Bean Peak (AR 03-09-03-331) in the Prescott system; and Carter (NA13,513), Veater (NA13,534), and Mir (NA13,235) along the middle Hassayampa in the Walnut Grove area (table 7.5). Vogel has also recently photo-documented hilltop sites on Burro Creek and Walnut Creek, in the Camp Wood area, and in Big Chino Valley, and elsewhere in this region. Site Stewards Tom and Sue Weiss, who assisted in the investigation of many of the above sites, have also visited others, looking for more line-of-sight connections. Of key importance is the fact that the Fiero site (NA13,195), part of a settlement system centered on Walnut Creek, has line of sight to Little Granite Mountain (Austin's Albee site, NA13,171), and other sites linked to it. This supports the hypothesis that the whole greater Prescott area was tied closely together by a dense network of line-of-sight relationships.

In the summer of 2004 Wilcox, at the invitation of BLM archaeologist John Rose, visited the Pima College Archaeological Field School directed by David Stephen near Black Butte. We visited the Ronnie site, NA14150, and Wilcox found that there is clear line of sight from this walled enclosure to the Mayes site, NA13229, the walled enclosure reported at Aztec Pass by Amiel Whipple in 1854 (Forman 1941). It is now pretty obvious that from the latter site that one could see many

Table 7.5 New Data on Selected Sites in the Greater Prescott Area Settlement System.

MNA Site No.	Other No.	No. of Rooms	Type	Record	Comments
13,229		None	Fort/ lookout	V, PA	Mayes (Aztec Pass); walled enclosure; entry
13,203		6+	Hilltop habitation	V	Hunt's Knoll
14,894		8	Hilltop habitation	V, PA	Hunt's Twins; walled enclosure
1899	09-06-23	None	Fort/ lookout	V; PA	Milligan; walled enclosure
822, 13,205		21	Hilltop habitation	V; PA	Indian Peak (Jackson); compound wall; entry; tower
15,364	09-06-183	25–40	Pueblo	V	B & B (Whipple's Pueblo)
14,250	09-01-162	None	Retreat	PA	Olsen; triangular compound; entry
4358; 13,182	09-01-59	5	Hilltop habitation	PA, V*	Blanton
13,408		several	Hilltop habitation?	PA, V*	Stricklin
13,195	09-06-05	None	Retreat	V; PA	Fiero; walled enclosure
13,230	09-06-36	None	Retreat	PA	McGroaty
13,220	09-06-119	2	Retreat	PA	Lerchen
13,549	09-06-145	1	Retreat	PA	Hunt
13,194	09-06-15	None	Retreat	PA	Ferguson
26,090		none	Retreat	PA	
26,093		none	Fort/ lookout	PA	

Table 7.5 Continued

MNA Site No.	Other No.	No. of Rooms	Type	Record	Comments
13,183	09-01-31	None	Fort/ lookout	V	Cheryl; walled enclosure
13,236		5+	Hilltop habitation	V	Molly G; compound wall; entry
13,237		3+	Hilltop habitation	V	Morgan; walled enclosure
13,530		None	Fort/ lookout	V	Wells
3525, 13,175		5	Retreat	V*	Ann T (Limestone Butte); walled enclosure; entry
13,171	09-03-27	6+	Retreat	V*	Albee; walled enclosure; entry
—	09-3-331	20–40	Hilltop habitation	V	Bean Peak
15,513		24	Hilltop habitation	V; PA	Carter; tower
13,534		None	Fort/ lookout	V	Veater

Record key: V = visited; PA = photographed from the air; V* = visited at our request

other hilltop sites in the Mount Hope area. From a local cowboy, Wilcox also confirmed what he and Vogel had seen in a 2004 flight, that there are no hilltop sites in the Mohon Mountains west of Mount Hope. Was there a buffer zone from Burro Creek westward to the Big Sandy, separating Patayan-Yuman populations to the west from Prescott Uto-Aztecan populations to the east? Continuing work on this fascinating issue is needed.

Was the sole purpose of a line-of-sight relationship to signal between nodes in a network—as we have largely assumed—or could the role of some sites have been to *monitor* the signaling of neighboring settlement systems, keeping one group informed about another? This seems like a plausible possibility. The Cheryl site, for example, is so situated on the northeast side of Big Chino Valley that many sites can be seen in the woodlands to the west and southwest, more than 10 miles (16 km) away. As a rule of thumb, we have assumed that signaling stations needed to be within 10 miles (16 km) of one another, and the networks we have described above conform to that premise. Yet this is an untested assumption. William Hardy (1888), a nineteenth-century observer of Yavapai smoke signaling in the greater Prescott area, reported, "I have known correct news concerning the movements of U.S. troops in war times to be smoked through at least three hundred miles in two or three hours, and news by courier five or six days later would prove the news by Indians to be correct." But how closely spaced were the signaling stations? We suggest that experimentation is needed to address this fundamental issue.

On December 1, 2002, a student, Brandon Hughart (2002), in a class on Southwestern archaeology being taught by Wilcox for the "Grand Canyon Semester" at Northern Arizona University, carried out an initial smoke-signal experiment. Teams were positioned on six hilltop sites (Townsend Butte, Horseshoe Butte, Estler Peak, Copper Mountain South, Boulder Maze, and Smith), fires were lit, and observations by eye and with binoculars were made; Joe Vogel flew above us and took photographs. In spite of Forest Service restrictions on the size of fires we were allowed to build, quite satisfactory results—for a first attempt!—were realized. Just how the Yavapai in the 1860s could send a plume of smoke 1,000 feet into the air (Hardy 1888), however, remains a mystery.

Conclusions

The anthropological meaning of hilltop sites cannot be understood by looking at the sites alone. Their relationships to one another and to the settlement systems in which they were elements or nodes are also crucially important. Comparison of the morphology of individual hilltop sites shows that they are highly variable, although subsets of them may share significant attributes, both morphologically and in terms of their relationships to other kinds of sites. Chronology, of course, is also crucially important, although often difficult to resolve with much precision. By postulating coherent behavioral models that have testable implications, we can hope to benefit by standing on the shoulders of those who have gone before us and by providing a firm foundation for future inquiry. We continue to seek ways to more fruitfully study a fascinating class of sites: those located with only the sky above, on hilltops.

Notes

1. Psalm 121:1, King James Version of the Bible. The semicolon and question mark have been added; Wilcox recalls a long-ago sermon in which the minister argued that on the hills were Canaanite temples, and that this is a query about how to know the truth, not an expression that it will necessarily be found on the hills. This interpretation seems like a suitable epigraph for the methodological discussion we present.

2. At the Amerind seminar the argument made by Wilcox (1979) that these walls were built as defense was misconstrued as having the form "If A, then B; B; therefore A"—which is a fallacy. To the contrary, the argument has the following form: Consider all alternative hypotheses to account for the construction of the walls, H1, H2, H3, . . . Hn. Testing each against the data then documented, it was found that only one was supported. Therefore, "in the absence of strong support for any alternative hypothesis, it is concluded that the defensive-wall hypothesis is currently the best supported and the most likely" (Wilcox 1979:28, emphasis added). Continued testing of all alternatives is desired (see below).

3. In 2003, Mark Hackbarth took Wilcox to see this small site. He reports seeing only two flakes and no pottery on it, but we saw two sherds that day. There is very little space behind these revetment walls, and their interpretation is still open to question.

4. This claim is tentative, being based on observations from Pepsi Cap but not yet confirmed by a visit to the Boulder Creek site.

5. When we became familiar with the extensive corpus of J. W. Simmons' writings at the Arizona State Museum, we found in it photographs of the Humboldt Ruin that set us to looking for it.

Acknowledgments

We warmly wish to thank Paul Fish, Suzanne Fish, and Elisa Villalpando for inviting us to participate in the two-day advanced seminar at the Amerind Foundation on trincheras sites, and both the Fishes, Elisa Villalpando, and Barbara Mills for the invitation to participate in the 2002 Southwest Seminar in Tucson. Many people have contributed enormously to the results reported here. Jerry Robertson, Jr. began this work with us, and we were greatly saddened when he recently passed away. We will miss him. We are especially grateful to the following Arizona Site

Stewards who have yet to find a hilltop they did not want to climb in short order: Shelley Rasmussen, Trudy Mertens, Al Enouen, Lila Elam, Tom and Sue Weiss, Jack and Georgia Burton, Bronwyn Butterfield, Judi and Rollie Myers, Sharon Olsen, and Terry Julin. Others who have shared data and helped record sites include Tom Wright, Don Mather, Jerry Ehrhardt and June Freden, Richard Lundin, Mary Spall, Judy Darbyshire, Cathy Baimonte, Paul Lindberg, Bill and Justine Kusner, Bob Dawson, and Gerry Haase. The Sharlot Hall Museum and especially Sandy Lynch have been most generous in cooperating with this project. Peter Pilles has graciously shared his wide and deep knowledge of this area, and with Kelley Hays Gilpin helped Wilcox identify sherd samples from sites in the upper and middle Verde Valley. Jan Bush of the Nature Conservancy helped us to gain access to a number of sites. Jim McKie, Prescott National Forest Archaeologist, has also been unfailingly gracious and helpful. Alan Ferg, Arizona State Museum, provided access to the J. W. Simmons archives. Jodi Griffith, Museum of Northern Arizona Exhibits Department, drafted the figures in her usual exquisite fashion. We look forward to working with all of you as the hilltop survey continues!

8

Crafting of Places

Mesoamerican Monumentality in Cerros de Trincheras and Other Hilltop Sites

Ben A. Nelson

What is the social and processual significance of "Mesoamerican" architectural elements found in Northwest Mexico and the American Southwest? The outstanding examples are ball courts and platform mounds, found most frequently in the Hohokam area. Colonnades are rarer. Roads and causeways, which are common and sometimes prominent, are curiously underexplored in terms of their origins and not often treated as Mesoamerican-inspired. *Cerros de trincheras* are another of the intriguing, Mesoamerican-derived architectural forms, although to my knowledge, Southwestern archaeologists have not treated them as such. When one adds these architectural and landscape-architectural features to the portable artifacts of Mesoamerican derivation (copper bells, conch shell trumpets, figurines, mirrors), it makes an impressive list of imports that calls for explanation.

This chapter is part of a renewed investigation of objects, symbols, and practices that were shared between prehispanic Mesoamerica and the prehistoric American Southwest (Nelson 1994, 1995, 2000, 2001, 2004, 2006; Nelson and Crider 2006). I start from the premise that these forms were Mesoamerican-derived because they appeared first in Mesoamerica and often were more elaborate there. Yet knowing the geographic origin does not go very far in explaining why people in northwest Mexico or the southwestern United States would trouble themselves to obtain or create such products. I assume that each of these items was associated with meaningful, central practices that defined social roles and relations through display and ritual. I further assume that the actors had ways of learning about Mesoamerican practices. Finally, I assume that departures from Mesoamerican practices are as important to understanding significance as are the conformities.

Scholars take a variety of approaches to understanding these shared traditions. Some, such as Pepper (1976), merely note that the Southwestern styles are "reminiscent" of Mesoamerica, while others (Di Peso et al. 1974b; Kelley and Kelley 1975; Turner and Turner 1999) argue for migration, intrusion, or direct control. These traditions probably represent something more than reminiscence, but less than direct intrusion (McGuire 1980; McGuire et al. 1994). Elson (1998) employs a cross-cultural approach to understanding platform mounds, demonstrating the strong probability that platform mounds were part of a strategy of social power. This uniformitarian approach is productive in dealing with aspects of architecture that are culturally indistinct and represent generic symbolism. Yet it leaves us with a limited understanding of how platform mounds resonated with other uniquely Native American symbols to create local social orders. The approach in this chapter is to examine examples of prehispanic Mesoamerican monumental architecture as a basis for suggesting structural analogies for their northern counterparts.

Monuments and Monumentalization

I think of monuments as structures meant to mark the significance of places to the living while pointing to people or events of enduring importance (Bradley 1998). Monuments were anchors in time, not only for territories and periodic gatherings, but also for social premises that required reinforcement. As such, the significance of monuments resided more in their practice-orienting properties and in the extension of social memory beyond the human life span. Physically, monuments were built of highly durable materials and were constructed so as to call attention to particular places. Size, height, color, materials, and design canons were manipulated in ways that conformed to Helms's (1993) skilled crafting. Monument builders evoked the supernatural by creating objects that were out of the ordinary, giving the messages associated with the product special credibility.

The fact that people intended a physical structure to endure does not imply that its meaning went unchanged (Bradley 2000). As with historical texts (Gillespie 1992), the authors altered meanings to suit the purposes of political actors in a given present. Also, similarities in form across space do not in themselves imply constancy of meaning across polities or regions. Probably one of the most common processes was to increase the size of the built features, but even such straightforward changes provided opportunities for shifts in meaning, for example, from an emphasis on the religious to the political. For these reasons, I use *monumentalization* in parts of this discussion, in parallel to Giddens's (1984) *structuration. Monumentalization* denotes the recursive, contextual, variable, and changing properties of monuments.

The fact that meanings attached to monuments vary does not mean that local meanings were entirely independent. Mesoamerican people held long-lived cultural ideals about cities and rulers and strove to replicate them, including in new places (Carrasco 2000). Some Mesoamerican monuments, such as Olmec colossal heads and thrones or altars, were materially stable and culturally central for centuries, only to go out of use, leaving us to muse about their meanings (Gillespie 1999). So it is with cerros de trincheras. Nevertheless, the ideals that cerros de trincheras embodied were present in other sites that provided a fund of reference material for the crafters, as they do for us. I suggest that the practice of referencing ideals and elaborating them over time, in consonance with prevailing styles, is one of the explanations for the spread of Mesoamerican traditions. Visible elements of "civilization" were drawn outward to the hinterlands by aspiring elites who sought effective power symbols expressed in terms of idealized people, places, and deities (Nelson 2006).

The cerro de trincheras phenomenon is the northernmost extension of a varied and extremely widespread kind of site structure. Following Binford (1982), site structure is the arrangement of facilities and artifacts on sites. The distinctions between cerros de trincheras and other hilltop sites become apparent in the discussion below. As a preliminary definition, cerros de trincheras are hilltop sites with residential terraces and areas of public architecture. The ones under consideration, in Sonora, Chihuahua, and Arizona, are outside Mesoamerica by any definition; they are also outside of the area often called the northern Mesoamerican frontier, which more or less encompasses Zacatecas and Durango (Kelley 1956).

As we shall see, the practice of turning landscape-dominating hilltops into sacred ceremonial places is a part of Mesoamerican monumentality. Other chapters in this volume give detail about the nature and distribution of cerros de trincheras. Haury (1976:93–94) suggests that the O'odham historically held dances on natural hills that were substitutes for pyramidal mounds; O'Donovan (2002) extends this idea to suggest that cerros de trincheras may be analogous to pyramids. It is not easy to solidify this idea of Mesoamerican derivation, yet as Haury (1976:93) states, there may be "no persuasive alternative" to the idea that such features were Mesoamerican-inspired.

The nearest roughly contemporary architectural relatives to the cerros de trincheras of Sonora and Chihuahua are in the interior of Mexico, not along the coast where many other signs of Mesoamerican-Southwestern interaction are encountered. Down coast, the nearest terraced hilltop site of which I am aware is Coamiles, on the coastal plain of Nayarit about 1230 km south of Trincheras, Sonora. In contrast, the distribution of cerros de trincheras in Sonora, Chihuahua, and Arizona nearly abuts that of the Loma San Gabriel sites (AD 200–1500) in Chihuahua and Durango (Brooks 1971; Foster 1985, 1995); that distribution, in turn, is contiguous with the Malpaso-Chalchihuites area, which contains elaborate hilltop sites of a kind that is even more common farther south in southern Zacatecas, Jalisco, and Guanajuato. The last sites appear to be most common ca. AD 500–1300. Thus, if one seeks regions from which meanings associated with cerros de trincheras are likely to derive, the most promising would seem to lie along the interior route.

If people who built cerros de trincheras used Mesoamerican models of monumentality to materialize ideologies of power, they should have used some of the specific elements—buildings, embellishments, open spaces, and connective features—as their counterparts in Mesoamerica. In addition to looking at individual types of features, we may compare the volume, durability, variety, energy consumed in construction, and contrasts between residential and public architecture to see whether Sonoran architects may have employed the same metaphors as their counterparts in Mesoamerica.

Similarities should also be apparent in landscape architecture, which I define here as modifications of landscape designed to resonate symbolically with town or village elements of the built environment. Patterns might include placement of ceremonial centers in relation to natural elements, modifications of slopes and ridgetops, and approach features such as roadways or causeways. They might also include the relative placement of residential and ritual features. Messages of social relationship, including power, are likely to be encoded in the architecture of central places. Differences may provide indications of specific Mesoamerican power construction strategies that were absent or little used in the societies that built cerros de trincheras.

Monumentalization and Emergent Social Power

I distinguish three kinds of hilltop sites that occur in Mexico. From north to south, there are (a) cerros de trincheras, (b) hilltop ceremonial centers, and (c) cities on hills. All three play on the natural potential of hilltops for monumentality; the builders selected prominent hills that were striking from a distance, and there is architectural evidence that each was a place of ritual significance. Yet they differ in important ways as well. The sites represent an array of sociopolitical complexity, their associated social systems varying in hierarchy, scale, differentiation, and number of interconnections among social components. This social variation is probably one reason, apart from historical contingency, why cerros de trincheras are not simply smaller versions of the other kinds of sites. The three types of sites represent a continuum of societies analogous to that of big man societies to chiefdoms in Polynesia or rural to urban societies in Mesopotamia, but of course in uniquely American forms.

The characteristics that cerros de trincheras shared and did not share with Mesoamerican hilltop sites help us to understand monumentality in the local context. Perhaps more important, they may allow us to perceive a process of monumentalization characteristic of emergent social power in northern Mesoamerica and beyond. In this trajectory or trajectories, peoples in transition toward hereditary inequality sometimes transformed selected hilltop sites from sacred natural places to paramount political centers and capitals.

Blanton (Blanton et al. 1993) believes that Monte Albán, which may be the archetypical city on a hill, came into being rapidly as what he labels the disembedded capital. In this model, competing polities of roughly equal power subordinated themselves to a new center that they created by mutual agreement and which they deliberately placed in a neutral, previously uninhabited spot. Flannery et al. (1981) and Marcus and Flannery (1996) date Monte Albán's transformation to urbanism ca. 150 BC, and suggest that it quickly spawned a series of similar but lesser centers in a secondary process that they label "synoikism" (Balkansky 1998). Similarly, the Tarascans created a new political landscape by founding new cities and deemphasizing old power centers such as Urichu (Pollard 1996; Pollard and Cahue 1999).

Creating disembedded capitals may be a strategy of urbanized peoples. Polities at that social scale may have been capable of mobilizing materials and labor, forcing practices to change, and reorienting themselves to new forms of rulership. Smaller-scale societies may have had alternative pathways, and it is also possible that archaeologists may have overlooked some of the initial processes of monumentalization in dealing with the depositional complexities of urban centers. A seemingly likely alternative to the disembedded-capital model, especially for regions where urbanism did not occur, was *placecrafting*.

Placecrafting was not a predetermined process but a succession of deliberate acts with changing purposes, a practice of constructing and reworking monuments over long periods. Important elements of this model are Binford's (Binford 1982) notions of place and palimpsest; Helms's (Helms 1993) skilled crafting, and Bradley's (1998, 2000) ideas about monuments and their preservation of ritual practice. The socially constructed hilltop began as a sacred natural spot on a ritual circuit. Suitable to sacralization because of cosmological connotations of the meeting of earth and sky, the hilltop became a place for marking seasonal and celestial changes as well as for rites of passage. Over time and with no determined outcome, ritual specialists became associated with the place as its significance changed. To enhance the effectiveness of ceremonies and maintain memory of the associated messages, they saw to the crafting of individual, small-scale monuments such as offertories and gnomens. Their own burials may have become such monuments, fixing ritual leaders in social memory as idealized ancestral community members.

Generations of placecrafters looked to already established social formations for sources of effective symbolism; in this case rich material was available from the south. They did not and probably could not have copied the corpus of urban symbols, as it must have contained messages about dominance and allegiance that were locally unacceptable. Adding their own twists and fitting symbols to local code, the crafters created products that resonated with regional sensibilities. In the process, the entire hilltop became monumentalized, that is, charged with significance and connection to changing social ideals.

On the surrounding landscape, which was itself altered by the presence of the crafted place, social units situated themselves in relation to the ceremonial center. Families built temporary dwellings at the site to participate in periodic gatherings; perhaps a wider range of celebrations began to occur. Such strategies may have led to conversion of the monumental zone into a continuously occupied ceremonial center. At some point the stakes became such that lineages or households translated ancestor veneration into political claims, appropriating religious power and transforming the sacred place into a center of political power. Symbolic statements of these changing relations, including architecture, were correspondingly elaborated. Even in the city on the hill, the culmination of placecrafting, one can still see the underlying glorification of ancestors, place, and cosmos serving to legitimate a constructed social order.

Nothing in this model of change is meant to imply gradualism, although it illustrates how gradual change may result in transformation. It is likely that "tipping points" (Gladwell 2000) occurred in which rapid political consolidation or religious movement may have changed the trajectory radically, giving political significance to a previously religious place. Also, I do not suggest that these processes are unique to hilltop locations; they could have occurred at any place that became a political capital, regardless of topography.

Cerros de trincheras, very impressive in local context, represent founding behavior in such a process, and may have marked locations of periodic gathering places where stakeholders maintained and frequently rebuilt temporary structures. McGuire et al. (1999) characterize Cerro de Trincheras as a continuously occupied town where a full range of daily activities was conducted and people lived out their lives. I am unsure that the place had reached that state or if it had, whether it had done so long before abandonment. Few of the structures except the monuments were made of permanent materials, and the nature of the debris is subject to alternative interpretation. Such inferences can best be appreciated through comparisons with other sites.

Cerros de Trincheras

As noted above, cerros de trincheras are hill sites that had small house plots set on terraces; some had separate areas of public architecture. The most extensively studied of the cerros de trincheras is Cerro de Trincheras, though others are known; McGuire, Villalpando, and their associates (McGuire and Villalpando 1991) have provided new understanding of that site's architectural characteristics. Fish and Fish (2004) characterize the landscape and other sites in the vicinity of Cerro de Trincheras. Hard and Roney (1998) describe a much earlier (ca. 1200 BC) example called Cerro Juanaqueña.

It is the height of the hill, rather than the artificial construction, that makes Cerro de Trincheras stand out on the landscape. The main architectural elements are terraces and house plots. There are also two areas of public architecture: a playing field or performance area at the base of the hill (La Cancha) and a spiral masonry structure at the top of the hill (El Caracol). The top of the hill is delimited by an enclosure that contains no house plots. This artificial construction would have been impressive to any local inhabitants, yet on a scale defined below by other sites, the cultural modifications appear less dramatic and the natural substructure more significant.

The number of terraces, more than 900, is impressive; McGuire and Villalpando estimate that at least 420 were residential. Most are on the steep north face of the hill overlooking the same section of river bottom where the town of Trincheras is located today. The terraces are typically a few meters wide and 15 to 30 m long; the vertical faces are rough stone retaining walls, typically .05 to 3 m high. A critical question is the length of time over which the terraces were built; if construction was spread over a century, the occupants would have needed to build only nine terraces per year to complete the site. The appearance of such a number of terraces over a much shorter time would imply more concerted social action.

Researchers have indicated that in one sector, terraces were higher and more substantial than elsewhere (McGuire et al. 1999). These same terraces also had somewhat different artifactual assemblages than the rest. This "wealthy barrio" contained evidence of elevated shell production (Vargas 2004) and distinctive ceramic assemblages (Gallaga 2002, 2004). Perhaps significantly, it was located high on the slope, nearest the open hilltop area with the Caracol structure. Perhaps house construction in this barrio was more costly in terms of labor and materials than in the other barrios, paralleling the differences in terrace construction.

One of the striking characteristics of Cerro de Trincheras is the contrast between the impermanence of the houses and the durability of the stone terrace substructures. Residential areas included brush structures, ramadas, and pithouses (McGuire et al. 1999). A few of the terraces had small stone platforms. Other than these and El Caracol on the crest and La Cancha at the base of the hill, few structures or living surfaces were built to last. These patterns allow the suggestion that most of the habitation structures at Cerro de Trincheras were not used year-round.

Another notable attribute of the site is its high ratio of sherds to lithics, apparently about 8:1 (Contreras 2002; Gallaga 2002). The ratio in assemblages from Hohokam settlements to the north is an order of magnitude lower. For example, at two pithouse sites and one Classic compound in Tonto Creek, the ratios encountered by Desert Archaeology researchers were all 1:1 (rounding to the nearest integer; Jeffery Clark, personal communication 2002). This difference possibly can be explained by archaeologists' collection strategies, unusually high water-carrying needs, or low availability of lithic materials. Another possibility, which seems consistent with the impermanence of the shelters, is that many daily activities conducted at the Tonto Creek sites were not conducted at Cerro de Trincheras.

The dead who came to rest at Cerro de Trincheras were deposited in the floor matrix of La Cancha, at the base of the hill. Although it may stretch our minds to do so, evidence suggests that we should view this interment pattern as a means of consecration. The nearest documented example may be the Electra site in San Luis Potosi, where multiple disarticulated skeletons were scattered between floor layers of the plaza (Pijoan Aguadé and Mansilla Lory 1996). The sense apparently was that the ancestors were returned to their underworld origins yet also kept close to the living. Commingling ancestors' bones and depositing them in a public space is unknown in the American Southwest, but is a variant of a pervasive practice in Mesoamerica that McAnany (1995) labels "living with the ancestors."

Hilltop Ceremonial Centers in Zacatecas

The *hilltop ceremonial centers* farther south in the Malpaso and Chalchihuites areas are markedly different from cerros de trincheras in some ways, yet are to some degree comparable in terms of architectural elements, site structure, and landscape architecture. My purpose here is not to make the simple point that the southern centers were more monumental than cerros de trincheras, but to observe that certain of their design principles were or were not employed in cerros de trincheras. I also am not attempting to establish a direct historical relationship, rather to compare different sets of architectural symbols within a broad tradition.

Our main comparative example is La Quemada, where I have worked since 1987. La Quemada is about 1,000 km southeast of Cerro de Trincheras, in the Malpaso Valley of Zacatecas. La Quemada was probably built in the AD 500s, and its main occupation was during the Epiclassic period (AD 600–900) (Nelson 1997; Trombold 1990). Thus, it was not a direct antecedent to Cerro de Trincheras.

La Quemada is one example of an architectural tradition that covered parts of modern Guanajuato, Jalisco, Nayarit, Zacatecas, and Durango, from ca. A.D. 500 to 1400. It now appears that La Quemada was at the northwestern edge of a cultural zone in which hilltop ceremonial centers were common. Archaeologists used to think of La Quemada as an isolated outpost but now know of similar Epiclassic period hilltop ceremonial centers throughout the Malpaso-Chalchihuites-Juchipila region, the Altos, the Bajío, and less commonly in Nayarit. La Quemada is similar ceramically and architecturally to Alta Vista and Cerro Motecuhuzoma, well-known contemporary ceremonial centers in the Suchil Branch Chalchihuites area.

Kelley characterizes the Chalchihuites-area site of Cerro de Motecuhuzoma as a miniature copy of La Quemada. Kelley (1985) suggests that when these latter centers were abandoned ca. AD 950–1000, their inhabitants moved to the north to join allies in the Guadiana branch of the Chalchihuites area. Occupation there persisted until about AD 1350

(Ganot R. and Peschard F. 1995), which means that some Guadiana branch sites were probably contemporary with Cerro de Trincheras. Hilltop sites during this period include Schroeder, Cañon del Molino, and probably Hervideros. La Quemada thus seems to be a model for—or have to have followed the same model as—some of these latter sites. The hilltop ceremonial centers, which belonged to a number of different polities, may have been part of the historical inspiration for the late hilltop ceremonial centers in Durango, and thereby for cerros de trincheras.

As at cerros de trincheras, the main elements of hilltop ceremonial centers are residential terraces and public architecture. Terraces formed the flat spaces necessary for living surfaces and building foundations and made the hilltop more visually imposing and difficult to scale. Though identical in fundamental principles to those of Cerro de Trincheras, these terraces are quite different in morphology. They are well faced with cut stone masonry, which is not as pleasant as Chaco Canyon's finest, but in general more carefully finished than that of Cerro de Trincheras. La Quemada has far fewer terraces than Cerro de Trincheras—about 60 as opposed to 900—but fewer than half of the latter may be residential, and the number for La Quemada does not include an extensive system of agricultural terraces at the base of the hill. Most important, the residential terraces at La Quemada are much grander, some measuring over 100 m long, and quite a few over 30 m wide.

The features atop the terraces at La Quemada were more varied and substantial than those at Cerro de Trincheras. Rather than topping their terraces with simple, lightweight houses and gardens, the Quemadeños built substantial structures of stone, adobe, or sometimes both. They plastered, decorated, and intensively maintained their terraces. In addition to being plastered, many of the outward-facing terrace walls were coated with *cal*, or whitewash. This devotion to architectural maintenance may have been in part a response to erosion; unmaintained adobe buildings on top of rock rubble would have a tendency to disintegrate. Only two terraces have been extensively excavated, but evidence from the surface and from several limited excavations indicates that everywhere in the site, efforts were made to maintain polished, perfected architectural forms. We cannot doubt that strong social signals emanated from these highly visible features.

On each terrace, a series of structures surrounded a main patio, which was defined by banquettes. The banquettes typically formed a U shape, while bedrock formed the upslope side of the patio. The inhabitants placed stone-lined drains beneath patio floors and structures to address the drainage problems inherent in such arrangements. They plastered all patio and outdoor banquette surfaces, and even covered bedrock with plaster where it emerged within a patio-banquette complex.

The smallest patios were focal points for house groups. On a single terrace, several sets of rooms could open onto minor patios; sets of these patio groups were arrayed around a major patio. The occupants of patio groups may have been nuclear family households, and the whole terrace a larger kin unit such as a polygamous or extended family.

Some terraces, possibly all, had ritual architecture consisting of small-scale replicas of more public temples, altars, and ball courts. Terrace 18, for example, had a ball court with a playing surface of 4 × 10 m in its main patio. It also had a temple—a large room that opened onto the main patio—in which ancestral remains were apparently curated (Nelson et al. 1992). Other terraces had central altars, and some had pyramids. This replication of public ceremonial facilities in household contexts is not found at Cerro de Trincheras.

Most of the public ritual architecture at La Quemada was in the site's monumental core. Structures in that part of the site, including terraces, tended to be larger and more substantial than those located elsewhere. No single residential structure stood out as monumental, however, and the basic patio-banquette design was replicated throughout the site and also throughout the valley. Many, though not all, of the buildings in the core were built of cut stone masonry rather than adobe. On the flanks of the site, adobe-block construction dominated and terraces tended to be smaller and lower.

The architects of La Quemada emphasized both exclusivity and connectedness, playing on the landscape as much as on the internal structure of the site. Massive walls enclosed the parts of La Quemada not walled off by cliffs. Staircases and causeways permitted movement among the terraces on the steepest parts of the site, some on alignments that continued out into the Malpaso Valley as roads (Trombold 1991). Some of the destinations of the roads were other hilltops, which in some cases also had monuments. Road-building is an extension of the placecrafting process outward from the isolated monument to embrace and ritualize the entire local landscape (Medina González 2000).

Mesoamerican archaeologists have recently realized that many settlements are structured to replicate cosmological principles (Ashmore and Sabloff 2002); for example, the north-south axis of Lowland Maya sites probably represents a vertical cosmological axis. Medina González (2000) has explored the symbolic significance of the architecture of La Quemada and successfully links it to Huichol cosmology. Many of the architectural elements and roads are plausible expressions of a sky-earth-underworld complementarity that is fundamental to Mesoamerican religions. Lelgemann's (1996) analysis indicates that La Quemada architects employed a standard Mesoamerican measurement unit, and were as concerned as other Mesoamerican architects with astronomical alignments.

As at Cerro de Trincheras, La Quemada's architects reserved flatter parts of the hill for public or specialized structures and created open spaces that were probably used ritually. Also as at Cerro de Trincheras, there were both upper and lower ceremonial spaces. The ceremonial spaces at La Quemada included a huge colonnaded hall facing an unusually large plaza, a long ball court, a pyramid, and a citadel at the north end of the site.

Relations to surrounding villages as well as to the land seem to have been encoded in landscape architecture. People in almost any village in the Malpaso Valley could see and be seen from La Quemada, and were physically and symbolically connected to it by roads. The roads led to other prominent landscape features, as well as to inhabited sites, and oriented processions that were probably astronomically and calendrically organized and linked with performances and feasts. Many constituencies may have jointly maintained La Quemada (Wells 2000), each constructing a terrace to monumentalize its ancestral past.

As at Cerro de Trincheras, the dead were ritually deposited at La Quemada, but in different ways. Stacks, bundles, and suspended sets of long bones and skulls were kept above and below ground, indoors and outdoors, in public and residential spaces (Nelson et al. 1992). We are still sorting out the information, but there may have been as many as six different disposition patterns. Some of the individuals may have been enemies rather than ancestors, but the evidence suggests that ancestors' bones were an important part of this ceremonial center. The remains of historically significant human beings on a highly visible hilltop would help create a sense of space, place, time, community, and status.

Cities on Hills

All of the above-mentioned hilltop ceremonial centers might have been inspired by a single cosmological model of *cities on hills*. The latter were urban centers of bureaucratized, militaristic states, exemplified during the Epiclassic period (AD 600–900) by Xochicalco (González Crespo et al. 1995; Hirth 1995, 2000; López Luján et al. 1995) and Teotenango (Piña Chan 1973)—two of the cities that apparently filled the power void left by the collapse of Teotihuacan.

Central Mexican cities on hills contained many of the above-described elements on a yet grander scale. Some monuments, such as the famous Danzantes of Monte Albán, exhibit written records of conquest (Marcus 1992). Causeways connected separate parts of the sites; large, level areas were dedicated to public architecture, and up to several thousand residential terraces occupied the hillslopes. At Xochicalco, moats, walls, and staircases physically divided the residential areas into what Hirth describes as "wards." Hirth (2000) suggests that some of the central iconographic messages on the Temple of Quetzalcoatl at Xochicalco were about tribute-taking, following Monte Albán's practice in naming the rulers of subjugated places (Marcus 1980, 1992). Multiple, massive ball courts were interspersed with pyramids and palaces.

In the mortuary traditions of the cities on hills, a seemingly constant theme was the glorification of ancestral leaders. The tombs of Monte Albán are one example (McCafferty and McCafferty 1994): semisubterranean structures marked with huge stones, with interiors embellished with an iconography of death and the afterlife. Rich arrays of grave goods accompanied the principals. Again, the ancestors were accorded a permanent status in the life of the community, selected ones playing particularly powerful roles.

In a sense, mentioning these urban centers last is a backward representation of the processes that probably led to the monumentality of Cerro de Trincheras. The Mesoamerican cities probably inspired the cerros de trincheras and hilltop ceremonial centers, rather than vice versa. According to Flannery et al. (1981), Monte Albán was an urban center by 150 BC, preceding the northern examples by several centuries. Monte Albán continued to be occupied as La Quemada arose, and though it clearly suffered setbacks similar to those of Teotihuacan, it was a demographic center when the Spaniards arrived. Cities on hills had to have been known over great distances and spans of time.

Discussion

The similarities and differences between Cerro de Trincheras and other hilltop sites have important implications for social phenomena in their respective regions. How might lived experience at the sites have been similar or different?

There are important structural parallels between cerros de trincheras and Zacatecan hilltop ceremonial centers, and even Central Mexican cities on hills. It is reasonable to think of cerros de trincheras as ultimately referring to an idealized city on a hill, home to powerful social and religious leaders capable of conquest as well as deliverance. In addition to the hilltop setting, features common to all three kinds of places included residential and public architecture, specially prepared open places, staircases, and smaller-scale replicas of the central-site features at other places on the landscape. Also, remains of the dead were maintained in ways that made them impossible to ignore.

In both cerros de trincheras and hilltop ceremonial centers, the buildings nearest the public ceremonial area tend to be the most substantially constructed. Both kinds of sites have high and low ceremonial grounds, although Cerro de Trincheras appears to be the only one of its kind to have this arrangement. The selection of hilltops to make statements of relatedness among people, land, and power does not seem coincidental. A gradation of ritual treatments of ancestors, from commingling them in the floor of a plaza at the foot of the hill to enshrining them individually in tombs at the top, associated the ancestors with the crafted places. Ceremonialists in both regions probably combined sounds and sights to create lasting impressions associated with social power. Symbolic connections with other hilltops and villages in the valley floor were reinforced in a variety of material and nonmaterial ways.

La Quemada's leaders seem to have been more concerned with, or more successful in getting social energy applied to, the elaboration of these themes. A much larger percentage of built space was devoted to ceremonial structures than at Cerro de Trincheras, and La Quemada has a considerably greater variety of monumental forms. La Quemada's monumentality extends beyond the ceremonial center and encompasses the whole Malpaso landscape in ways that one does not find in the Magdalena Valley. Causeways lead dramatically to constructed monuments and were occasionally fitted with small wayside monuments in the form of pyramid-shaped altars like those found in the ceremonial center.

Clearly, monumentality diminished considerably to the north. Structures were more ephemeral, the hilltops were less modified, and some of the main features of monumentality found at hilltop ceremonial centers were absent; one does not find pyramids or colonnades at Cerro de Trincheras, for example. This pattern is consistent with broadly distributed as opposed to concentrated social power, a possibility that must be investigated with other classes of remains. The absence of pyramids and magnificent monumental buildings seems to indicate that hierarchical principles were absent or limited, or else not expressed as clearly in architecture.

The modest degree of monumentality at Cerro de Trincheras is consistent with the lack of evidence for the postmortem aggrandizement of individual lineages' ancestors, practices for which there is evidence at the Zacatecas and Durango hilltop ceremonial centers. Alta Vista has a complex pyramidal tomb on its main plaza (Aveni et al. 1982); La Quemada has 13 pyramids, including one at the north end of its 75-m-long ball court (Nelson 1997). The one La Quemada pyramid that has been excavated systematically contained a ritual burial (Lelgemann 2000). At the same site, it was customary to fill in houses to create substructures for later dwellings; by analogy with other parts of Mesoamerica, one could expect that these platforms contain the memorialized remains of ancestors.

Other striking differences are the sizes of terraces and the nature of the structures that they supported. At La Quemada, one finds temple and ball court monuments replicated inside house groups, a pattern which seems to indicate the appropriation of social power by lineages or similar social units. At Cerro de Trincheras, such monumentality as there was seems to have been more public. Individual households did not have ball courts or pyramids. Terraces and structures at Cerro de Trincheras were also small, possibly indicating that nuclear families rather than more extended groups occupied individual terraces. The social units responsible for the construction of terraces and houses either possessed small labor forces by comparison with those that built the house groups at La Quemada, or chose to invest in construction less heavily.

Conclusions

McGuire et al. (1999) paint Cerro de Trincheras as a town of house and garden plots where residents lived an everyday life. Portions of the town had more evidence of craft activities, and some areas were ceremonial. This characterization is an advance over the vague notion of the site as a trading center responsible for moving shell into the Hohokam region. Yet it seems wise to consider the possibility that many of the residences were only part-time dwellings used for periodic gatherings, as suggested by the low durability of house structures and the unusual artifact ratios.

Mesoamerican perspectives suggest additional conceptions of meaning and process. Central to these conceptions are notions of place (Basso 1996; Binford 1982; Bradley 2000), crafting (Helms 1993), monumentality (Bradley 2000), memory (Carrasco 2000), and ritual landscape (Medina González 2000). Cerro de Trincheras represents early phases in a monumentalization process that in other places went on to produce a hilltop ceremonial center or even a city on a hill. In this view, the *cerro* was first a sacred place for periodic use. Throughout its particular local trajectory, the character of the central place was continuously reworked, its powers perhaps increasingly exploited for political purposes. Whether Cerro de Trincheras in fact achieved the status of town, or had only become a place for periodic gatherings, is a question that in my opinion remains unanswered.

In any event, placecrafting at hilltop sites is testimony to a spectrum of social power unique to the Americas, but in some ways analogous to the continuum found in Melanesia and Polynesia. There, anthropologists have documented a range of social formations including big-man societies and open, traditional, and stratified chiefdoms (Chowning 1979; Godelier 1999; Goldman 1970; Kirch and Sahlins 1992; Lemmonier 1991; Sahlins 1958, 1963). Oceanian strategies of status enhancement emphasized competitive feasting, antagonistic exchange, control of craft specialization, and warfare. Mesoamerican elites and those in the Northwest/Southwest may also have used all of these strategies. Yet a series of recent studies demonstrates that economic approaches to prestige were downplayed at La Quemada (Nelson 2006). I would argue that in these northern regions the ideologies depended heavily on linkages among power, cosmology, time, distance, and place. Architectural creations designed to reinforce these linkages are a major class of evidence for understanding the varieties of ancient indigenous American social power.

Acknowledgments

I thank Paul Fish, Suzanne Fish, and Elisa Villalpando for inviting me to participate in the Trincheras meetings, John Ware for his gracious hosting and management of the Amerind Foundation seminar, and Barbara Mills for organizing the Southwest Symposium at which I read an early version of this chapter. I also thank Randall McGuire and Elisa Villalpando for inviting me to comment on the subsequent Society for American Archaeology symposium. Margaret Nelson, Christopher Fisher, and two anonymous reviewers provided very useful comments, although they are not responsible for my corruptions of their ideas. I am grateful to Jeffery Clark and Desert Archaeology, Inc., for providing ceramic data from the Tonto Basin sites. The fieldwork at La Quemada was conducted with the permission of the Instituto Nacional de Antropología e Historia, and I am indebted to Joaquin Garcia Barcena, Lorena Mirambell, Alejandro Martinez Muriel, Jose Luis Perea, Jose de la Cruz Pacheco Rojas, Peter Jimenez Betts, and Baudelina Garcia, of that institution. Financial support came from the National Science Foundation (Grants 8806238 and 0211109), the National Endowment for the Humanities, the Wenner-Gren Foundation for Anthropological Research, the Foundation for the Advancement of Mesoamerican Studies, and an anonymous private donor.

9

Concluding Observations

Perspectives from the Hill Towns of Oaxaca

Stephen A. Kowalewski

Four Questions

What Are Trincheras Sites?

Trincheras sites, or *cerros de trincheras*, is a colloquial, nontechnical term for hills in the Basin and Range province that have artificial terraces or other rockwork. This is the consensus definition reached by the Amerind Foundation seminar. It is a behaviorally neutral definition, implying nothing about function, cultural affiliation, or age. The geographical limiting criterion is useful. Not all hills used by people anywhere are cerros de trincheras. Trincheras sites may have certain behavioral or formal parallels to hilltop sites of the Mogollon Rim, the Colorado Plateau, or Mesoamerica, but the shared characteristics do not automatically make sites in those areas part of the phenomenon considered here.

Why Are Trincheras Sites Significant?

For people outside of archaeology and within our discipline, cerros de trincheras have an importance greater than their small numbers might suggest. They are spectacular and enduring. Trincheras sites are still visible as monuments (as discussed in Nelson's chapter). From the ground or from the air, their images present views into the past that are rarely afforded by other archaeological sites in Basin and Range country. Their rockwork—terraces, walls, enclosures, paths, etc.—offer ready material for the imagination and for the testing of ideas about past community organization. As described in the preceding chapters of this volume, trincheras sites have attracted the attention of major figures in the history of archaeology and geography and have become subjects of varying interpretations and of methodological and theoretical debate. This book also demonstrates that significant scientific advances have been made toward understanding cerros de trincheras.

What Is New in This Book?

If one's ideas about trincheras congealed before 1998, it is time to toss them out and read this book. Thirty years ago there was far more interpretation of and speculation about trincheras sites than there were data about them. Since then, archaeological investigation aimed at trincheras sites and their larger contexts has produced much more information, and many surprises. There is now much better basic information from mapping, regional surveys, surface collections, excavations, floral and faunal studies, environmental work, and chronology. The authors of this volume have directed most of the trincheras research in the last 20 years. This is the first synthesis and comparison of the sites using the new information. The book is selective, for not all trincheras sites or regions with trincheras sites could be covered equally. The authors do synthesize and compare all the major mapping-plus-excavation projects in Chihuahua, Sonora, and Arizona.

This book provides considerable new detail on activities at trincheras sites. The authors offer further documentation on modes of construction and performance characteristics of various types of rock features. Like other sites, cerros de trincheras have to be seen in their local, regional, and macroregional contexts. Much research still needs to be done in this regard, but this is the first time so much of the settlement system context has been described.

What Are the Broader Conclusions?

Cerros de trincheras are distinctive and special to the Basin and Range province, but they are not a unitary phenomenon. To use the term *cerro de trincheras* does not imply particular situational, formal, cultural, functional, or behavioral characteristics, because the sites differ from one another in all these respects, and because some share characteristics with certain hilltop sites outside this area. For example, there are trincheras sites whose main feature is a rock enclosure at the top of the hill, there are others with small, separate terraces, and still others have long, free-standing walls. Some date to 1250 BC and others to AD 1250. Trincheras sites are not all the same thing.

By emphasizing that trincheras sites are not a unitary phenomenon, we also mean that these sites will not have a single interpretation. It is simply and demonstrably not true that "trincheras sites were [agricultural] or [ceremonial] or [fortifications] or [refuges] or [monuments]"—because as a class not all of the sites were any of these things, primarily or perhaps even in part. Some have little public architecture, others were poor defensive sites, and others have no more space to cultivate plants than the average apartment house balcony. In short, there is no single explanation for trincheras sites. This does not mean that there are not viable, testable explanations to come out of controlled comparisons, within and beyond the Basin and Range province. Each of the chapters in this volume describes regional cerros de trincheras phenomena and compares these to those in other regions.

The cerros de trincheras phenomenon is at least 2,700 years old. The span includes very different cultural contexts, from the Late Archaic or Early Agricultural periods through the early "Pottery Neolithic" to Classic Hohokam and late prehistoric times. Trincheras site construction and occupation was episodic, sometimes occurring for durations of two centuries or less, separated in some cases by several hundred years of little or no use.

The surface and excavated remains of domestic and other activities at most trincheras sites undercut any general hypothesis of a predominantly agricultural use. Possible garden space and well-documented agricultural features such as waffle gardens and water diversions are found in limited areas at some trincheras sites, including Cerro Prieto. There are no trincheras sites where the predominant rock features are agricultural. Instead, garden features seem to be integral to domestic space or were small "infield" plots near residences.

Larger trincheras sites with domestic features were sometimes among the top population centers of their regions. In some cases cerros de trincheras villages may have had higher densities of population than contemporary valley-floor settlements. These large populations and higher densities raise questions about whether cerros de trincheras communities were organized differently from their valley-floor contemporaries.

This issue is relevant to the Arizona and Sonora sites, and also to the Cerro Juanaqueña Early Agricultural period system, where presumably the cerro de trincheras communities were more tightly bound than those of their neighbors.

The older and oft-heard idea that trincheras sites were places of temporary refuge or retreat in time of war receives little support here. To clarify, the refuge hypothesis would have trincheras sites constructed as special, prebuilt fortifications where people would have moved from their settlements on valley floors for brief times—weeks, months, a season—under threat of raids or war. As shown by McGuire and Villalpando, and by Downum, the sites with the most excavation evidence exhibit instead the full range of domestic architecture and artifacts to be found in the permanent valley-floor settlements. The quantities of artifacts are likewise similar to those expected in permanently occupied villages. Some of the trincheras sites with the lowest surface densities of domestic artifacts are also those with feeble defensive characteristics, for example SON F:10:130 in the Cerro de Trincheras settlement system (chap. 6). It is difficult to prove that a settlement was *never* a temporary refuge, but this particular response to threat has little or no empirical support in this part of the Southwest.

The military suitability of trincheras—for some sites and at some times more than others—should not be denied. Quite a few of the sites described in these pages were fortified villages or hamlets, including the Juanaqueña system, Tumamoc Hill in the Tucson Basin, and some trincheras sites in the Papaguería (e.g., DD:6:1, Stacey 1974:143–148). Cerro de Trincheras was a town with good defensive (and thus offensive) capabilities. The Tucson and Phoenix basins do not have the amount of fortification and other evidence of warfare as do some of their outlying upland regions (e.g., the settlement systems described in chapter 7 by Wilcox et al.). The temporary-refuge idea has little support, yet settlements were built on hilltops and fortified in varying degrees.

In other ways besides warfare the character and mix of activities at trincheras sites had much to do with the roles they played in local, regional, and macroregional social systems. In the Tortolita phase (AD 550–650), Tumamoc Hill must have been an important central place in the Tucson Basin. It had a fairly large population, and although some areas on the top of the hill were bulldozed during twentieth-century construction, earlier accounts describe what must have been considerable ceremonial space (chap. 3). One intriguing result of the comparisons in this volume is the pattern of stone "corrals" of similar sizes and associations. Sites with corrals had importance in ceremonies practiced over very extensive areas and quite different archaeological traditions, from at least the Cerro de Trincheras region north into the mountains beyond the Phoenix Basin (chap. 6).

To me the research in this volume shows that trincheras sites were usually *central places* in networks of other places. Central places offer special goods or services not available in households or in ordinary settlements (the inhabitants of central places may carry out basic activities). Central places may be ranked by the numbers and types of functions they provide. This is clear for the northwestern Sonora settlement system (chaps. 5 and 6), where the main center, Cerro de Trincheras, had more and larger architectural facilities for ceremonies. Smaller trincheras sites in the region often had ceremonial areas, but these were fewer and smaller. Other places were central places as well, for example, the larger Tortolita-phase villages such as Valencia Vieja in the Tucson Basin, and the platform mound sites in the Classic period Marana Community. Yet cerros de trincheras were special in their mix of functions and distinctive in their architecture and hilltop situation.

In sum, the trincheras research described in this volume reached four general conclusions:

1. Trincheras hills are not a unitary phenomenon. They are not all the same thing and therefore cannot be accounted for by a single label or explanation.
2. Cerros de trincheras have great time depth and were built and used in quite different cultural systems. Minimally, there were episodes of trincheras site construction about 1250 BC, 300 BC, AD 500, AD 1000–1200, and AD 1200–1450.
3. Recent research summarized in this book provides detailed documentation of the natural settings, many types of rock construction, domestic architecture, artifacts, and floral and faunal remains. This new evidence shows (a) that trincheras sites were used for multiple purposes and (b) that the mix of features and activities varies considerably between trincheras sites.

4. The character of cerros de trincheras, including the types of architectural features and activities, can be better understood when these sites are analyzed as parts of local, regional, and macroregional settlement systems.

These same four conclusions also apply to research on hilltop terraced sites in Mesoamerica, specifically Oaxaca in southern Mexico, which has many such sites and is the area I know best. There are many parallels between what we have been finding out about hilltop terraced sites in Oaxaca and the trincheras site research in the Northwest/Southwest. In the following pages I draw on these parallels to illustrate in greater detail the results that I have just outlined.

Oaxaca Perspectives on Trincheras Research

In the (Oaxaca) Beginning: Monte Albán

I saw my first hilltop terraced site in Oaxaca in 1970. I did not know what I was seeing. This was Monte Albán, the most famous archaeological site in Oaxaca. At the time, all archaeological attention was on the monumental architecture around the Main Plaza. Another terraced hilltop site I saw but did not understand was the Fortress at Mitla. I walked up that hill many times, seeing the artifacts on the sides of the hill and noting that there was Classic period occupation in addition to the fortress walls and the standing adobe structures inside the walls, which dated later, in the A.D. 1300s. But I did not realize that I was walking up and down across residential terraces. My ignorance of hilltop terraced sites and their prominence in the archaeological record was shared, for no one knew much about these sites.

When Richard Blanton began the Monte Albán mapping project in 1971, he used terraces as the units of collection and analysis (Blanton 1978). Monte Albán covers the top and sides of a mountain that rises 500 m above the valley floor. It looms over modern Oaxaca City just as Tumamoc Hill looks over downtown Tucson. In three field seasons Blanton's project mapped more than 2,000 residential terraces, roads, houses, pyramid mounds, water control features, craft specialization areas, a large defensive wall, and a probable market plaza. He conclusively demonstrated that Monte Albán was not a vacant ceremonial center or a necropolis (it had been called that in the literature), but a real city. Monte Albán's founding date was in the Middle Formative, about 500 BC. At that time, 2,000 km to the north, the earliest occupation on the hilltop terraced site of Cerro Juanaqueña was already ancient history, having been abandoned for some 600 years.

Residential or Agricultural Terraces?

A basic fact demonstrated by the Monte Albán Survey and Mapping Project, and confirmed again and again by survey and excavation, is that the terraces in settlements were overwhelmingly residential, not agricultural. Virtually the entire surface area of these terraces was taken up by buildings, patios, paved floors, stairs, ramps, walkways, and walls. There was no space for milpa and little for kitchen gardens, although a few garden plants, maguey, nopal, and trees (*cazahuate*, *guaje*, etc.) probably were planted around terrace edges.

Several additional observations concerning agricultural terraces come from our experience since the Monte Albán project. First, there are pre-Columbian agricultural terraces in Oaxaca that can be recognized archaeologically. These are cross-drainage chains of substantial terraces and retaining walls, called *lama-bordos*; smaller check-dam terraces; and broad, contour terraces on hillside slopes (Kirkby 1972; Smith and Price 1994; Spores 1969). All continue to be made today, and except for some contour terraces, they are distinct from residential terraces. Second, we have sometimes had difficulty in identifying terraces at the lower boundaries of residential terrace settlements. In one kind of situation, a hill meets the valley floor rather abruptly, and its residential terraces run all the way to the bottom of the slope. Because of alluviation we may not see any surface indication of archaeological remains that may have continued onto the valley floor. This may be like the north side of Cerro de Trincheras. Another problem, which is fairly common, is our difficulty in identifying the last, lowest residential terraces on slopes that are recently cultivated. Farmers plow, modify, or obliterate ancient terraces, and build new ones; artifacts may end up below inhabited terraces as refuse tossed from above, or they work their way downslope by plowing or erosion. These factors can make it difficult to tell if one is on a residential terrace, an ancient agricultural terrace, or a modern agricultural terrace.

Why Live up There?

As we clambered up- and downslope all day on the Monte Albán project, our recurring question was, "Why did those crazy people go to the trouble of living up here?" The same sentiment is echoed in the first lines of chapter 3, "Why on earth would anyone want to live atop Tumamoc Hill?" After 30 years and many field seasons of climbing up and down terraced slopes, here is the best I can do for an answer (with the disclaimer that archaeology is not paleopsychology). First, the question is a bit ethnocentric. It is not likely that Monte Albán's or Tumamoc's builders and inhabitants were as bothered by the mountain slopes as we are. Still, living atop high hills seems wasteful of energy unless there are reasons for doing so. In some cases people moved onto hills under duress. They had to because other communities were doing so and the threat of war was immediate. The threat cannot be shown in all cases, however, and in Oaxaca hilltop terraced settlements persisted as communities for centuries after their initial founding. I therefore add a consideration contained in a statement by Christian Downum in chapter 4: "cerros de trincheras [were] rather aggressive political and symbolic statements, designed to send a message to other groups on the landscape regarding territorial control and political power. . . . highly visible monuments commemorating the power (and implied threat) represented by a cooperating village unit or other population aggregate." In other words, the energetic cost of hilltop life was offset if membership in a highly cooperative group afforded certain rights, privileges, protections, access, and clout. It was not just the warfare—there are two significant processes at work—but also the simultaneous formation of new social groups with new collective institutions. One material manifestation of the cooperative institutions is rockwork and slope modification requiring planning and labor beyond the household scale. If my interpretation of what Downum suggests is true, then a comparison of hilltop terrace-site households with those on valley floors should show the fruits of these corporate advantages. Why did people live up on the hills? The best answer I can give is that hilltop sites had social, politico-economic, and offensive-defensive advantages. Being part of a cooperating group was worth the climb (as you yell to the kids if they complain when you send them for water).

Evolving Field Methods

In 1974 I did a systematic survey of about 250 km^2 surrounding Monte Albán, in the central part of the Valley of Oaxaca. Here we used techniques for valley floor survey developed by Basin of Mexico researchers and brought to Oaxaca by Blanton. I encountered two hilltop terrace sites, El Mirador and Loma de la Concepción. I had 1:5,000 scale aerial photos, not the 1:1,000 photos that we had used on the Monte Albán project. I had to work out another technique for terrace mapping so we would have results comparable to the Monte Albán study but still cover all the sites in the 250 km^2. It was a methodological problem not resolved until the next major project, when we were confronted with dozens of hilltop terraced sites, many of them with hundreds of terraces.

We returned to the Valley of Oaxaca in 1977 to survey its southern arm and its northern, Etla branch. We worked out techniques to efficiently map terraces and terraced sites in the context of a regional survey. We drew each terrace in pencil on 1:5,000 aerial photos. We took notes on each terrace, assessed their phases of occupation from the ceramics, noted other artifacts, and measured the terraces by pacing. Where terraces were dense and easy to find, as at certain parts of Jalieza, a good crew of two people (such as Fausto Olivera and Laura Finsten) could map 120 terraces a day. That's much faster than at Monte Albán, but we were sacrificing detail, such as a collection for every terrace, in favor of regional coverage. Also, by 1977 we were more experienced with hilltop terrace sites, and we were able to separate essential from redundant information. We mapped all the terraces at every site whose terraces were substantially intact. By the end of the 1980 field season we had surveyed all of the Valley of Oaxaca, finding about 2700 sites and 6,353 components. Of these, 358 components had residential terraces and in 134 components terracing was a substantial part of the settlement. The sample of residential terraces mapped amounted to some 9,000 (Kowalewski et al. 1989, 1:34–35; more illustrations of Valley of Oaxaca terraced sites and aerial photos showing mapping techniques are in Kowalewski 1990).

Hilltop Terraced Sites Were Not Refuges

By this time we could reject several suggestions that always seem to come up. Were the terraced sites retreats or refuges used in times of conflict? The answer, with only a handful of possible exceptions, is no. The amount of ordinary domestic debris, the longevity of occupation, and the investment in substantial construction all argue strongly against the idea that terraced hilltop sites were temporary refuges. McGuire and Villalpando make the same case for Cerro de Trincheras, and I agree with them. The hilltop terraced sites in Oaxaca were in most cases villages and towns, and likewise the large cerros de trincheras in the Cerro de Trincheras settlement system.

The Valley of Oaxaca has several hilltop terrace sites that, one might argue, were paired with nearby valley-floor towns. Santa Ana Tlapacoyan, in the southern part of the valley, is one such case: a defensible hilltop terrace site is across the river and only 2 km from a contemporary valley-floor town of about the same size. This is similar to the Tucson and Cerro Prieto situations, where cerros de trincheras are parts of multi-site platform mound communities. But again it is difficult to claim that the hilltop site is a refuge for the valley towns when the former has the same range of domestic structures, artifacts, and refuse as the latter.

Gary Feinman, Linda Nicholas, and their colleagues have shown through stratigraphic excavation what we already had thought from surface evidence (Feinman et al. 2002). At El Palmillo, near Santiago Matatlán in the eastern arm of the Valley of Oaxaca, the terraces have a record of habitation and remodeling stretching over hundreds of years, with all the domestic features and artifact types found in excavations at valley-floor sites. The next level of analysis should contend with the more subtle issue of the ways in which households in hilltop terrace communities were different from those in valley-floor communities.

Central Places

After the 1977 and 1980 field seasons, we realized that Monte Albán was not alone in being a hilltop terraced site. It wasn't only a question of why Monte Albán, but why so many people all over the Valley of Oaxaca were living in high, out-of-the-way places. For the six phases from 500 BC to AD 900, from 40 to 60 percent of the total population lived at hilltop terraced sites (after AD 900 the figure falls to 20 percent) (Elam 1989:404). We addressed this question with two lines of research. One brought out the defensive characteristics of hilltop terrace sites. The other was to use our field observations on the terraces and their artifacts to show that hilltop terrace sites had multiple functions and roles in the regional system.

J. Michael Elam, who as a member of the 1980 project saw his share of hilltop terraced sites, made the case for defensibility (1989). Elam was careful not to say that defense was the only function of terraced sites. His argument was based on design characteristics of terraces and terraced sites that match military designs cross-culturally. He was also aware of David Wilcox's paper that had made a similar argument for Tumamoc Hill. He compared the Valley of Oaxaca hilltop terrace sites (especially those of the Early Classic) to legionary fortresses of the Roman Principate, concluding that both types of sites "(1) monitored and maintained their respective system's limits, (2) were propaganda showpieces of the power of their systems, (3) served as centers for production, distribution, and trade, (4) were administrative centers of frontier areas, (5) were magnets for the attraction and exploitation of immigrants, and (6) were centers for the dissemination of their respective system's culture" (Elam 1989:394).

There is a potential problem of logic in the idea of a system or supralocal defensive ring in a basin such as the Valley of Oaxaca, the Tucson Basin, or the San Pedro Valley. Except for a few basaltic hills in the middle of the Valley of Oaxaca, and Monte Albán, which is a sedimentary rock remnant on the valley floor, the suitable places for a settlement with terraces are of course the encircling foothills or the mountains. The sites will thus by necessity line up on the edge of the valley. If there are enough of them, the sites will be intervisible. To demonstrate a supralocal system of strong points, other factors need to be brought to bear, as Wilcox et al. do in chapter 7. (The site classification in that chapter makes reasonable distinctions, but the names for the categories, such as lookouts and retreats, are behaviorally loaded, as the authors acknowledge.)

As part of the excellent, holistic Juanaqueña project, Hard and Roney have carried out the cross-cultural study of hilltop settlements that, given all the hilltop sites in Oaxaca, we should have done years ago.

Elam had drawn on studies of war in the Classical world, but the cases cited in chapter 2 are from a broader range of societies. (It may be useful to consult Ungar's *Archaeological Problem of Defense: Historic Settlement Patterns in the Var Valley System, Southwestern France* [1978]. She must have had trincheras sites in mind, having worked with Stacey on sites in the Papaguería.) One interpretation of the Juanaqueña Early Agricultural settlement system is that the people who built the early cerros de trincheras did so because as (newly arrived?) farmers they needed protection from surrounding hunter-gatherer groups. Another interpretation would reverse the explanation: to counter pressure from surrounding groups, local people built trincheras sites—and as a consequence of the rather sudden nucleation, sedentism, and larger group size, had to intensify food production, thus committing themselves to maize agriculture. This latter scenario would be similar to a fairly common cross-cultural pattern of "intensification under duress" (Kowalewski 2003). Much more needs to be known about groups along and around the Rio Casas Grandes before, during, and after the Juanaqueña episode.

In both Oaxaca and the Northwest/Southwest, terraced sites are multiple phenomena and have multiple explanations. Similarities exist among subsets, especially when the chronology of construction and use can be determined. Hilltop terraced sites in Oaxaca were not at all alike. Some had more defensive features than others. They varied considerably in size, public architecture, number of terraces, terrace dimensions, period of occupation, amount of craft production, distribution of wealthier households within the settlement, and longevity. We subjected our surface survey data on these hilltop terraced-site variables to exhaustive multivariate regression and cluster analyses. The analysis (Kowalewski et al. 1989, 1:240–245) turned up no strong patterning or clustering along any of these dimensions. The terraced sites seemingly had developed a resistance to typology. For the Early Classic, however, which had the most and best-preserved terraced sites, there was some weak patterning—tendencies rather than bounded types. We found three subsets of terraced sites that had somewhat distinctive mixes of functions: centers with administrative and production/exchange functions; production and exchange centers; and strategic, garrison or short-term, military sites. More intensive collecting and excavating would be necessary to confirm these assignments. As a step in this direction, Finsten (1996) analyzed large, intensively collected surface samples from Jalieza, a multicomponent terraced site of urban proportions that we had identified as a center with administrative and production/exchange functions. She showed how both terraces and artifacts varied along dimensions of social stratification, craft specialization, and time.

There were geographical patterns in the distribution of these three types of Early Classic centers. Places with administrative functions were centers of local territories. Places with the most evidence for production and exchange were located in the eastern or Tlacolula arm of the valley, where there was generally more emphasis on craft production, not only at hilltop sites. The small, short-term sites interpreted as having more exclusively military functions were situated at strategic points on the valley's edges.

Another geographical pattern that emerged from this study was the complementary distribution of labor-rich/land-poor hilltop communities versus land-rich/labor-poor valley-floor communities. The valley-floor towns seemed to have had larger numbers of wealthier households, larger mounds, more elaborate tombs, more elaborate iconographic display objects, and more possibilities for irrigation than the hilltop towns. This dichotomy suggests a flow of labor between hilltop communities and large valley-floor estates. Carefully designed research and more excavation data are required, first to verify the geographical pattern and then to assess the difficult problem of flow or interdependence.

The point is that variation in the goods and services provided by central places—in this case hilltop terraced sites—depends on the roles that centers play in a regional social system. Note, for example, the differences between Cerro de Trincheras and the small, farming settlements around it on the valley floor, and the variation in ceremonial facilities among the hilltop sites in the Cerro de Trincheras regional system (chaps. 5 and 6). As is illustrated by Tumamoc Hill and the Tucson Basin data in general (chaps. 3 and 7), regional systems change over time, and so do the roles played by their component settlements. At Tumamoc, there are at least two distinct periods of occupation, and in successive periods the earlier ruins were taken over, modified, and likely obliterated in some cases (chap. 3).

Hilltop Town Planning

In 1990, I worked with Laura Finsten on a survey of 1,000 km^2 in Peñoles, an area adjoining the Valley of Oaxaca to the west (Finsten 1996). Peñoles is all mountains. All the archaeological sites are on ridgetops (like Hard and Roney's "limited options" coding category, chap. 2). All sites larger than a hamlet had to have terraces. Many of these terrace sites are very well preserved. We again had to adjust our survey techniques, this time to the mountainous terrain. We wanted to take advantage of the opportunity to map well-preserved sites while still covering a large region. Because the Peñoles mountains are forest-covered, aerial photos were of little help. By 1990, however, the Mexican government had published excellent 1:50,000 scale topographic maps. We used these to locate ourselves and to plot sites. We mapped architecture (terraces, walls, mounds, plazas, etc.) on graph paper and, in an elaborate process, combined the field drawings with the contour lines of the topographic maps to make site maps (Smith 1993).

Mapping the well-preserved terraced sites in Peñoles produced unanticipated results. We realized that sites differed in how the residential terraces were built and arranged. The layouts came in two forms (actually two ends of a continuum, with hybrids and other possible layouts in between). The most common form was a cascade of small, often interconnected, usually single-house terraces (fig. 9.1). Most sites had this layout, and variations on this theme were also the most common forms in the Valley of Oaxaca. The other layout we saw in Peñoles was the doughnut, or concentric rings of long terraces, on which several houses shared the common terrace and retaining wall (fig. 9.2). These terraces were sometimes 70 m or more long. They followed the contour around a conical peak and were usually arranged in several tiers, one below the other. There are also several examples of the concentric-ring layout in the Valley of Oaxaca. We began to realize that the concentric ring sites were earlier (Late Formative to Early Classic), and the terrace cascades were later (Classic and Postclassic). This was our first clue of a strong temporal pattern, the significance of which we would understand only in 1999, after our work farther west in the Mixteca Alta.

Our 1999 Central Mixteca Alta Settlement Pattern Project (Balkansky

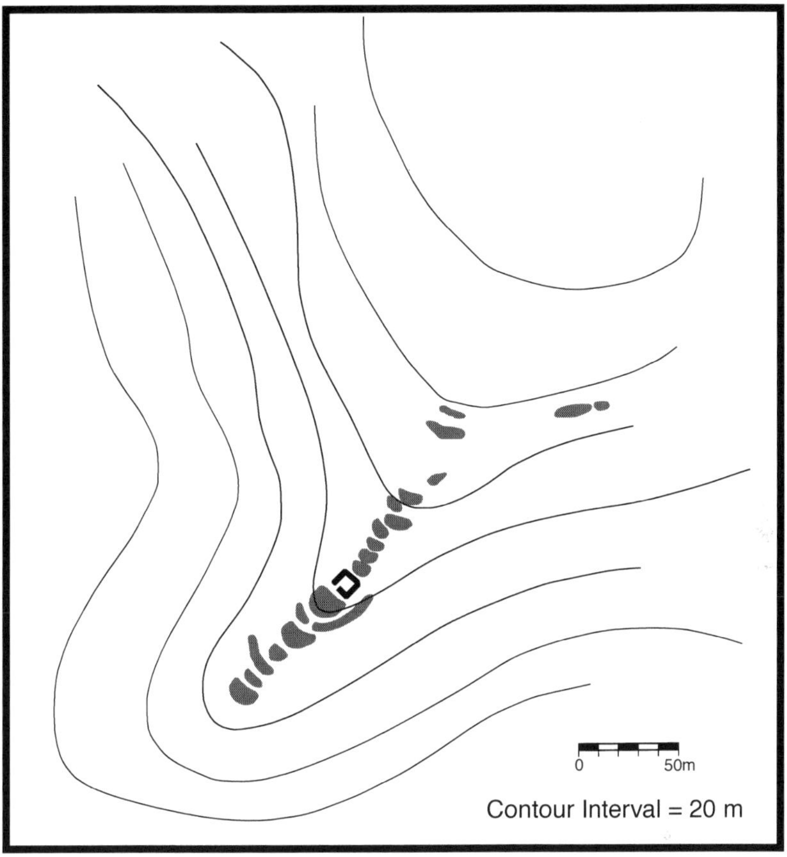

9.1 A portion of ET-SMP-RO-3, a simple, one-terrace-wide cascade.

et al. 2000) provided a whole new perspective on the old question about why people would live on hilltops and at a place like Monte Albán. The Mixteca Alta is west and north of Peñoles. Our project, together with the earlier surveys in the Teposcolula Valley and Huamelulpan, covered about 1500 km^2. The terrain consists of very small valleys surrounded by mountains. Hilltop terrace sites are common, but because the soils are so eroded, residential terraces were often not preserved. Nevertheless, we mapped dozens of terraced sites.

A striking difference between the central Mixteca Alta and our earlier study areas has to do with the layouts of terraces. In Peñoles we found

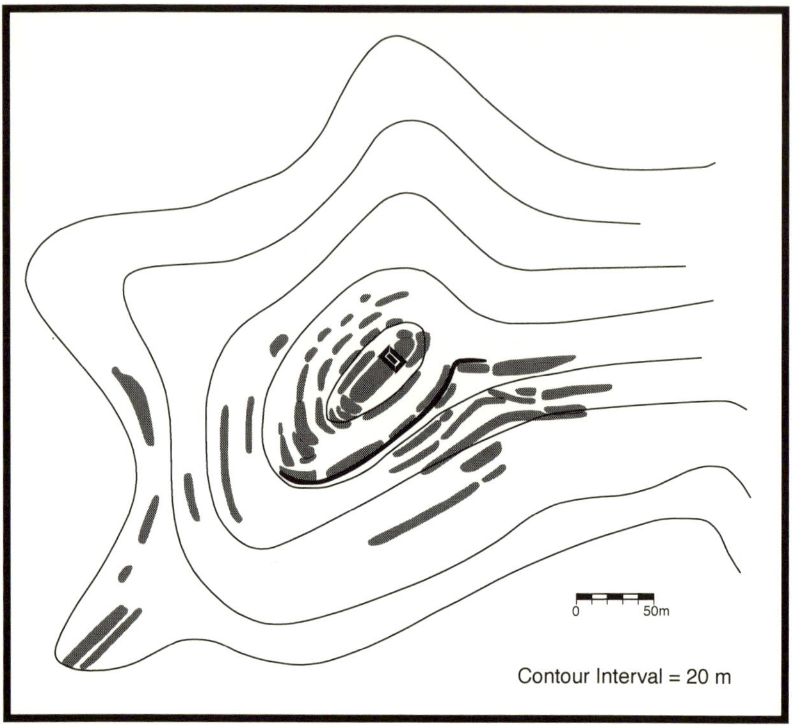

9.2 A portion of NO-SDN-OA-1, a knob with concentric rings of terraces, some sharing a high, common wall.

more concentric-ring terrace layouts than in the Valley of Oaxaca. Moving farther west, into the central Mixteca Alta, the concentric-ring layout became even more prevalent, and the other type (the cascade of terraces) was less common.

Why were concentric rings of terraces favored in one area (the central Mixteca Alta), and cascades of single terraces in Peñoles and the Valley of Oaxaca? People could have constructed settlements with either layout type in all these places. One thing is clear: the concentric-ring layout is early. This is the form of the earliest hilltop terraced sites in the Mixteca Alta, dating to the Late Formative, 300–100 BC. During this period almost all the villages and towns were "doughnut sites," often with 4- to 5-m-high retaining walls. Virtually all people in much of the Mixteca Alta lived in such communities during the Late Formative.

Local to Macroregional Context, over Time

We now have a better sense of the sequence of events that involved the origins and spread of hilltop terraced sites. As it turns out, the founding of Monte Albán was part of this history. The following is a five-step sequence for highland central Oaxaca, in which broad-scale political-economic processes play out differently in the central Mixteca Alta, Peñoles, and the Valley of Oaxaca.

1. Early and Middle Formative, to 500 BC. All over highland Oaxaca, from the Valley of Oaxaca through the Mixteca Alta, people lived in clusters of villages and hamlets, usually with a larger head town. These settlement clusters were on and adjacent to well-watered, valley-floor land. There were more people in the Mixteca Alta than in the Valley of Oaxaca.

2. Middle Formative, 500–300 BC. Some people moved to hilltop sites adjacent to the valley floors. This may have happened at one or two places in the Mixteca Alta, but the major move was the establishment of Monte Albán. If Monte Albán was founded as a new, regional capital to counter outside competition (Blanton 1978), the Mixteca Alta's large population would be a prime candidate for that competition. In any case, the founding of Monte Albán set off an urban transformation of the Valley of Oaxaca, affecting almost every aspect of the cultural system and inducing rapid growth (Blanton et al. 1999). The Mixteca Alta was not so totally transformed (yet) and did not grow as much.

3. Late Formative, 300–100 BC. The Valley of Oaxaca continued to grow and urbanize rapidly. A few hilltop terrace sites were added, probably of the concentric-ring layout. In the Mixteca Alta, a very different process occurred. Almost all valley floor settlements were abandoned, and their inhabitants constructed scores of fortified hill towns with concentric rings of terraces (Kowalewski et al. 2006). These were a new kind of collectively organized community. We see this as a response to violence from within the Mixteca Alta or from without. Monte Albán and the new Valley of Oaxaca state may have been one threat.

4. Terminal Formative, 100 BC–AD 200. In the Valley of Oaxaca the growth that had characterized this region slowed, and in some areas there was a retraction and nucleation of settlement. In the Mixteca Alta, almost all of the fortified hill towns were abandoned. Large expanses of territory were left unoccupied. Population consolidated into a handful of large, dense, urban settlements, which included large terraced sites. These urban clusters would have been the political competitors or peers of Monte Albán.

5. Transition and Early Classic, AD 200–500. Population grew in all areas, and urbanization and differentiation of settlement types increased. In the Mixteca Alta, the areas left vacant during the previous period were reoccupied. Most of the old fortified hill towns were also reoccupied, and new hilltop terraced sites were built. There were nonterraced sites too, and hilltop terraced sites displayed a greater variety of sizes, forms, and functions than they had in the Late Formative. The increasing differentiation was also true for the Valley of Oaxaca.

In the sequence just summarized, macroregional political turmoil played a crucial role in shaping regional settlement systems. The history of hilltop terraced sites is closely linked to these events. Monte Albán and perhaps one or two would-be competitors in the Mixteca Alta were the first hilltop terraced sites. Within 200 years, by the Late Formative, the wave had grown—especially in the Mixteca Alta, where terraced hill forts became the predominant settlement type in a militarized landscape. These were collective or communal hill towns, a new type of community that may have lived on for a long time thereafter. By the Early Classic, terraced hill towns had diversified in form and function, becoming, like other settlements, differentiated centers in complex regional divisions of labor (see Heredia Espinoza 2005 for a comparative study of social stratification in large hilltop terraced sites in the Mixteca Alta).

What about the problem of site layouts—concentric rings of long terraces versus cascades of small ones? It is at the earlier sites, those built to counter the threat of violence, where the concentric ring is typical. Because of the tight packing of terraces, the high and continuous retaining walls, and the controlled access from one level of terraces to the next, the concentric ring design had clear military advantages. The long, high retaining walls and multiple-house terraces also point to a suprahousehold cooperation in design and labor. We have interpreted these early hill towns as collectives in which the organizational emphasis was given to the community level of integration.

Cascades of small, single-house terraces did not require as much community-level design or commitment. In hilltop sites dominated by narrow cascades of small terraces, the organizational emphasis would not have been on the town itself. Instead, no one level of integration—household, barrio, community, or polity—stands out. This tended to occur more often in the Epiclassic and Postclassic periods, especially in Peñoles and the Valley of Oaxaca.

The distinction between concentric rings of long terraces versus cascades of many small terraces has no exact parallel in the Northwest/Southwest. However, it may be productive to think along similar lines. Could the layouts of terraces and other rockwork suggest different kinds of organizations and communities? Cerro de Trincheras has multihouse terraces with long retaining walls; many of the small terraces share the same contour. When the town was occupied, the tiers of houses would have been quite visible (jacal construction can be substantial). Especially when viewed from the north, where most other settlements in the Magdalena Basin system were located, the array of houses and terraces at Cerro de Trincheras must have been very imposing. Cerro de Trincheras must have looked like a pueblo. Cerro Juanaqueña was also quite compact; Cerro Prieto had a looser layout.

New Insights from Excavations

Downum (chap. 4) reminds us that many things about cerros de trincheras and their past activities are not knowable without excavation. In Oaxaca, the El Palmillo project in the eastern Valley of Oaxaca has been singularly important in this regard (Feinman et al. 2002). In 2002 Verónica Pérez Rodríguez returned to excavate commoners' house terraces at Nicayuhu, a Postclassic site in the Mixteca Alta that had originally been surveyed and mapped by Laura Stiver (Pérez Rodríguez 2003; Stiver 2001). Pérez found domestic structures with multiple construction stages and remodelings, indicating protracted use. Her excavations also contributed to our understanding of how terraces were built. One can create a flat place on a slope by the cut-and-fill method, that is, by cutting into the slope and shifting the resulting fill outward, behind a retaining wall. Pérez's excavations on multiple terraces found little evidence of cutting, however, so building terraces was not a cut-and-fill, but a pure fill operation. This was also true at El Palmillo (Feinman et al. 2002). The fill typically contained habitation refuse, but its source is not known.

Pérez also sectioned long, 1- to 1.5-m-wide terraces very similar to the narrow terraces excavated at Cerro de Trincheras (chap. 5), with similar results. I suspect that McGuire and Villalpando are correct in suggesting that such terraces probably had plantings, perhaps agaves. Similar features are common at hilltop terraced sites in the Mixteca. As at Cerro de Trincheras, they typically are on the lower slopes, below residential terraces, often but not always immediately below broader, taller terraces. We think that the narrow terraces stabilized cleared slopes and would have been especially important where there was heavy pedestrian traffic. Planting agaves or trees would also help stabilize the slope.

Conclusions

In referring to the exciting and substantial recent progress in trincheras site research in the Northwest/Southwest, I may inadvertently convey the impression that all the riddles have been solved. That is not the case. We recognize that cerros de trincheras vary, and that they vary in relation to their role in the local, regional, and macroregional social systems of their times. Yet we also realize how little work has been done and how much more we need to do before we can claim control over the most basic issues. Still, the other participants in this trincheras project have cleared away a lot of the *monte*, the thorny and spiny scrub, so that the outlines of the rockwork are now clear.

Acknowledgments

I thank John Ware and the Amerind Foundation, and the Southwest Symposium, for providing an exceptional environment and forum for learning, and the organizers and participants for allowing me the opportunity to learn. The National

Science Foundation, the Canadian Social Science and Humanities Research Council, and the National Geographic Society funded our Oaxaca settlement pattern research over the years, and the Instituto Nacional de Antropología e Historia and its Centro INAH Oaxaca provided permissions and support. I thank the many participants of the survey projects, and Verenice Heredia, Verónica Pérez, and Charlotte A. Smith for their criticisms of my ideas as this chapter formed.

Photographing Trincheras Sites

Adriel Heisey

Coming down from the sky to fly slow circles around a trincheras site feels like a boyhood dream come to life: a windswept hill, ringed with stone walls old as a medieval cathedral, but holding stories only the dirt can tell, and I have flown in on a mission. If I can, I will bring home something genuinely new: a picture of this place from a point in space just far enough away to encompass the setting, but close enough to show the character of the rocks, so that we might understand it all a little better.

It is debatable what value these pictures would have on their own, but when teamed up with the work of those who toil in thought and deed to lay out the facts of the place, the images are pedigreed. As their maker, I too experience a transformation at the hands of the investigators. I am granted a new way of seeing, in which subtle traces on the landscape spring forward to meet my inquisitive eyes.

The excitement of coming upon these ancient bulls-eyes on high-points in wild and hilly terrain makes them seem more visible to my brain than they are to the camera, and thus I have my challenge. Through the tools of my trade, I must tease out these modest features and give them the chance to signal to us their mystery and import. In this task I am fortunate to work in the air, because there I can capitalize on one of the human brain's most powerful abilities: to recognize patterns. When shown a well-made aerial photograph of a *cerro de trincheras*, even the uninitiated viewer will have a eureka moment, as if a long-dormant message has leaped from the rocks and found its mark in a living host. Volleys of questions may follow, but those are the province of the researchers in this volume, and the photograph has done its job.

The flying is no small part of why I love this work. There is a special place in the sky, just above the highest plants, but far below the altitude of our people-moving aircraft, where human flight seems almost magical. Our era of innovation and high-tech materials has given us a multitude of ways to achieve it: the hang glider, the parasail, the powered paraglider, the powered parachute, the sailplane, the ultralight, and of course the helicopter. I have flown all of these craft and have chosen the ultralight airplane as my workhorse because it gives me the best compromise between power and agility.

The particular plane I fly is 15 years old at the time this volume is being published, and it has served me well. Virtually every one of its 1,600 flight hours has been dedicated to seeking out photographs, so I have formed a bond with it that is seasoned and true. By strapping the control stick to my right knee, I can fly the plane without using my hands. I hold the camera to my eye and compose my photographs just as I would on the ground. This might sound woefully improvised, but the truth is that it works beautifully. When I am circling above my subject, in light that begs for remembering, and the camera is glued to my eye, flying the plane with my leg feels completely natural. It is an extension of my body. What is more, through it I am part of the place. I feel heat from the elevated rocks below me, and cool air over green fields and watercourses. My wings tremble and quake with the energy of small currents wafting around me. I smell the odors of the earth and the life upon it. I see jackrabbits and coyotes and songbirds as a vulture might see them—and then I see vultures.

One afternoon over Cerro de Trincheras in Sonora, I found myself in the midst of scores of giant black birds. They sauntered in great spirals, riding the chimney of sun-warmed air rising from the cerro's summit. They did not appear to begrudge my presence even though surely I was a noisy, smelly, and ungainly interloper by their standards. I could see individual birds turning their heads to look at me as they soared past, but they seemed unperturbed. At first I felt on the verge of panic, knowing that very little of me or my airplane could survive an impact with a buzzard. As the seconds passed without event I realized that they were skilled at evading me, and gradually I relaxed. In every direction there were dark wingspans tilting lazily in the buoyant air. I never had such a sensation of space as *volume*—and of my movement in it—as in this moment.

Below me, the rocks crowning the cerro were plastered with white splotches. The buzzards had obviously roosted on the handiwork of the trincheras builders for a long time. These ancient scavengers, perhaps descended from the dinosaurs, are among nature's most revolting to our modern sensibilities. Yet some human societies hold them sacred as hygiene workers in the natural order, and even as agents of transformation. As I flew among the vultures, immersed in their element, I realized that I would leave, but they would remain. I imagined them settling at sunset on the walls I was merely here to photograph. In the absence of the original occupants, this was their home. Perhaps they were indeed fitting stewards of mysteries we will pursue but never fully grasp.

BIBLIOGRAPHY

Abadie, Maurice

1924 Minorities of the Sino-Vietnamese borderland: With special reference to Thai tribes. Translated by Walter E. J. Tips. [*Les races du Haut-Tonkin de Phone-Tho à Lang-Son.*] Société d'Éditions Géographiques Maritimes et Coloniales, Paris.

Adams, E. Charles

1991 *The Origin and Development of the Pueblo Katsina Cult.* University of Arizona Press, Tucson.

Adams, Karen R.

1994 A Regional Synthesis of *Zea mays* in the Prehistoric American Southwest. In *Corn and Culture in the Prehistoric New World*, edited by Sissel Johannessen and Christine A. Hastorf, pp. 273–302. Westview Press, Boulder, Colo.

1998 Plant Remains Recovered from Juanaqueña, a Late Archaic (3000 B.P.) Trincheras Site in Northern Chihuahua. Manuscript on file, Center for Archaeological Research, University of Texas at San Antonio.

1999a Plant Remains Recovered in 1998 from Cerro Juanaqueña, Cerro Vidal, and Cerro los Torres, Trinchera Sites in Northern Chihuahua. Manuscript on file, Center for Archaeological Research, University of Texas at San Antonio.

1999b Plant Remains Recovered in 1999 from Cerro Juanaqueña, Cerro El Canelo, and the Floodplain Site. Manuscript on file, Center for Archaeological Research, University of Texas at San Antonio.

2000 Data Tables of the 2000 Field Season Plant Remains from the Trincheras Project. Data on file, Center for Archaeological Research, University of Texas at San Antonio.

Adler, Michael A.

1989 Ritual Facilities and Social Integration in Nonranked Societies. In *The Architecture of Social Integration in Prehistoric Pueblos*, edited by William D. Lipe and Michelle Hegmon, pp. 35–52. Occasional Paper No. 1. Crow Canyon Archaeological Center, Cortez, Col.

Adriani, Nicolaus, and Albertus Christiaan Kruyt

1950 *The Bare'e-speaking Toradja of Central Celebes (the East Toradja).* Translated by Jenni Karding Moulton. 4 vols. Noord-Hollandsche Uitgevers Maatschappij, Amsterdam.

Andrews, Roy C.

1919 Exploring Unknown Corners of the "Hermit Kingdom." Electronic document, eHRAF, http://ets.umdl.umich.edu/cgi/e/ehraf/ehraf, accessed May 15, 2003.

Apter, David E.

1967 *The Political Kingdom in Uganda: A Study in Bureaucratic Nationalism.* Princeton University Press, Princeton.

Arizona Daily Star

1919 Evidence of Ancient Civilization Found West of Tucson. *Arizona Daily Star* 23:1. Tucson.

Ashmore, Wendy A., and A. Bernard Knapp

1999 *Archaeologies of Landscape: Contemporary Perspectives.* Blackwell, Oxford.

Ashmore, Wendy, and Jeremy A. Sabloff

2002 Spatial Orders in Maya Civic Plans. *Latin American Antiquity* 13:201–215.

Austin, Ken

2000 The Mountain Patayan People of West Central Arizona. In *Archaeology in West Central Arizona: Proceedings of the 1996 Arizona Archaeological Council Prescott Conference*, edited by Thomas N. Motsinger, Douglas R. Mitchell, and James M. McKie, pp. 63–74. Sharlot Hall Museum Press, Prescott, Arizona.

Aveni, Anthony F., Horst Hartung, and J. Charles Kelley

1982 Alta Vista (Chalchihuites), Astronomical Implications of a Mesoamerican Ceremonial Outpost at the Tropic of Cancer. *American Antiquity* 47:316–335.

Bahr, Donald M.

1994 *The Short, Swift Time of Gods on Earth: The Hohokam Chronicles.* University of California Press, Berkeley.

Balkansky, Andrew

1998 Urbanism and Early State Formation in the Huamelulpan Valley of Southern Mexico. *Latin American Antiquity* 9:37–67.

Balkansky, Andrew K., Stephen A. Kowalewski, Verónica Pérez Rodríguez, Thomas J. Pluckhahn, Charlotte A. Smith, Laura R. Stiver, Dmitri Beliaev, John F. Chamblee, Verenice Y. Heredia Espinoza, and Roberto Santos Pérez

2000 Archaeological Survey in the Mixteca Alta of Oaxaca, Mexico. *Journal of Field Archaeology* 27:365–389.

Bandelier, A. F.

1892 *Final Report of Investigations among the Indians of the Southwestern United States, Carried on Mainly in the Years from 1880 to 1885.* Papers of the Archaeological Institute of America, American Series, Vol. 4, Pt. 2. Cambridge University Press, Cambridge.

Barker, Stephen F.

1974 *The Elements of Logic.* 2nd ed. McGraw-Hill, New York.

Barnett, Franklin

1974 *Excavation of Main Pueblo at Fitzmaurice Ruin—Prescott Culture in Yavapai County, Arizona.* Museum of Northern Arizona Special Publication, Flagstaff.

Barrett, Samuel Alfred

1908 The Ethno-geography of the Pomo and Neighboring Indians. In *University of California Publications in American Archaeology and Ethnology,* edited by Frederic Ward Putnam, vol. 4, pp. 1–107, 118–245, 330–332. University of California Press, Berkeley.

Barth, Fredrik

1953 *Principles of Social Organization in Southern Kurdistan.* Universitetets Etnografiske Museum Bulletin No. 7. Brødrene Jørgensen A/S, Oslo.

Barton, R. F.

1922 *Ifugao Economics.* University of California Press, Berkeley.

1938 *Philippine Pagans: The Autobiographies of Three Ifugaos.* George Routledge and Sons, London.

Basso, Keith H.

1996 *Wisdom Sits in Places: Landscape and Language among the Western Apache.* University of New Mexico Press, Albuquerque.

Becker, C.

1924 Family Property and Maternal Rights. Translated by Elizabeth Knight. *Journal for Buddhism and Related Fields* 6:127–138, 300–310.

Beek, Walter E. A. van

1990 Harmony versus Autonomy: Models of Agricultural Fertility among the Dogon and the Kapsiki. In *Creative Communion: African Models of Fertility and the Regeneration of Life,* edited by Anita Jacobson-Widding and Walter van Beek, pp. 285–305. Uppsala Studies in Cultural Anthropology No. 15. Uppsala University, Uppsala.

Belgrave, C. Dalrymple

1923 *Siwa: The Oasis of Jupiter Ammon.* John Lane, London.

Bellwood, Peter

1971 Fortifications and Economy in Prehistoric New Zealand. *Proceedings of the Prehistoric Society* 37:56–95.

Bennett, Wendell C., and Robert M. Zingg

1935 *The Tarahumara: An Indian Tribe of Northern Mexico.* University of Chicago Press, Chicago.

Bernard-Shaw, Mary

1990 *Archaeological Investigations at the Lonetree Site, AA:12:120 (ASM), in the Northern Tucson Basin.* Technical Report No. 90-1. Center for Desert Archaeology, Tucson.

Bernatzik, Hugo Adolf

1970 *Akha and Miao: Problems of Applied Ethnography in Farther India.* Translated by Alois Nagler. Human Relations Area Files, New Haven.

Berry, Michael S.

1982 *Time, Space, and Transition in Anasazi Prehistory*. University of Utah Press, Salt Lake City.

Best, Elsdon

1924 *The Maori*. 2 vols. Board of Maori Ethnological Research, Wellington, New Zealand.

Betancourt, Julio L., and Raymond M. Turner

1990 Tucson's Santa Cruz River and the Arroyo Legacy. Manuscript on file, Arizona State Museum Library, University of Arizona, Tucson.

Beyer, H. Otley, and Roy Franklin Barton

1911 An Ifugao Burial Ceremony. *Philippine Journal of Science* 6:227–252.

Binford, Lewis R.

1982 The Archaeology of Place. *Journal of Anthropological Archaeology* 1:5–31.

Bishop, Isabella Bird

1898 *Korea and Her Neighbors: A Narrative of travel, with an Account of the Recent Vicissitudes and Present Position of the Country*. Revell, New York.

Blackwood, Beatrice

1935 *Both Sides of Buka Passage: An Ethnographic Study of Social, Sexual and Economic Questions in the North-Western Solomon Islands*. Clarendon Press, Oxford.

Blanton, Richard E.

1978 *Monte Albán: Settlement Patterns at the Ancient Zapotec Capital*. Academic Press, New York.

Blanton, Richard E., Gary M. Feinman, Stephen A. Kowalewski, and Linda M. Nicholas

1999 *Ancient Oaxaca: The Monte Albán State*. Cambridge University Press, Cambridge.

Blanton, Richard E., Stephen A. Kowalewski, Gary M. Feinman, and Laura Finsten

1993 *Ancient Mesoamerica: A Comparison of Change in Three Regions*. 2nd ed. Cambridge University Press, Cambridge.

Blau, Harold, Jack Campisi, and Elisabeth Tooker

1978 Onondaga. In *Northeast*, edited by Bruce G. Trigger, pp. 491–499. *Handbook of North American Indians*, Vol. 15, William C. Sturtevant, general editor, Smithsonian Institution, Washington, D.C.

Blom, Frans, and Oliver La Farge

1927 *Tribes and Temples: A Record of the Expedition to Middle America Conducted by the Tulane University of Louisiana in 1925*. 2 vols. The Tulane University of Louisiana, New Orleans.

Bonar, H.A.C.

1883 Notes on the Capital of Korea. *Transactions of the Asiatic Society of Japan* 11:243–259.

Bostwick, Todd W.

2001 Look to the Sky: Another View of Hilltop Sites in Central Arizona. In *The Archaeology of Ancient Tactical Sites*, edited by John R. Welch and Todd W. Bostwick, pp. 37–54. Arizona Archaeologist No. 32. Arizona Archaeological Society, Phoenix.

Bouroncle Carreón, Alfonso

1964 Contribution to the Study of the Aymara. Translated by Sidney Muirden. *América Indígena* 24(2, 3): 129–169, 233–269.

Bowen, Thomas

1972 A Survey and Re-evaluation of the Trincheras Culture, Sonora, Mexico. Manuscript on file, Arizona State Museum Archives, Tucson.

1976a Esquema de la historia de la cultura Trincheras. In *Sonora: antropología del desierto*, edited by Beatríz Braniff C. and Richard S. Felger, pp. 347–363. Colección Científica 27. Instituto Nacional de Antropología e Historia, SEP, Centro Regional del Noroeste, Mexico.

1976b *Seri Prehistory: The Archaeology of the Central Coast of Sonora, Mexico*. Anthropological Papers of the University of Arizona No. 27. University of Arizona Press, Tucson.

Bradley, Richard

1998 *The Significance of Monuments: On the Shaping of Human Experience in Neolithic and Bronze Age Europe*. Routledge, London.

2000 *An Archaeology of Natural Places*. Routledge, London.

Brand, Donald D.

1935a Prehistoric Trade in the Southwest. *New Mexico Business Review* 4:202–209.

1935b The Distribution of Pottery Types in Northwest Mexico. *American Anthropologist* 37:287–305.

1938 Aboriginal Trade Routes for Sea Shells in the Southwest. *Yearbook of the Association of Pacific Coast Geographers* 4:3–10.

1943 The Chihuahua Culture Area. *New Mexico Archaeologist* 6–7(3):115–158.

Brandt, Vincent S. R.

1971 *A Korean Village between Farm and Sea*. Harvard University Press, Cambridge, Massachusetts.

Braniff C., Beatríz

1990 The Identification of Possible Elites in Prehispanic Sonora. In *Perspectives on Southwestern Prehistory*, edited by P. Minnis and C. Redman, pp. 173–183. Westview Press, Boulder.

1992 *La frontera protohistórica Pima-Ópata en Sonora, México. Proposiciones arqueológicas preliminares*. 3 vols. Instituto Nacional de Antropología e Historia, Mexico, D.F.

Brooks, Richard H.

1971 Lithic Traditions in Northwestern Mexico, Paleo-Indian to Chalchihuites. Unpublished Ph.D. dissertation, University of Colorado, Boulder.

Brown, David E.

1994 *Biotic Communities: Southwestern United States and Northwestern Mexico.* University of Utah Press, Salt Lake City.

Bryan, Edwin H., Jr.

1924 Preliminary Report on the Lau Group, Fiji. Manuscript on file, Bernice P. Bishop Museum Library, Honolulu.

Buechler, Hans C., and Judith-Maria Buechler

1971 *The Bolivian Aymara.* Case Studies in Cultural Anthropology. Holt, Rinehart and Winston, New York.

Burling, Robbins

1963 *Rengsanggri: Family and Kinship in a Garo Village.* University of Philadelphia Press, Philadelphia.

Burrus, Ernest J.

1971 *Kino and Manje, Explorers of Sonora and Arizona.* Sources and Studies for the History of the Americas Vol. 10. Jesuit Historical Institute, Rome.

Busia, Kofi Abrefa

1951 *The Position of the Chief in the Modern Political System of the Ashanti: A Study of the Influence of Contemporary Social Change on Ashanti Political Institutions.* Ph.D. dissertation, University of Oxford, London. Oxford University Press for the International African Institute, London.

Buxton, David R.

1949 The Shoan Plateau and Its People: An Essay in Local Geography. *Geographical Journal* 114:157–172.

Byrkit, James

1988 The Palatkwapi Trail. *Plateau* 59(4):1–44.

Cable, John S., and David E. Doyel

1987 Pioneer Period Village Structure and Settlement Pattern in the Phoenix Basin. In *The Hohokam Village: Site Structure and Organization,* edited by David E. Doyel, pp. 21–70. AAAS Publication No. 87-15. Southwestern and Rocky Mountain Division of the American Association for the Advancement of Science, Glenwood Springs, Colo.

Carles, W. R.

1888 *Life in Corea.* Macmillan, London.

Carpenter, John P.

1997 Passing through the Netherworld: New Insights from the American Museum of Natural History's Sonora-Sinaloa Archaeological Project (1937–1940). In *Prehistory of the Borderlands: Recent Research in the Archaeology of Northern Mexico and the Southern Southwest,* edited by John P. Carpenter and M. Guadalupe Sanchez, pp. 113–127. Arizona State Museum Archaeological Series No. 186. University of Arizona, Tucson.

Carrasco, David

2000 *Quetzalcoatl and the Irony of Empire: Myths and Prophecies in the Aztec Tradition*. University Press of Colorado, Boulder.

Carter, William E.

1965 *Aymara Communities and the Bolivian Agrarian Reform*. University of Florida Monographs No. 24. University of Florida Press, Gainesville.

Cazes, M. H., and A. Jacquard

1981 Mating Structure in the Dogon Population in the Tabi Massif. *Social Biology* 28:281–292.

Chamberlin, T. C.

1890 The Method of Multiple Working Hypotheses. *Science* old ser.15:92–96.

1897 The Method of Multiple Working Hypotheses. *Journal of Geology* 5:837–848.

Chesky, Jane

1942 The Wikita. *Kiva* 8:3–5.

Choudhury, Bhupendranath

1958 *Some Cultural and Linguistic Aspects of the Garos*. B. N. Dutta Barooah, B. L., Lawyer's Bookstall, Gauhati, Assam.

Chowning, Ann

1979 Leadership in Melanesia. *Journal of Pacific History* 14:66–84.

Christenson, Andrew L.

2000 Petrographic Analysis of Sands, Self-Tempered Clays, and Prehistoric Ceramics from the Prescott Area. In *Archaeology in West Central Arizona: Proceedings of the 1996 Arizona Archaeological Council Prescott Conference*, edited by Thomas Motsinger, Douglas R. Mitchell, and James M. McKie, pp. 155–164. Sharlot Hall Museum Press, Prescott, Ariz.

Cieza de Leon, Pedro de

1883 *The Second Part of the Chronicle of Peru*. Translated and edited by Clements R. Markham. Works Issued by the Hakluyt Society No. 68. Hakluyt Society Publications, London.

Ciolek-Torrello, Richard (editor)

1998 *Early Farmers of the Sonoran Desert: Archaeological Investigations at the Houghton Road Site, Tucson, Arizona*. Technical Series No. 72. Statistical Research, Tucson.

Clark, Charles Allen

1932 *Religions of Old Korea*. Revell, New York.

Clemmer, Richard O.

1995 *Roads in the Sky: Hopi Indians in a Century of Change*. Westview Press, Boulder, Colo.

Cline, Walter

1936 *Notes on the People of Siwah and El Garah*. General Series in Anthropology No. 4. George Banta, Menasha, Wisc.

Cobo, Bernabé

1893 *Historia del Nuevo Mundo* [History of the New World]. Translated by Ariane Brunel. Sociedad de Bibliófilos Andaluces Vol. 4. E. Rasco, Seville.

Colton, Harold S.

1936 The Rise and Fall of the Prehistoric Population of Northern Arizona. *Science* 84 (2181):337–343.

1937 The Eruption of Sunset Crater as an Eye Witness Might Have Observed It. *Museum of Northern Arizona Museum Notes* 10(4):9–12.

1939 *An Archaeological Survey of Northwestern Arizona, Including the Descriptions of Fifteen New Pottery Types*. Museum of Northern Arizona Bulletin No. 16. Northern Arizona Society of Science and Art, Flagstaff.

1946 *The Sinagua: A Summary of the Archaeology of the Region of Flagstaff, Arizona*. Museum of Northern Arizona Bulletin No. 22. Northern Arizona Society of Science and Art, Flagstaff.

Conklin, Harold C.

1967 Some Aspects of Ethnographic Research in Ifugao. *Transactions of the New York Academy of Sciences* Ser. 2, 30(1):99–121.

Contreras, Eréndira

1998 Litica tallada del sitio Cerro de Trincheras. Manuscript on file, Cerro de Trincheras Project, Centro INAH Sonora, Hermosillo.

2002 La litica tallada del Proyecto Cerro de Trincheras. Paper presented at the 67th Annual Meeting of the Society for American Archaeology, Denver.

Cortina-Borja, Mario, and Leopoldo Valiñas

1989 Some Remarks on Uto-Aztecan Classification. *International Journal of American Linguistics* 55(2):214–239.

Courlander, Harold

1982 *Hopi Voices: Recollections, Traditions, and Narratives of the Hopi Indians*. University of New Mexico Press, Albuquerque.

Crown, Patricia L.

1994 *Ceramics and Ideology: Salado Polychrome Pottery*. University of New Mexico Press, Albuquerque.

Darling, Frank Fraser (editor)

1955 *West Highland Survey: An Essay in Human Ecology*. Oxford University Press, London.

Davidson, Janet

1987 The Paa Maori Revisited. *Journal of the Polynesian Society* 96:7–26.

Davis, Edward H.

1920 *The Papago Ceremony of Vítkita*. Indian Notes and Monographs Vol. 3, No. 4. Museum of the American Indian, New York.

Dean, Jeffrey S., William H. Doelle, and Janet Orcutt

1994 Adaptive Stress, Environment, and Demography. In *Themes in Southwest*

Prehistory, edited by George J. Gumerman, pp. 53–86. School of American Research Press, Santa Fe.

Department of Economics and Statistics, Assam, Shillong

1963 *Report on Rural Economic Survey in United K & J. Hills*. Assam Government Press, Shillong.

Derry, Gregory N.

1999 *What Science Is and How It Works*. Princeton University Press, Princeton, N.J.

Diehl, Michael W.

1996 *Archaeological Investigations of the Tucson Pressed Brick Company*. Technical Report No. 96–13. Center for Desert Archaeology, Tucson.

Diguet, Edouard

1908 *Les Montagnards du Tonkin*. AMS Press, New York.

Di Peso, Charles C.

1958 *The Reeve Ruin of Southeastern Arizona: A Study of a Prehistoric Western Pueblo Migration into the Middle San Pedro Valley*. Publication No. 8. Amerind Foundation, Dragoon, Ariz.

1974 *Casas Grandes: A Fallen Trading Center of the Gran Chichimeca*. Amerind Foundation Series No. 9 vol. 2. Amerind Foundation and Northland Press, Dragoon, Arizona and Flagstaff, Arizona.

1979 Prehistory: The Southern Periphery. In *Southwest*, edited by Alfonso Ortiz, pp. 152–161. *Handbook of North American Indians*, Vol. 15, William C. Sturtevant, general editor, Smithsonian Institution Press, Washington, DC.

1983 The Northern Sector of the Mesoamerican World System. In *Forgotten Places and Things: Archaeological Perspectives on American History*, edited by Albert E. Ward, pp. 11–22. Contributions to Anthropological Studies No. 3. Center for Anthropological Studies, Albuquerque.

Di Peso, Charles C., John B. Rinaldo, and Gloria Fenner

1974a *Casas Grandes: A Fallen Trading Center of the Gran Chichimeca*. Amerind Foundation Series No. 9, Vol. 8. Amerind Foundation and Northland Press, Dragoon, Arizona and Flagstaff, Arizona.

1974b *Casas Grandes: A Fallen Trading Center of the Gran Chichimeca*. Amerind Foundation Series No. 9, Vol. 4. Amerind Foundation and Northland Press, Dragoon, Arizona, and Flagstaff, Arizona.

Doelle, William H., Allen Dart, and Henry D. Wallace

1985 *The Southern Tucson Basin Survey: Intensive Survey along the Santa Cruz River*. Institute for American Research Technical Report 85–3, Tucson.

Doelle, William H., and Henry D. Wallace

1991 The Changing Role of the Tucson Basin in the Hohokam Regional System. In *Exploring the Hohokam: Prehistoric Desert Peoples of the American Southwest*, edited by George J. Gumerman, pp. 279–345. University of New Mexico Press, Albuquerque.

Doolittle, William E.

1988 *Pre-Hispanic Occupance in the Valley of Sonora, Mexico*. Anthropological Papers of the University of Arizona No. 48. University of Arizona Press, Tucson.

Downs, Richard E.

1956 *The Religion of the Bare'e-speaking Toradja of Central Celebes*. Uitgeverij Excelsior, 's-Gravenhage.

Downum, Christian E.

1986 The Occupational Use of Hill Space in the Tucson Basin: Evidence from Linda Vista Hill. *Kiva* 51:219–232.

1988 Classic Period Platform Mound Communities of the Lower Santa Cruz River Basin, ca. A.D. 1050–1450. National Register of Historic Places Multiple Property Documentation. Report prepared for Arizona State Historic Preservation Office, Arizona State Parks Department, Phoenix. Manuscript on file, Arizona State Museum, University of Arizona, Tucson.

1992 The Sinagua. *Plateau* 63(1):1–32.

1993 *Between Desert and River: Hohokam Settlement and Land Use in the Los Robles Community*. Anthropological Papers of the University of Arizona No. 57. University of Arizona Press, Tucson.

1995 Archaeological Investigations at Linda Vista Hill, 1980–1987. In *Archaeological Investigations at Los Morteros: A Prehistoric Settlement in the Northern Tucson Basin*, edited by Henry D. Wallace, pp. 1155–1183. Anthropological Papers No. 17. Center for Desert Archaeology, Tucson, Arizona.

Downum, Christian E., and Allen Dart

1986 *Archaeological Studies at AZ BB:13:223 (ASM) and Nearby Sites in the Santa Cruz Industrial Park, Tucson, Arizona*. Technical Report No. 86–3. Institute for American Research, Tucson.

Downum, Christian E., John E. Douglas, and Douglas B. Craig

1985 Community Structure and Agricultural Strategies at Cerro Prieto (AZ AA:7:11). In *Proceedings of the 1983 Hohokam Symposium*, edited by Alfred E. Dittert and Donald E. Dove, pp. 545–556. Occasional Paper No. 2. Arizona Archaeological Society, Phoenix.

1993 The Cerro Prieto Site. In *Between Desert and River: Hohokam Settlement and Land Use in the Los Robles Community*, by Christian E. Downum, pp. 53–97. Anthropological Papers of the University of Arizona No. 57. University of Arizona Press, Tucson.

Downum, Christian E., Paul R. Fish, and Suzanne K. Fish

1981 Hohokam Terraces and Agricultural Production in the Tucson Basin. Paper presented at the 46th Annual Meeting of the Society for American Archaeology, San Diego.

1994 Refining the Role of Cerros de Trincheras in Southern Arizona Settlement. *Kiva* 59:271–296.

Doyel, David E.

1991 Hohokam Cultural Evolution in the Phoenix Basin. In *Exploring the Hohokam: Prehistoric Desert Peoples of the American Southwest*, edited by George J. Gumerman, pp. 231–278. University of New Mexico Press, Albuquerque.

Drew, Frederic

1875 *The Jammu and Kashmir Territories*. E. Stanford, London.

Drobnjaković, Borivoje M.

1973 *Jasenica: Anthropological Research*. Serbian Ethnographic Archives of the Serbian Royal Academy Vol. 25. Human Relations Area Files, New Haven.

Du Bois, Cora

1944 *The People of Alor*. University of Minnesota Press, Minneapolis.

Dumia, Mariano A.

1979 *The Ifugao World*. New Day, Quezon City, Republic of the Philippines.

Dupas, Pierre

1929 Note on the Collective Storehouses of the Western High Atlas (Tribes of the Ida ou Mahmoud and the Seksaoua) [Note sur les magasins collectifs du Haut-Atlas (Tribus des Ida ou Mahmoud et des Seksaoua)]. Translated by Helen Bluhm. *Hespéris, archives berbères et Bulletin de l'institut* 9:303–322.

Ekholm, Gordon

1939 Results of an Archaeological Survey of Sonora and Northern Sinaloa. *Revista Mexicana de Estudios Antropológicos* 3:7–11.

Elam, J. Michael

1989 Defensible and Fortified Sites. In *Monte Albán's Hinterland, Part II: Prehispanic Settlement Patterns in Tlacolula, Etla, and Ocotlan, the Valley of Oaxaca, Mexico*, edited by Stephen A. Kowalewski, Gary M. Feinman, Laura Finsten, Richard E. Blanton, and Linda M. Nicholas, vol. 1, pp. 385–408. Memoirs of the Museum of Anthropology No. 23. University of Michigan, Ann Arbor.

Ellis, Florence Hawley

1974 The Hopi: Their History and Use of Lands. In *Hopi History and Ethnobotany*, edited by Harold S. Colton. Garland, New York.

Elson, Mark

1998 *Expanding the View of Hohokam Platform Mounds: An Ethnographic Perspective*. University of Arizona Press, Tucson.

Ember, Carol R., and Melvin Ember

1992 Resource Unpredictability, Mistrust, and War: A Cross-Cultural Study. *Journal of Conflict Resolution* 36:242–262.

Eppley, Lisa G.

1990 Lonetree Chipped and Ground Stone Analysis. In *Archaeological Investigations at the Lonetree Site, AA:12:120 (ASM), in the Northern Tucson Basin*, edited by Mary Bernard-Shaw, pp. 127–148. Technical Report No. 90-1. Center for Desert Archaeology, Tucson.

Euler, Robert C., and Henry F. Dobyns

1962 Excavations West of Prescott, Arizona. *Plateau* 34:69–85.

Ezzo, Joseph A., and William L. Deaver

1998 *Watering the Desert: Late Archaic Farming at the Costello-King Site.* Technical Series No. 68. Statistical Research, Tucson.

Fallers, Lloyd A.

1964 The Modernization of Social Stratification. In *The King's Men: Leadership and Status in Burganda on the Eve of Independence*, edited by Lloyd A. Fallers, pp. 117–157. Oxford University Press, London.

Fallers, Margaret Chave

1960 *The Eastern Lacustrine Bantu (Ganda and Soga).* Ethnographic Survey of Africa: East Central Africa Pt. 11. Sidney Press, Bedford, England.

Farmer, Malcolm F.

1957 A Suggested Typology of Defensive Systems of the Southwest. *Southwestern Journal of Anthropology* 13:249–266.

Feinman, Gary M., Linda M. Nicholas, and Helen R. Haines

2002 Houses on a Hill: Classic Period Life at El Palmillo, Oaxaca, Mexico. *Latin American Antiquity* 13:251–278.

Fenton, William, and Elisabeth Tooker

1978 Mohawk. In *Northeast*, edited by Bruce G. Trigger, pp. 466–480. *Handbook of North American Indians*, Vol. 15, William C. Sturtevant, general editor, Smithsonian Institution, Washington, D.C.

Fewkes, Jesse Walter

1912 *Antiquities of the Upper Verde River and Walnut Creek Valleys, Arizona.* 28th Annual Report, 1906–1907, pp. 181–220. U.S. Bureau of American Ethnology, Washington, D.C.

Filipović, Milenko S.

1954 *Folk Religion among the Orthodox Population in Eastern Yugoslavia (Some Remarks and Considerations).* Harvard University Press, Cambridge.

Finsten, Laura

1996 Periphery and Frontier in Southern Mexico: The Mixtec Sierra in Highland Oaxaca. In *Pre-Columbian World Systems*, edited by Peter N. Peregrine and Gary M. Feinman, pp. 77–96. Prehistory Press, Madison, Wisc.

Firth, Raymond

1959 *Economics of the New Zealand Maori. 2nd ed.* R. E. Owen, Wellington, New Zealand.

Fish, Paul R., and Suzanne K. Fish

1989 Hohokam Warfare from a Regional Perspective. In *Cultures in Conflict: Current Archaeological Perspectives. Proceedings of the Twentieth Annual Conference of the Archaeological Association of the University of Calgary*, edited by Diana Claire Tkaczuk and Brian C. Vivian, pp. 112–129. University of Calgary Archaeological Association, Calgary.

2000 The Marana Mound Site: Patterns of Social Differentiation in the Early Classic Period. In *The Hohokam Village Revisited*, edited by David E. Doyel, Suzanne K. Fish, and Paul R. Fish, pp. 245–275. Southwestern and Rocky Mountain Division of the American Association for the Advancement of Science, Fort Collins, Colo.

Fish, Paul R., Suzanne K. Fish, George J. Gumerman, and J. Jefferson Reid

1994 Toward an Explanation for Southwestern "Abandonments." In *Themes in Southwest Prehistory*, edited by George J. Gumerman, pp. 135–163. School of American Research, Santa Fe.

Fish, Paul R., Suzanne K. Fish, Austin Long, and Charles Miksicek

1986 Early Corn Remains from Tumamoc Hill, Southern Arizona. *American Antiquity* 51:563–572.

Fish, Suzanne K.

1995 Mixed Agricultural Technologies in Southern Arizona and Their Implications. In *Soil, Water, Biology, and Belief in Prehistoric and Traditional Southwestern Agriculture*, edited by H. Wolcott Toll, pp. 101–116. Special Publication No. 2. New Mexico Archaeological Council, Albuquerque.

1999 Cerro de Trincheras Settlement and Land Use Survey. Report to the National Geographic Society for Grant 5856–97. Report on file, Arizona State Museum Archives, Tucson.

Fish, Suzanne K., and Paul R. Fish

1994 Comparative Aspects of Hohokam Communities. In *The Ancient Southwestern Community: Models and Methods for the Study of Prehistoric Social Organization*, edited by W. H. Wills and Robert D. Leonard, pp. 119–130. University of New Mexico Press, Albuquerque.

2000a The Institutional Contexts of Hohokam Complexity and Inequality. In *Alternative Leadership Strategies in the Prehispanic Southwest*, edited by Barbara J. Mills, pp. 154–167. University of Arizona Press, Tucson.

2000b In the Trincheras Heartland. Paper presented at the 65th Annual Meeting of the Society for American Archaeology, Philadelphia.

2004 In the Trincheras Heartland: Initial Insights from Full-Coverage Survey. In *Surveying the Archaeology of Northwest Mexico*, edited by Gillian E. Newell and Emiliano Gallaga, pp. 47–63. University of Utah Press, Salt Lake City.

Fish, Suzanne K., Paul R. Fish, and Christian E. Downum

1984 Hohokam Terraces and Agricultural Production in the Tucson Basin, Arizona. In *Prehistoric Agricultural Strategies in the Southwest*, edited by

Suzanne K. Fish and Paul R. Fish, pp. 55–71. Anthropological Papers No. 33. Department of Anthropology, Arizona State University, Tempe.

Fish, Suzanne K., Paul R. Fish, and John H. Madsen

1989 Classic Period Hohokam Community Integration in the Tucson Basin. In *The Sociopolitical Structure of Prehistoric Southwestern Societies*, edited by Steadman Upham, Kent G. Lightfoot, and Roberta A. Jewett, pp. 237–267. Westview Press, Boulder, Colo.

1990 Analyzing Regional Agriculture: A Hohokam Example. In *The Archaeology of Regions: The Case for Full-Coverage Survey*, edited by Suzanne K. Fish and Stephen A. Kowalewski, pp. 189–218. Smithsonian Institution Press, Washington, DC.

1992a Early Sedentism and Agriculture in the Northern Tucson Basin. In *The Marana Community in the Hohokam World*, edited by Suzanne K. Fish, Paul R. Fish, and John H. Madsen, pp. 11–19. Anthropological Papers of the University of Arizona No. 56. University of Arizona Press, Tucson.

1992b Evidence for Large-Scale Agave Cultivation in the Marana Community. In *The Marana Community in the Hohokam World*, edited by Suzanne K. Fish, Paul R. Fish, and John H. Madsen, pp. 73–87. Anthropological Papers of the University of Arizona No. 56. University of Arizona Press, Tucson.

1992c *The Marana Community in the Hohokam World*. Anthropological Papers of the University of Arizona No. 56. University of Arizona Press, Tucson.

Flannery, Kent V., Joyce Marcus, and Stephen A. Kowalewski

1981 The Preceramic and Formative of the Valley of Oaxaca. In *Archaeology*, edited by Jeremy A. Sabloff, pp. 48–93. *Supplement to the Handbook of Middle American Indians*, vol. 1, Victoria Reifler Bricker, general editor. University of Texas Press, Austin.

Fontana, Bernard L., J. Cameron Greenlear, and Donnelly D. Cassidy

1959 A Fortified Arizona Mountain. *Kiva* 25(2):41–52.

Forman, Grant

1941 *A Pathfinder in the Southwest, The Itinerary of Lieutenant A. W. Whipple during His Explorations for a Railway Route from Fort Smith to Los Angeles in the Years 1853 & 1854*. University of Oklahoma Press, Norman.

Fortes, Meyer, Robert W. Steel, and P. Ady

1947 Ashanti Survey, 1945–1946: An Experiment in Social Research. *Geographical Journal* 110:149–179.

Foster, Michael S.

1985 The Loma San Gabriel Occupation of Zacatecas and Durango, Mexico. In *The Archaeology of West and Northwest Mesoamerica*, edited by Michael S. Foster and Phil C. Weigand, pp. 327–352. Westview Press, Boulder, Colo.

1995 The Loma San Gabriel Culture and Its Suggested Relationships to Other

Early Plainware Cultures of Northwest Mesoamerica. In *The Gran Chichimeca: Essays on the Archaeology and Ethnohistory of Northern Mesoamerica*, edited by Jonathan E. Reyman, pp. 179–207. Avebury, Brookfield, Vt.

Fritz, Gayle, Karen R. Adams, Robert J. Hard, and John R. Roney

1999 Evidence for Cultivation of *Amaranthus* sp. (Amaranthaceae) 3000 Years Ago at Cerro Juanaqueña, Chihuahua. Paper presented at the 22nd Annual Conference of the Society of Ethnobiology, Oaxaca, Mexico.

Fuller, Steven L., and James N. Morris

1991 Excavations at Knobby Knee Stockade: A Basketmaker III–Pueblo III Habitation. In *Archaeological Excavations on the Hovenweep Laterals*, by James N. Morris, pp. 59–325. Four Corners Archaeological Project Report No. 16. Complete Archaeological Services Associates, Cortez, Colo.

Gabel, Norman E.

1931 Martinez Hill Ruins: An Example of Prehistoric Culture of the Middle Gila. Unpublished master's thesis, University of Arizona, Tucson.

Gallaga M., Emiliano

1997 La cerámica polícroma de Cerro de Trincheras, Sonora, México. Tesis de licenciatura, Escuela Nacional de Antropología e Historia, Mexico.

2001 Informe Area A.1. Manuscript on file, Cerro de Trincheras Excavation Project, Centro INAH Sonora, Hermosillo.

2002 Tepalcates Trinchereños: The Ceramic Analysis from Cerro de Trincheras, Sonora, Mexico. Paper presented at the 67th Annual Meeting of the Society for American Archaeology, Denver.

2004 A Spatial Distribution Analysis of the Shell and Polychrome Ceramics at the Cerro de Trincheras Site, Sonora, Mexico. In *Surveying the Archaeology of Northwest Mexico*, edited by Gillian E. Newell and Emiliano Gallaga, pp. 47–63. University of Utah Press, Salt Lake City.

Ganot R., Jaime, and Alejandro A. Peschard F.

1995 The Archaeological Site of Cañon del Molino, Durango, México. In *The Gran Chichimeca: Essays on the Archaeology and Ethnohistory of Northern Mesoamerica*, edited by Jonathan E. Reyman, pp. 146–178. Avebury, Brookfield, Vt.

Garcia, Angela, Barnaby V. Lewis, J. Andrew Darling, and Amadeo Rea

2002 In Search of the Sacred: TCP Inventory and Heritage Preservation on the Traditional Lands of the Akimel O'odham and Pee Posh Peoples. Manuscript on file, Cultural Resource Management Program, Gila River Indian Community, Sacaton, Ariz.

Geddes, Arthur

1955 *The Isle of Lewis and Harris: A Study in British Community*. University Press, Edinburgh.

Giddens, Anthony
1984 *The Constitution of Society: Outline of the Theory of Structuration.* Polity Press, Cambridge, England.
Gifford, Edward W.
1936 Northeastern and Western Yavapai. *University of California Publications in American Archaeology and Ethnology* 34:247–354.
Gillespie, Susan D.
1992 *The Aztec Kings: The Construction of Rulership in Mexican History.* University of Arizona Press, Tucson.
1999 Olmec Thrones as Ancestral Altars: The Two Sides of Power. In *Material Symbols: Culture and Economy in Prehistory*, edited by John E. Robb, pp. 224–253. Center for Archaeological Investigations Occasional Paper No. 26. Southern Illinois University, Carbondale.
Glacken, Clarence J.
1953 *Studies of Okinawan Village Life.* Scientific Investigations in the Ryukyu Islands (SIRI) Report No. 4. Pacific Science Board, National Research Council, Washington, D.C.
Gladwell, Malcolm
2000 *The Tipping Point: How Little Things Can Make a Big Difference.* Little, Brown, Boston.
Godelier, Maurice
1999 *The Enigma of the Gift.* Translated by Nora Scott. University of Chicago Press, Chicago.
Godwin-Austen, H. H.
1876 Further Notes on the Rude Stone Monuments of the Khasi Hill Tribes. *Journal of the Anthropological Institute of Great Britain and Ireland* 5:37–41.
Goldman, Irving
1970 *Ancient Polynesian Society.* University of Chicago Press, Chicago.
González Crespo, Norberto, Silvia Garza Tarazona, Hortensia de Vega Nova, Pablo Mayer Guala, and Giselle Canto Aguilar
1995 Archaeological Investigations at Xochicalco, Morelos: 1984 and 1986. *Ancient Mesoamerica* 6:223–236.
Goodwin, Grenville
1942 *The Social Organization of the Western Apache.* University of Chicago Press, Chicago.
Graham, David Crockett
1937 The Customs of the Ch'uan Miao. *Journal of the West China Border Research Society* 9:13–70.
Greenleaf, J. Cameron
1975 The Fortified Hill Site near Gila Bend. *Kiva* 40:213–282.

Greenwald, Dawn
1997 Ground Stone from Cerro de Trincheras, Sonora, Mexico. Manuscript on file, Cerro de Trincheras Excavation Project, Binghamton University, Binghamton, N.Y.

Gregor, Mary J. F., and Ruth M. Crichton
1946 *From Croft to Factory: The Evolution of an Industrial Community in the Highlands*. Discussion Books, A.J.J. Ratcliff, general editor. Thomas Nelson and Sons, London.

Gregory, David A.
2001 Variation and Trend during the Early Agricultural Period. In *Excavations in the Santa Cruz River Floodplain: The Early Agricultural Period Component at Los Pozos*, edited by David A. Gregory, pp. 255–280. Anthropological Papers No. 21. Center for Desert Archaeology, Tucson.

Griaule, Marcel, and Germaine Dieterlen
1986 *The Pale Fox*. Continuum Foundation, Chino Valley, Ariz.

Groube, Leslie M.
1970 The Origin and Development of Earthwork Fortifications in the Pacific. In *Studies in Oceanic Culture History*, edited by Roger C. Green and M. Kelly, pp. 133–164. Pacific Anthropological Records No. 11. Bishop Museum, Honolulu.

Gurdon, Phillip Richard Thornhagh
1907 *The Khasis*. David Nutt, London.

Haas, Jonathan
1990 Warfare and the Evolution of Tribal Polities in the Prehistoric Southwest. In *The Anthropology of War*, edited by Jonathan Haas, pp. 171–189. Cambridge University Press, Cambridge.

Haas, Jonathan, and Winifred Creamer
1993 Stress and Warfare among the Kayenta Anasazi of the Thirteenth Century. *Fieldiana: Anthropology* n.s. 21.
1996 The Role of Warfare in the Pueblo III Period. In *The Prehistoric Pueblo World, A.D. 1150–1350*, edited by Michael Adler, pp. 205–213. University of Arizona Press, Tucson.
1997 Warfare among the Pueblos. *Ethnohistory* 44:235–261.

Hack, John T.
1942 *The Changing Physical Environment of the Hopi Indians of Arizona*. Papers of the Peabody Museum of American Archaeology and Ethnography Vol. 35, No. 1. Harvard University, Cambridge.

Hansen, Henry Harald
1961 *The Kurdish Woman's Life: Field Research in a Muslim Society, Iraq*. Nationalmuseet, Copenhagen, Denmark.

Hard, Robert J., and William L. Merrill
1992 Mobile Agriculturalists and the Emergence of Sedentism: Perspectives from Northern Mexico. *American Anthropologist* 94:601–620.

Hard, Robert J., and John R. Roney

1998 A Massive Terraced Village Complex in Chihuahua, Mexico, 3000 Years before Present. *Science* 279:1661–1664.

1999 *An Archaeological Investigation of Late Archaic Cerros de Trincheras Sites in Chihuahua, Mexico: Results of the 1998 Investigations.* Report to the Consejo de Arqueología, Instituto Nacional de Antropología e Historia, Mexico City. Center for Archaeological Research Special Report No. 25. University of Texas at San Antonio, San Antonio.

2004 Late Archaic Period Hilltop Settlements in Northwestern Chihuahua. In *Identity, Feasting, and the Archaeology of the Greater Southwest*, edited by Barbara Mills, pp. 276–294. University Press of Colorado, Boulder.

2005 The Transition to Farming on the Rio Casas Grandes and in the Southern Jornada Mogollon Region. In *The Late Archaic across the Borderlands: From Foraging to Farming*, edited by Bradley J. Vierra, pp. 141–186. University of Texas Press, Austin.

2007 Early Farming and Warfare in Northwest Mexico. With contributions by Karen R. Adams, Gayle J. Fritz, J. Kevin Hanselka, Lee Nordt, Kari M. Schmidt, Bradley J. Vierra. In preparation, to be submitted to the University of Utah Press, Salt Lake City.

Hard, Robert J., José E. Zapata, Bruce K. Moses, and John R. Roney

1999 Terrace Construction in Northern Chihuahua, Mexico: 1150 BC and Modern Experiments. *Journal of Field Archaeology* 26:129–146.

Hardy, William H.

1888 Early Trouble with Indians–1866. *Mohave County Miner*, December 8, 1888. Copy on file, Munk Library of Arizoniana, Southwest Museum, Los Angeles.

Hartmann, Gayle Harrison

1997 *Archaeological Investigations at the Silverbell Coachline Site, AZ AA:12:321 (ASM), in Marana, Arizona.* Archaeology Report No. 13. Old Pueblo Archaeology Center, Tucson.

Hartmann, Gayle H., and William K. Hartmann

1979 Prehistoric Trail Systems and Related Features on the Slopes of Tumamoc Hill. *Kiva* 45:39–69.

Hastings, James R., and Raymond M. Turner

1965 *The Changing Mile: An Ecological Study of Vegetation Change with Time in the Lower Mile of an Arid and Semiarid Region.* University of Arizona Press, Tucson.

Haury, Emil Walter

1962 The Greater American Southwest. In *Courses toward Urban Life*, edited by Robert J. Braidwood and Gordon R. Willey, pp. 106–131. Viking Fund Publications in Anthropology No. 32. Aldine, Chicago.

1976 *The Hohokam: Desert Farmers & Craftsmen.* University of Arizona Press, Tucson.

Hayden, Julian, and Charlie R. Steen

1937 The Vikita Ceremony of the Papago. Southwestern Monuments Monthly Report, April 1937. Department of the Interior, National Park Service, Globe, Ariz. Manuscript on file, Arizona State Museum Library, University of Arizona, Tucson.

Hegmon, Michelle

1989 The Styles of Interaction: Ceramic Style and Pueblo I Integrative Architecture in Southwestern Colorado. In *The Architecture of Social Integration in Prehistoric Pueblos*, edited by William D. Lipe and Michelle Hegmon, pp. 125–142. Occasional Papers No. 1. Crow Canyon Archaeological Center, Cortez, Colo.

Heidke, James M.

2003 Tortolita Phase Ceramics. In *Roots of Sedentism: Archaeological Excavations at Valencia Vieja, A Founding Village in the Tucson Basin of Southern Arizona*, edited by Henry D. Wallace, pp. 145–192. Anthropological Papers No. 29. Center for Desert Archaeology, Tucson.

Heidke, James M., and Judith A. Habicht-Mauche

1998 The First Occurrences and Early Distribution of Pottery in the North American Southwest. *Revista de Arqueología Americana* 14:65–99.

Heidke, James M., R. Jane Sliva, Deborah L. Swartz, and Jennifer A. Waters

1996 Artifact and Archaeobotanical Analyses. In *Limited Excavation at the Eastern Margin of the Hodges Site*, edited by Deborah L. Swartz, pp. 15–39. Technical Report No. 96-6. Center for Desert Archaeology, Tucson, Arizona.

Helms, Mary W.

1993 *Craft and the Kingly Ideal: Art, Trade, and Power*. University of Texas Press, Austin.

Heredia Espinoza, Verenice Y.

2005 The Nature of Governance in Secondary Centers of the Classic Period, Mixteca Alta, Oaxaca, Mexico. Unpublished Ph.D. dissertation, Department of Sociology and Anthropology, Purdue University, West Lafayette, Ind.

Herold, Laurance C.

1965 *Trincheras and Physical Environment along the Rio Gavilán, Chihuahua, Mexico*. Publications in Geography; Technical Paper No. 56-1. Department of Geography, University of Denver, Denver.

Hill, Jane H.

2001 Proto-Uto-Aztecan: A Community of Cultivators in Central Mexico? *American Anthropologist* 103:913–934.

Hinsley, Curtis M., and David R. Wilcox (editors)

2002 *The Lost Itinerary of Frank Hamilton Cushing. Frank Hamilton Cushing and the Hemenway Southwestern Archaeological Expedition, 1886–1889*, Vol. 2. University of Arizona Press, Tucson.

Hinton, Leanne, and Lucille J. Watahomigie

1984 *Spirit Mountain: An Anthology of Yuman Story and Song*. University of Arizona Press, Tucson.

Hinton, Thomas B.

1955 A Survey of Archaeological Sites in the Altar Valley, Sonora. *Kiva* 21:1–12.

Hirth, Kenneth G.

1995 Urbanism, Militarism, and Architectural Design: An Analysis of Epiclassic Sociopolitical Structure at Xochicalco. *Ancient Mesoamerica* 6:237–250.

2000 *Archaeological Research at Xochicalco: 1. Ancient Urbanism at Xochicalco: The Evolution and Organization of a Pre-Hispanic Society*. University of Utah Press, Salt Lake City.

Hoben, Allan

1973 *Land Tenure among the Amhara of Ethiopia: The Dynamics of Cognatic Descent*. University of Chicago Press, Chicago.

Holliday, William G.

1974 *Archeological Investigations in the Cave Creek Drainage, Tonto National Forest, Arizona*. Archeological Report No. 1. USDA Forest Service, Southwest Region, Albuquerque.

Hoover, J. W.

1941 Cerros de Trincheras of the Arizona Papagueria. *Geographical Review* 31:228–239.

Howard, Jerry B.

1990 Los Hornos: Site Structure and Community Patterning at a Large Hohokam Village. In *One Hundred Years of Archaeology at La Ciudad de los Hornos*, edited by David R. Wilcox, Jerry B. Howard, and Rueben H. Nelson, pp. 73–121. Publications in Archaeology No. 16. Soil Systems, Phoenix.

2000 Quantitative Approaches to Spatial Patterning in the Hohokam Village: Testing the Village Segment Model. In *The Hohokam Village Revisited*, edited by David E. Doyel, Suzanne K. Fish, and Paul R. Fish, pp. 167–195. Southwestern and Rocky Mountain Division of the American Association for the Advancement of Science, Fort Collins, Colo.

Howard, W. A., and T. M. Griffiths

1966 *Trincheras Distributions in the Sierra Madre Occidental, Mexico*. Geography Technical Papers No. 66-1. University of Denver, Denver.

Hoyningen-Huene, Paul

1993 *Reconstructing Scientific Revolutions: Thomas S. Kuhn's Philosophy of Science*. Translated by Alexander T. Levine. University of Chicago Press, Chicago.

Huckell, Bruce B.
1984 The Paleo-Indian and Archaic Occupation of the Tucson Basin: An Overview. *Kiva* 49:133–145.
Huckell, Bruce B., and Lisa W. Huckell
1984 Excavations at Milagro, a Late Archaic Site in the Eastern Tucson Basin. Manuscript on file, Arizona State Museum Archives, University of Arizona, Tucson.
Hughart, Brandon
2002 Still Smokin': Testing an Archaic Communication System. Manuscript on file, Anthropology Department, Museum of Northern Arizona, Flagstaff.
Hulbert, Homer B.
1906 *The Passing of Korea*. Doubleday, New York.
Hull, Richard W.
1976 *African Cities and Towns before the European Conquest*. Norton, New York.
Huntington, Ellsworth
1904 Fieldnotes. Manuscript on file at the Yale University Library Archives, New Haven.
1913 The Fluctuating Climate of North America. In *Annual Report of the Smithsonian Institution 1912*, pp. 383–412. Smithsonian Institution, Washington, D.C.
1914 *The Climatic Factor as Illustrated in Arid America*. Carnegie Institution of Washington Publication No. 192. Carnegie Institution, Washington, D.C.
Hyde, George E.
1974 *The Pawnee Indians*. University of Oklahoma Press, Norman.
Ingrams, William Harold
1938 The Hadhramaut: Present and Future. *Geographical Journal* 92:289–312.
Izady, Mehrdad
1992 *The Kurds: A Concise Handbook*. Taylor and Francis, Washington, D.C.
Jenness, Diamond
1959 *The People of the Twilight*. University of Chicago Press, Chicago.
Johnson, Alfred E.
1960 The Place of the Trincheras Culture of Northern Sonora in Southwestern Archaeology. Unpublished master's thesis, Department of Anthropology, University of Arizona, Tucson.
1963 The Trincheras Culture of Northwestern Sonora. *American Antiquity* 29:174–186.
Johnson, J.C.A.
1940 The Kurds of Iraq. *Geographical Magazine* 10:382–393.

Kagwa, Apolo, May M. Edel, and John Roscoe
1934 *The Customs of the Baganda.* Translated by Ernest B. Kalibala. Columbia University Press, New York.
Katzer, Keith
1985 A Geomorphic Evaluation of the Agricultural Potential of Cerros de Trincheras. Manuscript on file, Desert Archaeology, Tucson.
1993 A Geomorphic Evaluation of the Agricultural Potential of Cerros de Trincheras. In *Between Desert and River: Hohokam Settlement and Land Use in the Los Robles Community,* by Christian E. Downum, pp. 91–95. Anthropological Papers of the University of Arizona No. 57. University of Arizona Press, Tucson.
Keeley, Lawrence H.
1996 *War before Civilization.* Oxford University Press, New York.
Kelley, J. Charles
1956 Settlement Patterns in North-Central Mexico. In *Prehistoric Settlement Patterns in the New World,* edited by Gordon R. Willey, pp. 128–202. Viking Fund Publications in Anthropology No. 23. Wenner-Gren Foundation for Anthropological Research, New York.
1985 The Chronology of the Chalchihuites Culture. In *The Archaeology of West and Northwest Mesoamerica,* edited by Michael S. Foster and Phil C. Weigand, pp. 269–288. Westview Press, Boulder, Colo.
Kelley, J. Charles, and Ellen A. Kelley
1975 An Alternative Hypothesis for the Explanation of Anasazi Culture History. In *Collected Papers in Honor of Florence Hawley Ellis,* edited by Theodore R. Frisbie, pp. 178–223. Papers of the Archaeological Society of New Mexico No. 2. Hooper, Norman, Okla.
Kenyon, Kathleen
1960 Excavations at Jericho (1957–58). *Palestine Exploration Quarterly,* 91:88–113.
Kennedy, John G.
1978 *Tarahumara of the Sierra Madre: Beer, Ecology, and Social Organization.* AHM Publishing, Arlington Heights, Ill.
Kerr, George H.
1958 *Okinawa: The History of an Island People.* C. E. Tuttle, Rutland, Vt.
Khaleque, Kibriaul
1988 Garo of Bangladesh: Region, Ritual and World View. In *Further Studies of Religions and World Views,* edited by Anthony R. Walker, pp. 129–156. Contributions to Southeast Asian Ethnography No. 7, Tan Chee Beng and Anthony R. Walker, general editor. Board of Editors, Columbus, Ohio.
Kidder, Alfred V.
1962 *An Introduction to the Study of Southwestern Archaeology, with a Preliminary Account of the Excavations at Pecos.* Reprint. Yale University Press,

New Haven. Originally published 1924, Papers of the Phillips Academy Southwest Expedition I, Phillips Academy, Andover, Mass.

Kidder, Tristram R.

2002 Mapping Poverty Point. *American Antiquity* 67:89–101.

Kirch, Patrick V., and Marshall Sahlins

1992 *Anahulu: The Anthropology of History in the Kingdom of Hawaii.* University of Chicago Press, Chicago.

Kirkby, Michael J.

1972 *The Physical Environment of the Nochixtlan Valley, Oaxaca.* Publications in Anthropology No. 2. Department of Anthropology, Vanderbilt University, Nashville.

Kiwanuka, M.S.M. Semakula

1972 *A History of Buganda from the Foundation of the Kingdom to 1900.* African Publishing, New York.

Kniffen, Fred B.

1939 Pomo Geography. In *University of California Publications in American Archaeology and Ethnology*, edited by A. L. Kroeber, Robert H. Lowie, and R. L. Olson, vol. 6, 353–399. University of California Press, Berkeley.

Kowalewski, Stephen A.

1990 Scale and Complexity: Issues in the Archaeology of the Valley of Oaxaca. In *Debating Oaxaca Archaeology*, edited by Joyce Marcus, pp. 207–270. Anthropological Papers No. 84. Museum of Anthropology, University of Michigan, Ann Arbor.

2003 Intensification under Duress. Paper presented at the 68th Annual Meeting of the Society for American Archaeology, Milwaukee.

Kowalewski, Stephen A., Gary M. Feinman, Laura Finsten, Richard E. Blanton, and Linda M. Nicholas (editors)

1989 *Monte Albán's Hinterland, Part II: Prehispanic Settlement Patterns in Tlacolula, Etla, and Ocotlan, the Valley of Oaxaca, Mexico.* 2 vols. Memoirs of the Museum of Anthropology No. 23. University of Michigan, Ann Arbor.

Kowalewski, Stephen A., Gary M. Feinman, Linda M. Nicholas, and Verenice Y. Heredia

2006 Hilltowns and Valley Fields: Great Transformations, Labor, and Long-Term History in Ancient Oaxaca. In *Labor in Cross-Cultural Perspective*, edited by E. Paul Durrenberger and Judith Marti, 197–216. Society for Economic Anthropology Monograph No. 22. Altamira Press, Lanham, Md.

Kroeber, A. L.

1953 *Handbook of the Indians of California.* California Book Company, Berkeley.

Kroeber, Clifton B., and Bernard L. Fontana

1986 *Massacre on the Gila: An Account of the Last Major Battle between American Indians, with Reflections on the Origin of War.* University of Arizona Press, Tucson.

Kuhn, Thomas

1962 *The Structure of Scientific Revolutions.* University of Chicago Press, Chicago.

Kwiatkowski, Lynn M.

1994 *Malnutrition, Gender, and Development in Ifugao, an Upland Community in the Philippines.* Ph.D. dissertation, University of California, Berkeley. University Microfilms, Ann Arbor.

La Barre, Weston

1948 *The Aymara Indians of the Lake Titicaca Plateau.* American Anthropological Association Memoir Series No. 68. American Anthropological Association, Menasha, Wisconsin.

Ladefoged, Thegn H., and Richard Pearson

2000 Fortified Castles on Okinawa Island during the Gusuku Period, AD 1200–1600. *Antiquity* 74:404–412.

Lambrecht, Francis

1929 *Ifugaw Villages and Houses.* Publications of the Catholic Anthropological Conference Vol. 1, No. 3. Catholic Anthropological Conference, Washington, D.C.

1932 *The Mayawyaw Ritual.* Publications of the Catholic Anthropological Conference Vol 4, No. 1. Catholic Anthropological Conference, Washington, D.C.

1957 The Mayawyaw Ritual VII. Hunting and Its Ritual. *Journal of East Asiatic Studies* 6:1–28.

Lange, Richard C., and William L. Deaver

1989 Photographs of Los Morteros Artifacts. In *The 1979–1983 Testing at Los Morteros (AZ AA:12:57 ASM), a Large Hohokam Village Site in the Tucson Basin,* compiled by Richard C. Lange, pp. 305–316. Arizona State Museum Archaeological Series No. 177. University of Arizona, Tucson.

Langer, Debra R.

1997 Site Formation Processes and Ceramics at Cerro de Trincheras. Bachelor's honors thesis, Binghamton University, Binghamton, N.Y.

Larson, Stephen M.

1972 The Tumamoc Hill Site near Tucson. *Kiva* 38:95–102.

1979 The Material Culture Distribution on the Tumamoc Hill Summit. *Kiva* 45:71–81.

LeBlanc, Steven A.

1982 The Advent of Pottery in the Southwest. In *Southwestern Ceramics: A Comparative Review,* edited by Albert H. Schroeder, pp. 27–57. Arizona Archaeologist No. 15. Arizona Archaeological Society, Phoenix.

1999 *Prehistoric Warfare in the American Southwest.* University of Utah Press, Salt Lake City.

LeBlanc, Steven A., and Glen E. Rice

2001 Southwestern Warfare: The Value of Case Studies. In *Deadly Landscapes: Case Studies in Prehistoric Southwestern Warfare,* edited by Glen E. Rice and Steven A. LeBlanc, pp. 239–287. University of Utah Press, Salt Lake City.

Lebra, William P.

1966 *Okinawan Religion: Belief, Ritual, and Social Structure.* University of Hawaii Press, Honolulu.

Lee, Hoon K.

1936 *Land Utilization and Rural Economy in Korea.* University of Chicago Press, Chicago.

Lekson, Stephen H.

1986 *The Great Pueblo Architecture of Chaco Canyon, New Mexico.* University of New Mexico Press, Albuquerque.

2002 War in the Southwest, War in the World. *American Antiquity* 67:607–624.

Lelgemann, Achim

1996 Orientaciones Astronómicas y el Sistema de Medida en La Quemada, Zacatecas, México. *Indiana (Berlin)* 14:99–125.

2000 *Proyecto Ciudadela de La Quemada, Zacatecas.* Informe final al Consejo de Arqueología, Instituto Nacional de Antropología e Historia, Bonn, Germany.

Lemmonier, Pierre

1991 From Great Men to Big Men: Peace, Substitution and Competition in the Highlands of New Guinea. In *Big Men and Great Men: Personifications of Power in Melanesia,* edited by Maurice Godelier and Marilyn Strathern, pp. 7–27. Cambridge University Press, Cambridge.

Lindauer, Owen, and Bert Zaslow

1994 Homologous Style Structures in Hohokam and Trincheras Art. *Kiva* 59:319–344.

Lindeman, Michael W.

2003 Plain Ware and Red Ware Horizon Architectural Style. In *Roots of Sedentism: Archaeological Excavations at Valencia Vieja, a Founding Village in the Tucson Basin of Southern Arizona,* edited by Henry D. Wallace, pp. 35–122. Anthropological Papers No. 29. Center for Desert Archaeology, Tucson.

Ling, Shun-shêng, and Yih-fu Ruey

1947 *Hsiang-hsi Miao-tsu Tiao-ch'a Pao-kao* [A Report on an Investigation of the Miao of Western Hunan]. Monograph Series A, No. 18. The Institute of History and Philology, Shanghai.

Linton, Ralph

1933 *The Tanala: A Hill Tribe of Madagascar.* Publications of the Field Museum of Natural History No. 317, Anthropological Series Vol. 22. Field Museum of Natural History, Chicago.

Lister, Robert

1958 *Archaeological Excavations in the Northern Sierra Madre Occidental, Chihuahua and Sonora.* University of Colorado Press, Boulder.

López Luján, Leonardo, Robert H. Cobean T., and Alba Guadalupe Mastache F.

1995 *Xochicalco y Tula.* Consejo Nacional para la Cultura y las Artes, Jaca Book, Mexico.

Lumholtz, Carl

1902 *Unknown Mexico: A Record of Five Years' Exploration of the Western Sierra Madre; in the Tierra Caliente of Tepic and Jalisco; and among the Tarascos of Michoacan,* vols. 1 and 2. Charles Scribner's Sons, New York.

1912 *New Trails in Mexico.* Charles Scribner's Sons, New York.

Lyons, Patrick

2001 Winslow Orange Ware and the Ancestral Hopi Migration Horizon. Unpublished Ph.D. dissertation, Department of Anthropology, University of Arizona, Tucson.

Mabry, Jonathan B.

1998 Architectural Variability and Site Structures. In *Archaeological Investigations of Early Village Sites in the Middle Santa Cruz Valley: Analyses and Synthesis,* edited by Jonathan B. Mabry, pp. 209–244. Anthropological Papers No. 19. Center for Desert Archaeology, Tucson.

1999 Summary and Interpretations. In *Prehistoric Uses of a Developing Floodplain: Archaeological Investigations on the East Bank of the Santa Cruz River at A-Mountain,* edited by Jonathan B. Mabry, Michael W. Lindeman, and Helga Wöcherl, pp. 88–98. Technical Report No. 98-10. Desert Archaeology, Tucson.

Mair, Lucy Phillip

1934 *An African People in the Twentieth Century.* Stephen Austin and Sons, Hertford, England.

Mange, Juan Mateo

1926 *Luz de tierra incógnita en la América Septentrional y diario de las exploraciones en Sonora.* Publicaciones del Archivo General de la Nación 10. Mexico City.

Maquet, Jacques J.

1961 *The Premise of Inequality in Ruanda: A Study of Political Relations in a Central African Kingdom.* Oxford University Press, London.

Marcus, Joyce

1980 Zapotec Writing. *Scientific American* 242:50–64.

1992 *Mesoamerican Writing Systems: Propaganda, Myth, and History in Four Ancient Civilizations.* Princeton University Press, Princeton, N.J.

Marcus, Joyce, and Kent V. Flannery
1996 *Zapotec Civilization: How Urban Society Evolved in Mexico's Oaxaca Valley*. Thames and Hudson, London.

Martínez, Júpiter
2001a Informe Area B.5. Manuscript on file, Cerro de Trincheras Excavation Project, Centro INAH Sonora, Hermosillo.
2001b Informe Area B.6. Manuscript on file, Cerro de Trincheras Excavation Project, Centro INAH Sonora, Hermosillo.

Masse, Bruce W.
1979 An Intensive Survey of Prehistoric Dry Farming Systems near Tumamoc Hill in Tucson, Arizona. *Kiva* 45:141–186.

Masters, William Murray
1953 Rowanduz: A Kurdish Administrative and Mercantile Center. Unpublished Ph.D. dissertation, University of Michigan, Ann Arbor.

McAnany, Patricia A.
1995 *Living with the Ancestors: Kinship and Kingship in Ancient Maya Society*. University of Texas Press, Austin.

McCafferty, Sharisse D., and Geoffrey G. McCafferty
1994 Engendering Tomb 7 at Monte Albán: Respinning an Old Yarn. *Current Anthropology* 35:143–166.

McCormack, Anna P.
1964 Khasis. In *Ethnic Groups of Mainland Southeast Asia*, edited by Frank M. Lebar, Gerald C. Hickey, and John K. Musgrave, pp. 105–112. Human Relations Area Files, New Haven, Connecticut.

McGee, W. J.
1895 The Beginning of Agriculture. *American Anthropologist* 8:350–375.
1898 *The Seri Indians*. Seventeenth Annual Report of the Bureau of American Ethnology. Smithsonian Institution, Washington, D.C.
2000 *Trails to Tiburón: The 1894 and 1895 Field Diaries of W. J. McGee*. University of Arizona Press, Tucson.

McGinnies, William G.
1981 *Discovering the Desert: Legacy of the Carnegie Desert Botanical Laboratory*. University of Arizona Press, Tucson.

McGregor, John M.
1998 You Take the Highlands and I'll Take the Low: An Analysis of Area E at Cerro de Trincheras, Trincheras, Sonora, Mexico. Unpublished master's thesis, Binghamton University, Binghamton, New York.

McGuire, Randall H.
1980 The Mesoamerican Connection in the Southwest. *Kiva* 46:3–38.
1991 On the Outside Looking In: The Concept of Periphery in Hohokam Archaeology. In *Exploring the Hohokam: Prehistoric Desert Peoples of the American Southwest*, edited by George J. Gumerman, pp. 347–382. University of New Mexico Press, Albuquerque.

1998 A Comparison of Terraced Settlements in the Southwest/Northwest and in Mesoamerica. Paper presented at the 63rd Annual Meeting of the Society for American Archaeology, Seattle.

McGuire, Randall H., E. Charles Adams, Ben A. Nelson, and Katherine A. Spielmann

1994 Drawing the Southwest to Scale: Perspectives on Macroregional Relations. In *Themes in Southwest Prehistory*, edited by George J. Gumerman, pp. 239–265. School of American Research Press, Santa Fe.

McGuire, Randall H., and Ann Valdo Howard

1987 The Structure and Organization of Hohokam Shell Exchange. *Kiva* 52:113–146.

McGuire, Randall H., and María Elisa Villalpando

1989 Prehistory and the Making of History in Sonora. In *Archaeological and Historical Perspectives on the Spanish Borderlands West*, edited by David Hurst Thomas, pp. 159–177. Columbian Consequences Vol. 1. Smithsonian Institution Press, Washington, D.C.

1991 Proyecto reconocimiento arqueológico en el Valle de Altar. Informe presentado al Consejo de Arqueología del INAH, México.

1993 *An Archaeological Survey of the Altar Valley, Sonora, Mexico*. Arizona State Museum Archaeological Series No. 184. University of Arizona, Tucson.

1994 Proyecto arqueológico Cerro de Trincheras. Informe final de la temporada de campo 1991. Reconocimiento de superficie y levantamiento topográfico. Informe al Consejo de Arqueología del INAH, México.

McGuire, Randall H., María Elisa Villalpando, James P. Holmlund, and Maria O'Donovan

1993 Cerro de Trincheras Mapping Project, Final Technical Report to the National Geographic Society for Grant #4454–91. Report on file, State University of New York, Binghamton.

McGuire, Randall H., María Elisa Villalpando, Victoria D. Vargas, and Emiliano Gallaga

1999 Cerro de Trincheras and the Casas Grandes World. In *The Casas Grandes World*, edited by Curtis F. Schaafsma and Carroll L. Riley, pp. 134–146. University of Utah Press, Salt Lake City.

McKim, Fred

1947 *San Blas: An Account of the Cuna Indians of Panama; The Forbidden Land: Reconnaissance of Upper Bayano River, R.P., in 1936: Two Posthumous Works*. Etnografiska Museet, Göteborg.

McLeod, Malcolm D.

1981 *The Asante*. British Museum, London.

McNamee, William D.

1992 Excavations at Cloud Blower Stockade (5DL121b): A Late Basketmaker III Habitation. In *Archaeological Excavations on Reach III of the Dove Creek Canal*, edited by William D. McNamee and Nancy S. Hammack, pp. 3.1–3.33. Four Corners Archaeological Project Report No. 18. Complete Archaeological Services Associates, Cortez, Colo.

McNamee, William D., and Nancy S. Hammack (editors)
1992 *Archaeological Excavations on Reach III of the Dove Creek Canal.* Four Corners Archaeological Project Report No. 18. Complete Archaeological Services Associates, Cortez, Colo.

Medina González, José H.
2000 El paisaje ritual del Valle de Malpaso. Tésis de licenciatura en arqueología, Escuela Nacional de Antropología, Instituto Nacional de Antropología y Secretaría de Educación Publica, Mexico, D.F.

Messing, Simon D., and M. Lionel Bender
1985 *Highland Plateau Amhara of Ethiopia.* Human Area Relations Files, New Haven, Conn.

Meulen, D. van der, and H. Von Wissmann
1932 *Hadramaut: Some of Its Mysteries Unveiled.* E. J. Brill, Leyden.

Meyer, Hans
1916 *Die Barundi: Eine volkerkundliche Studie aus Deutsch-Ostafrika* [The Barundi: An Ethnological Study of German East Africa]. Translated by Helmut Handzik. Ott Spamer, Leipzig.

Meyerowitz, Eva Lewin-Richter
1974 *The Early History of the Akan States of Ghana.* Red Candle Press, London.

Milbrath, Robert Steven
1986 *Institutional Development and Capital Accumulation in a Complex of Basque Worker Cooperatives.* Ph.D. dissertation, University of Michigan. University Microfilms, Ann Arbor.

Miller, Wick R.
1984 The Classification of Uto-Aztecan Languages Based on Lexical Evidence. *International Journal of American Linguistics* 50(1):1–24.

Minturn, Penny Dufoe, and Lorrie Lincoln-Babb
1995 Human Remains from Trincheras: Son F:10:2. Manuscript on file, Cerro de Trincheras Excavation Project, Binghamton University, Binghamton, New York.

Moisley, Henry A.
1962 *Uig: A Hebridean Parish.* Department of Geography, University of Nottingham, Glasgow.

Montagne, Robert
1930 *The Berbers and the Makhzen in the South of Morocco: Essay on the Political Transformation of the Sedentary Berbers (the Chleuh Group).* Translated by Jean Winchell. Librairie Félix Alcan, Paris.

Moore, Andrew M. T.
1978 *The Neolithic of the Levant,* vols. 1 and 2. Unpublished Ph.D. dissertation, Oxford University.

Moose, Robert J.

1911 *Village Life in Korea.* M. E. Church, Nashville.

Morgan, Lewis Henry, and Herbert M. Lloyd

1901 *League of the Ho-Dé-No-Sau-Nee or Iroquois*, vol. 1. Dodd and Mead, New York.

Morris, Earl H.

1928 *An Aboriginal Salt Mine at Camp Verde, Arizona.* Anthropological Papers Vol. 30, Pt. 3. American Museum of Natural History, New York.

Motsinger, Thomas N.

2000 Ceramic Figurines at the Hassayampa Ruin and Simmons' "Room Creek Effigy Culture." In *Archaeology in West Central Arizona: Proceedings of the 1996 Arizona Archaeological Council Prescott Conference*, edited by Thomas N. Motsinger, Douglas R. Mitchell, and James M. McKie, pp. 145–154. Sharlot Hall Museum Press, Prescott, Ariz.

Murie, James R.

1914 Pawnee Indian Societies. *Anthropological Papers of the American Museum of Natural History* 11(7):543–644.

Nakane, Chie

1967 *Garo and Khasi: A Comparative Study in Matrilineal Systems.* Mouton, Paris.

Nelson, Ben A.

1994 Outposts of Mesoamerican Empire and Architectural Patterning at La Quemada, Zacatecas. In *Culture and Contact: Charles C. DiPeso's Gran Chichimeca*, edited by Anne I. Woosley and John C. Ravesloot, pp. 173–190. University of New Mexico Press, Albuquerque.

1995 Complexity, Hierarchy, and Scale: A Controlled Comparison between Chaco Canyon, New Mexico, and La Quemada, Zacatecas. *American Antiquity* 60:597–618.

1997 Chronology and Stratigraphy at La Quemada, Zacatecas, Mexico. *Journal of Field Archaeology* 24:85–109.

2000 Aggregation, Warfare, and the Spread of the Mesoamerican Tradition. In *The Archaeology of Regional Interaction: Religion, Warfare, and Exchange across the American Southwest and Beyond*, edited by Michelle Hegmon, pp. 317–337. University of Utah Press, Salt Lake City.

2001 Northwestern Mexico. In *Oxford Encyclopedia of Mesoamerican Cultures: The Civilizations of Mexico and Central America*, edited by Davíd Carrasco, Anthony F. Aveni, Elizabeth H. Boone, John K. Chance, William L. Fash, Linda Manzanilla, and William B. Taylor, vol. 2, pp. 385–388. Oxford University Press, New York.

2004 Current and Future Directions in Northwest Mexican Archaeology. In *Surveying the Archaeology of Northwest Mexico*, edited by Gillian E. Newell and Emiliano Gallaga, pp. 289–296. University of Utah Press, Salt Lake City.

2006 Mesoamerican Objects and Symbols in Chaco Canyon Contexts. In *The Archaeology of Chaco Canyon: An Eleventh-Century Pueblo Regional Center*, edited by Stephen H. Lekson, pp. 339–372. The School for American Research Press, Santa Fe, N.M.

Nelson, Ben A., and Destiny Crider
2006 Posibles pasajes migratorios en el Norte de México y el Suroeste de los Estados Unidos durante el Epiclásico y el Postclásico. In *Reacomodos demográficos del Clásico al Postclásico en el Centro de México*, edited by L. Manzanilla, pp. 75–102. Instituto de Investigaciones, Universidad Nacional de México, Mexico, D.F.

Nelson, Ben A., J. Andrew Darling, and David A. Kice
1992 Mortuary Patterns and the Social Order at La Quemada, Zacatecas. *Latin American Antiquity* 3:298–315.

Noguera, Eduardo
1958 *Reconocimiento arqueológico en Sonora.* Dirección de Monumentos Prehispánicos, Informe No. 10. Instituto Nacional de Antropología e Historia, Mexico.

North, Chris D.
2001 *The Tonto Hills Project: Results of Archaeological Testing and a Cultural Resources Overview for the Desert Foothills Region Surrounding Carefree, Maricopa County, Arizona.* SWCA Cultural Resources Report No. 01-310, Phoenix.

North, Chris D., Louise Senior, and Michael S. Foster
2003 *An Archaeological Survey and Ethnohistoric Study of the Verde Wild and Scenic River Corridor.* SWCA Cultural Resources Report No. 02-415. Phoenix.

O'Donovan, Maria
1997 Confronting Archaeological Enigmas: Cerro de Trincheras, Cerros de Trincheras and Monumentality. Unpublished Ph.D. dissertation, State University of New York, Binghamton.
2002 *New Perspectives on Site Function and Scale of Cerro de Trincheras, Sonora, Mexico: The 1991 Surface Survey.* Arizona State Museum Archaeological Series No. 195. University of Arizona, Tucson.
2004 The Role of Cerro de Trincheras Sites in the Northwest Mexican and American Southwest Landscape. In *Surveying the Archaeology of Northwest Mexico*, edited by Gillian E. Newell and Emiliano Gallaga, pp. 27–45. University of Utah Press, Salt Lake City.

Ott, Sandra
1981 *The Circle of Mountains: A Basque Shepherding Community.* Clarendon Press, Oxford.

Otterbein, Keith F.
2000 A History of Research on Warfare in Anthropology. *American Anthropologist* 101:794–805.

Pagès, G.

1933 *Un royaume hamite au centre de l'Afrique: au Ruanda sur les bords du Lac Kivu (Congo Belge)* [A Hamitic Kingdom in the Center of Africa: In Ruanda on the Shores of Lake Kivu (Belgian Congo)]. Mémoires, Institut Royal Colonial Belge, Section des Sciences morales et politiques, Collection in-80 Vol. 1. Librairie Falk Fils, Brussels.

Palau Martí, Montserrat

1957 *The Dogon*. Translated by Frieda Schütze. Presses Universitaires de France, Paris.

Parin, Paul, Fritz Morganthaler, and Goldy Parin-Matthey

1963 *The Whites Think Too Much: Psychoanalytic Investigations among the Dogon in West Africa*. Translated by Frieda Schütze. Atlantis Verlag, Zurich.

Paulme, Denise

1940 *Social Organization of the Dogon (French Sudan)*. Translated by Frieda Schütze. Éditions Domat-Montchrestien, F. Loviton, Paris.

Pennington, Campbell W.

1963 *The Tarahumar of Mexico: Their Environment and Material Culture*. University of Utah Press, Salt Lake City.

Pepper, George H.

1976 The Exploration of a Burial Room in Pueblo Bonito, New Mexico. In *Putnam Anniversary Volume*, 2nd ed., edited by F. Boas, pp. 196–252. G. D. Strechert, New York.

Pérez Rodríguez, Verónica

2003 Household Intensification and Agrarian States: Excavation of Houses and Terraced Fields in a Mixtec Cacicazgo. Unpublished Ph.D. dissertation, Department of Anthropology, University of Georgia, Athens.

Pijoan Aguadé, Carmen María, and Josefina Mansilla Lory

1996 Prácticas rituales en el norte de Mesoamérica: evidencias en Electra, Villa de Reyes, San Luis Potosí. *Arqueología* 4:87–96.

Pilles, Peter J., Jr.

1981 The Southern Sinagua. *Plateau* 53(1): 6–17.

Piña Chan, Román (editor)

1973 *Teotenango, segundo informe de exploraciones arqueológicas*. Dirección de Turismo, Gobierno del Estado de México, Mexico, D.F.

Pitts, Forrest R., William P. Lebra, and Wayne P. Suttles

1955 *Post-war Okinawa*. National Research Council, Pacific Science Board, Washington, D.C.

Playfair, Alan

1909 *The Garos*. David Nutt, London.

Pollard, Helen

1996 La transformación de elites regionales en Michoacán central. In *Las cuencas del occidente de México: epoca Prehispánica*, edited by Eduardo

Williams and Phil C. Weigand, pp. 131–156. El Colegio de Michoacán, with CEMCA and ORSTOM, Zamora, Michoacán.

Pollard, Helen Perlstein, and Laura Cahue

1999 Mortuary Patterns of Regional Elites in the Lake Patzcuaro Basin of Western Mexico. *Latin American Antiquity* 10:259–280.

Price, Mary

2000 Cerro de Trincheras Area B.1 Report. Manuscript on file, Cerro de Trincheras Excavation Project, Binghamton University, Binghamton, New York.

Pringle, Robert Maxwell

1968 *The Ibans of Sarawak under Brooke Rule*. University Microfilms, Ann Arbor.

Radcliffe-Brown, A. R.

1922 *The Andaman Islanders: A Study in Social Anthropology*. University Press, Cambridge.

Rappaport, Roy A.

1968 *Pigs for the Ancestors: Ritual in the Ecology of a New Guinea People*. Yale University Press, New Haven.

Ray, Benjamin C.

1991 *Myth, Ritual, and Kingship in Buganda*. Oxford University Press, New York.

Raymond, Albert

1952 Skull Mesa Ruins. Manuscript on file, NA Additional Site Information, Museum of Northern Arizona, Flagstaff.

Rice, Glen E.

2001 Warfare and Massing in the Salt and Gila Basins of Central Arizona. In *Deadly Landscapes: Case Studies in Prehistoric Southwestern Warfare*, edited by Glen E. Rice and Steven A. LeBlanc, pp. 289–329. University of Utah Press, Salt Lake City.

Rice, Glen E., and Steven A. LeBlanc (editors)

2001 *Deadly Landscapes: Case Studies in Prehistoric Southwestern Warfare*. University of Utah Press, Salt Lake City.

Richards, Audrey Isabel

1966 *The Changing Structure of a Ganda Village: Kisozi, 1892–1952*. East Africa Publishing House, Nairobi.

Robequain, Charles

1929 *Le Thanh Hoá. Étude géographique d'une province annamite*. English translation. Translated by C. A. Messner. Publications de l'École Française d'Extrême-Orient 23–24. 2 vols. G. Van Oest, Paris.

Robles, Manuel

1973 *El arroyo Bcoachi y el tráfico de conchas trincheras*. Museo de la Universidad de Sonora, Hermosillo.

Rohn, Arthur
1974 Payne Site Investigations. *Southwestern Lore* 40:50–52.
Roney, John R.
1999 Canador Peak: An Early Pithouse Period Cerro de Trincheras in Southwestern New Mexico. In *La Frontera: Papers in Honor of Patrick H. Beckett,* edited by Meliha S. Duran and David T. Kirkpatrick, pp. 173–184. Archaeological Society of New Mexico, Albuquerque.
Roney, John R., and Robert J. Hard
2002 Early Agriculture in Northwestern Chihuahua. In *Traditions, Transitions, and Technologies: Themes in Southwestern Archaeology: Proceedings of the 2000 Southwest Symposium,* edited by Sarah Schlanger, pp. 160–177. University Press of Colorado, Boulder.
2003 Late Archaic Villages on the Rio Casas Grandes. *Archaeology Southwest* 17(2):11.
2004 A Review of Cerros de Trincheras in Northwest Chihuahua. In *Surveying the Archaeology of Northwest Mexico,* edited by Gillian E. Newell and Emiliano Gallaga, pp. 127–148. University of Utah Press, Salt Lake City.
Rongmuthu, Dewan Sing (compiler)
1960 *The Folk Tales of the Garos.* University of Gauhati, Department of Publications, Gauhati, India.
Roosevelt, Archie, Jr.
1947 The Kurdish Republic of Mahabad. *Middle East Journal* 1:247–269.
Roscoe, John
1911 *The Baganda: An Account of Their Native Customs and Beliefs.* Macmillan, London.
1915 *The Northern Bantu: An Account of Some Central African Tribes of the Uganda Protectorate.* Cambridge University Press, Cambridge.
Roth, Barbara J.
1996 Regional Land Use in the Late Archaic of the Tucson Basin: A View from the Upper Bajada. In *Early Formative Adaptations in the Southern Southwest,* edited by Barbara J. Roth, pp. 37–48. Monographs in World Archaeology No. 5. Prehistory Press, Madison, Wisc.
Rowe, John Howland
1946 Inca Culture at the Time of the Spanish Conquest. In *Handbook of South American Indians: 2. The Andean Civilizations,* edited by Julian H. Steward, pp. 183–330. Smithsonian Institution Bureau of American Ethnology Bulletin No. 143, Washington, D.C.
Russell, Frank
1908 *The Pima Indians.* 26th Annual Report of the Bureau of American Ethnology, 1904–1905, U.S. Government Printing Office, Washington, D.C.

1975 *The Pima Indians*. Reprinted. University of Arizona Press, Tucson. Originally published 1908, *26th Annual Report of the Bureau of American Ethnology to the Secretary of the Smithsonian Institution*, 1904–1905. U.S. Government Printing Office, Washington, D.C.

Sahlins, Marshall

1958 *Social Stratification in Polynesia*. American Ethnological Society, Seattle.

1963 Poor Man, Rich Man, Big Man, Chief: Political Types in Melanesia and Polynesia. *Comparative Studies in History and Society* 5:285–303.

Sakihara, Mitsugu

1987 *A Brief History of Early Okinawa Based on the Omoro Soshi*. Honpa Shoseki Press, Tokyo.

Sandin, Benedict

1967 *The Sea Dayaks of Borneo: Before White Rajah Rule*. Macmillan, London.

Sandomingo, Manuel

1954 *Historia de Sonora: tiempos prehistoricos*, vol 1. Manuel Sandomingo, Agua Prieta, Sonora, Mexico.

Sassaman, Kenneth E.

2005 Structure and Practice in the Archaic Southeast. In *North American Archaeology*, edited by Timothy R. Pauketat and Diana DiPaolo Loren, pp. 79–107. Blackwell, Oxford.

Sauer, Carl, and Donald D. Brand

1931 Prehistoric Settlements of Sonora, with Special Reference to Cerros de Trincheras. *University of California Publications in Geography* 5(3): 67–148.

Schaafsma, Polly

2000 *Warrior, Shield, and Star*. Western Edge Press, Santa Fe.

Schaefer, Stacy B., and Peter T. Furst

1996 The Crossing of the Souls: Peyote, Perception, and Meaning among the Huichol Indians. In *People of the Peyote: Huichol Indian History, Religion & Survival*, edited by Stacy B. Schaefer and Peter T. Furst, pp. 138–168. University of New Mexico Press, Albuquerque.

Schaepe, David M.

2006 Rock Fortifications: Archaeological Insights into Precontact Warfare and Sociopolitical Organization among the Sto:Lo of the Lower Fraser River Canyon, B.C. *American Antiquity* 71(4):671–705.

Schmidt, Kari M., and Jennifer E. Nisengard

2000 1999 Excavations: A Report on the Faunal Remains from Cerro Juanaqueña, Cerro El Canelo, and the Floodplain Site, Chihuahua, Mexico. Manuscript on file, Center for Archaeological Research, University of Texas at San Antonio.

Schroeder, Albert H.

1954 Four Prehistoric Sites near Mayer, Arizona, Which Suggest a New Focus. *Plateau* 26:103–107.

Schwalen, H. C., and R. J. Shaw

1957 *Ground Water Supplies of the Santa Cruz Valley of Southern Arizona between Rillito Station and the International Boundary*. Bulletin No. 288. Arizona Agricultural Experimental Station, University of Arizona, Tucson.

Shaul, David L., and Jane H. Hill

1999 Tepimans, Yumans, and Other Hohokam. *American Antiquity* 63:375–396.

Simmons, J. W.

n.d. J. W. Simmons Papers. Manuscript on file, Arizona State Museum Archives, University of Arizona, Tucson.

Simmons, Marc

1979 History of Pueblo-Spanish Relations to 1821. In *Handbook of North American Indians*, edited by Alfonso Ortiz, pp. 178–193, Vol. 9, William C. Sturtevant, general editor, Smithsonian Institution Press, Washington, D.C.

Sinha, Tarunchandra

1966 *The Psyche of the Garos*. Anthropological Survey of India, Government of India, Calcutta.

Slaughter, Mark C., and Heidi Roberts

1996 *Excavation of the Gibbon Springs Site: A Classic Period Village in the Northwestern Tucson Basin*. SWCA Archaeological Report 94–87. SWCA, Tucson.

Sliva, R. Jane

1998 Flaked Stone Artifacts. In *Archaeological Investigations of Early Village Sites in the Middle Santa Cruz Valley: Analyses and Synthesis*, edited by Jonathan B. Mabry, pp. 299–356. Anthropological Papers No. 19. Center for Desert Archaeology, Tucson.

2003 Valencia Vieja and Changing Perspectives on Early Ceramic Period Flaked Stone Technology. In *Roots of Sedentism: Archaeological Excavations at Valencia Vieja: A Founding Village in the Tucson Basin of Southern Arizona*, edited by H. D. Wallace, pp. 335–362. Anthropological Papers No. 29. Center for Desert Archaeology, Tucson.

Smets, George

1946 The Structure of the Barundi Community (Ruanda-Urundi Territory, Central Africa). *Man* 46:12–16.

Smith, Charlotte A.

1993 Prehistoric Mixtec Social Organization: The Architectural Evidence. Unpublished master's thesis, Department of Anthropology, University of Georgia, Athens.

Smith, Fay Jackson, John L. Kessell, and Francis J. Fox

1966 *Father Kino in Arizona*. Arizona Historical Foundation, Phoenix.

Smith, Ian W. G.

1990 Historical Archaeology in New Zealand: A Review and Bibliography. *New Zealand Journal of Archaeology* 12:85–119.

Smith, Michael E., and T. Jeffrey Price

1994 Aztec-Period Agricultural Terraces in Morelos, Mexico: Evidence for Household-Level Agricultural Intensification. *Journal of Field Archaeology* 21:169–179.

Spoerl, Patricia M., and George J. Gumerman (editors)

1984 *Prehistoric Cultural Development in Central Arizona: Archaeology of the Upper New River Region*. Center for Archaeological Investigations Occasional Paper No. 5. Southern Illinois University, Carbondale.

Spores, Ronald

1969 Settlement, Farming Technology, and Environment in the Nochixtlan Valley. *Science* 166:557–569.

St. John, Donald Patrick

1981 *The Dream-Vision Experience of the Iroquois: Its Religious Meaning*. Ph.D. dissertation, Fordham University, New York. University Microfilms, Ann Arbor.

Stacy, Valeria Kay Pheriba

1974 Cerros de Trincheras in the Arizona Papagueria. Unpublished Ph.D. dissertation, Department of Anthropology, University of Arizona, Tucson.

1977 Activity Patterning at Cerros de Trincheras in Southcentral Arizona. *Kiva* 43:11–17.

Stanley, C.V.B.

1912 The Oasis of Siwa. *Journal of the African Society* 11:290–324.

Steel, Robert W.

1948 The Population of Ashanti: A Geographical Analysis. *Geographical Journal* 112:64–77.

Stefánsson, Vilhjalmur

1914 *The Stefánsson-Anderson Arctic Expedition of the American Museum: Preliminary Ethnological Report*. Anthropological Papers Vol. 14, Part 1. American Museum of Natural History, New York.

Stegmiller, P. F.

1921 The Religious Life of the Khasi. *Anthropos* 16:407–411.

Steindorff, Georg

1904 *Durch die Libysche Wüste zur Amonsoase* [Through the Libyan Desert to the Oasis of Amon]. Translated by Theodore J. Ziolkowski. Land und Leute, Monographien zur Erdkunde Vol. 19. Verlag von Velhagen und Klasing, Bielefeld.

Stephenson, John B.

1984 *Ford, A Village in the West Highlands of Scotland: A Case Study of Repopulation and Social Change in a Small Community*. University Press of Kentucky, Lexington.

Steward, Julian H.

1937 Ecological Aspects of Southwestern Society. *Anthropos* 32:87–104.

1955 Lineage to Clan: Ecological Aspects of Southwestern Society. In *Theory of Culture Change: The Methodology of Multilinear Evolution*, edited by Julian H. Steward, pp. 151–172. University of Illinois Press, Urbana.

Stiver, Laura R.

2001 Prehispanic Mixtec Settlement and State in the Teposcolula Valley of Oaxaca, Mexico. Unpublished Ph.D. dissertation, Department of Anthropology, Vanderbilt University, Nashville.

Stone, Connie L.

2000 The Perry Mesa Tradition in Central Arizona: Scientific Studies and Management Concerns. In *Archaeology in West Central Arizona: Proceedings of the 1996 Arizona Archaeological Council Prescott Conference*, edited by Thomas Motsinger, Douglas R. Mitchell, and James M. McKie, pp. 205–214. Sharlot Hall Museum Press, Prescott, Ariz.

Stone, Glenn D., and Christian E. Downum

1999 Non-Boserupian Ecology and Agricultural Risk: Ethnic Politics and Land Control in the Arid Southwest. *American Anthropologist* 101:113–128.

Stuiver, Minze, Paula J. Reimer, and Thomas F. Braziunas

1998 High-precision Radiocarbon Age Calibration for Terrestrial and Marine Samples. *Radiocarbon* 40:1127–1151.

Sturler-Raemaekers, M. de

1953 Towns and Architecture of the Hadhramaut. *Royal Central Asian Journal* 40:241–248.

Swanson, Steven J.

1997 Atalayas of Paquimé: A GIS Analysis of Prehistoric Communication Features. Unpublished master's thesis, Department of Anthropology, University of Oklahoma, Norman.

2003 Documenting Prehistoric Communications Networks: A Case Study in the Paquimé Polity. *American Antiquity* 68:753–767.

Swartz, Deborah L., and Michael W. Lindeman

1997 The Stone Pipe Site, AZ BB:13:425 (ASM). In *Archaeological Investigations of Early Village Sites in the Middle Santa Cruz Valley: Descriptions of the Santa Cruz Bend, Square Hearth, Stone Pipe, and Canal Sites*, edited by Jonathan B. Mabry, Deborah L. Swartz, Helga Wöcherl, Jeffrey J. Clark, Gavin H. Archer, and Michael W. Lindeman, pp. 281–417. Anthropological Papers No. 18. Center for Desert Archaeology, Tucson.

Talayesva, Don, and Leo W. Simmons

1942 *Sun Chief: The Autobiography of a Hopi Indian.* H. Millford, Oxford University Press, London.

Tanaka, Masako U.

1974 *Kinship and Descent in an Okinawan Village.* Ph.D. dissertation, University of Rochester, Rochester, New York. University Microfilms, Ann Arbor.

Tanner, Clara Lee Fraps

1936 Blackstone Ruin. *Kiva* 2:9–12.

Thompson, Laura

1940 *Fijian Frontier.* Studies of the Pacific No. 4. American Council Institute of Pacific Relations, San Francisco.

Titiev, Mischa

1971 *Old Oraibi: A Study of the Hopi Indians of the Third Mesa.* Reprinted. Kraus Reprint, New York. Originally published 1944, Papers of the Peabody Museum of American Archaeology and Ethnology Vol. 22, No. 1, Harvard University, Cambridge.

Tower, Donald Bayley

1945 *The Use of Marine Mollusca and Their Value in Reconstructing Prehistoric Trade Routes in the American Southwest.* Papers of the Excavators Club Vol. 2, No. 3. Excavators Club, Cambridge, Mass.

Trigger, Bruce G.

1990 Monumental Architecture: A Thermodynamic Explanation of Symbolic Behavior. *World Archaeology* 22:119–132.

Trombold, Charles D.

1990 A Reconsideration of the Chronology for the La Quemada Portion of the Northern Mesoamerican Frontier. *American Antiquity* 55:308–323.

1991 Causeways in the Context of Strategic Planning in the La Quemada Region, Zacatecas, Mexico. In *Ancient Road Networks and Settlement Hierarchies in the New World,* edited by Charles D. Trombold, pp. 145–168. Cambridge University Press, Cambridge.

Tschopik, Harry, Jr.

1951 *The Aymara of Chucuito, Peru.* Anthropological Papers of the American Museum of Natural History vol. 44, part 2. American Museum of Natural History, New York.

Turnbull, Colin M.

1962 *The Forest People.* Simon and Schuster, New York.

Turnbull, Harold Frederick

1981 *The Importance of Population Structure and Birth Order Specific Selection in Relation to the Maintenance and Distribution of the Rhesus Blood Group Polymorphism in Human Populations. Evidence That Birth Order Specific Marriage and Migration Patterns in a Spanish Basque Village Mask the*

Opportunity for Incompatibility Selection. Ph.D. dissertation, University of California, Riverside. University Microfilms, Ann Arbor.

Turner, Christy G., and Jacqueline A. Turner

1999 *Man Corn: Cannibalism and Violence in the Prehistoric American Southwest*. University of Utah Press, Salt Lake City.

Tuthill, Carr

1947 *The Tres Alamos Site on the San Pedro River, Southeastern Arizona*. Amerind Foundation Publication No. 4. Amerind Foundation, Dragoon, Arizona.

Tweney, Ryan D., Michael E. Doherty, and Clifford R. Mynatt

1981 *On Scientific Thinking*. Columbia University Press, New York.

Underhill, Ruth M.

1946 *Papago Indian Religion*. Columbia University Contributions to Anthropology No. 33. Columbia University, New York.

Ungar, Catherine Anne

1978 The Archaeological Problem of Defense: Historic Settlement Patterns in the Var Valley System, Southwestern France. Unpublished Ph.D. dissertation, Department of Anthropology, University of Arizona, Tucson.

Urla, Jacqueline Louise

1987 *Being Basque, Speaking Basque: The Politics of Language and Identity in the Basque Country*. Ph.D. dissertation, University of California, Berkeley. University Microfilms, Ann Arbor.

Valehrach, Emil M., and Bruce S. Valehrach

1971 *Excavations at Brazaletes Pueblo*. The Arizona Archaeologist No. 6. Arizona Archaeological Society, Phoenix.

van Waarden, Nora

1984 Hilltop Sites in Central Arizona: An Analysis of Their Functional Relationships. Unpublished master's thesis, Arizona State University, Tempe.

Vargas, Victoria D.

1997 The Marine Shell Artifacts at Cerro de Trincheras. Manuscript on file, Cerro de Trincheras Excavation Project, Binghamton University, Binghamton, New York.

2004 Shell Ornaments, Power, and the Rise of Cerro de Trincheras: Patterns through Time at Trincheras Sites in the Magdalena River Valley, Sonora. In *Surveying the Archaeology of Northwest Mexico*, edited by Gillian E. Newell and Emiliano Gallaga, pp. 65–76. University of Utah Press, Salt Lake City.

Vega, Garcilasco de la

1871 *El Inca. The Royal Commentaries of the Yncas Part I*. Translated by Clements R. Markham. Hakluyt Society Series 1, Vols. 41 and 45. Hakluyt Society Publications, London.

Villalpando, María Elisa, John P. Carpenter, Guadalupe Sánchez de Carpenter, and Mayela Pastrana Oliver

1999 Salvamento arqueológico la playa. Informe de la Temporada 1997–1998. Manuscript on file, Centro INAH de Sonora, Hermosillo.

Villa Rojas, Alfonso

1945 *The Maya of East Central Quintana Roo*. Carnegie Institution of Washington, Washington, D.C.

Villaverde, Juan, and L. E. Case

1909 The Ifugaos of Quiangan and Vicinity. Translated and edited by Dean C. Worcester. *Philippine Journal of Science* 4:237–262.

Vokes, Arthur W.

2003 Personal Ornaments of Shell and Stone from Valencia Vieja. In *Roots of Sedentism: Archaeological Excavations at Valencia Vieja, a Founding Village in the Tucson Basin of Southern Arizona*, edited by Henry D. Wallace. Anthropological Papers No. 29. Center for Desert Archaeology, Tucson, in press.

Wagner, Ulla

1972 *Colonialism and Iban Warfare*. OBE-Tryck, Stockholm.

Walker, William H.

1995 Ceremonial Trash? In *Expanding Archaeology*, edited by James M. Skibo, William H. Walker, and Axel E. Nielsen, pp. 67–79. University of Utah Press, Salt Lake City.

Wallace, Henry D.

1983 The Mortars, Petroglyphs, and Trincheras on Rillito Peak. *Kiva* 48:137–246.

1987 Regional Context of the Prehistoric Rancho Vistoso Sites: Settlement Patterns and Socioeconomic Structure. In *Settlement in the Cañada del Oro Valley, Arizona. The Rancho Vistoso Survey Project*, edited by Douglas B. Craig and Henry D. Wallace, pp. 117–166. Institute for American Research Anthropological Papers No. 8, Tucson.

1988 Ceramic Boundaries and Interregional Interaction: New Perspectives on the Tucson Basin Hohokam. In *Recent Research on Tucson Basin Prehistory: Proceedings of the Second Tucson Basin Conference*, edited by William H. Doelle and Paul R. Fish, pp. 313–348. Institute for American Research Anthropological Papers No. 10, Tucson.

1995 Summary and Concluding Remarks. In *Archaeological Investigations at Los Morteros: A Prehistoric Settlement in the Northern Tucson Basin*, edited by Henry D. Wallace, pp. 801–835. Anthropological Papers No. 17. Center for Desert Archaeology, Tucson.

2003 Prelude. In *Roots of Sedentism: Archaeological Excavations at Valencia Vieja, a Founding Village in the Tucson Basin of Southern Arizona*, edited by Henry D. Wallace, pp. 1–23. Center for Desert Archaeology, Tucson.

Wallace, Henry D. (editor)

1995 *Archaeological Investigations at Los Morteros: A Prehistoric Settlement in the Northern Tucson Basin.* Anthropological Papers No. 17. Center for Desert Archaeology, Tucson.

Wallace, Henry D., and William H. Doelle

2001 Classic Period Warfare in Southern Arizona. In *Deadly Landscapes: Case Studies in Prehistoric Southwestern Warfare*, edited by Glen E. Rice and Steven A. LeBlanc, pp. 239–287. University of Utah Press, Salt Lake City.

Wallace, Henry D., James M. Heidke, and William H. Doelle

1995 Hohokam Origins. *Kiva* 60:575–618.

Wallace, Henry D., and Michael W. Lindeman

2000 Foundations of Hohokam Political Organization. Paper presented at the 65th Annual Meeting of the Society for American Archaeology, Philadelphia, Pennsylvania.

2004 Valencia Vieja and the Origins of Hohokam Culture. In *Roots of Sedentism: Archaeological Excavations at Valencia Vieja, a Founding Village in the Tucson Basin of Southern Arizona*, edited by Henry D. Wallace, pp. 371–406. Center for Desert Archaeology, Tucson.

Walters, Lorenzo D.

1926 The Papagos' Last Stand. *Progressive Arizona* 3:26–27.

Wang, Hsing-ju

1948 *Hainin Tao chih Miao-jen* [The Miao People of Hainan Island]. Translated by Te-Kong Tong. Chung-kuo Pien-chiang Yen-chiu Shin [Institute for Chinese Frontier Studies] Series B, No. 2. Chu-hai University, Canton.

Wasley, William W.

1968 Archaeological Survey in Sonora, Mexico. Paper presented at the 33rd Annual Meeting of the Society for American Archaeology, Santa Fe.

Wedel, Waldo Rudolph

1936 *An Introduction to Pawnee Archaeology.* Bureau of American Ethnology Bulletin No. 112. Smithsonian Institution, Washington, D.C.

Wellman, Kevin D. (editor)

1999 *The Tortolita Phase in the Tortolita Foothills: Investigations at the Triangle Road Site (AZ BB:9:87 [ASM]), Oro Valley, Arizona.* Archaeological Report No. 97-161. SWCA Environmental Consultants, Tucson.

Wells, E. Christian

2000 Pottery Production and Microcosmic Organization: The Residential Structure of La Quemada, Zacatecas. *Latin American Antiquity* 11:21–42.

Weltfish, Gene

1965 *The Lost Universe, with a Closing Chapter on* The Universe Regained. Basic Books, New York.

Wetterstrom, Wilma

1986 *Food, Diet, and Population at Prehistoric Arroyo Hondo Pueblo, New Mexico.* School of American Research Press, Santa Fe, New Mexico.

Whittlesey, Stephanie M.

1995 Mogollon, Hohokam, and O'otam: Rethinking the Early Formative Period. *Kiva* 60:465–480.

Wilcox, David R.

1979 Warfare Implications of Dry Laid Masonry Walls on Tumamoc Hill. *Kiva* 45:15–38.

1986 The Tepiman Connection: A Model of Southwestern-Mesoamerican Interactions. In *Ripples in the Chichimec Sea*, edited by F. Joan Mathien and Randall H. McGuire, pp. 135–153. Southern Illinois University Press, Carbondale.

1989 Work Plan for the 1989 MNA/NAU Archaeological Field School. Manuscript on file, Museum of Northern Arizona Library, Flagstaff.

2004 Review of *New Perspectives on Site Function and Scale of Cerro de Trincheras, Sonora, Mexico: The 1991 Surface Survey* by Maria O'Donovan. *Journal of Anthropological Research* 60:309–310.

Wilcox, David R., and Jonathan Haas

1994 The Scream of the Butterfly: Competition and Conflict in the Prehistoric Southwest. In *Themes in Southwest Prehistory*, edited by George J. Gumerman, pp. 211–238. School of American Research, Santa Fe.

Wilcox, David R., and Jim Holmlund

2007 *The Archaeology of Perry Mesa and Its World.* Bilby Research Center Occasional Paper No. 3. Northern Arizona University, Flagstaff.

Wilcox, David R., Donald Keller, and David Ortiz

2000 Long-Distance Exchange, Warfare, and the Indian Peak Ruin, Walnut Creek, Arizona. In *Archaeology in West Central Arizona: Proceedings of the 1996 Arizona Archaeological Council Prescott Conference*, edited by Thomas Motsinger, Douglas R. Mitchell, and James M. McKie, pp. 119–144. Sharlot Hall Museum Press, Prescott, Arizona.

Wilcox, David R., and Stephen M. Larson

1979 Introduction to the Tumamoc Hill Survey. *Kiva* 45:1–14.

Wilcox, David R., Stephen M. Larson, Bruce W. Masse, Gayle H. Hartmann, and Alan Ferg

1979 A Summary of Conclusions and Recommendations of the Tumamoc Hill Survey. *Kiva* 45:187–195.

Wilcox, David R., Thomas R. McGuire, and Charles Sternberg

1981 *Snaketown Revisited.* Arizona State Museum Archaeological Series No. 155. University of Arizona, Tucson.

Wilcox, David R., Gerald Robertson, Jr., and J. Scott Wood

1999 Perry Mesa: Arizona's First Gated Community. *Plateau Journal* (Summer):44–61.

2001a Organized for War: The Perry Mesa Settlement System and Its Central Arizona Neighbors. In *Deadly Landscapes: Case Studies in Prehistoric Southwestern Warfare*, edited by Glen E. Rice and Steven A. LeBlanc, pp. 141–194. University of Utah Press, Salt Lake City.

2001b Antecedents to Perry Mesa: Early Pueblo III Defensive Refuge Systems in West Central Arizona. In *Deadly Landscapes: Case Studies in Prehistoric Southwestern Warfare*, edited by Glen E. Rice and Steven A. LeBlanc, pp. 109–140. University of Utah Press, Salt Lake City.

Wilcox, David R., Joseph P. Vogel, Tom and Sue Weiss, and Neil Weintraub

2007 The Hilltop Defensive and Communication System of the Greater Prescott Area, A.D. 1100 to 1275, and Their Cohonina Neighbors. In *Prescott to Perry Mesa: 4,000 Years of Adaptation, Innovation, and Change in Central Arizona*, edited by Christine K. Robinson and Cory David Breternitz. Sharlot Hall Museum Press, Prescott, Ariz.

Winner, Irene

1971 *A Slovenian Village: Zerovnica.* Brown University Press, Providence, Rhode Island.

Wishart, David J.

1979 The Dispossession of the Pawnee. *Annals of the Association of American Geographers* 69(3):382–401.

Wolf, Arthur H.

1975 Robert Fletcher Gilder: Archeologist for the Museum. *Museum Notes* 54, *UNL News* 55(11). University of Nebraska State Museum, Lincoln.

Wood, J. Scott

1987 *Checklist of Pottery Types for the Tonto National Forest: An Introduction to the Archaeological Ceramics of Central Arizona.* The Arizona Archaeologist No. 21. Arizona Archaeological Society, Phoenix.

Wood, J. Scott, and David R. Wilcox

2001 Agua Fria. *Archaeology Southwest* 15(1):12–13.

Woodward, Arthur

1936 A Shell Bracelet Manufactory. *American Antiquity* 2:117–125.

Zavala, Bridget

1998 Building Trincheras: An Analysis of Architectural Features at Cerro de Trincheras. Unpublished master's thesis, State University of New York, Binghamton.

Zirakzadeh, Cyrus Ernesto

1985 *Popular in the Basque Region of Spain: A Study in Political Anthropology.* Ph.D. dissertation, University of California, Berkeley. University Microfilms, Ann Arbor.

Zulaika, Joseba

1988 *Basque Violence: Metaphor and Sacrament.* Basque Series. University of Nevada Press, Reno.

ABOUT THE CONTRIBUTORS

CHRISTIAN DOWNUM received his Ph.D. from the University of Arizona in 1988. He is Associate Professor and Director of the Anthropology Laboratories at Northern Arizona University. His research interests focus on the history of Southwest archaeology, ceramic dating, political ecology, and the prehispanic cultures of the U.S. Southwest. Publications include *Between Desert and River*, published by the University of Arizona Press, and *Archaeology of the Pueblo Grande Platform Mound*, published by the Pueblo Grande Museum.

PAUL R. FISH received his Ph.D. from Arizona State University in 1976. He is Curator of Archaeology at the Arizona State Museum and Professor of Anthropology at the University of Arizona and coordinates the Southwest Land, Culture and Society program jointly sponsored by the Department of Anthropology and the Arizona State Museum. Current research interests and publications pertain to the organization of middle range societies, the Hohokam of southern Arizona, and complex pre-European fishermen of southeast coastal Brazil.

SUZANNE K. FISH received her Ph.D. from the University of Arizona. She is Curator of Archaeology at the Arizona State Museum and Professor of Anthropology at the University of Arizona. Her research interests include ethnobotany, traditional agriculture, emergent political complexity, the U.S. Southwest and northwestern Mexico, and coastal Brazil. Publications include the *Marana Community in the Hohokam World* (with Paul Fish and John Madsen), published by the University of Arizona Press, the *Hohokam Village Revisted* (with David Doyel and Paul Fish), published by the American Association for the Advancement of Science.

ROBERT J. HARD received his Ph.D. in anthropology from the University of New Mexico in 1986 and is currently an associate professor of anthropology at the University of Texas at San Antonio. He has published, also with John Roney, an article in the journal *Science*, and they are completing a book on Cerro Juanaqueña. They and their colleagues have initiated a new project farther south in Chihuahua to continue to explore early agricultural and *cerros de trincheras* sites with the continued support of the National Science Foundation.

STEVE KOWALEWSKI received his Ph.D. from the University of Arizona and taught at the City University of New York for three years before coming to the University of Georgia, where he is Professor of Anthropology. He has done archaeological survey in Mesoamerica and the U.S. Southeast. His research interests are regional analysis, political economy, and human ecology. Recent publications include "Scale and the Explanation of Demographic Change: 3500 Years in the Valley of Oaxaca," in *American Anthropologist*, and *Ancient Oaxaca: The Monte Albán State* (with Richard Blanton, Gary Feinman, and Linda Nicholas), published by Cambridge University Press.

RANDALL MCGUIRE received his Ph.D. from the University of Arizona in 1982 and is now Professor of Anthropology at New York State University, Binghamton. His research encompasses social theory, inequality and stratification, historical archaeology, and northwest Mexico and the Southwest United States. Recent publications include "Contested Pasts: Archaeology and Native Americans," in *A Companion to Social Archaeology*, edited by L. Meskell and R. Preucel (Blackwell), and "Although They Have Petty Captains, They Obey Them Badly: The Dialectics of Prehispanic Western Pueblo Social Organization," in *American Antiquity* (with Dean Saitta).

BEN NELSON received a Ph.D. in anthropology from Southern Illinois University and specializes in the archaeology and ethnoarchaeology of social inequality in Mesoamerica and the American Southwest. His interests include changing complexity and connectivity among populations in those regions. His recent publications include "Elite Residences in West Mexico," in *Palaces of the Ancient New World: Form, Function, and Meaning*, edited by J. Pillsbury and S. T. Evans (Dumbarton Oaks Research Library and Collection, Washington, D.C.), and "Mesoamerican Objects and Symbols in Chaco Canyon Contexts," in *The Archae-*

ology of Chaco Canyon: An Eleventh-Century Pueblo Regional Center, edited by S. H. Lekson (SAR Press). He is Professor of Anthropology and Associate Director of the School of Human Evolution and Social Change at Arizona State University.

JOHN RONEY received his M.A. from Eastern New Mexico University in 1985. He has recently retired after a 31-year career with the Bureau of Land Management and now divides his time between cultural resource consulting and research in northwestern Mexico. His field research includes investigations throughout the Southwest and western Great Basin; he is widely recognized for his expertise on the archaeology of northwest Mexico.

JUDITH ROWE Taylor obtained an M.S. in botany from Purdue University, after which she studied fine art at Herron School of Art, Indianapolis, Indiana. Ms. Taylor served as a site steward for the Arizona State Historic Preservation Office (SHPO) and was regional coordinator for the Bumble Bee area until she moved to Washington in 2002. Her publications focus on central Arizona rock art, and she currently teaches a continuing education class about rock art at North Seattle Community College, Seattle, Washington.

M. ELISA VILLALPANDO is a research archaeologist with the Centro Regional Sonora of the Instituto Nacional de Antropología e Historia. Aside from the trincheras phenomenon, her research interests include Seri ethnography and prehistory, the transition to agriculture, ethnohistory, and shell production and exchange. Current publications include four chapters (Los Antiguos Cazadores-Recolectores en Sonora, Los Nómades de Siempre en Sonora, Las Rutas de Intercambio en Sonora, and En Sonora) in *La Gran Chichimeca: El Llugar de Las Rocas Secas*, edited by Beatriz Braniff, and *Boundaries and Territories: Prehistory of the U.S. Southwest and Northern Mexico*.

JOSEPH VOGEL is a retired computer programmer with Eastman Kodak, with BSEE and MBA degrees. The owner of two small airplanes, he has been using them to locate and photo-document archaeological sites, over 400 of which have been reported to the Museum of Northern

Arizona. He is an Arizona Site Steward who monitors sites for federal and state agencies.

HENRY D. WALLACE received his M.A. from the University of Arizona in 1980 and is Research Director at Desert Archaeology, Inc. in Tucson. His research focuses on ceramic iconography and seriation and the Hohokam archaeological culture of southern Arizona. Recent publications include major monographs on the Hohokam sites of Los Morteros and Valencia Vieja, published in the Anthropological Papers of Desert Archaeology.

DAVID R. WILCOX received a B.A. from Beloit College in 1966 and a Ph.D. from the University of Arizona in 1977, both in anthropology. Now a Senior Research Anthropologist, from 1988 to 2006 he was the head of the Department of Anthropology at the Museum of Northern Arizona, where his long-term research program focuses on the history of anthropology and museums, the archaeology of the greater Flagstaff area, and synthesis of Southwestern archaeology at multiple scales of analysis. The research he and colleagues began on Perry Mesa has expanded to a "hilltop survey" in all of west-central Arizona and to an investigation of the fourteenth-century Hopi macro-economy.

JON SCOTT WOOD received his M.A. in anthropology from Arizona State University. As Archaeologist for the Tonto National Forest for over 30 years, he is recognized for expertise on the prehispanic and early historic indigenous cultures of central Arizona. Topical interests include ceramic typology, settlement patterns, and the development of complex organizations.

INDEX